ENGLAND'S MARITIME EMPIRE

TURNING POINTS

General Editor: Keith Robbins
Vice Chancellor, University of Wales Lampeter

This ambitious new programme of books under the direction of *Professor Keith Robbins* (already General Editor of Longman's very successful series Profiles in Power) will examine moments and processes in history which have conventionally been seen as 'turning points' in the emergence of the modern world. By looking at the causes and long-term consequences of these key events, the books will illuminate the nature of both change and continuity in historical development. There are numerous titles in active preparation, and the following are already available:

The Bomb: Nuclear Weapons in their Historical, Strategic and Ethical Context
D.B.G. Heuser

England's Maritime Empire: Seapower, Commerce and Policy, 1490–1690
David Loades

The End of the Ottoman Empire, 1908–1923
A.L. Macfie

The Paris Commune, 1871
Robert Tombs

ENGLAND'S MARITIME EMPIRE

Seapower, Commerce and
Policy, 1490–1690

DAVID LOADES

Longman

An imprint of **Pearson Education**

Harlow, England · London · New York · Reading, Massachusetts · San Francisco
Toronto · Don Mills, Ontario · Sydney · Tokyo · Singapore · Hong Kong · Seoul
Taipei · Cape Town · Madrid · Mexico City · Amsterdam · Munich · Paris · Milan

Pearson Education Limited
Edinburgh Gate
Harlow
Essex CM20 2JE
England

and Associated Companies throughout the world

Visit us on the World Wide Web at:
www.pearsoneduc.com

First published 2000

ISBN 0–582–35628–8 PPR
ISBN 0–582–35629–6 CSD

British Library Cataloguing-in-Publication Data
A catalogue record for this book is available from the British Library

Library of Congress Cataloging-in-Publication Data
A catalog record for this book is available from the Library of Congress
Loades, D. M.
      England's maritime empire : seapower, commerce, and policy 1490–1690 / David
Loades.
          p.   cm. — (Turning points)
      Includes bibliographical references and index.
      ISBN 0–582–35629–6 — ISBN 0–582–35628–8 (pbk.)
      1. Great Britain—History, Naval—16th century.   2. Great Britain—History,
Naval—17th century.   3. England—Commerce—History—16th century.
4. England—Commerce—History—17th century.   5. England—Economic
conditions—16th century.   6. England—Economic conditions—17th century.
7. Great Britain—Colonies—History.   I. Title.   II. Turning points (Longman (Firm))

DA86.L6   2001
359'00941'09031—dc21

                                                                                        00–028193

Set by 35 in 11/13pt Baskerville MT
Typeset by 35
Produced by Pearson Education Asia Pte Ltd.
Printed in Singapore

CONTENTS

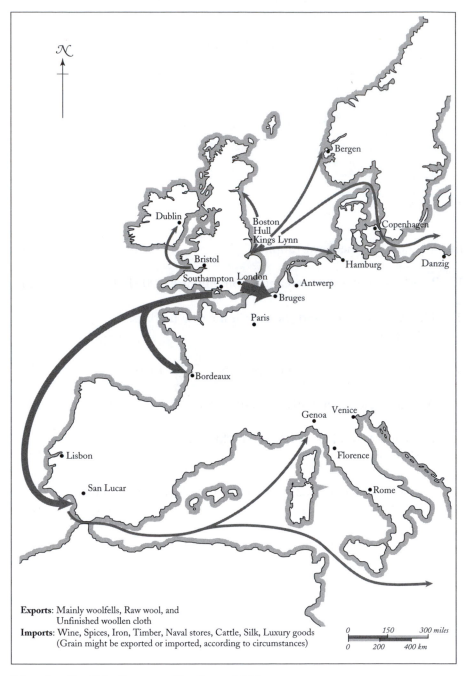

Map 1   English Overseas Trade, *c.* 1500

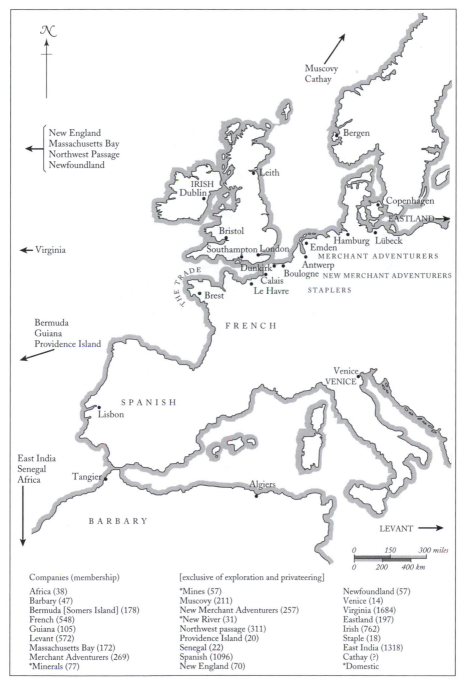

N

Muscovy
Cathay

New England
Massachusetts Bay
Northwest Passage
Newfoundland

Bergen

IRISH
Dublin

Leith

Copenhagen

EASTLAND

Bristol

Hamburg Lübeck

Virginia

Southampton London
Dunkirk
Calais
Le Havre
Brest

Emden
MERCHANT ADVENTURERS
Antwerp
Boulogne NEW MERCHANT ADVENTURERS
STAPLERS

THE TRADE

FRENCH

Bermuda
Guiana
Providence Island

Venice
VENICE

SPANISH
Lisbon

East India
Senegal
Africa

Tangier

Algiers

BARBARY

LEVANT

| 0 | 150 | 300 miles |
| 0 | 200 | 400 km |

Companies (membership)

[exclusive of exploration and privateering]

Africa (38)	*Mines (57)	Newfoundland (57)
Barbary (47)	Muscovy (211)	Venice (14)
Bermuda [Somers Island] (178)	New Merchant Adventurers (257)	Virginia (1684)
French (548)	*New River (31)	Eastland (197)
Guiana (105)	Northwest passage (311)	Irish (762)
Levant (572)	Providence Island (20)	Staple (18)
Massachusetts Bay (172)	Senegal (22)	East India (1318)
Merchant Adventurers (269)	Spanish (1096)	Cathay (?)
*Minerals (77)	New England (70)	*Domestic

Map 2   Elizabethan and Jacobean Companies
Source: T.K. Rabb, *Enterprise and Empire, 1575–1630* (New Haven, 1967)

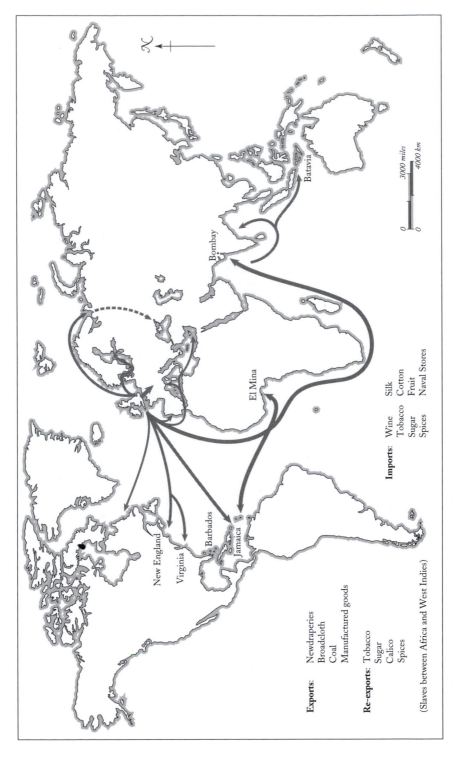

Exports: Newdraperies
Broadcloth
Coal
Manufactured goods

Re-exports: Tobacco
Sugar
Calico
Spices

(Slaves between Africa and West Indies)

Imports: Wine   Silk
Tobacco Cotton
Sugar   Fruit
Spices   Naval Stores

New England
Virginia
Barbados
Jamaica

Bombay
Batavia
El Mina

3000 miles
4000 km

Map 3   English Overseas Trade, c. 1650

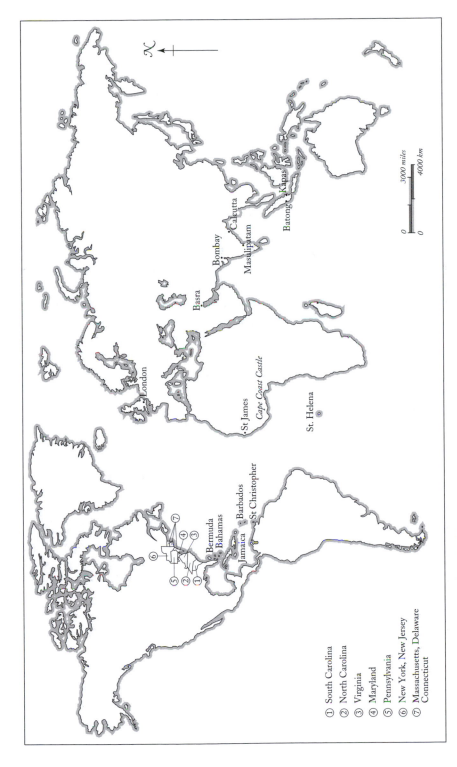

Map 4 The English Empire, 1690

① South Carolina
② North Carolina
③ Virginia
④ Maryland
⑤ Pennsylvania
⑥ New York, New Jersey
⑦ Massachusetts, Delaware
   Connecticut

London
Basra
Bombay
Masulipatam
Calcutta
Batong
Kipas
St James
Cape Coast Castle
St. Helena
Barbados
St Christopher
Bermuda
Bahamas
Jamaica

3000 miles
4000 km
0
0

PREFACE

As historical studies have become more diversified, and specialisms more esoteric, it has become increasingly difficult for the student to see the wood for the trees. One regrettable consequence of this has been for social and economic history to drift away from the history of politics and institutions. In the course of some recent correspondence, a distinguished economic historian dismissed political history as an old-fashioned chronicle of kings and battles, from which he totally dissociated himself. Yet kings and battles, nobles and parliaments, shaped much of the context in which ordinary people lived, and carried on their laudable private activities.

Kings imposed taxes and customs dues, requisitioned ships, and fought wars which resulted in embargoes and confiscations. As soon as a merchant began to look further than the nearest town, the affairs of kings and princes impinged upon him. Even when kings seldom troubled themselves with the affairs of commerce, the reverse was not true. International trade, in particular, is so much bound up with the histories of kings and battles that the two things should never be studied in isolation. But that is what normally happens. Economic history, naval history and conventional political history are treated as distinct disciplines, and even when they appear side by side in the same textbook they are given separate chapters.

Consequently the transformation of policy which moved England from being a small and conventional late medieval kingdom into a world imperial power, a transformation at once political, naval and commercial, has never been looked at as a whole. It took about 200 years, and progressed through a number of distinct stages, each of which could be called a 'turning point'. These stages do not correspond with the conventional divisions of political history, and yet without political will economic forces alone would not have brought them about. It is also a story of remarkable success. No wonder eighteenth-century Englishmen felt that God was pleased with them. At the end of the twentieth century the wheels have turned another cycle, and the English no longer feel particularly successful, or favoured. But perhaps they should think again. Without the tough-minded ambition and independence of the New Englanders, would the United States be the power which it now is? Without the legacy of the East India Company and the Raj, would India ever have become the world's most populous democracy? Without the commercial revolution, would there ever have been an industrial revolution? Why is English the world's most widely spoken language, and association football the world's most ubiquitous sport? It is in the strange history of early modern England that the answers to all these questions lie, and it is only by putting the merchants, the seamen, the preachers and the politicians together that we can reach a true understanding of them.

Since this book was conceived, and largely written, Peter Padfield has published his well-received work *Maritime Supremacy and the Opening of the Western Mind* (John Murray, 1999) with a somewhat similar agenda. However, although our periods overlap, the core of our interpretations is rather different. Professor Padfield is more interested than I am in battles, but more important, his focus is much later. It is my contention that several of the most critical changes in English policy and attitudes had already taken place before the Armada, whereas all the essential characteristics of eighteenth-century policy were in place by 1690. Although more was achieved in the eighteenth century, the seismic changes which converted England from a minor land power to a major sea power mostly took place in the sixteenth century, along with similarly potent changes in government and religion, to which they are closely related.

I have consequently written this book, not as a critique of Peter Padfield, and certainly not under the illusion that I have achieved a unique insight, but in order to lay down a thesis for others to challenge, develop or refute. It started with an invitation from Andrew Maclennan of Addison Wesley Longman (as it then was) to write about 'turning points', and it has been built up partly on my own research and partly on the research of others. Where I have used the latter, this is always acknowledged, but I do not wish to blame anyone else for my mistakes and misunderstandings. My main gratitude is to friends and colleagues in the Navy Records Society, who have encouraged me to think about the ways and means of sea power, and to my wife, Judith, for her constant encouragement and support.

Medieval England was not a sea power. From the Norman Conquest until the early sixteenth century successive kings strove, with varying degrees of success, to maintain an imperial ascendancy on both sides of the Channel. This ascendancy, when it existed, was not called an *Imperium*, because the only entity entitled to that designation was the Holy Roman Empire. However, between 1066 and 1453 the King of England also held, at various times, the Duchies of Normandy, Aquitaine and Gascony, and the Counties of Anjou, Maine, Touraine and Poitou. From 1340 onward the Plantagenets styled themselves kings of France, in respect of a plausible claim advanced by Edward III on the death of Charles IV,[1] and in 1420 by the Treaty of Tours seemed likely to make that claim good. At that point Henry V held over half of France by conquest, and the 'English Empire' was at its widest extent. Less than half a century later this whole fragile ascendancy had collapsed, and the only remnants of a once-mighty collection of fiefs and titles were the town and Pale of Calais, and the Channel Islands. Edward IV, Richard III and Henry VII continued to style themselves 'King of France', but made no serious attempts to make good their pretensions. Richard's reign was very brief, but Edward and Henry both dealt with France pragmatically. Their priorities remained continental, but neither was anxious to wage war, except for immediate and very tangible gains. Henry VIII was more ambitious. Three times – in 1512, 1522 and 1543 – he launched attacks on France which were primarily intended to restore a significant English bridgehead on the other side of the Channel. However, the world had moved on since the days of Agincourt, and not even Henry expected to conquer his powerful neighbour. His efforts were not entirely without success. He took Tournai and Thérouanne in 1513, and Boulogne in 1544, but the policy which these gains represented had become an expensive anachronism. After his death in 1547 it was quietly abandoned, and English aspirations to continental ascendancy disappeared.

For over 400 years the sea had been a highway, linking the various parts of the realm which the King of England ruled. France, the principal antagonist and threat, was for much of this time virtually landlocked. Brittany was an independent duchy, and English control of Gascony meant that direct access to the Atlantic was denied. Picardy and Normandy, when these were in French hands, offered reasonable outlets to the North Sea and the Channel, but direct royal control was never strong. Access to the Mediterranean was more reliable, but even that was not consistent, and it is largely irrelevant to this discussion. The main sea powers in northern waters were the Flemings, the Hanseatic League and (before 1397) the King of Norway.[2] The Flemings were usually friendly to the English for reasons of their own, and the Hanse were not belligerent unless they were seriously upset, a situation which the Plantagenets avoided until 1449. The kings of Norway were a declining force after the twelfth century, and in any case seldom interfered so far south. Consequently the post-conquest kings of England had never felt that it was worth their while to maintain an expensive war fleet, except for a few very brief periods. The normal need was for transports to ship men, horses and supplies across the Channel, and such vessels were taken up, either by indenture or by established systems of ship service, from the various port towns. Although they were required in large numbers, it was for limited periods, and the risk of such ships being attacked at sea was negligible. By the thirteenth century the largest single contributor was the collective known as the Cinque Ports, but London and other east coast ports such as Yarmouth were also important.[3]

Before the fourteenth century fighting ships were usually galleys, because combats only occurred in estuaries and other sheltered coastal waters. The technological limitations of both shipwrights and navigators meant that deep-water sea battles using large sailing ships were a virtual impossibility.[4] At the same time galleys were fragile, ill equipped to cope with stormy northern seas, and needed careful storage when not in use. Unsurprisingly, the biggest galley building programme embarked upon by an English king was triggered by a threat from France. Between 1284 and 1293 a 'naval base' for the construction and operation of galleys was built near Rouen, and in 1295 a fleet of French Mediterranean galleys made the hazardous voyage across the Bay of Biscay to harass the Channel Islands and the south coast ports. Edward I responded by building a fleet of his own, but it may not have seen much action as the threat soon receded.[5] There had been 'galley sheds' at Rye and at Southampton earlier in the century, and these may have been refurbished at this time, but such vessels were a short-term asset and soon disappeared from the records. Although subsequent English kings used oared warships in small numbers, this late thirteenth-century effort does not seem to have been repeated. This was not for lack of need. Between 1335 and 1340 a new French galley fleet, reinforced by Genoese and other squadrons from the Mediterranean, raided the English coast on several occasions, burned Southampton and took Guernsey. There was real fear of a large-scale French invasion, and England's naval defences seem to have been almost non-existent. This was partly because Edward III had virtually no strategic imagination, and for years consistently failed to appreciate the importance of sea power. It was also partly because naval organisation was rudimentary; by the time a fleet could be assembled in response to a threat, the enemy had struck and gone. English seamen were also notoriously undisciplined. The men of the Cinque Ports, for example, were fierce fighters and famous pirates, but they were just as liable to attack their own side as the enemy. A feud between the Ports and Yarmouth, for example, went on for centuries and cost many lives.[6]

However, lessons were slowly learned. In the course of the war which began in 1330, the English began to claim the 'sovereignty of the seas'. This certainly did not reflect any military superiority, but rather a desire to claim the Channel (not 'the seas' in general) as English territorial water – a consequence of Edward's claim to the sovereignty of both shores. Having made such a claim, even Edward (who did not believe in anything which could not be done on horseback) began to understand the desirability of making it real. In 1339 the Franco-Genoese alliance appeared to have everything its own way. Hastings was burned in May, and Plymouth raided. However, in July the Genoese ships mutinied and went home, and in October a sizeable French fleet was destroyed by storms. Finally, in 1340, the English began to enjoy some success at sea. In January ships from the Cinque Ports raided Boulogne and Dieppe, burning a number of French galleys. In May Tréport was also raided, and then in July an English sailing fleet under the command of Lord Morley attacked and virtually annihilated a rather larger French fleet at Sluys.[7] The French lost 190 ships and nearly 18,000 men. Ironically, after a dismal record going back half a century, and against a background of indecisive raid and counter-raid, it was the English fleet which won the first really decisive victory. Sluys did not make England a sea power, but it did give Edward effective control of the Channel for a number of years, to substantiate his claims. It also seems to have prompted some development in both the office and jurisdiction of Lord Admiral.[8] There was no new strategic thinking. Sluys had happened by accident rather than by tactical skill, and Edward continued to raise his fleets by the traditional methods, but he did now build and retain a few ships of his own, notably the *Cog Thomas*, which served him as what would later be called a flagship.

Continental preoccupations inevitably meant treating the sea as a highway, rather than a moat or a power base, and it was a measure of English success that 85 per cent of the fighting took place on French soil. However, England was also part of a complex of offshore islands, and in that context the sea was a rather different element. Before the Norman Conquest, English power had related not to the King of France or the Count of Flanders, but to the kings of Norway, Denmark and Scotland, to the lords of the Isles, and to Irish and Welsh chieftains. Although like all other invaders, the Saxons had come by sea, once settled they seem both literally and meta-phorically to have burned their boats. By the end of the eighth century Northumbria, Kent and even Wessex were being raided more or less at will by predators generally known as 'Vikings', although they seem to have come from a number of different places. In the middle of the ninth century it must have seemed that the Danes were about to treat the Saxons as the Saxons had treated their British predecessors.

However, the English monarchy proved to be both tough and resilient. In a reign lasting from 877 to 899 Alfred of Wessex turned back the Danish assault, and developed new methods of defence, both on land and sea. Exactly what his warships were is a matter of controversy, but they were successful in both repelling and deterring raids,[9] making the Danes who had already settled a more manageable proposition. In the reign of his grandson Aethelstan, the Old English monarchy reached its apogee. Hav-ing succeeded as King of Wessex and Mercia in 924, Aethelstan annexed Northumbria in 927, and in the same year the kings of Scotland and Strath-clyde acknowledged his overlordship. Between then and his death in 939 he maintained his ascendancy in the north and west largely by sea power, sending a fleet as far as Caithness in 934.[10] In spite of setbacks under his brothers Eadmund and Eadred between 939 and 957, his nephew Edgar recovered this full ascendancy between 959 and 975, undergoing a sym-bolic imperial coronation in 973, when he was rowed on the Dee by eight tributary princes from Wales, Scotland and Ireland. Edgar's son Aethelred is not normally remembered as a successful ruler, because of his defeat at the hands of Sweyn Forkbeard, but during his reign the English fleet re-mained powerful, and was effective in maintaining his control over the Irish Sea and the Western Approaches. In 1000 he led a successful expedition to Cumberland and the Isle of Man. During the troubled half century which followed, the Crown of England, whether in English or in Danish hands, continued to command a strong fleet, and the English overlordship of the Celtic west continued to be recognised. It was only after the Norman Conquest, when the king's attention was consistently elsewhere, that this supremacy lapsed, and when the Anglo-Norman lords began to move west and north in the twelfth century, they found a changed situation.

South Wales was vulnerable to land-based infiltration and invasion, and that began to happen before the end of the eleventh century, without any significant maritime involvement. However, the next step, the so-called Anglo-Norman invasion of southern Ireland, was a different proposition. This did not at first involve the King of England, and it was not so much an invasion as an increasing involvement of Anglo-Norman marcher lords based in South Wales in the political structure of the Irish Sea littoral.[11] Richard FitzGilbert, Earl of Pembroke, desiring to escape from the attentions of his overlord, crossed to Ireland with the assistance of Diarmait MacMurchada of Leinster, whose daughter he married. It was MacMurchada who provided the ships to cover this crossing, and FitzGilbert became a powerful ally in the web of Irish politics. Naturally MacMurchada's enemies, particularly Rory O'Connor of Connaught, the High King, struck back in the same way. Another Anglo-Norman adventurer, John de Courcy, had married the daughter of the King of Man, and with his help had established a strong foothold in Ulster. De Courcy appealed to his overlord, Henry II, and in 1171 the King of England launched an expedition across the Irish Sea, for which the sea power was provided by Man and the Western Isles.[12] By the end of the twelfth century the English had a powerful foothold in Ireland, but no sea power to maintain it – the opposite of the situation in King Edgar's time. This did not matter so long as communications across the Irish Sea were undisturbed, or some local power existed to provide protection. It was a vulnerable and unsatisfactory situation, but for the next hundred years English kings were too busy at their front doors to bother much about the tradesman's entrance.

Even when English energies were directed westwards, there was an extraordinary failure to understand the strategic situation. Edward I's Welsh campaigns after 1277 provide an excellent series of examples. The Welsh princes did not have a fraction of Edward's military resources, but the terrain was a splendid ally against any overland campaign. Time and again English forces became bogged down, and were forced to retreat, sodden and starving, in the face of the slightest resistance. Eventually Edward subdued North and mid-Wales by building a ring of powerful and immensely expensive castles, when the same effect could have been achieved at a fraction of the cost by bringing his armies in by sea. The Welsh had no sea power of their own to resist such landings, and no reliable allies. The English were not short of ships. Workmen and timber were brought in for the castles by sea, and the completed fortresses were supplied in the same way. The small English boroughs of places like Conway and Caernarfon were cut off by their hostile hinterlands, and depended entirely upon their sea lanes for survival.[13] But neither Edward nor his successors learned the lesson. English communications around North Wales and across the Irish Sea remained almost entirely unprotected, except by self-help, until the Tudor period. In the north the situation was rather similar. No English fleet challenged the kings of Man or the lords of the Isles as Aethelstan's had done. Man remained a Norse kingdom, in uncertain and fluctuating relations with the King of Norway himself, until it was taken by Alexander III of Scotland in 1266. In 1290 it was held by the Earl of Ulster as a fief of the

English Crown, but it passed backwards and forwards uneasily between English and Scottish suzerainty, until it was finally captured by Edward III in 1333, and bestowed upon William Montague, Earl of Salisbury, who presumably had enough sea power to maintain himself, even if his overlord showed little further interest in him.

Scotland, like Wales, was seen by the English as a straightforward military problem. However, the country not only had an enormous coastline in relation to its size, it also had two distinct seafaring traditions. The power of the lords of the Isles, which was not subjected to the kings of Scots until the fifteenth century, and which covered the inner and outer Hebrides, and much of the mainland coast from Argyll northwards, was maintained by fleets of what were normally called galleys. The term is misleading, because galleys of Mediterranean type would not have lasted five minutes in those turbulent waters. They seem to have been Scandinavian *esnecca*, or 'snakes', which were fast and seaworthy, but not specifically designed for fighting.[14] The east coast of Scotland, on the other hand, put out trading ships of the same type as those which sailed from the Humber or the Tyne, and in rather similar numbers. The ship service available to the King of Scots was not great in relation to that of his southern neighbour, but was greater in proportion than his military resources, and had the big advantage of being close to where it was likely to be needed. However, when it came to serious warfare, the Scots were survivors rather than victors. Edward I's last campaign of 1303 is a case in point. His main army advanced up the east coast, supported by a transport fleet of about 30 sailing ships, while the Earl of Ulster attacked from the west with almost 200 vessels raised in Ireland and the Isles, most of which must have been very small. By 1304 victory appeared to be complete, but two years later the country was in arms again, and this time Robert the Bruce had enough support in the west to prevent any repetition of an attack from that quarter. Edward's treaty with France in 1303 had also angered the Flemings, who now joined forces with the Scots at sea to make a formidable combination, which prevented the English from bringing in supplies from the east. The campaign of 1307 was aborted by Edward's death, and over the next few years the Scots acquired a complete ascendancy in the Irish Sea, attacking Man and Ulster at will. The English defeat at Bannockburn in 1314 cannot be attributed to any failure to command the seas, east or west, but one of the consequences was that Scottish ships took the initiative in the North Sea, as they already had in the Irish Sea, and raided English shipping as far south as the Thames. When Edward III redeemed his father's mistakes in 1333–34, he was able to use his ships to blockade Berwick and force it to surrender. The balance of power had now tilted back in England's favour and Scottish raids on the east coast ceased to be a problem, but the English were virtually excluded

from the Western Isles, and Scotland's back door was consequently access-
ible to her friends.

The Scots did not go away, and in spite of their defeats retained their
independence and capacity for hostile action, but for the rest of his long life
Edward III's priorities were elsewhere. His victory at Sluys gave him an
ascendancy over the French at sea, but that did not extend to their allies,
and in 1349 a formidable fleet of Castilian ships came north to collaborate
in an attack on England. Castile was probably the most powerful maritime
power with access to the Atlantic at this point, so the threat was no light
one. However, in August 1350 in an action off Winchelsea which went
down in the English chronicles as 'espagnols sur mer', a fleet of almost 50
Castilian warships was dispersed and repulsed.[15] This was not a victory to
compare with Sluys, and was probably only one of a series of actions, but it
effectively broke up the attacking force. An outbreak of civil strife in Castile
soon after caused the southerners to withdraw, and for about a decade the
English enjoyed a precarious ascendancy undisturbed. The war continued,
and there was much coming and going, but no action at sea until the
French punctured their rival's complacency by raiding and destroying
Winchelsea in 1360. Soon after, in the same year, the Treaty of Bretigny
brought a lull in the war. In spite of some significant successes, nothing had
really changed. At one point Edward had as many as 40 of his own ships,
but in the latter part of his reign this dwindled away again to three or four.
Naval infrastructure, as distinct from commands on active service, remained
minimal – a single Clerk of the Ships, who usually had numerous other
things to do. The only gesture to the increasing size and handiness of sailing
ships was a store of prefabricated wooden castles, which could be added to
merchant ships when they were 'taken up', and removed when they were
returned to their owners. The king paid the crews of the ships when they
were in his service and tonnage for the ships themselves, but not during the
weeks or months which might elapse between their requisitioning and actually being used.[16] Time so spent was financial loss to the owners for which
they were never compensated, although the king might occasionally pay for
a ship which was actually lost in service.

It is not surprising that merchants complained bitterly against the war,
because they felt that they were paying for it twice over. Not only did the
king take their money in taxes, he also took their capacity to earn it. Nor
did the war benefit them in any way. Belligerent markets were closed to
them, and the sea lanes, which were hazardous enough in normal times,
became even more so. As Nicholas Rodger has recently pointed out, the
climate of hostilities which prevailed in the fourteenth century made peaceful commerce a virtual impossibility.[17] Every merchant went armed for self-
defence, and turned pirate when the opportunity offered. However, there

were some compensations. By 1360 it was customary for the most valuable traffic – wool to the Low Countries and wines from Bordeaux – to travel together in convoy under the escort of a small number of fighting ships. The collective security of the fleet was probably more important than the escort, but either way a method of reducing the risks of transit had been found. By the early fifteenth century it was normal for the ships of all the larger merchant companies to travel together, both in war and peace, and irrespective of whether royal escorts were provided or not. However, the connection between commerce and sea power, so obvious in the Mediterranean, and axiomatic to later generations of Englishmen, had not yet been made.

Genoa and Venice had built their power upon the sea, not by using the round ships of their merchants for fighting but by using their commercial wealth to keep the seas, for the safe passage of trade and for the opening of reluctant markets by the persuasions of force. Once in existence, a war fleet of such dimensions became an instrument of policy in itself, and an exploitable asset. Both the Genoese and the Grimaldi of Monaco rented parts of their galley fleets to the French during the Hundred Years War,[18] and Edward III also hired such ships from time to time. After the decline of Norway, the nearest equivalent in the north was the Hanseatic League. The fleets of the League were not designed for military purposes; they were convoys on a grand scale, but they had considerable muscle, as successive kings of Denmark found when they tried to exercise their control over the Sound. The kings of France and England needed flourishing ports to provide the ships and seamen for their confrontational policies, but neither seems to have drawn the obvious conclusion than an active promotion of trade would increase their power. Edward III in particular seems to have considered 'merchants matters' as beneath him, except when it came to borrowing money from the Staplers. In spite of the critical importance of commercial wealth, the English Crown made no systematic attempt to 'keep the seas' between the Norman Conquest and the Tudor period, and the lack of a professional navy in the Mediterranean sense was both a cause and a consequence of that omission.

After a lull in the early 1360s, following the Treaty of Bretigny, the situation steadily deteriorated. English intervention in the Castilian civil war served only to strengthen the victor, Henry of Trastamara, in his alliance with the French, and to return Castilian warships to the north. At the same time the King of Denmark, who could always find reasons to pick a quarrel with the English, joined the French and the Scots in threatening naval attacks. A series of disasters followed: a raid on Portsmouth; the capture of the Earl of Pembroke and his treasure *en route* to Poitou; the loss of La Rochelle.[19] Between 1369 and 1372 a crisis developed, and was met with a large shipbuilding programme over the next two years. The fleet thus created certainly operated, but it seems to have achieved small success and in 1375 an entire convoy on its way to the Bay of Bourgneuf was captured by the Castilians with a total loss of £18,000. English vitality was clearly sinking with their aged king, and within a few days of his death in 1377 a combined French and Castilian fleet swept along the south coast, destroying nearly a dozen towns between Rye and Plymouth, and holding the Isle of Wight to ransom. Responses were made over the next two years, not entirely without success, but they could not stem the tide of defeat. In 1380 the Channel Islands were lost, Winchelsea was destroyed, and an attack on Gravesend directly threatened London.[20] It is no coincidence that in the same year the last ships of Edward III's royal squadron were sold. In the face of these catastrophes, the government of Richard II showed neither intelligence nor flexibility. Efforts were still concentrated upon raising fleets of transports to ferry men and horses across the Channel, and no serious attempts were made either to defend the coasts or to protect English ships at sea. Fortunately a combination of bad weather and their own internal divisions prevented the French from exploiting this weakness to the full, and after 1381 the war subsided through a series of inconclusive truces. Just before the general truce of 1389 the Earl of Arundel did succeed in capturing a Franco-Castilian convoy in the straits of Dover, but this went only a small way towards restoring the pride and reputation which had been so hammered over the previous 20 years.

After 1400 both France and England were plagued by internal weaknesses. Hostilities became sporadic, and largely unofficial. French and Scottish support for the Glyndwr revolt after 1404 gave it a kind of spurious significance and again exposed the weaknesses of the English castles, but it did not prevent it from being suppressed.[21] Most of the hostilities at sea were in the nature of large-scale piracy – opportunistic and unpredictable – rather than organised campaigns. Henry IV did have a few ships of his own, and the office of Clerk of the Ships continued, but the problem, as always, was money. Ship service was cheap (for the Crown) and useful for short expeditions. Requisitioning was less cheap and caused much resentment, but it could be used for extended service. Both were slow to mobilise. Only a regular royal fleet in a constant state of readiness could have provided the speed and strength of response which was required in these years, and that was considered prohibitively expensive, given that the decisive battles were always going to be fought on land.

It was not until about 1409, as the king's son Prince Henry began to take a hand in affairs, that a new direction of thinking can be detected. The accounts of John Starlyng, who was Clerk of the Ships from 1410 to 1412, survive, and reflect a moderate level of activity, although it is very hard to tell how many ships he had in his care at any given time.[22] When they were on active service they were controlled by the Lord Admiral, and paid through a Treasurer appointed by him. When Henry IV died in 1413, his heir had already decided to renew the war with France, and had begun to build up his sea power in preparation. Royal fleets did occasionally appear between 1400 and 1412. In 1405 Thomas of Lancaster, the king's second son, as Lord Admiral led a fleet which burned Harfleur and several other towns on the Norman coast, in retribution for raids on Portland and Falmouth in the previous year. However, the normal method of response had become licensed self-help. When Caernarfon and Harlech were attacked in 1404, the city of Bristol was instructed to send out five ships to encounter the raiders; and in the same year the king granted authorisations similar to the later letters of marque to two Bristol captains to 'go upon' the French at their own expense and keep the proceeds.[23] This type of operation clearly had an appeal to both sides. In 1405 a company of merchants, either disgruntled with the king's failure to protect their trade, or perhaps scenting a golden opportunity for profit, petitioned for a licence to keep the seas, not against an identified enemy, but against pirates and raiders in general. They offered to set out their own ships, in return for standard tonnage payments, the bulk of the prizes taken (less the Lord Admiral's 20 per cent), and a commission of Admiralty jurisdiction under the Great Seal. It seems to have been in response to this petition that commissions were issued to Nicholas Blackburne and Richard Clitherowe, as the admirals of this volunteer fleet in April 1406.[24] Later in the same year Blackburne and Clitherowe escorted Princess Philippa to Denmark, and charged £166 13s 4d for their services. On reflection, Henry seems to have felt that this was a diminution of his honour, because the commissions were withdrawn in the following year, and the king declared that henceforth it would be the Lord Admiral's function to protect trade. As an explicit commitment, this was a new departure of momentous significance, but for the time being it had little effect. The Earl of Kent's notion of discharging this newly identified responsibility was to conduct a very old-fashioned raid on the Breton coast in 1408, in the course of which he was killed. Over the next few years a measure of relief was provided, not by military action but by political means. So bad had the situation become in western European waters generally, and so serious the threat to prosperous commerce, that between 1408 and 1410 the kings of England and France and the Duke of Burgundy concluded a series of maritime truces, which by depriving the pirates of the connivance of their governments, reduced the problem to manageable proportions.[25]

Henry V, who throughout his reign was to show a much keener military intelligence than his predecessors, was earnest to preserve this situation. In 1414 a statute declared piracy, and the breaking of the maritime truces, to be high treason; no armed ship (which meant just about any merchant going further than the next port) was to put to sea without entering into a bond or recognisance not to attack friendly or neutral vessels.[26] In the context this can be seen as part of the king's preparations for renewed war, but it was also a fresh approach to the urgent problem of keeping the seas. His intention was to reassure both his own merchants and their trading partners, particularly the Flemings and the Hanse, and as there were relatively few complaints over the next few years, it seems to have worked in the short term. Henry was probably the first English king since Aethelred to have a proper understanding of the meaning of sea power. By 1414 he already possessed one Great Ship, the *Jesus* of 1,000 tons, and six or seven smaller vessels. Three more Great Ships (over 400 tons) were laid down in the same year, and a small fleet of balingers. These latter were a bit like the Norse *esnecca*, in that they were more seaworthy than galleys, and could be moved by either oar or sail. They varied between 50 and 120 tons in burden, and were useful for scouting and communications as well as in countering galleys. By the end of the war in 1420 the king had a war fleet of about 30 vessels, the largest number for nearly a century, and including four Great Ships of over 500 tons.

His naval tactics were a mixture of the traditional and the innovative. When his invasion army sailed for France in August 1415 it was transported and escorted in the usual way, a large fleet of nearly 150 merchant ships having been mobilised for the purpose. However, before it sailed, three patrols had also been set up to cover the coast between Plymouth and King's Lynn. The average size of a patrol was four ships, and it is not known how long they were at sea, so their usefulness must have been very limited, but the idea of using standing patrols to keep the seas was new.[27] Moreover in 1416 a deliberate attempt was made to secure control of the Narrow Seas (English Channel) by challenging a large-scale sea battle – the sort of result which had been achieved accidentally at Sluys. The occasion was provided by a French attempt to recover the town of Harfleur, which was besieged on land and blockaded from the sea. This fleet was a formidable armament, consisting of about 200 French ships of various sizes, reinforced with eight large Genoese carracks. The English raised rather more ships and organised them around such of the king's Great Ships as were then in service (probably three). On 15 August the English attacked, battle being joined in the narrow channel opposite the town. The result was as decisive as Sluys, although somewhat less destructive, with three of the Genoese carracks being captured, and two driven aground. The siege of Harfleur was broken, and the English command of the seas was not challenged again for the remainder of the war.[28] There was further innovation in 1417. The king led another expedition to Normandy, but instead of calling upon his own merchants for transport, he listened to their inevitable complaints and hired his transports in Holland, his own ships providing the convoy. This operation was preceded spectacularly, if somewhat unnecessarily, by a sweep of the Channel conducted by 40 ships drawn mainly from the Cinque Ports, but led by four or five of the king's Great Ships, including two of the carracks taken the previous year.

Until 1420 it looked as though Henry had a long-term naval strategy in mind, but that soon turned out to have been an illusion. The king's understanding of sea power, so much superior to that of his predecessors, encompassed only the war with France. As soon as the war was over, the patrols were discontinued and the Great Ships mothballed. By the terms of his will, drawn up shortly before his death in 1422, most of the 40-odd ships of which he died possessed were to be sold to pay his debts. England's command of the seas, which in any case had never extended beyond Ushant, disappeared as quickly as it had been created. As far as the keeping of the seas was concerned, the victorious reign of Henry V was just another false dawn. Between 1423 and 1425 William Soper, the Clerk of the Ships, and his fellow commissioners raised rather more than £1,000 by the sale of 22 ships, many of them officially described as 'debilis', or worn out. By 1430 only two of the Great Ships remained afloat, and five years later the balinger *Little Jesus* was the only vessel still in Soper's charge.[29] For a number of years the Clerk's accounts show him spending and receiving no more than £5 or £6 a year. In 1436 a huge fleet of over 500 vessels was raised to transport an army for the relief of Calais, but no more than two or three of these belonged to the king, and two years later they seem to have been taken out of the hands of the Clerk and handed over to 'royal shipmasters'. In 1452 the last naval stores at Southampton were sold, and the office of Clerk was allowed to lapse.

Although the war restarted after Henry's death, and continued in fits and starts until 1453, the minority council of Henry VI had no naval strategy at all, a fact which contributed significantly to England's ultimate defeat. The lessons of the previous reign were completely ignored. When ships were needed, they were raised mainly by indenture. Traditional ship service had declined, partly because the Cinque Ports were no longer the force they had been and partly because newer centres like Bristol and London did not have similar obligations. An indenture was simply a contract between the king and a particular commander to raise a given number of ships, for a specified period and at a specified rate. It was often used to raise a large fleet for a short period, but could equally be applied to smaller numbers and more extended service – in other words 'keeping the seas'. A number of sums paid to individuals 'pro salva custodia maris' suggests that such a system was in regular use during the 1430s and 1440s.[30] Unfortunately, such a method cost money whether it was effective or not, and as early as 1436 there was a return to the commission system tried in the reign of Henry IV. Groups of merchants from eight or nine ports clubbed together to raise a fleet of about 30 ships under the command of John Scot of Calais and John Milbourne of London, who then received commissions of authority from the king.[31] The maritime truces of the early century had long since broken down, and the temptation to recoup their losses by indiscriminate marauding must have been very great. Such a system cost the Crown virtually nothing, and some of the merchant communities liked it, but they were suffering from very short vision. The Lord Admiral had no control over these poachers turned gamekeepers, and when a fleet of them took an entire Hanseatic convoy in 1449, it resulted in an embargo on English trade with both Danzig and the Low Countries, and cost Henry VI £4,500 in compensation, which he could ill afford. He could have run his own patrols for several years at less expense.

By 1450 a policy issue had emerged which was to play a very important part in the ensuing debates. Dissatisfaction with the war, and the way in which it was being handled, was almost universal. Some writers, like Lydgate, Hoccleve and Gower, denounced warfare in general as being morally indefensible and physically destructive.[32] Others, and particularly the anonymous author of *The Libelle of Englyshe Polycye*, had a vision which was both more subtle and more positive. Peace meant uninterrupted commerce, and commerce meant prosperity; but peace was more than the absence of senseless strife between unreconstructed monarchs. It also meant a freedom to come and go, particularly upon the seas, without being in danger of robbery, assault and murder.

> But many lands would seek peace out of need;
> The sea well kept, it must be done for dread.
> Thus will Flanders need to have unity
> And peace with us, and it will not be otherwise
> Within short while, and ambassadors
> Will be here soon to treat for their succour.
> This unity is pleasing to God,
> And peace after the wars variance;
> The end of battle is peace surely
> And power causes true, lasting peace.[33]

This power was to be sought upon the seas. In other words the secret of peace, prosperity and security for England lay in the development of a strong navy. In Dover and Calais the king had 'two eyes ... to keep the narrow seas', and it was his responsibility, not that of the merchant communities themselves, to maintain law and order within those waters over which he claimed control. At about the same time, in 1435, that veteran of the French wars Sir John Fastolf declared that 'the sea [should] be kept mightily, as well for the king's worship and the realm's as for the salvation of the merchandise', and emphasised the disadvantages of using uncontrolled commissions, because it was so difficult to ensure that such privateers 'be not suffered to take nor rob the kings very true friends and ancient allies, instead of the enemies'.[34] John Capgrave, writing about ten years after the *Libelle*, was one of a number of authors who pointed out that the King of England was, whether he liked it or not, a 'sea king' and that his honour required him to be powerful in that element. In 1442 the House of Commons even went so far as to specify that the 'welfare and defence of this realm of England' required eight ships to be constantly at sea. As the French war sank towards its final ignominious end, there were voices already declaring that this defeat had been willed by God, who had a different role in mind for England, and pointing explicitly to the ways in which they expected that to happen.

However, if that was the case, it made no impression upon Henry VI, or those who tried to govern in his name. Defeat in France was followed, first by the temporary but total incapacity of the king himself, and then by the disintegration of his government. In the decisive battles of 1460 and 1461 the private fleet of Richard Neville, Earl of Warwick, supporting the Yorkist cause, defeated such power as Henry was able to send against him, and played a large part in the Yorkist victory which placed Edward IV upon the throne.[35] This should have given the new king a different insight into sea power from the first. His own father, the Duke of York, had declared in 1454 that what England needed was a proper naval administration 'to the intent that all your navy be ready together, and of power to assemble in such place as is most convenient for the assembling of them, for to break the puissance of the navy of the said adversary before their assembling' – a traditional, but perfectly sound strategy which was simply incapable of realisation with the system of mobilisation then in use. However, if Edward did have an understanding of the meaning of sea power, it emerged only very slowly and incompletely. This was partly because he remained committed to the military culture of chivalry, which was enjoying its last and most exotic flowering in contemporary Burgundy, and partly because his resources were extremely limited. His first priority had to be the restoration of royal government at home; everything else was makeshift. He purchased a small number of his own ships, which were used both for trading and communications, and built the first royal carvel, the *Edward*, at Dunwich in 1464, but he continued the late Lancastrian practice of entrusting these vessels to 'royal shipmasters', until he finally revived the office of Keeper of the Ships in 1480. It was not that he lacked for good advice. Just as there had been no shortage of voices telling Henry VI how he could best uphold his honour and the realm's safety, so in 1476, in *The Governance of England*, Sir John Fortescue declared:

> And though we have not alway war upon the sea, yet it shalbe necessary that the king have always some fleet upon the sea, for the repressing of rovers, saving of our own merchants, our fishers, and the dwellers upon our coasts, and that the king keep alway some great and mighty vessels for the breaking of an army when any such shall be made against him upon the sea . . .[36]

All the ideas necessary for a new defensive naval strategy based upon the keeping of the seas were present in the late fifteenth century, but the necessary connection with political will, and hence with resources, had not yet been made.

Change came about in the first place because of some decisive shifts in the relationship between the Crown and the mercantile communities. In respect of the early Middle Ages, it is impossible to speak meaningfully of 'England's overseas trade'. Each port town exported the products of its own hinterland, and such other items as could be conveniently transported to it, exchanging these for whatever could be obtained in the partner town or towns. The ships involved were small and technically unsophisticated, so that voyages even across the Narrow Seas were hazardous, and the pattern of trade was limited and opportunistic. Down to the end of the thirteenth century the merchants who ventured abroad tended to travel in groups to the great fairs, taking a miscellaneous selection of goods with them. By that time Mediterranean trade was already much better organised and large-scale. Such cities as Venice and Genoa had become rich on long-distance trade, and had translated those riches into power by the creation of war fleets.

English trade development was driven mainly by two commodities, wine inward and wool outward. By 1400 Bordeaux was exporting 90,000–100,000 tuns a year, the bulk of which came to England. So important was this trade that the capacity of trading ships in general came to be measured in wine casks. The trade in raw wool began to expand at the end of the twelfth century, but cannot be quantified until regular customs records begin in 1275. By that time about 30,000 sacks were being exported every year, every sack containing some 250 fleeces.[37] The customs dues were based upon the principle that no person or chattel could be removed from the realm without the king's consent. Any person leaving the realm, except by the king's specific order, consequently required a licence for which a fee was payable, and all commodities were charged at fixed rates. Imports were not at first customable.

Because of its large scale and high value, the wool trade was the first to be placed under monopolistic control, when the Company of the Staple was formed in 1343, and given the exclusive right to ship wool to the Low Countries, which was the principal market. The staple, or control point through which the trade must pass, was located originally at Bruges. The Staplers were given extensive privileges, and their monopoly was guaranteed by the Crown. In return they paid heavy customs dues, and were expected to underwrite the king's debts, even lending him money directly from time to time. This was a new kind of partnership between the Crown and the mercantile community, because hitherto the king had dealt only with towns or groups of towns, granting them privileges in return for ship service. The Staplers were a chartered company, whose membership was not confined to a single town, although the logic of both wealth and management quickly caused it to be dominated by London.

In 1407 a similar company was established to control the trade in unfinished cloth, as more wool began to be spun and woven in England. This company, which grew largely out of the London Mercers, began in a small way about 1350, and by 1440 was exporting nearly 60,000 cloths a year, mainly also to the Low Countries.[38] The Merchant Adventurers, as they were called, were in a sense ill named because they showed no interest in venturing beyond the Narrow Seas, but they became extremely prosperous, and by the mid-fifteenth century their annual convoy to the Low Countries was one of the pivotal events of the northern economic year. The Adventurers enjoyed a similar relationship with the Crown to that of the Staplers, but with one significant exception. The export duties on cloth remained significantly lower than those on raw wool. Whether this was a calculated plan to encourage the English clothiers, or more or less accidental, is not clear, but by the later fifteenth century its effects were very noticeable. By 1480, when the Merchant Adventurers exceeded 60,000 cloths for the first time, the Staplers exports had shrunk to about 10,000 sacks, having reached 45,000 in 1355. By the reign of Edward IV, although the Staplers clung to their privileges with great tenacity, the Adventurers were wealthier, more numerous, and much more important to the Crown.

The circumstances of Edward's accession, his constant need for support, and perhaps a native political shrewdness, brought him closer to the merchant community, and particularly to the City of London, than any previous king. Although it is very unlikely that he ever gave commercial interests priority when they conflicted with his ambitions in foreign or dynastic policy, where there was no such conflict he was prepared to go out of his way to be supportive. Some of this concern was cheap and largely cosmetic. Edward knighted more aldermen of London than any of his predecessors, welcomed them (and their wives) at court, and even invited them to his hunting parties.[39] This conviviality cost very little, either politically or financially, and created a useful climate of goodwill. The king also traded substantially in his own right, using factors who were often Italians, and usually his own ships, of which he had between five and ten during most of his reign. These ships were also leased out to individual merchants, or to groups, when they were not needed for the king's purposes. This was not a new idea, but Edward pursued it more systematically, and his example encouraged his nobles to follow suit. Not everyone was impressed by this 'hands on' approach. John Russell, the Bishop of Lincoln and author of the 'Croyland Chronicle', was slightly scandalised that a king should so demean himself:

> This same king in person, having equipped ships of burden, laded them with the very finest wools, cloths, tin, and other products of his realm, and, like a man living by merchandise, exchanged goods for goods, both with the Italians and Greeks, through his factors . . .[40]

The consequences of this attitude were numerous, and far from straightforward. In the first place English merchants did not speak with a single voice on any issue. Hostility to aliens was very general, and occasionally erupted into violence. This had to be suppressed, and the positions of the strangers protected. More seriously, the Staplers and the Merchant Adventurers were constantly at loggerheads. Not only did the Staplers pay high taxes, but they had also assumed responsibility for paying the garrison of Calais, where their staple was by this time located. They felt, understandably, that this gave them a special claim to the king's favour, and his tendency to prefer the Adventurers, not only in London but also in other ports, was much resented. Relations with the Hanseatic League also caused constant problems. The Hanse not only enjoyed a monopoly of bringing Baltic products to England, they also largely controlled the return trade in English cloth, much to the rage of the Merchant Adventurers, who struggled in vain to secure reciprocal privileges in the Hanse ports. At the same time east coast ports such as Lynn, Boston and Hull depended heavily upon the Hanse presence, and their merchants were much less hostile than the Londoners.[41] Edward conducted a constant diplomatic dialogue with the League, aimed at improving the position of his own subjects within the overall pattern. Because the League towns themselves did not speak with one voice, or pursue a common interest, he had some success, but never enough to satisfy the London Adventurers, who became increasingly aggressive.

The seizure of several English vessels in the Sound in June 1468, allegedly for illegal trading, precipitated a crisis. The English council embargoed Hanseatic trade and arrested the merchants based at the Steelyard, the London Hanse headquarters. There followed a period of total confusion.

Cologne broke ranks with the rest of the League and came to a separate understanding with England. Edward was first imprisoned and then deposed by the Earl of Warwick, taking refuge in the Low Countries in 1470. The restored Lancastrian government was opposed to any settlement with the Hansards, which prompted Hamburg and Lübeck to launch a destructive privateering campaign against English shipping. By 1471, when Edward recovered his Crown, there was full-scale war at sea, although the fact that many of the Hanse towns were acting separately, and English privateering was completely uncoordinated and uncontrolled, gave it more the appearance of a spontaneous free-for-all.

So damaging was this situation to all concerned that, as soon as he had recovered full control of the government, Edward began to seek a settlement.[42] The internal divisions of the League made this slow work, and although the outlines of an agreement were in place by 1473, the main members of the community did not accede to the Treaty of Utrecht until 1474, and Danzig not until 1476. The privileges of the Hanse in England were confirmed, and reciprocity was not secured, so from the point of view of the Merchant Adventurers all their efforts and losses had been for nothing. On the other hand, they had learned that a total breakdown of relations, such as they had just witnessed, was the worst situation of all. Relations continued to be tense and unsatisfactory, but the flow of trade was resumed. What had become clear was that the English Crown no longer felt that it could leave its merchants to fight their own battles, a view which was shared by the dukes of Burgundy and the kings of Denmark. Once commerce had become a proper concern of international diplomacy, the fortunes of an association like the Hanseatic League, which had no common sovereign, were likely to decline.

During the latter part of his reign the evidence of Edward's interest in the affairs of merchants and seamen increased and diversified. He took over an earlier practice of paying bounties for the building of large ships, and in 1474 offered a specific reward to Bristol shipwrights to construct a carvel on the Portuguese model.[43] He encouraged foreign craftsmen to settle in England and teach their skills, and encouraged his own mariners to look further afield for their trade. He seems to have been particularly interested in the opportunities created by the Portuguese voyages of the mid-century. A Bristol merchant first appeared in the Azores in 1470, and as early as 1465 two Englishmen, John Lockton and Richard Whittington, brought the king a present of lions from the Barbary coast of North Africa. When the Portuguese reacted angrily to what they saw as intrusions on their territory, the king endeavoured in February 1481 to persuade Pope Sixtus IV to declare the Guinea trade open to all comers. He did not succeed, but he had demonstrated his willingness to use political pressure in support of commercial endeavour. All these interventions seem to have been in response to initiatives from the merchants themselves. In spite of his willingness to be supportive, Edward had no policy of his own, nor any particular vision of the ways in which maritime enterprise could promote the interests of the realm. When he licensed Thomas Croft and his associates in 1480 to carry their trade to any place known or unknown, it was certainly in response to a petition from a group intending to carry out a voyage of exploration. These adventurers may (or may not) have been the first Europeans since the tenth century to reach the North American mainland, but nothing very much came of their voyage, and the king's interest was not sustained.[44]

As we have seen, the practice of merchant ships travelling in convoy for mutual protection went back a long way, and kings had occasionally provided escorts in the past, but Edward made a regular habit of 'wafting', as it came to be called. Although he did not have a navy in the later sense, or even in the sense that Henry V had had, by the 1470s he certainly owned some ships which were primarily intended for fighting. Guns had first been used at sea in the middle of the fourteenth century, but for some time they were considered to be exotic and not very useful weapons. However, Edward's carvels carried a modest number of serpentines, which were reasonably effective for anti-personnel purposes, and certainly inspired fear in less sophisticated opponents. So the king regularly provided 'wafters', at a price, for the wool and cloth fleets, and also for the fishing fleets which were beginning to cross to the Newfoundland banks. Such ships were not numerous, and not particularly effective against pirates, whose activities continued to be troublesome, but they represented an awareness on the king's part that he had a responsibility to protect his subjects on the seas. The revival of the office of Clerk of the Ships with the appointment of Thomas Roger in 1480 therefore represented slightly more than a return to the earlier Lancastrian position. Edward died at the early age of 41, and it is impossible to guess how far these preliminary indications might have been carried over another 20 years or so, which would have included the momentous voyages at the end of the century.

Although he was not particularly successful in combatting piracy at sea, the king was determined to convince all those concerned of his seriousness in addressing the problem. This included the payment of compensation where necessary to restore good relations with trading partners. Henry VI had done the same, but had reaped little benefit. Edward was more systematic. The Treaty of Utrecht with the Hanse involved payments totalling £10,000, and the merchants of Guipuzcoa in northern Spain received a further £4,000 at the same time. In 1472 by the Treaty of Chateaugiron with Brittany, Breton merchants were compensated for earlier losses by being licensed to import goods into England without paying customs.[45] At the same time the king showed a willingness to act against those of his own subjects who were notorious offenders. The town of Fowey in Cornwall was excluded from the Treaty of Chateaugiron, and two years later all the shipowners and captains belonging to the town were arrested, and their property was confiscated. Edward himself issued letters of reprisal to two Breton merchants who had been plundered by the men of Portsmouth, authorising some £3,000 of recoveries against the commerce of the town. By 1483 English piracy had been contained, not by sea power but by jurisdictional action. Of course the depredations of other nationals could not be controlled by the same means, and although a certain amount could be achieved by way of international agreements, Sir John Fortescue had been quite correct to argue that only by 'keeping the seas' with a strong fleet could the peace of commerce, and of the coastal communities, be guaranteed.

Consequently, as we approach the period with which this study is mainly concerned, a number of the elements required for important change were already in place. However, in spite of a long seafaring tradition and a large number of active merchants, English navigational science was far behind that of the Iberians, and its shipbuilding was imitative and unenterprising. Tide tables and rutters, or coastal location maps, were recent importations from the Mediterranean, and most seamen used nothing more sophisticated than a sounding line and a compass to supplement their personal knowledge of currents, shoals and channels. At a time when the Portuguese had rounded Cape Bodajor, and were rapidly approaching the southern point of Africa (sometimes by way of inadvertent excursions to Brazil), it is very doubtful whether any English seaman had the necessary skill to find the Cape Verde Islands. There are, as we have seen, later reports of Bristol mariners finding their way across the Atlantic before 1490, but they are unauthenticated, and if they happened at all, they may well have been unintentional. The kind of charts which were already being prepared at Sagres were unknown in northern Europe. Observational instruments such as the cross stave and the astrolabe, generally used in the Mediterranean, were known to some but little used. Although a bewildering number of names are used to describe English ships of the fourteenth and fifteenth centuries, these terms relate mainly to fine gradations of size. Virtually all were clinker-built, single-masted and square-rigged. By the middle of the fifteenth century, however, that situation was beginning to change, thanks partly to Henry V's taste for two-masted dromonds and carvels of southern origin. Lateen-rigged mizen masts begin to appear, greatly enhancing the sailing qualities of the ships concerned. Most, however, continued to be small. Of 47 English ships 'taken up' by the Crown between 1449 and 1451, only 7 were of 200 tons or more, and 28 were of less than 100 tons burden.[46] English shipwrights were capable of building Great Ships, but the demand was small, and that was the point of the bounties and other encouragements offered by the Crown, particularly after 1460. Carvels with three or even four masts were beginning to appear before the end of Edward's reign, but it was only after his death that the first carracks of Portuguese design were built in England. Before 1480 maritime ambition in England, whether of a commercial or a military kind, was very limited in scope and confined to a small minority of the community. The Crown's interest flickered uncertainly, but offered no consistent guidance or support outside the traditional limits of English trading experience. In short, there was no effective leadership or ambition.

Notes

1. Edward's mother, Isabella, was the sister of Charles IV, but it was contrary to the custom of France (the 'Salic Law') to allow a woman to succeed, and uncertain whether she could transmit a claim. Edward advanced his claim in 1328, but it was ignored and he was in no position to press it. The Crown passed instead to Philip, Count of Valois, who was the son of Charles, a younger brother of Philip IV (Charles IV's father), and consequently a first cousin to the late king. As relations with France deteriorated through the 1330s, Edward revived his claim in 1337, and from 1340 styled himself 'King of France'.

2. The politics of Scandinavia in the fourteenth century were fluid and confused. The line of Norwegian kings was preserved, but they were almost entirely preoccupied with conflicts involving their nobles and their neighbours. The country was also severely weakened by the Black Death. In 1397 Margaret, the widow of King Haakon VI, and regent for her son, Eric, brought about the so-called Union of Kalmar, bringing the three kingdoms together. This ensured that internal strife would continue to weaken Scandinavia throughout the fifteenth century.

3. The Cinq[ue] Ports consisted of Hastings, Romney, Hythe, Dover and Sandwich. In the thirteenth century they were bound by their charter to produce 57 ships for the king's service, to serve for fourteen days at their own cost. T. Rymer, *Foedera, conventiones, literae . . . et acta publica* (London, 1704–35), I, 53.

4. Ian Friel, *The Good Ship: Ships, Shipbuilding and Technology in England, 1200–1520* (London, 1995); Gillian Hutchinson, *Medieval Ships and Shipping* (London, 1994).

5. N.A.M. Rodger, *The Safeguard of the Sea* (London, 1997), 82.

6. Ibid., 126.

21

7. J. Sumption, *The Hundred Years War. I: Trial by Battle* (London, 1990), 321–7.

8. Sir Travers Twiss, *The Black Book of the Admiralty* (London, 1871–76).

9. Rodger, *Safeguard*, 11–14; Arne E. Christensen, *The Earliest Ships: The Evolution of Boats into Ships* (London, 1996).

10. D. Whitelock, ed., *English Historical Documents, c.500–1042* (London, 1979), 278.

11. M.T. Flanagan, 'Strongbow, Henry II and Anglo-Norman intervention in Ireland', in J. Gillingham and J.C. Holt, eds, *War and Government in the Middle Ages: Essays in Honour of J.O. Prestwich* (Woodbridge, 1984).

12. Sean Duffy, 'The first Ulster Plantation: John de Courcy and the Men of Cumbria', in T.B. Barry, R. Frame and K. Simms, eds, *Colony and Frontier in Medieval Ireland: Essays Presented to J.F. Lydon* (London, 1995).

13. M. Prestwich, *Edward I* (London, 1988), 214–16.

14. R.C. Anderson, *Oared Fighting Ships* (London, 1962); Friel, *The Good Ship*.

15. C.F. Richmond, 'The war at sea', in K. Fowler, ed., *The Hundred Years War* (London, 1971), 96–121.

16. D. Loades, *The Tudor Navy* (Aldershot, 1992), 12.

17. Rodger, *Safeguard*, 117–30.

18. Henri, Marquis de Terrier de Loray, *Jeanne de Vienne, Amiral de France, 1341–1396* (Paris, 1877), 82–3.

19. J.W. Sherborne, 'The battle of La Rochelle and the War at Sea, 1372–5', *Bulletin of the Institute of Historical Research*, 42, 1969, 17–29.

20. Charles de La Roncière, *Histoire de la Marine Française* (Paris, 1899–1932), II, 67–8.

21. R.R. Davies, *The Revolt of Owain Glyndwr* (Oxford, 1995).

22. Public Record Office (PRO) E101/44/17. S.E. Rose, *The Navy of the Lancastrian Kings* (Navy Records Society, London, 1982), 266.

23. C.F. Richmond, 'English naval power in the fifteenth century', *History*, 52, 1967, 1–15. Letters of marque were commissions to 'go upon' the king's enemies in time of war.

24. Rymer, *Foedera*, VIII, 447.

25. D. Loades, 'The kings' ships and the keeping of the seas, 1413–1480', *Medieval History*, 1, 1990, 93–104.

26. Ibid.

27. C. Richmond, 'The keeping of the seas during the Hundred Years War, 1422–1440', *History*, 49, 1964, 283–98.

28. R.A. Newhall, *The English Conquest of Normandy, 1416–1424* (London, 1924), 29–33; Sir Nicholas Nicolas, *A History of the Royal Navy* (London, 1847), II, 419–25.

29. Rose, *Navy of the Lancastrian Kings*; Loades, 'The king's ships'.

30. PRO E403/724; Richmond, 'The keeping of the seas', 292 and n.

31. *Calendar of the Patent Rolls*, 52 vols (London, 1891–1916), *1429–1436*, 509, 510, 512, 515, 608, 609; Loades, *Tudor Navy*, 23.

32. Ben Lowe, *Imagining Peace: A History of Early English Pacifist Ideas* (Philadelphia, 1997), 129–41.

33. *The Libelle of Englyshe Polycye*, ed. Sir George Warner (Oxford, 1926), 54–5 (lines 1082–91).

34. J. Stevenson, ed., *The Wars of the English in France during the Reign of Henry VI* (Rolls Series, London, 1861–64), II, ii, 583.

35. C. Ross, *Edward IV* (London, 1974), 22–40.

36. Sir John Fortescue, *The Governance of England*, ed. C. Plummer (Oxford, 1885), 248.

37. T.H. Lloyd, *The English Wool Trade in the Middle Ages* (Cambridge, 1977).

38. Ibid.

39. Ross, *Edward IV*, 353–4.

40. 'Historiae Croylandensis Continuatio', in *Rerum Anglicarum Scriptores Veterum*, ed. W. Fulman (Oxford, 1684), 569; Ross, *Edward IV*, 352.

41. J.D. Fudge, *Cargoes, Embargoes and Emissaries: The Commercial and Political Interaction of England and the German Hanse, 1450–1510* (Toronto, 1995), 18–50.

42. Ibid., 51–80.

43. Ross, *Edward IV*, 352.

44. D.B. Quinn, 'Edward IV and exploration', *Mariners Mirror*, 21, 1935, 275–84; Quinn, 'The argument for the English discovery of America between 1480 and 1494', *Geographical Journal*, 127, 1961, 227–85.

45. Ross, *Edward IV*, 207–8.

46. D. Burwash, *English Merchant Shipping, 1460–1540* (Toronto, 1947), 188–9.

CHAPTER ONE

The Crown and the Mercantile Community, 1490–1547

Edward's premature death on 9 April 1483 resulted in a totally unnecessary crisis. He left two sons, Edward aged twelve and Richard aged nine. He also left an apparently loyal and reliable younger brother, Richard of Gloucester, perfectly capable of exercising a regency over the next six years or so. Royal minorities were regrettable lapses of dynastic concentration, but this one did not look particularly threatening. However, for reasons which are still disputed, Richard did not choose to follow the script. His relations with the queen dowager and her kindred had been uneasy, but not overtly hostile.[1] However, once the king was dead, he chose to regard them as a serious threat to his own security. This somewhat neurotic attitude probably resulted from an awareness that the young Edward V was much closer to his maternal uncle, Anthony Woodville, Earl Rivers, than he was to Richard himself.[2] Perhaps he knew something about that relationship which is not on record. However, he mobilised his personal affinity against the Woodvilles, had the late king's sons declared bastards, and seized the Crown himself. In the process he executed Edward IV's Chamberlain and confidant Lord Hastings without trial, and Edward V and his brother disappeared in the Tower of London. These actions split the English political nation right down the middle, and paralysed public policy for about five years. Richard's case rested ostensibly upon a canonical technicality relating to Edward IV's marriage, but really upon the fact that an adult king of proven competence was preferable to a child, and that primogeniture was only a custom as far as the Crown was concerned, not a law.[3]

Not surprisingly, his brief reign was conducted in a state of siege. His erstwhile ally Henry Stafford, Duke of Buckingham, rebelled, but was defeated and executed before the end of 1483.[4] There were two possible alternatives to Richard as king. One was his nephew Edward, Earl of Warwick, the eight-year-old son of the Duke of Clarence, and the other was Henry Tudor, who styled himself Earl of Richmond and had a shadowy hereditary claim going back through the Beauforts to John of Gaunt.[5] Edward was not only younger than the princes who had disappeared, he was also in Richard's hands, so the attentions of all those who opposed the king began to focus on Henry Tudor. The particulars of his rise do not need to concern us. He was supported by the French, because Charles VIII wanted to keep England weak and divided; he was supported by the survivors of the Woodville affinity, and he was supported by long-time Lancastrians who had always regarded Edward IV as an intruder. With this threat building up against him, Richard could establish only the barest outline of a normal policy. He had been accepted without enthusiasm by the City of London, and given time would no doubt have sought to continue his brother's good relations there. He continued Thomas Rogers in office as Clerk of the Ships, but did not add to the modest stock of ships which he had taken over.[6] In 1484 he mobilised a small fleet against Scottish threats in the North Sea, and won an engagement, but his main maritime concern was to patrol the coasts of Brittany and France, to give early warning of Henry's activity. Early in 1485 he decided to build up a fleet against this threat, but the only consequence was the launching of one ship, the *Governor*, and by the late summer it was too late.[7] In August Richmond with a very modest force of no more than 2,000 men, mostly French mercenaries, and a few ships, made a landfall in south-west Wales. Richard appears to have made no attempt to intercept him, but instead advanced into the Midlands to confront the invaders.

Henry's strength lay not so much in his own followers, who had been augmented to no more than 5,000 in his march through Wales, as in the ambivalence with which Richard was regarded.[8] When the armies came face to face at Bosworth Field, a part of Richard's much larger force did not engage, and Thomas Stanley changed sides. The king was defeated and killed. A long historiographical tradition going back to the Tudors themselves has represented this battle as a key turning point in English history, but it certainly did not look that way at the time. Instead, the omens for Henry VII's success were distinctly unpromising. He had no experience, no personal following, and no established family position. What he did have was intelligence and a refreshing pragmatism, which turned these apparent disadvantages to good account. Having no experience and no affinity also meant that he had no inhibiting commitments, beyond a promise to marry Edward IV's daughter Elizabeth.[9] He had no originality of mind, but he was able to take things as he found them, and shape his policies as he went along. For the first two years his own security was top of the agenda, and it is only after the defeat of Lambert Simnel at Stoke in 1487 that we can speak of him taking policy initiatives, and becoming proactive rather than reactive. It is therefore all the more surprising that he must have taken an important decision in respect of his ships before the end of 1486. At some point during 1487 two large new carracks, later named the *Sovereign* and the *Regent*, were laid down. These were state-of-the-art fighting ships, one of 450 tons and the other of 600, modelled on Portuguese and French proto-types, and costing (probably) over £1,000 each.[10] The reason for making so significant an investment at this stage is not entirely clear. The ships were launched at some point in 1488, but were not immediately deployed. Nor did they represent the beginning of a major shipbuilding programme; Henry commissioned only another four or five ships of modest size during the remaining 20 years of his reign.[11] There is no evidence to suggest that they were part of an ambitious policy intention which was subsequently aborted, and the most likely answer is that they were for show. Warships were symbols of power, and the English were a seafaring people. These heavily armed ships – the *Regent* carried over 300 guns – were intended as a signal, both to deter possible aggression and to reassure his own subjects that he intended to keep the seas.

Having made this gesture, Henry's naval policy, if it can be so described, was just as low-key and piecemeal as Edward IV's had been. He totally failed to intercept Simnel's invasion from Ireland in June 1487, or to keep any ships in the Irish Sea at all as far as we know.[12] Some support, probably not including either of the capital ships, was sent to the rebels against James III of Scotland in 1489, but was defeated at sea by Sir Andrew Wood.[13] In 1492, in fulfilment of his treaty obligation to Brittany, and in order to indicate his displeasure and alarm at the personal union of Brittany with France brought about by the marriage of the Duchess Anne to Charles VIII, Henry launched 14,000 men across the Channel. Such an expedition required a large fleet of transports, and the king chartered these in Holland and Flanders rather than in England.[14] Whether this was because sufficient numbers were not available at home, or in order to spare the feelings and pockets of the English merchants, is not clear. As we have seen, Edward IV had done the same in 1475. A confrontation with Scotland, brought about by the manoeuvrings of Perkin Warbeck, led to a fleet being sent north in 1497. Some 25 ships are listed as having taken part in this expedition, but the accounts relate only to private ships 'taken up', so whether any of the king's warships were used is not clear.[15] Nor is much known about the outcome. The fleet certainly reached the Forth, but whether a shot was fired in anger is nowhere recorded. Like so much that Henry did, this campaign seems to have been primarily a gesture.

In spite of his capital ships, there is very little evidence that he had any-thing which could be dignified as a naval policy. Like Edward, and indeed Richard, before him, he provided 'wafters' for the Merchant Adventurers, and charged them for the service. Even so, he insisted upon his own priorities. In 1491 he declined the responsibility on the grounds that the presence of English warships in Netherlands waters might be seen as provocative, but the following year he provided both ships and soldiers without demur.[16] He paid bounties in a somewhat erratic manner to encourage merchants to build larger ships, and he looked after the modest number of ships which he owned himself. Thomas Rogers died in harness in January 1488, and was succeeded by William Commersall, who was in turn succeeded in 1495 by Robert Brygandyne. Some of Rogers's and Brygandyne's accounts survive.[17] They are hard to interpret, but appear to show a responsible policy of repair and maintenance, with ships passing in and out of the Clerk's care as they went on active service, or were leased to merchants for their proper occasions. In the late 1490s Brygandyne was dispensing about £1,000 a year in the king's service. This included nearly £200 for a new dock at Portsmouth, and that provision has been the subject of some speculation. The term 'dokking' had been customarily used to mean hauling a ship out of the water on a suitable mud flat, and building a temporary enclosure round it while it was caulked or repaired. However, this 'dokk' at Portsmouth was clearly an excavation, lined with timber and emptied with pumps when the ship had entered it. There is no suggestion that it was an innovation, and the 'head' of the dock was sealed and unsealed manually with tons of clay and stones.[18] It also formed a nucleus around which other services became established, notably a forge and a storehouse. Previously the king's ships had been 'dokked' in the Hamble, and the storehouse had been located at Southampton, but the new Great Ships seem to have been too big for the Hamble and the whole operation was transferred to Portsmouth. The harbour there had been partly fortified by Henry V, and Henry VII added at least one more tower.[19] Whether he deliberately intended to create an embryonic naval base, or whether that is just the way it looks with the benefit of hindsight, cannot really be determined. What we can be sure of is that Henry did not have an ambitious naval programme, or any intention of going beyond what his more competent predecessors had done for a couple of centuries.

The same may be said of his relations with the mercantile community. It is no more realistic to speak of a government 'economic policy' in the late fifteenth century than it is to speak of Gross National Product. The prosperity of London was important to the king for a variety of reasons. The customs of its port formed one of the largest single items in the Crown's ordinary revenue, and a new Book of Rates was promulgated in July 1507. By 1526 London accounted for 11 per cent of the total assessed lay wealth of the kingdom.[20] With a population of between 50,000 and 60,000 in 1500 it had only about 2 per cent of the manpower, but serious social or economic disruption so close to the centre of government could pose a real threat, as Jack Cade and his followers had demonstrated in 1450. London's support for Edward, both in 1460 and in 1471, had been crucial to his success. On the other hand, Henry had no intention of allowing commercial interests to take precedence over security. In 1493, when he was particularly exasperated with Maximilian and the Burgundians over their support for Perkin Warbeck, he embargoed all English trade with the Low Countries, including Antwerp, a prohibition which remained in place until February 1496.[21] A few years later, when he was similarly concerned to secure the surrender of the 'White Rose', Edward de la Pole, Earl of Suffolk, Henry ordered a further suspension of trade, which began in May 1502. He did not secure his objective, and the suspension was not officially lifted until 1506, but the resumption of negotiations in 1504 caused it to be largely ignored thereafter.[22] As a result of this political interference, the export of English broadcloths, which was the worst affected as well as being both the best recorded and by far the most important, tended to fluctuate considerably from year to year. The fact that the general trend was steadily upward (from 50,878 in 1485–91 to 81,835 in 1503–09) owed less to the king's hot and cold attitude than to the dynamics of the trade itself.[23] When he chose, Henry could be very supportive, and secured the insertion of favourable trading clauses in both his main treaties with the Low Countries, the *Intercursus Magnus* of 1496 and the *Intercursus Malus* ten years later.

The king listened to important interest groups like the Merchant Adventurers and the Merchant Staplers, and responded positively when his other concerns did not take precedence. A large number of statutes regulating different aspects of trade can be traced directly to petitions by the parties involved, including the Navigation Acts of 1486 and 1489.[24] Sometimes the Commons themselves petitioned the king, as they did to secure the recital of the statute of 17 Edward IV c.1, requiring alien merchants to disburse the profits of their English trade within England.[25] To anyone unfamiliar with the procedures of the late medieval parliament, these numerous acts look like the work of an active and involved government, but that was not the case. Very often acts were pushed through by one interest group, and promptly repealed in the next session by pressure from another. The king did resort to statute, but only when his own interests, or what he regarded as the interests of the community as a whole, were involved. In the first parliament of the reign, for example, he required that aliens made denizens should continue to pay customs at the alien's rate, and should not 'cover' goods for other aliens.[26] He also insisted that no acts concerning merchandise should prejudice the merchants of the Hanse. This led to direct conflict with the Merchant Adventurers, who were trying to do just that. Statutes concerning vagabondage and the control of enclosure also emanated from the council, but need not concern us here.

Henry's concern to defuse tension between the Merchant Adventurers and the Hanse also extended to the former's relations with the Merchant Staplers. The Staplers had been the first, and by far the greatest, merchant company of the late fourteenth and early fifteenth centuries, but by Henry's reign they were in steady decline. This was partly because the trade in raw wool was heavily taxed, and partly because reviving population levels and other less obvious factors had led to a steadily increasing demand by domestic cloth manufacturers. In 1450 they had exported about 10,000 sacks, but between 1491 and 1497 the average was no more than 7,434, and that dropped still further to 5,074 between 1503 and 1509.[27] By 1490 some of the Staplers were attempting to recover their prosperity by trading cloth themselves, in defiance of the Adventurers monopoly. They did this, not so much by intruding upon the Adventurers' staple markets in Flanders, Brabant, Holland and Zeeland, as by using their own staple port of Calais.[28] As the Adventurers were also forced to use Calais while the Low Countries were embargoed, there was considerable confusion. After several disputes, in 1497 the king resorted to statute in an attempt to resolve the quarrel. The act of 12 Henry VII c.6 did not address the issue directly, but rather authorised the Adventurers to set an entry fine of 10 marks (£6 13s 4d) for freedom of the fellowship.[29] This was considerably less than they had been accustomed to charge, but had the effect of giving them statutory authority to admit or exclude whoever they wished. It also reaffirmed that no one might trade in unfinished cloth who was not free of the company. This in turn meant that the Adventurers were now at liberty to exclude Staplers from their own fellowship if they wished to do so, while maintaining their monopoly control. This should have clarified the legal position, but unfortunately did not. In 1505 the parties were before the King's council, who ruled, without reference to the statute, that members of each company could trade in the other's commodity, provided that they submitted to the jurisdiction of the appropriate court in respect of any transaction in dispute.[30] A few weeks later the Staplers were back, complaining that the Adventurers had seized cloths belonging to members of their fellowship at Calais in order to force them to become free of the Adventurers as well. The statute of 1497 had clearly authorised such action, but the council ordered the Adventurers to return the cloths and to cease their campaign of harassment.[31] The waters were now thoroughly muddied, and the controversy continued unresolved into the next reign.

What this inconclusive dispute demonstrates is that the king had no policy respecting the relative merits of cloth and wool exports, and probably no real understanding of the issues. He tried with some seriousness of purpose to prevent two of his most important merchant companies from feuding. This was partly because it was his duty to keep the peace and partly because it was in his interest to have a unified trade in England's most valuable export commodity. In that way it became a much more effective political lever. For the same reason he showed an active interest in the way in which the Adventurers organised themselves. They had for some time had a Governor and Court in the Low Countries, to exercise and defend the privileges which they had been granted there, and in 1486 an Act of Common Council in London created a similar Court, mainly for the purpose of organising the annual fleets.[32] For the time being the Adventurers had no headquarters of their own in London; they met at the Mercers Hall, and used the Mercers Wardens as their officers.[33] However, the king desired that they should be as similar as possible to their rivals the Staplers, and in 1505 he issued letters patent, setting up a Governor and Court of Assistants (34 in number) in London.[34] He also stipulated that the outports should be represented on this Court, again wishing to defuse a rumbling dispute in order to unify the trade.

Henry's reign as a whole was one of increasing prosperity. More ships were being built; trade with Spain increased significantly with the improvement in diplomatic relations; and the value of goods paying the petty customs in London went up from £126,000 in 1485 to £226,000 in 1509.[35] Apart from London, statistics are hard to come by, and do not tell a consistent story. The trade of Southampton declined when the London merchants moved their business back to the capital, and their Italian partners followed them. The petty customs of the port of Boston in Lincolnshire, although fluctuating wildly from year to year, dropped away from an average of £621 10s 0d between 1475 and 1480 to £223 17s 0d between 1504 and 1509, largely because of the disappearance of the Hanseatic merchants.[36] On the other hand, using the same periods, Hull increased from £2,244 6s 8d to £5,302 10s 0d. None of this had very much to do with the king, although the payment of bounties at 5s a ton may have encouraged some merchants to build rather larger ships than they might otherwise have done. Statistics here are unobtainable, and even the tonnage necessary to qualify for a subsidy was not clearly laid down. It probably depended upon individual negotiation and the circumstances of the moment, but the lower limit seems to have been no more than 80 tons.[37] However, the number of vessels benefiting should probably be counted in dozens rather than hundreds over the whole reign.

Only in one respect did Henry show any serious interest in seafaring, as distinct from the revenue advantages of trade. English maritime enterprise in the late Middle Ages is poorly documented, but the glimpses which can be obtained are significant. By 1478 English ships were carrying cloth to Pisa and Livorno, although not in significant quantities. At about the same time the first Bristol merchants appeared in the Azores, although it appears that in that case the shipping was Portuguese.[38] In 1479 English traders were noticed (and even living) on Chios, and two years later in Oran. Not everyone was content with the easy option of trading to northern Europe, and probably the exclusive attitudes of the London controlled companies encouraged merchants from the outports to seek alternatives. The use of royal warships (such as the *Sovereign*), which were hired for these voyages, added to their security, and the Florentines, who were often at odds with their Italian neighbours, were willing to encourage the English presence.[39] By 1480, and perhaps as early as 1420, seamen from the east coast ports had re-established contact with Iceland, and discovered the rich cod fisheries off Newfoundland, although there is no evidence that they landed there. It is normally argued that the English were well off the pace being set by the Iberians when it came to navigational and cartographic skills, and in terms of hard evidence that must be accepted. However, if these vaguely reported enterprises were real, perhaps that judgement should be modified. Regular and successful visits to the Newfoundland banks could not have been carried out by seamen who were virtually helpless out of sight of land.

Moreover, Bristol ships may have gone still further. In the next generation it was persistently believed that they had made a landfall in 'Brazil' about ten years before Columbus set off on his momentous voyage.[40] If such an event did occur, it is surprising that it was not properly recorded, but if it happened more or less by accident, and with no tangible consequences, nobody at the time may have thought that it was of much significance. However, something must have prompted John Cabot, a Genoese of Venetian citizenship, to look to Bristol in 1495 when he was planning that ambitious enterprise which was to give Henry VII his only experience of maritime patronage. Cabot was trying to emulate Columbus by seeking a passage to Asia through a more northerly latitude, so it was natural that he should look to the King of England for support. Normally, one would have expected a relatively uninformed outsider to have looked also to London, which was by far the largest seaport. Cabot, however, went to Bristol, where he found not only interest but ships and seamen suitable for his purpose.[41] He must also have found a modest level of investment, because his negotiations with the king, although successful up to a point, did not produce any money. On 5 March 1496 Cabot was granted letters patent authorising him to undertake a voyage of discovery, using up to five ships of any tonnage, and to investigate 'quascumque insulas, patrias, regiones sive provincias gentilium et infidelium [quorumcumque], in quacumque parte mundi positas, quae Christianis omnibus ante haec tempora fuerunt incognitae' ('whatever islands, countries, regions or provinces, heathen or infidel . . . in whatsoever part of the world they may be found, previously unknown to Christian people').[42]

He was empowered to claim any lands so discovered for the Crown of England, but specifically instructed to avoid anywhere already claimed by the King of Spain. He was authorised to keep any profits accruing from the voyage, less 20 per cent payable to the king, but he was to bear the whole cost of the expedition himself. Cabot attempted to carry out his mission later that year, but was turned back by storms, and it was not until May 1497 that he finally crossed the Atlantic, with one small ship and eighteen men, presumably all that his modest resources would run to.[43] He hoisted the English flag at some point on the North American mainland, probably in what is now Maine, and was back in England by 6 August.

So far Henry could hardly claim to have been a generous promoter, and his initial reward to Cabot (£10) was out of proportion with the achievement, especially as he received more than a fair share of the credit which the Genoese gained for his exploit. However, as was often the case with Henry, once he was satisfied with the service he was being given, his attitude changed. On 13 December 1497 Cabot was awarded a pension of £20 a year (about £20,000 in contemporary money), which was clearly a retainer to keep him in English service, and the king listened with some enthusiasm to his further plans. On 3 February 1498 he issued Cabot with fresh letters patent, supplementing those of the previous year.[44] This time the restriction was removed, and the expedition was authorised to explore the coast southward from its original landfall, even if this did mean contact with the Spaniards. Not more than six ships of up to 200 tons were specified, and this time the king provided one himself. The others were financed by the merchants of Bristol and London. Expectations seem to have been high, and volunteers were recruited without difficulty. In early May 1498 John Cabot and his small fleet set out again – and sailed into oblivion.[45] No record remains of the fate of the expedition, and Cabot himself certainly died, but it is possible that one or more ships returned, bringing such disappointing news of their success that all official interest evaporated.

Somehow by 1501 Henry knew that whatever land Cabot had discovered, it was not Asia, and it did not appear to be particularly rich. In Bristol, however, this was not devastating news. After all, the Spanish Indies were not Asia either, but they were still turning out to be valuable colonies. Further letters patent were obtained in 1501 and 1502, setting out regulations and privileges for colonies and new trading companies, enterprises in which John Cabot's son Sebastian was actively involved.[46] The king was benevolent, but strictly non-participatory, as he had been in 1496, and that may have been one of the reasons why these exalted plans came to nothing.

By 1506 a company of adventurers to the New Found Lands had been established, again a gesture of confidence by potential investors, but requiring no more than complaisance from Henry. As far as we know, no trade resulted and the patents remained dead letters.[47] By 1508 the emphasis had shifted away from the New Found Lands themselves, and Sebastian proposed a new expedition to find a route to Asia via the north – what would later be known as the north-west passage. Fresh investment was attracted, and the king's blessing given. By later standards this voyage was quite successful, and seems to have penetrated into Hudson Bay long before Hudson. However, it did not deliver on its primary objective, and by the time it returned, Henry VII was dead.[48]

The old king may not have done very much to encourage maritime enterprise, but he had responded positively when approaches were made to him. If John Cabot had not died, he might have been tempted to do more, but even when he was most persuaded and engaged, it was a low priority. The fitting out of one ship, and the granting of sundry patents, which cost Henry nothing, do not represent a very significant commitment. It was more, however, than his son was prepared to make. When Richard Hakluyt was celebrating the maritime achievements of the English, just after the Armada, he was naturally anxious to present the queen's father in a positive light. As a result he produced some very dubious stories as though they were established fact. For example, in 1516 'Sir Thomas Pert, knight' and Sebastian Cabot are alleged to have made a voyage to Brazil, Santo Domingo and Puerto Rico, with the king's support.[49] There is no evidence that Sebastian was in England, except as a visitor, after 1512, when he was paid 20s for providing the king with a map, and Sir Thomas Pert does not appear to have existed at all. The person referred to is Thomas Spert, who in 1516 was the master of the king's Great Ship, the *Mary Rose*, and also a yeoman of the Chamber.[50] He became Clerk Controller of the Navy in 1524, and was knighted in 1535. Spert was an experienced seaman, and may indeed have made such a voyage, with or without Sebastian Cabot, but there is no other record of it, and the king's support is purely hypothetical. Four years later Henry is alleged to have urged a group of sceptical London merchants to support another scheme of Cabot's 'for the New Island', but nothing came of it. Slightly more substantial is the claim, originating with Robert Thorne, that the king sent out 'two fair ships well manned and victualled' in May 1527 'for the discovery of the north parts'. One of these ships, the *Dominus Vobiscum*, was cast away; the other made a landfall, and returned in October with nothing else accomplished.[51] There is no record evidence for this voyage either, but Thorne himself was real enough, and certainly urged maritime enterprises upon Henry. Thorne also supported another scheme of Sebastian Cabot's in 1525. By that time Cabot was in the service of

Charles V, and his attempt to reach China was ventured on the Emperor's behalf, but he was obviously still in touch with his friends in England, because Thorne backed him and Roger Barlow actually sailed on the voyage.[52]

By 1530 we are on slightly firmer ground. There is no good reason to doubt the enterprise of William Hawkins, who, in that year, 'armed out a tall and goodly ship of his own of the burthen of 250 tons, called the *Pole of Plymouth*, wherein he made three long and famous voyages to the coast of Brazil, a thing in those dayes very rare, especially to our nation'.[53] Hawkin's exploits were well known, and his son John was still alive when Hakluyt was writing. However, even Hakluyt did not claim that Henry had provided anything more tangible than permission, although he alleged that the king had been hugely impressed when Hawkins brought back with him a 'savage king', who was duly presented at court. Hawkins's motive had not been discovery but trade, and he was sufficiently successful to persevere for a while, but without any organised backing such a solitary effort was unlikely to get far in the long run, and no one was interested in exploiting the openings which Hawkins had made. Rather different was the enterprise of 'Mr. Hore of London', who 'being much given to the study of cosmography' in 1536 persuaded a group of about 50 gentlemen to join him in a voyage of discovery 'upon the northwest parts of America'. The king, says Hakluyt, accorded the enterprise his 'good favour and countenance', but nothing more, so presumably the gentlemen were the subscribers.[54] Two ships were fitted out, the *Trinity* and the *Minion*, and about 30 of the backers actually went on the voyage. After hair-raising privations, they lost both their ships and made their way back in a French vessel which they had managed to hijack. Hore seems to have achieved nothing, which must have discouraged other similar ventures for many years.

Henry was not indifferent to trade, or to the wellbeing of London, particularly towards the end of his reign when his financial problems began to mount, but his priorities were consistently elsewhere. Most particularly his Great Matter – the divorce followed by the break with Rome – left all his merchants in Habsburg territories very vulnerable. This was especially the case with those trading out of Seville and San Lucar, because many Spaniards chose to regard Henry's repudiation of Catherine as an insult to their nation. Moreover the king's renunciation of papal jurisdiction left all his subjects abroad in a tight spot. If they disowned his actions, they were in trouble when they came home; if they supported him, they were in trouble where they were, and in Spain that meant the attentions of the Inquisition.[55] Charles did not order any general policy of exclusion or harassment, but local officials took the law into their own hands. Men were imprisoned and questioned; ships and cargoes were seized, not consistently but in a random and arbitary fashion which discouraged all but the most resolute. Trade with Spain declined sharply, and because of Spanish rule and influence in Italy, the promising late fifteenth-century developments there also withered. In 1545 Robert Reneger of Southampton became so exasperated with the manner in which officials at San Lucar were confiscating his property that he took the law into his own hands, and seized an incoming Spanish ship from the Indies, with a cargo worth many thousands of ducats.[56] The Emperor's ambassador in London complained vigorously, but Henry's council sympathised with Reneger, and issued only a formal censure for what was, in truth, a major act of piracy. Anglo-Habsburg relations, which were already strained following the peace of Crespy in 1544, declined still further.

At the same time intensified Ottoman activity in the Mediterranean spelled the end of the hopeful Levantine adventures of Henry VII's reign. Rhodes had fallen to the Turks in 1522, and by 1540 Ottoman influence over the minor Muslim states of the North African coast was rapidly increasing. The corsair stronghold of Algiers became a dependency in 1534, when its most famous captain Khair ad Din, known as Barbarossa, entered the sultan's service. Charles V's massive effort to take the city in 1541 failed, and the security of Christian shipping continued to decline.[57] It did not matter to Khair ad Din that the Spanish and the English were at loggerheads. Henry, like his father, had originally been willing to make the occasional warship available for Mediterranean voyages, but as the situation deteriorated it became clear that one or two armed ships were no longer sufficient, and like the merchants themselves, he withdrew.

This contraction, which also involved the abandonment of hopeful earlier probes down the West African coast, looks like a serious setback, but at the time it was insignificant except to the individual traders themselves. The same period, between 1510 and 1550, saw the rise and rise of Antwerp.[58] Thanks to its canny handling of political relations with Maximilian and the Archduke Philip in the late fifteenth century, the city had been able to take over much of the trade which had previously flowed to Ghent, Ypres and Bruges. Also enjoying a superb strategic position, by 1500 Antwerp was already becoming the great entrepôt and clearing house of north European trade. The Portuguese spice staple was located there in 1501, and it was in Antwerp that French wine, woad, salt and corn were traded for Hanseatic flax, skins and timber – and English woollen cloth. By 1510 the latter was probably the most valuable single commodity, and Henry VIII, no less than his father, took the politics of this seriously. As the value of the trade increased, embargoes became more potent weapons; but they were double-edged. As we have seen, between 1490 and 1509 the cloth staple had moved backwards and forwards between Calais and Antwerp in accordance with the state of diplomatic relations. That continued to be the case in the early years of the new reign, and there were periods of intensive negotiation, particularly between 1509 and 1515, in which the king was actively engaged.[59] If Henry ever did urge his merchants to look further afield, it was probably in the context of one of these early involvements. Thereafter Thomas Wolsey, soon to be Lord Chancellor and Cardinal, assumed the direct responsibility, and in 1520 the key treaty, long worked for, was finally negotiated. All legal proceedings arising from earlier toll disputes were abrogated. The subjects of each prince were to enjoy liberty of commercial intercourse, and pay such dues as had been originally agreed in 1496.[60]

Shortly after, encouraged by this new security, the Merchant Adventurers established their principal headquarters in a privileged 'English house' in Antwerp, and their trade boomed. So great was the mutual advantage accruing from this treaty that political interference with the trade became for many years less volatile. Even in 1528 when there was a 'phoney war' between Henry and Charles, Wolsey and Margaret of Savoy, the regent of the Netherlands, managed to patch together a series of truces to protect the merchants.[61] In spite of his chagrin over Henry's treatment of his aunt, Charles V never attempted to make either Antwerp or the Merchant Adventurers the butt of his anger. As Stephen Vaughan, later Henry's financial agent, pointed out in 1531: 'the emperor in no wyse sufferith anything to be done in vyolacion or breche of such intercourse or covenauntes as have been concluded bytwyn hym and the kynges hyghnes'.[62]

There were, of course, alarms. In 1533 there was a panic among the English merchants, which led them to make special representations in Brussels, but the new regent, Mary of Hungary, was reassuring, pointing out that it was not in the Emperor's interest to inhibit so profitable a business. More seriously, in 1538, following the Truce of Nice, Henry was convinced that England was about to be invaded, and shipping on both sides was 'stayed'. However, the crisis passed, for reasons which had nothing whatsoever to do with commerce. Thomas Cromwell, the king's chief minister, reduced the customs rates for aliens, and although this may not have pleased the Adventurers, it helped to get the trade flowing again.[63] From 1538 to 1546 Henry maintained Vaughan as his financial agent, and as Vaughan's biographer has pointed out, the king's diplomacy in the Low Countries during those years was principally directed to securing favourable trading concessions.[64] By 1547 the annual shipment of broadcloths from London to Antwerp had risen to over 125,000 (a 75 per cent increase during the reign), so it is not surprising that both the merchants and the king were content, and prepared to regard the virtual demise of the southward trade with something akin to equanimity.[65] It was also on the security of the immense value of this trade that Henry began to borrow money on the Bourse in 1545. Over the same period the proportion of the trade passing through Blackwell Hall in London had risen from about 50 per cent to over 80 per cent. A lot of eggs were beginning to gather in one basket.

In a world increasingly dominated by kings, the Hanseatic League was something of an anachronism. However, as long as the various cities which comprised it held together, it continued to be powerful, controlling as it did a virtual monopoly of Baltic produce, particularly naval supplies. Edward IV's Treaty of Utrecht continued to govern the position of the Hanse in England throughout Henry VII's reign.[66] The king was not averse to threatening Hanseatic privileges from time to time, either to make a political point or to sweeten the Merchant Adventurers, but it made very little difference to their position, and the first parliament of Henry VIII's reign confirmed the Treaty of Utrecht in full.[67] However, the failure of reciprocity for English merchants in the Baltic continued to rankle, and in 1513 Wolsey delivered a sharp rebuke to the Germans, warning them that they should not presume upon their privileges, which they enjoyed by the king's grace. By the time of the Treaty of London in 1518, Wolsey was coming to agree with the Londoners, who claimed that the position of the Hanse was detrimental, not only to the interests of English commerce, but to those of the Crown itself. In 1519 the Adventurers sent a petition to the council, alleging that the Germans were selling their goods retail in London, contrary to the City's charter, and Wolsey convened a meeting with the League at Bruges in 1520.[68] Realising which way the wind was blowing, the Hanse delegates delayed and prevaricated. Any renegotiation of the Treaty of Utrecht must be to their disadvantage. On the other hand, they knew that it was only freedom from military commitments which enabled Henry to take a tough line. As soon as he became involved in war again, he would reconsider his position. Moreover, even in decline the League could still muster 60 ships of war, as it did in September 1522, and that was twice as many as Henry could deploy at that date. Consequently in 1523 the king backed off, leaving the Hanseatic privileges virtually unchanged, and the Merchant Adventurers fuming with frustration.[69] In 1529 they returned to the charge with a fresh list of grievances, but although Henry sympathised with both their sentiments and their intentions, he could not afford to make any further enemies at that juncture.

During his time as Chancellor, Sir Thomas More used the search for heretical books as a pretext to harass the Steelyard, and a brief suspension was imposed in 1535. In 1539 the Senate of the League struck back with a list of its own grievances, particularly complaining that the English government held the Steelyard merchants collectively responsible for depredations to English shipping carried out by one member city. For this the King's council was quite unrepentant, and rumours began to circulate that the Hanseatic privileges would be revoked altogether.[70] Tension continued to be high until 1542, when the return of war again persuaded Henry not to press his merchants' complaints. He urgently needed the naval supplies which the League alone could guarantee, and backed off again in return for consignments of spars and rigging which reached him in 1544. By the following year relations had recovered sufficiently for the League to provide Henry with three vessels for service in the Channel.[71]

Although they did not produce any conclusive results, the king's sparrings with the Hanse throughout his reign not only provide excellent examples of the interface between commerce and politics but also a foreshadowing of the role which government might be expected to play in the future. Unlike Antwerp, the trade to the Baltic was not simply a question of commercial prosperity; it also involved national security. The time was bound to come when the English government would have to insist that a significant part, at least, of the trade in naval stores was in the hands of its own subjects. Henry VIII's decision to maintain a standing navy would make it eventually imperative that the power of the Hanse should be broken.

What prompted the king to this momentous shift of policy is not really known. As we have seen, in the past navies had come and gone in accordance with the exigencies of war. The king's responsibility to 'keep the seas' for the security of his coasts and merchants had been enunciated, and even acknowledged, but had never been effectively addressed. Henry had inherited about half a dozen ships from his father, and possibly a couple more in building, but this was no more than had been available to Henry VII himself, or to Richard. When he had decided that he wanted a war with France, which he did soon after his accession, and certainly by 1511, the young king began to collect ships. The *Mary Rose* and the *Peter Pomegranate*, which may have been laid down before April 1509, were launched in 1510; the *Lion* was taken from the Scots in 1511; and no fewer than fourteen others, varying in tonnage from 120 to 900, were purchased or built in 1512.[72] By the time that the war finished in 1514, Henry had 29 warships of various sizes – a similar fleet to that which Henry V had possessed in 1420.

By that time there had already been some signs that the new king was thinking differently. The accounts of John Heron, the Treasurer of the Chamber, show that an enhanced level of activity antedated the war. Not only were ships prepared and rigged (apparently at the king's expense) to waft the Merchant Adventurers fleet in June 1511, but in the following month three further men of war escorted other, unnamed merchants to Zeeland, and in August of the same year 'arrearages' were paid 'for defending the merchants against rovers'.[73] In less than three years, and in peacetime, Heron expended nearly £5,000 on naval activity, and that did not include any of the routine maintenance costs, which were borne by Robert Brygandyne, who was still the Clerk of the Ships. Moreover, during the war several steps were taken to enlarge the naval infrastructure. New docks were constructed in 1512 at Limehouse and at Erith in Kent. Storehouses were built at Erith and at Deptford – substantial brick buildings intended to last – and a Keeper of the Storehouses was appointed.[74] Both this Keeper and the Clerk of the Ships were then placed under the supervision of a new officer called the Clerk Controller, a Gentleman of the Chamber named John Hopton.[75] It seems clear that by 1512 at least Henry had decided not to dispose of his war fleet in the customary manner, and in July 1514, when hostilities were coming to an end, fourteen ships were mothballed at Deptford and Erith. Their ordnance was returned to the Tower of London, and most of their rigging handed over to Hopton for storage. Each ship was then placed on a care and maintenance basis, with a skeleton crew.[76] A few older vessels were disposed of and the rest, about a dozen in number, were kept in commission for winter patrols and other regular service.

The naval administration created in 1512 was not particularly sophisticated. There was no clear chain of command, and no departmental structure. The officers' functions overlapped, and they seem to have accounted separately. Nevertheless they represented a major advance in strategic thinking, and Henry's decision to mothball half his fleet in July 1514 must be ranked in importance with his decision to break with the papacy, or to dissolve the monasteries. One possible reason for this course of action is that he saw himself as a 'warrior king', and had no intention of remaining at peace for long. Pretexts for war were easy to find in Renaissance Europe, and Henry had not yet discovered how limited his resources were. Another possibility is simply that the king had a boyish enthusiasm for warships. When he found out, just before the war, that James IV of Scotland had a Great Ship (the French-built *Michael*), larger than any which he possessed, he immediately ordered the construction of a 'super dreadnaught' which was launched in 1513 as the *Henry Imperial*, or *Henry Grace à Dieu*, of 1,500 tons.[77] More significantly, Henry seems to have been personally responsible for the design of the 800-ton *Great Galley*, and is supposed to have strutted about in a cloth of gold sailor suit at her launching in 1515. This ship was properly a galleasse rather than a galley, and carried a gun deck over the oarsmen. Even knowledgeable Italians were impressed, but the fact that she remained in service until 1538 probably owed more to the king's interest than to her performance.[78] Both ships and facilities continued to be constructed after the war, but not at the same rate. In addition to the *Great Galley*, the small *Katherine Plesaunce* was built in 1518, and the 300-ton *Mary Gloria* purchased in 1517. Also in 1517 a new basin or 'pond' was constructed at Erith, to shelter some of the Great Ships 'aflote' during the winter.[79]

As far as the operation of the navy was concerned, a heightened level of ordinary activity was more obvious than success in battle. Whether the regular, all-the-year-round patrols actually captured many pirates must be doubted, but they probably deterred the more blatant infringements, and the first 20 years of Henry's reign saw fewer complaints and protests than either before or after. Sir Edward Howard used royal ships to defeat the Scottish rover Sir Andrew Barton in 1511, and that eased the pressure on the east coast ports, but the fortunes of war in 1512–14 were mixed. Howard showed some tactical imagination when he attacked the French fleet at Brest in 1512, but the resulting engagement was inconclusive, and in the following year he was defeated and killed in an attack on French galleys on the same coast.[80] Nevertheless, the English fleet 'kept' the Channel successfully, and the coast was raided only once, when Brighton was attacked in 1514. However important Henry thought his ships to be, there is no sign that he, or any of his captains, had any coherent strategy for the use of the navy he was creating. Nor did the English at this stage have any particular technological advantages. The *Mary Rose* appears to have been built with ports to carry side-firing guns, but she was neither as big nor as well armed in that mode as the *Michael*, launched only two years later.[81] It was Scottish rather than English sea fighting capacity which was precocious at this stage, and arguably if the two fleets had encountered, the English would have come off worst. However, Scotland was poor, even by comparison with England, and the effort proved impossible to sustain, especially after James was killed at Flodden in 1513. In 1520 English warships were still clinker-built, and only a few of them carried the new heavy guns. Henry had inherited his father's interest in artillery, and established a new gunfoundry at Hounsditch in 1511, but he still imported most of his naval guns from Mechlin and it was not until 1543 that the newer and more effective cast iron guns began to be made in England. Nevertheless, when war returned in 1522, Henry had a larger, better maintained and more available fleet than any of his predecessors had enjoyed.

The second French war of 1522–25 did not see any major innovations. A second dock was excavated at Portsmouth, and brewhouses and bakehouses built there, indicating that it was perceived as a permanent base and victualling station, not merely a convenient rendezvous.[82] The fleet saw some action, both against the Scots and the French, with mixed but not discreditable results. Five new, mainly small, ships were acquired, three of them built, while the retirement of Brygandyne and the death of Hopton brought new men into the naval offices, particularly Thomas Spert and William Gonson. Both Spert and Gonson were experienced seamen, which neither Brygandyne nor Hopton had been, and Gonson became increasingly important over the next decade. Although he was theoretically, as

Storehouse Keeper, the least senior, Wolsey trusted him.[83] Until the latter's fall in 1529, he was responsible for routine naval administration, as for most other aspects of day-to-day government. Although Spert accounted separately, Gonson began to handle most of the money, usually on specific warrants, but sometimes on general warrants which gave him considerable discretion in the allocation of funds. This he continued to do after 1530, but the king's attention was distracted by other issues, and Wolsey's application was sadly missed. The navy was not exactly neglected. Three small ships were built during the war, and two more added in 1530 and 1532. Money continued to be spent, but large wooden ships deteriorate fast, whether in use or not, and it seems that a large backlog of maintenance built up. In 1536 Eustace Chapuys, the Imperial ambassador, reported with a hint of satisfaction (he did not like Henry's policies) that although the King of England had many great ships, they were in such a poor state that it would take eighteen months to get them to sea.[84] Chapuys almost certainly exaggerated, and by the time that he wrote Thomas Cromwell had already awoken to the danger. Six ships were either built or rebuilt between the beginning of 1535 and the end of 1536, including both the *Peter Pomegranate* and the *Mary Rose*, and Henry proudly and deliberately showed them off to the French ambassador.

By this time all warships were being built with gun decks, and using the stronger carvel construction, but as yet this had had no effect on fighting tactics. Instructions issued in 1530 make it clear that warships were still expected to fight individually, and to use their guns primarily to 'soften up' the opposition for boarding.[85] Cromwell was proud of his achievement in modernising the navy, but his years in power did not see any foreign war, and war continued to be the catalyst for major change. There was a major invasion scare in 1539, but Henry was persuaded to direct most of his emergency defence expenditure into coastal fortifications, and the navy benefited little. Ships were mustered during the summer, as were the county militias, and the king seems to have been satisfied with their state of readiness. In spite of the fact that he now had nearly 40 ships of his own, most of those called upon at this time were privately owned, as they would have been in the past. The state of the English merchant marine is hard to quantify, but the number of English ships recorded as entering and leaving port had been steadily and sometimes dramatically increasing for about a century.[86] More particularly, they were getting larger. There are no surveys before Elizabeth's reign, but the number of references to ships of over 200 tons grew decade by decade, particularly in major ports such as Bristol and London. Henry had no difficulty in mobilising his defence force, but private warships were a thing of the past. Long-distance traders were always armed up to a point, but not adequately for naval auxiliaries, and the main expenditure involved in this mobilisation arose from the provision and shipping of guns. It may have been satisfaction with this aspect of his preparations which caused the king to divert so much money into places like Calshott Castle. Although the *Henry Grace à Dieu* was rebuilt (and reduced in size) in 1540, no new ship was added to the fleet between 1538 and 1542. Then war came again, and there were further significant developments.

By this time Henry had given up his earlier grandiose ambition to reconstruct the empire of Henry V, but he still regarded the French as his natural enemies, and the Scots as rebellious subjects. As we have seen, much of his diplomacy, particularly after 1540, was directed towards rebuilding the Imperial alliance, and his merchants benefited from that considerably. By 1542 he had come to an understanding with Charles which involved a resumption of those hostilities which had been suspended in 1525, when a different political agenda had supervened.[87] The war which followed, however unnecessary it may have been, was reasonably successful. The Scots were heavily defeated at Solway Moss, opening the way for the Treaty of Greenwich in which they accepted a marriage between their infant queen and Henry's son, Edward. Boulogne was taken from the French, and a massive French invasion attempt in 1545 was frustrated.

On the other hand, it was hugely expensive – over £2 million between 1542 and 1546 – and that was to have serious repercussions. The navy was greatly expanded. Over the same four years no fewer than 24 ships, ranging from 100 to 700 tons, were built, purchased or taken as prizes.[88] Two, or perhaps three, were lost. It was during this war also that English gunfounders finally mastered the art of casting iron cannon, which they were producing in significant quantities by 1546. Letters of marque were granted for the first time on 20 December 1544.[89] The Admiralty Court had for many years issued letters of reprisal, authorising aggrieved merchants to recover their losses by direct action when other methods had failed. This proclamation, however, enabled the king's subjects to make war upon the Scots and the French at their own expense, keeping the whole proceeds for themselves. It was probably not an original idea, but it opened a very important chapter in English maritime history. Piracy was as old as shipping, but the day of the privateer was just dawning. Most important of all, as the war was coming to an end, the naval administration was reorganised. The immediate cause of this was probably the death of William Gonson in 1544. Gonson had quickly commended himself to Cromwell in the same way that he had to Wolsey, and for ten years before his death had been acting as *de facto* Treasurer of the Navy. Between 1545 and 1546 the existing three officers were replaced by a council of six, called the Council for Marine Causes.[90] To the Clerk of the Ships and Clerk Controller were added a Treasurer, a Surveyor and Rigger, a Master of Naval Ordnance and a Vice-Admiral or Lieutenant. The new council, which was presided over by the Lieutenant, was responsible to the Lord Admiral, but was given a large degree of autonomy, and constituted in effect as a department of state, similar to the Exchequer or, more appropriately, the Ordnance Office, upon which it was probably modelled. Each officer was given clearly defined responsibilities, an appropriate salary, and generous expenses. The Admiralty had been born.

We do not know who was responsible for this important innovation. It has the appearance of an initiative by Thomas Cromwell, but Cromwell had been executed in 1540, and we have no evidence that he had ever addressed the problem of naval management, being content to work through Gonson. It may have been Henry's own idea, as the reorganisation of the council in 1535–36 probably was; or it may have come from the initiative of the new Lord Admiral, John Dudley, Viscount Lisle. Lisle, who was appointed in 1543, had been a close associate of Cromwell, and sympath- ised with many of his methods.[91] He was also an intelligent and innovat- ive commander. His fighting instructions, issued in 1545, show him to have been a student of the latest French and Spanish thinking. For the first time he envisaged his ships manoeuvring and fighting in formation, using their guns systematically rather than at random.[92] A few years ago it was argued that Lisle's pursuit of the French fleet, following the stand-off in the Solent in 1545, saw the first use of the synchronised broadside.[93] This now seems doubtful, but, as we shall see, Lisle was a man with an innovative streak in him, and a genuine interest in maritime affairs.

When Henry died in January 1547, he therefore left a very different situation from that which he had inherited. London was twice the size that it had been in 1509, and the trade of the Merchant Adventurers was about twice as valuable. Instead of some half a dozen ships, he left a standing navy of over 50 vessels, controlled by the most sophisticated administration in Europe. He had three dockyards, with storehouses and other facilities, a fortified naval base at Portsmouth, gunfoundries, and a semi-permanent workforce of carpenters and shipwrights managed by full time masters. There were no colonies, however, and long-distance trade had withered. Outside the arts of war and courtly love, the king had no imagination.

Not all Englishmen shared this myopia. Robert Thorne, who was based in Seville until the going there got too rough, invested money in Cabot's voyage of 1525–26, so that two of his friends, Roger Barlow and Henry Latimer, could go on the voyage and bring back valuable topographical information.[94] It was probably Thorne also who urged in 1526 that Henry should buy the spice island claims which Charles V was reported to be willing to sell. The king, who had no money at that point, did not respond, and when the Emperor did sell his claim in 1529 it was to the Portuguese. When Thorne published his *Geographia* in 1531, it contained an appeal to

Henry to promote the discovery of a north-west passage, but there was no response from the preoccupied monarch. At some point Thorne himself purchased a ship in Spain, ostensibly for a voyage of discovery, but it is not clear that he ever went, and if he did it was never followed up.[95] Ten years later Barlow also wrote a geographical treatise, the 'Brief some . . .', and presented it to the king, but it was never printed, and it is not clear whether Henry ever read it.[96] In 1541 the Privy Council actually debated sending an expedition in search of a route to 'Tartary'. Who was behind this uncharacteristic initiative is not clear, because Lisle did not become a councillor until 1543, but even if the idea was seriously intended, nothing came of it.

Henry had scientific interests, but they were much closer to home, and very practical. Guns fascinated him, and he could get quite absorbed by ballistics when applied to breaching a fortress, or sinking a ship. It was probably this personal interest which ensured that English guns, when they were eventually produced, were of good quality and standardised design. He was treated to a number of demonstrations, and again this may have been partly responsible for the fact that, even at this stage, the English navy was using specialised sea-gunners, rather than relying upon soldiers. The king was also interested in hydrography and in maps, but again with immediate objectives in mind. Surveys of Dover harbour and of the fortifications of Calais and Portsmouth were commissioned, and the Frenchman Jean Rotz was appointed Hydrographer Royal in 1542. Rotz presented a treatise to Henry in the same year, and seems to have been friendly with Roger Barlow, some of whose work he incorporated with his own.

Rotz was not the only Frenchman working in England at this time. Jean Maillard, also a mathematician and cosmographer, was also serving Henry, and there seems to have been a number of others, irrespective of the fact that England and France were at war at the time, and such cartographic information could be sensitive.[97] Rotz became a naturalised Englishman, but several of the others did not, and the question of their motivation remains unanswered. The king was certainly a patron, but not a particularly generous one. Huguenot sympathies have been suggested, but that seems unlikely. There was not a lot to choose between Henry and Francis in 1546 when it came to doctrinal heresy. More likely, perhaps, is the congenial atmosphere which was beginning to develop in certain quarters of the court and the City. The enigmatic John Dee, at this point in the early stages of his extraordinary career, was in London, and was in touch with Lisle, William Cecil, and others of that circle. Perhaps through Barlow, they also seem to have been communicating with the aged Cabot, who was showing an interest in returning to England. As Henry got older, and his health began to break down, his vision became still narrower. In 1546 he was preoccupied with retaining control of Boulogne, with forcing the Scots to honour the Treaty of Greenwich, and with the problem of preserving the royal supremacy if he should leave his heir as a minor. He was also burdened with debt. The cost of his last wars had forced him to borrow in Antwerp, and although by comparison with the borrowings of Francis or Charles, these operations were trivial, the debt still had to be serviced from a very modest ordinary revenue. The monastic lands, confiscated between 1536 and 1540, had mostly been sold. They had realised the enormous sum of over £1 million, but that had paid for less than half the war. More seriously, in 1545 Henry began to debase his coinage. Bi-metallic currencies were always tricky to manage, and there had been a debasement as early as 1526. That had been absorbed without difficulty, but the new situation was different. Rising population levels from the late fifteenth century, and the consequent increase in consumer demand, had begun to exercise a gentle inflationary pressure from about 1510 onward. By 1547 the increase had reached about 40 per cent over half a century or so, and was beginning to be noticed.[98] In these circumstances, tampering with the coinage was bound to have a very adverse effect upon confidence. When the king died, prices were set to rise steeply, and the pound sterling to decline sharply on the foreign exchanges. In 1546 also, Anthony Jenkinson set off from London to explore the possibilities of reopening trade with the Levant.

When Edward VI came to the throne, and a regency government was established in England, circumstances were conspiring to produce some momentous changes. Politically the country was vulnerable. Within a few weeks Francis I of France was also dead, and Henry II made no secret of his intention to recover Boulogne. The Scots had consistently refused to honour the Treaty of Greenwich, and had overthrown the government which negotiated it. Charles V regarded the religious reforms which soon began to be imposed in England with ill-concealed hostility. Inflation and debasement confronted the City of London with an economic storm. However, the country also had the means to cope with these problems. It had a navy which was at least the equal of any it was likely to meet, and a flourishing merchant marine. It also had voices very close to the centre of power – notably John Dudley, now Earl of Warwick – who were prepared to look for new ways ahead. As long as the Merchant Adventurers continued to make a massive profit shipping broadcloths to Antwerp, and as long as the government continued to depend upon the security of that trade, nothing very much was likely to happen. But should that comfortable pattern be disrupted, either by war or by economic crisis, then these potentialities might be realised.

Notes

1. The best general account of Richard's actions and motives is Charles Ross, *Richard III* (London, 1981). For the Woodville relationship specifically, see M.A. Hicks, 'The changing role of the Wydevilles in Yorkist politics to 1483', in C. Ross, ed., *Patronage, Pedigree and Power* (Stroud, 1979).

2. Ross, *Richard III*; D.E. Lowe, 'Patronage and politics: Edward IV, the Wydevilles and the Council of the Prince of Wales, 1471–1483', *Bulletin of the Board of Celtic Studies*, 29, 1980–82, 545–73.

3. Edward had been pre-contracted to marry Eleanor Butler when he actually married Elizabeth Woodville; but as Eleanor had died before Edward V was born, the canonical status of the impediment was not clear. R.H. Helmholz, 'The sons of Edward IV: a canonical assessment of the claim that they were illegitimate', in P.W. Hammond, ed., *Richard III: Loyalty, Lordship and Law* (London, 1986).

4. The best account of the events of the autumn of 1483 is given by Rosemary Horrox in *Richard III: A Study in Service* (London, 1989).

5. Henry's mother, Lady Margaret Beaufort, was the granddaughter of John Beaufort, Earl of Somerset, a son of John of Gaunt by his mistress Katherine Swynford. John had subsequently married Katherine and the Beauforts had been legitimated, but barred from the succession. There was a question over the legality of this bar. R.A. Griffiths and R.S. Thomas, *The Making of the Tudor Dynasty* (Gloucester, 1985).

6. C. Richmond, 'English naval power in the fifteenth century', *History*, new series, 52, 1967, 1–15.

7. C. Richmond, 'Royal administration and the keeping of the seas, 1422–1485' (University of Oxford D.Phil., 1962), 501–2.

8. S.B. Chrimes, *Henry VII* (London, 1972), 25–49; C. Richmond, '1485 and all that, or what was really going on at the Battle of Bosworth', in Hammond, ed., *Richard III*.

9. Chrimes, *Henry VII*, 22; see also the continuation of the Croyland Chronicle in *Rerum Anglicarum Scriptores Veterum*, ed. W. Fulman (Oxford, 1684).

10. M. Oppenheim, *Naval Accounts and Inventories of the Reign of Henry VII, 1485–8, 1495–7* (Navy Records Society, London, 1896). David Loades, *The Tudor Navy* (Aldershot, 1992), 39.

11. M. Oppenheim, *The History of the Administration of the Royal Navy, 1509–1660* (London, 1896), 36.

12. Chrimes, *Henry VII*; N.A.M. Rodger, *The Safeguard of the Sea* (London, 1997), 153–63.

13. F.W. Robertson, 'The rise of a Scottish navy, 1460–1513' (University of Edinburgh Ph.D., 1934), 46–8.

14. Ian Tanner, 'Henry VII's expedition to France in 1492: a study of its financing, organisation and supply' (University of Keele M.A., 1988); Rodger, *Safeguard*, 156.

15. Oppenheim, *Naval Accounts*, 82–132.

16. D.R. Bisson, *The Merchant Adventurers of England: The Company and the Crown 1474–1564* (London, 1993), 28–9.

17. Oppenheim, *Naval Accounts*, passim.

18. H.M. Colvin, *The History of the King's Works* (Oxford, 1963–73), IV, ii, 491; Ian Friel, 'The documentary evidence for maritime technology in later medieval England and Wales' (University of Keele Ph.D., 1990), 39–40. This dock was originally excavated in 1492, and enlarged and reinforced in 1494–95.

19. Colvin, *King's Works*, IV, ii, 488.

20. R. Schofield, 'The geographical distribution of wealth in England, 1334–1649', *Economic History Review*, 2nd series, 18, 1965, 483–510.

21. Chrimes, *Henry VII*, 232; J.F. Larkin and P.L. Hughes, *Tudor Royal Proclamations* (New Haven, 1964), I, 31, 18 September 1493.

22. Chrimes, *Henry VII*, 234; T. Rymer, *Foedera, conventiones, literae . . . et acta publica* (London, 1704–35), XIII, 105; *Calendar of State Papers, Venetian*, ed. Rawdon Brown *et al.* (London, 1864–98), I, 846.

23. D.C. Coleman, *The Economy of England, 1450–1750* (London, 1977), 64. P.H. Ramsey, 'Overseas trade in the reign of Henry VII', *Economic History Review*, 2nd series, 6, 1953, 173–82.

24. 4 Henry VII, c.10, *Statutes of the Realm (SR)*, II, 534.

25. 3 Henry VII, c.9, *SR*, II, 517.

26. 1 Henry VII, c.2, *SR*, II, 501.

27. R. Davis, *English Overseas Trade, 1500–1700* (London, 1973).

28. Bisson, *Merchant Adventurers*, 7–8.

29. 12 Henry VII, c.6, *SR*, II, 639.

30. *Calendar of the Patent Rolls, 1494–1509*, 52 vols (London, 1891–1916), 388.

31. G. Schantz, *Englische Handelspolitik gegen Ende des Mittelalters*, (Leipzig, 1881), I, 549.

32. E.M. Carus Wilson, 'The origin and early development of the Merchant Adventurers', *Economic History Review*, 4, 1932, 147–76; J. Imray, 'The Merchant Adventurers and their records', *Journal of the Society of Archivists*, 2, 1964, 457–67.

33. L. Lyell, 'The problems of the records of the Merchant Adventurers', *Economic History Review*, 5, 1934, 96–8.

34. Carus Wilson, 'Origin'.

35. Ramsey, 'Overseas trade'.

36. J.D. Fudge, *Cargoes, Embargoes and Emissaries: The Commercial and Political Interaction of England and the German Hanse, 1450–1510* (Toronto, 1995), 214–15.

37. Loades, *Tudor Navy*, 29–30.

38. G.V. Scammell, 'The English in the Atlantic Islands, 1450–1650', *Mariners Mirror*, 72, 1986, 295–317.

39. G.V. Scammell, *The World Encompassed: The First European Maritime Empires, c.800–1650* (London, 1981), 460.

40. Ibid., 461. P. McGrath, 'Bristol and America, 1480–1631', in K.R. Andrews, N.P. Canny and P.E.H. Hair, eds, *The Westward Enterprise* (Liverpool, 1978).

41. McGrath, 'Bristol and America'.

42. Rymer, *Foedera*, XII, 595.

43. J.A. Williamson, *The Cabot Voyages and Bristol Discovery under Henry VII* (London, 1962).

44. Ibid., 91–2, 220–3.

45. Ibid., 116–44.

46. Ibid., 145–72.

47. McGrath, 'Bristol and America', 89.

48. Chrimes, *Henry VII*, 230.

49. Richard Hakluyt, *The principall navigations, voiages and discoveries of the English nation* (London, 1589), 515.

50. Public Record Office (PRO) C66/700, m. 32; *Letters and Papers relating to the War with France, 1512–13*, ed. Alfred Spont (Navy Records Society, London, 1897), 3.

51. Hakluyt, *Principall navigations*, 517, referring to a letter written to the king by Thorne.

52. Thorne was based in Seville at the time. E.G.R. Taylor, *Tudor Geography, 1485–1583* (London, 1930), 48–52.

53. Hakluyt, *Principall navigations*, 520; Michael Lewis, *The Hawkins Dynasty* (London, 1969), 41–9.

54. Hakluyt, *Principall navigations*, 517; E.G.R. Taylor, 'Master Hore's voyage of 1536', *Geographical Journal*, 77, 1931, 469–70.

55. G. Connell Smith, *Forerunners of Drake* (London, 1954).

56. Ibid., 141; PRO SP1/200, ff. 95–6.

57. H.G. Koenigsberger, 'The empire of Charles V in Europe', in G.R. Elton (ed.), *The Reformation, 1520–1559*, New Cambridge Modern History II, 2nd edn (Cambridge, 1990), 364–5.

58. S.T. Bindoff, 'The greatness of Antwerp', in Elton (ed.), *The Reformation, 1520–1559*, 47–59. H. van der Wee, *The Growth of the Antwerp Market and the European Economy* (London, 1963).

59. Bisson, *Merchant Adventurers*, 80–2.

60. British Library (BL) MS Cotton Galba B.6, f. 144.

61. BL MS Cotton Galba B.9, ff. 49, 53, 123; Bisson, *Merchant Adventurers*, 85.

62. PRO SP1/68, f. 61, Vaughan to Cromwell, 20 November 1531.

63. Bisson, *Merchant Adventurers*, 88–9.

64. W.C. Richardson, *Stephen Vaughan: Financial Agent of Henry VIII* (Baton Rouge, 1953).

65. E. Carus Wilson and O. Coleman, *England's Export Trade, 1275–1547* (London, 1963).

66. Fudge, *Cargoes, Embargoes and Emissaries*, 89–165.

67. Bisson, *Merchant Adventurers*, 52.

68. L. Lyell and F. Watney (eds), *Acts of Court of the Mercers Company, 1453–1526* (London, 1936), 482. Bisson, *Merchant Adventurers*, 53.

69. BL Cotton Galba B.7, f. 217; PRO SP1/236, ff. 198–200.

70. PRO SP1/164, f. 392; Bisson, *Merchant Adventurers*, 56.

71. *Historical Manuscripts Commission, Calendar of the MSS of the Marquis of Salisbury* (1883–1940), I, 144. Bisson, *Merchant Adventurers*, 57.

72. Rodger, *Safeguard*, 476.

73. *Letters and Papers relating to the War with France*, ix and ns. Arrearages were sums owed on a previous account.

74. *Letters and Papers . . . of the Reign of Henry VIII*, ed. J. Gairdner *et al.* (London, 1862–1910), II, 4606; Loades, *Tudor Navy*, 68.

75. *Letters and Papers . . . of the Reign of Henry VIII*, I, iii, 3318.

76. PRO E36/13.

77. Oppenheim, *A History of the Administration of the Royal Navy*, 372–81. Rodger, *Safeguard*, 204–5.

78. R.C. Anderson, 'Henry VIII's *Great Galley*', *Mariners Mirror*, 6, 1920, 274–81.

79. BL Add. Charter 6289.

80. *Letters and Papers relating to the War with France*, 145–54, Edward Echyngham to Wolsey, 5 May 1513.

81. Rodger, *Safeguard*, 168.

82. PRO E315/317 f. 58; Loades, *Tudor Navy*, 80.

83. Loades, *Tudor Navy*, 74–6.

84. *Letters and Papers . . . of the Reign of Henry VIII*, VI, 1510, Chapuys to the Emperor, 9 December 1533.

85. Audley's fighting instructions of 1530; *Fighting Instructions, 1530–1816*, ed. J.S. Corbett (Navy Records Society, London, 1905), 15–17.

86. D. Burwash, *English Merchant Shipping, 1460–1540* (Toronto, 1947).

87. J.J. Scarisbrick, *Henry VIII* (London, 1968), 424–40.

88. Rodger, *Safeguard*, 477–8.

89. Larkin and Hughes, *Tudor Royal Proclamations*, I, 345.

90. C.S.L. Davies, 'The administration of the navy under Henry VIII: the origins of the Navy Board', *English Historical Review*, 80, 1965, 268–8.

91. D. Loades, *John Dudley, Duke of Northumberland* (Oxford, 1996).

92. Lisle's fighting instructions of 1545; *Fighting Instructions*, 20–3.

93. Peter Padfield, *Guns at Sea* (London, 1973), 33.

94. Taylor, *Tudor Geography*, 49.

95. Ibid., 51.

96. BL Royal MS 188 xxviii.

97. Rotz's treatise of hydrography remains in BL Royal MS 20E ix.

98. R.B. Outhwaite, *Inflation in Tudor and Early Stuart England* (London, 1969), 10.

CHAPTER TWO

The Antwerp Crisis and the Search for New Markets, 1547–1558

Debate continues about exactly what Henry was trying to achieve when his last will and testament was drawn up in January 1547. Although it is reasonably certain that he was still alive when it was given its final form, it is by no means clear that he was sufficiently *compos mentis* to know exactly what it said. Consequently we cannot be sure whether the honours and rewards which were handed out in February, and the form which the regency government took at the same time, were really in accordance with his wishes or not.[1] However, the uncertainty relates to means rather than ends. The king intended his son's minority to be controlled by that group in his final council which was led by Edward Seymour, Earl of Hertford, and included William, Lord Paget, and John Dudley, Viscount Lisle. To facilitate that, he had deliberately removed Stephen Gardiner, the conservative Bishop of Winchester, from the list of executors, and had excluded the Howards by the more drastic action of conviction for treason.[2] At the end of his life, Henry treasured three achievements: the begetting of a legitimate son, the capture and retention of Boulogne, and the establishment of the royal supremacy. His favour towards Seymour and his allies in the last months of his life can be explained in these terms. He might have trusted his widow, Catherine, or even Gardiner, to remain loyal to Edward; but he also trusted the Seymour group to defend both his conquest and his church. Whether he realised the Protestant proclivities of this group is not clear. Henry remained staunchly loyal to certain aspects of the traditional faith until the very end, and was still burning sacramentaries in the summer of 1546, but he had long been aware of the unorthodox views of his cherished Archbishop, Thomas Cranmer, and must have known something of the reforming attitudes of those whom he had chosen to teach his son and heir.[3] He may have deliberately not chosen to see their sacramental heresy (which they concealed), and believed that in every other respect their convictions made them ideal defenders of the royal supremacy. If that was his thinking, he was completely correct.

Within a fortnight of Henry's death, Seymour had created himself Duke of Somerset, and with the support of the majority of his fellow executors had constituted himself Lord Protector. The French war had been brought to an end by the Treaty of Camp in May 1546, and the Scottish war was dormant, but the problems which they had left to the new regime were formidable. Over four years the fighting had cost £2,135,000. Of this almost half, about £1 million, had been raised by alienating 65 per cent of the property acquired from the dissolution of the monasteries.[4] The rest was raised from parliamentary subsidies, loans both at home and abroad, and the debasement of the coinage. By contemporary standards Henry's straightforward debts were not enormous – about £100,000 in Antwerp and rather more in London – but the adulteration of the currency was an economic time bomb. The temptation had been overwhelming. Experiments conducted at the mint between 1542 and 1544 demonstrated that by reducing the silver content of the commonest coins (groats and testons) from the sterling standard of 11oz 2dwt per pound Troy to 9oz 2dwt, and minting at 48s to the pound, a profit of about 9 per cent could be achieved.[5] This meant that at the level of production for those years (£68,522) the profit would have been £6,045, and the face value of the coin would have remained the same. Over the next three years mint production soared as coin was energetically recycled: £149,000 in 1544–45, £440,000 in 1545–46, and £450,000 in 1546–47.[6] At the same time the fineness dropped further, first to 9oz and then to 6oz. Although the coinage continued to be at 48s, the profit by the spring of 1547 had reached about £250,000. The face value of the coin remained unchanged, but the real metallic value declined by nearly 50 per cent. It seems likely that those who knew how dangerous this was did not know what was happening, and those who knew what was happening did not understand the economics. The gold coinage was also debased, but to a lesser extent and was not minted in the same quantities; consequently the bi-metallic ratio became drastically distorted, the gold coin being seriously undervalued by comparison with the base silver, a fact which soon began to drive the gold coin out of circulation.[7]

The effects of these developments were only just beginning to show in 1547. Prices in the domestic markets had been rising gently since about 1510, and by 1545 had reached 225 from a base of 100 in 1500. There was, if anything, a slight drop in 1547, but in the following year inflation resumed strongly, reaching 275 in 1549.[8] With the benefit of hindsight, we can link this last surge to debasement, but that connection was not generally made at the time, when enclosers, regrators, bankers, and indeed businessmen in general were blamed for their anti-social greed. It now seems likely that the original trigger for inflation was rising population, pushing up consumer demand and increasing pressure on the land market. Contemporaries were accustomed to dearth, but it had been almost entirely linked to harvest failures and consequent food shortages. The harvests of the late 1540s were good, and there was no dearth in the traditional sense, yet prices continued to rise. It is not surprising that tempers also rose, and that scapegoats were sought. At the same time a rather similar situation was developing on the Antwerp exchange. In 1544 the pound sterling had exchanged at about 26s Flemish, peaking at 27s 2d in February.[9] By the summer of 1547 it had fallen to 22s 6d, having touched 22s in April. The council had the benefit of good financial advice from the London bankers, but either the experts did not spot the warning signs in time, or Somerset, having other priorities, chose to ignore them. As the pound weakened, it became more expensive to service and repay the king's debts. For whatever reason, and it probably had most to do with his decision to re-ignite the Scottish war, Somerset decided not only to continue the policy of debasement, but to accelerate it. Between April 1547 and July 1551 £1,628,000 worth of debased coin was passed into circulation. The silver content dropped from 6oz to 4oz, and even on one occasion to 3oz; and at the same time the minting went up from 48s to the pound to 72s, even touching 96s at one point; and the total profit of these four years reached nearly £1 million.[10]

The death of Francis I of France in April 1547 called the Treaty of Camp in question. Henry II made no secret of his intention to recover Boulogne, and this not only forced Somerset into a heightened state of military preparedness, it increased his determination to settle with the Scots before any serious attack could develop in the south. The profits of the mint were certainly needed, not so much to discharge Henry's debts as to cover current military expenditure. By the time that a peace was finally negotiated in March 1550, another £1.65 million had been added to Henry's war bill. At the same time, as a direct result of debasement, inflation was pushed over the 300 mark in both 1550 and 1551, and the exchange rate in Antwerp plummeted from 19s 7d in December 1549 to 12s 9d in July 1551.[11] In seven years sterling had lost over 50 per cent of its value. Given the much slower economic metabolism of the period, this would be equivalent to the present-day pound going from $1.65 to 80c in about a week.

It is not surprising that such a dramatic development had a serious effect upon trade. As the pound fell, the real price of English cloth fell with it, and became 'good cheap'. The number of cloths passing from London to Antwerp rose from 109,000 in 1544/45 to 132,000 in 1549/50, and the industry was stretched to meet the demand.[12] However, in a manner more familiar to the twentieth century than the sixteenth, boom was followed by bust.

The market had been oversupplied. In the summer of 1551 the council also embarked upon a remedial policy for the coinage, announcing a 25 per cent devaluation. This was mishandled, and caused both hardship and indignation at home, but it began the rehabilitation of sterling in Antwerp.[13] By October 1551 the pound was back to 19s 2d Flemish, and although this eased the pressure on government loans, it also meant that the price of English cloth rose by about 30 per cent, just at the point when it was becoming difficult to shift anyway. Demand for new cloth decreased sharply, and in 1551/52 only 85,000 cloths went out from Blackwell Hall to the Low Countries. In the short term the setback was no more than temporary. There are no figures for 1552/53, but 1553/54, when political relations between England and the Low Countries were unusually amicable, broke all records, with over 135,000 cloths crossing the Narrow Sea.[14] In the longer term, however, 1551/52 was a portent for greater storms ahead, as well as an immediate shock which jolted the Merchant Adventurers out of their complacency. For at least two generations the Adventurers had been accustomed to a steadily increasing trade. Memories of the political disruptions of the previous century had faded, and purely economic setbacks had been mild and of short duration. Now, however, it was clear that the staple market could not be trusted. In fact 1553/54 turned out to be almost the last boom year. Through the later 1550s exports fell away: to 113,000 in 1556/57; 109,000 in 1559/60; and 81,000 in 1560/61. After a final surge to 133,000 in 1561/62, the market fluctuated between 70,000 and 110,000 for about 20 years, falling as low as 53,000 in 1562/63.[15] By the mid-1560s politically inspired disruptions had begun again, and although the Low Countries trade remained the largest single outlet until well into the following century, the London/Antwerp axis was losing its security.

The crisis of 1551/52 in itself did not change anything, but coming when it did, it reinforced new ways of thinking which were already beginning to emerge. A symptom of this change was the return to England, at some point in 1547 or 1548, of Sebastian Cabot. Cabot had been in Spain, in the service first of Ferdinand and then of Charles, for nearly 40 years, much of that time as Charles's Pilot Major. He possessed not only a vast fund of navigational knowledge, but all the secrets of the *Casa de Contratacion*. He had, however, never become a naturalised Spaniard, remaining, officially, a subject of the King of England. He had also remained in touch with his English friends, and in October 1547 the Privy Council allocated the sum of £100 'for the transporting of one Cabot, a pilot, to come out of Hispania to serve and inhabit in England'.[16] This was a generous sum, and the wording of the grant suggests that Cabot intended to move his whole establishment permanently. He was a little over 60 years old, and although we know nothing about his dependants, a man of his position must have had at least a modest household. He appears to have returned to his old stamping ground in Bristol, and on 6 January 1549 was awarded an annuity of 200 marks (£166 13s 4d) out of the Exchequer, with arrears from Michaelmas 1548.[17] The Emperor was not happy. Not only was Cabot a valuable servant, the knowledge which he possessed threatened to destroy Iberian attempts to preserve the confidentiality of their cartographic information. In April 1549 he instructed his ambassador in London, Francois van der Delft, to demand Cabot's immediate return to Spain, and appears to have written in the same vein to Cabot himself.[18] This move triggered a prolonged game of cat and mouse, the truth of which remains extremely elusive. Somerset's initial response was one of sweet reason:

> The Protector answered that Sebastian had been recommended to them as a good and expert pilot by the Admiral, and having received his discharge from your Majesty's service in a letter written by your Majesty to the Council of the Indies which they [the English Council] handed over to me, as a subject of this kingdom he now desires to serve his king. But if it would further your Majesty's service . . . the Protector would be pleased to allow him to fulfill his mission, for although he has always been the king's subject, he is entirely and for that very reason at your Majesty's command and disposal . . .[19]

However by July, according to van der Delft, the duke had changed his tune, denying that he had ever promised to return Cabot to the Emperor's service. Somerset was not the only person to have forgotten what had been said such a short time before, because the ambassador then proceeded to wax indignant at his assertion that King Edward wished to employ the pilot himself:

> I challenged this unworthy retort, offering that neither he nor Cabot's secretary, who came to me several times at his request, had ever said that Cabot was being detained here on service duty; on the contrary I had been told that he was here because he needed rest, being an old man.[20]

Whatever Cabot's secretary (or anyone else) may have said, the Privy Council was not paying an expert navigator 200 marks a year to rest. Thereafter the web of confusion thickens. On 13 August, when Somerset's mind may well have been on more urgent matters, he told van der Delft that Cabot 'was old and infirm, and did nothing but pray that he might be allowed to remain in this kingdom', to which the ambassador commented 'This, Sire, is pure deceitfulnes, for Cabot came to me only 4 or 5 days ago, and begged me as hard as he could to get your Majesty to take him out of this country', claiming, apparently, that he had information of the greatest urgency to impart to the Emperor.[21] For the next three years the reports of successive Imperial ambassadors, first van der Delft, then Scheyfve and then Simon Renard, continue to tell the tale of Cabot, eager to go to the Emperor and held against his will by the English council.

The ambassadors clearly did not invent this story, and we must conclude that Cabot, for reasons of his own, wished them to believe that he was desperate to return to Imperial service. At the same time he was getting on with the business for which he had (presumably) come: working with members of the Privy Council to persuade the merchants of Bristol and London that the time was ripe for investment in voyages for the discovery of new markets. If he had really wanted to leave England, it is hard to see what was stopping him, apart from the thought of 200 marks a year. Moreover on 2 September 1549, not long before the Protector's fall, the council authorised a further £100 'for conducion of Sebastian Cabot', which suggests that they had no desire to detain him against his will, but were as confused as the ambassadors about his real intentions.[22] In spite of this helpfulness, and whatever he may have said, Cabot stayed, and in June 1550 collected a further £200 'by way of the King's reward', which may have been merely an inducement but is more likely to have been linked to continued good service.[23] An indication of what that service was is provided by the fact that on 4 June he was awarded an exemplification of the letters patent granted to his father, his brothers and himself on 5 April 1496 'touching the discovery of new lands', 'which letters have been accidentally lost as the said Sebastian has made oath in Chancery'.[24]

Cabot's idea seems to have been to seek a new route to China around the north of mainland Europe and Asia, what was later to be called 'the north-east passage', and his backers on the council included the Earl of Warwick, who had taken over the effective regency from the Protector, the earls of Arundel and Bedford, and Lord Paget. According to Hakluyt, 'certain grave citizens of London' had consulted him 'for the removal of the great stagnation of trade resulting from the disturbed and warlike state of the continent', but it is clear that he also had the backing of the Crown.[25] As early as January 1551 Scheyfve had discovered that Cabot was working with 'a certain Jehan Ribault, a Frenchman' and some Englishmen who had sailed with Cabot before 'to discover some islands, or to seek a road to the Indies'. It was the latter, of course, which interested the Emperor and probably lay behind his obvious desire to detach the old pilot from his English service.

How quickly the scheme progressed, and what setbacks it may have suffered, we do not know, but according to Hakluyt by the spring of 1553 it was all set up and ready to go. The method employed was standard business practice. A group was formed, each member of which put up a fixed sum of money as his share of the 'venture', in return for a proportionate share of the profit at the end of the voyage. However, both the size and the composition of the group was unprecedented for an enterprise of this kind. Some 240 individual shares were sold at £25 each, raising a capital of £6,000, and the shareholders included Privy Councillors, courtiers and other royal servants, as well as the usual merchants (mostly of London) who formed the majority.[26] Individual councillors and officials had done business in the city for generations, but collaboration on this scale was new. Moreover, as the declared object of the voyage was the discovery of new lands and new markets rather than direct trade, there was little immediate profit in prospect. The king was interested, even enthusiastic, but his health was poor by the spring of 1553, and it is unlikely to have been his will which drove the enterprise forward. The momentum almost certainly came from the head of government himself, the Earl of Warwick (Duke of Northumberland from November 1551), who as Lord Admiral had probably been the man who commended Cabot to the council in the first place. The opposition which might have been anticipated from the conservative Merchant Adventurers was critically reduced by this forceful patronage, as well as by the uncertainties of the existing market, and several leading Adventurers were among the Cathay shareholders.

Because the whole nature of the enterprise required that it should be followed up if any profit was to be derived from it, the contributors were constituted into a company to trade with China. Cabot was appointed Governor, and a royal charter of incorporation was applied for. Instructions were drawn up, probably in March or April although dated 9 May, by Cabot himself, and three ships were prepared, manned and victualled.[27] The command was given to Sir Hugh Willoughby as Captain General, with the experienced Richard Chancellor as Pilot General. The ownership of these vessels is unclear, but almost certainly within the London merchant community. One of them was called the *Edward Bonaventure*, but it was not the royal warship of that name, which was very much larger and quite unsuitable for a voyage of discovery. The others were the *Bona Speranza* and the *Confidentia*. On 10 May 1553 this important expedition set out, the young king, who believed himself to be convalescent, sitting at a window in Greenwich palace to watch it pass.[28]

While these preparations were at their height, on 10 April, Cabot called upon the Imperial ambassador to tell him about 'the voyage to the North East', and apparently to repeat his request to be readmitted to the Emperor's service.[29] Charles responded in a letter which arrived on the day of Edward's death, demanding his release from all commitments in England. In the confusion which then followed as the Duke of Northumberland endeavoured to settle the Crown on his daughter-in-law Jane Grey, and was defeated by the lawful heir, Mary, it is not surprising that Cabot's affairs were neglected. In early September he went back to the ambassador, demanding to know what was happening about his recall, and Renard observed that 'the people of London set great store by the captain's service, and believe him to be possessed of secrets concerning English navigation'. This was undoubtedly true, and might make them opposed to his release.[30] However, Mary could refuse her mentor nothing, and on 19 October Renard reported that Cabot had obtained leave of the queen 'to go towards your Majesty'.[31] He did not, however, go. Instead, on 15 November he wrote to Charles, explaining that he was too ill to travel, and would have to convey his vital information in writing. This turned out to be a circumstantial tale about how the Duke of Northumberland, in collaboration with the French, had planned to send a force of 4,000 men to build a fort at the mouth of the Amazon, and to attack Peru overland; 'that they might succeed in their evil designs . . . Boisdauphin [the French ambassador who had been recalled in April 1553] took with him £2000 which the Duke gave him to make a beginning'.[32] This cannot have been the equally essential information which he had been so anxious to impart in 1549, and it is hard to know what to make of it. By the time Cabot wrote, the Duke of Northumberland was dead, and his supporters in prison or in disgrace. There was not the remotest chance that Mary's council would pick up, or even conceal, such a scheme − if it had ever existed. Charles took it seriously enough to make a number of further enquiries, not because he feared attack from England but because it might just possibly represent a French intention. Meanwhile, Cabot stayed in England.

On 20 November, five days after he had claimed to be incapacitated by illness, Renard reported that the Chancellor had countermanded the queen's permission, and had refused him leave to go.[33] Thereafter the whole question of his return to Imperial service disappears from the agenda. He not only stayed in England; he was actively involved in promoting a number of other voyages, and became officially Governor of the Muscovy Company when that was finally chartered after Richard Chancellor's return, in 1555. In November 1555 his annuity was renewed, and although he surrendered it in May 1556, it was immediately regranted jointly in survivorship with William Worthington.[34] Quite what the advantage of this was is elusive, but it certainly appears to have been done on Cabot's initiative, and not as a result of any falling out with the English government.

It is hard to overemphasise the importance of Cabot's knowledge and initiative in creating a new and more enterprising culture in the City of London. His vast experience, and prestige as the former Pilot Major of the world's greatest colonial power, gave him great influence. Close association with the Duke of Northumberland made no difference, because many of the original Cathay Company shareholders, and the subsequent members of the Muscovy Company, were Mary's councillors as well. In this respect at least the change of regime in July 1553 made no difference; and it is clear that the search for a north-east passage was his idea. He was highly regarded and well rewarded, so the mystery over his real attitude to England is hard to fathom. He came of his own free will, stayed, and was active beyond his years or expectation. In April 1550, when he had already been agitating for months to 'go to' the Emperor, the English council told the ambassador 'that as for Sebastian Cabot, he of himself refused to go either into Spain or towards the Emperor, and that he being of that mind and the king of England's subject, no reason or equity would that he should be forced or compelled to go against his will'.[35] Unless we believe that all politicians are compulsive liars, he was clearly telling his English associates one thing, and the Imperial ambassador the opposite. Why remains a mystery, but if we judge by actions rather than words, then he was probably one of the most creative servants employed by the English Crown during the mid-century period. Cabot died in England, full of years and honour, in 1557.

London had responded positively to his ideas, but it had its own agenda as well, and the long-running feud between the Merchant Adventurers and the Hanseatic League featured prominently. As we have seen, Henry had valued the friendship of the Hanse at the end of his reign, but the difficulties afflicting the cloth trade in 1551/52 brought matters to a head. From 1546 onward, Hanseatic merchants began to increase the number of undyed cloths which they were shipping direct to Hamburg. This did not matter while the main trade to Antwerp was booming, but by 1551 it constituted serious, and most unwelcome, competition.[36] There was also a diplomatic incident in Danzig in 1547, where it was alleged that an English ship had been seized, and the King of England insulted. The Hanseatic parliament attempted to smooth ruffled feathers, but the Danzigers were uncooperative and in 1548 the English council applied pressure by forbidding certain selected exports.[37] In June 1549 Edward officially resurrected the old grievance of reciprocity, and demanded that the League cease providing naval support to the Scots.[38] The Hanse prevaricated, and there was a further major incident in 1551 when another English ship was seized in Danzig and its cargo impounded. The owner, Richard Bannester, complained to the council, and Edward wrote an angry letter demanding restitution and compensation.[39] Danzig refused both, and this gave the London Adventurers the pretext they needed for an all-out onslaught. In January 1552 a long and comprehensive list of grievances was presented to the council. Their main complaints were: first, lack of that reciprocity which was supposed to have been guaranteed by the Treaty of Utrecht; second, that the Germans were taking cloth out of London, ostensibly for their own domestic market, and then reselling it in Antwerp in direct competition with the Adventurers; and third, that they were abusing their import privileges by 'colouring' the goods of other aliens, who should have paid unprivileged customs.[40] The council then summoned the merchants of the London Steelyard to defend their privileges, which they did in a number of documents. The issue was adjudicated on 9 February.

Given the increasingly close relationship between the City and the council since 1547, the outcome was probably a foregone conclusion, but it none the less represented a dramatic departure from over 70 years of precedent:

> Notwithstanding that divers requests have been made, as well by the king's majesty's father as by his majesty, for the present redress of such wrongs as have been done to the English merchants contrary to the said treaty [Utrecht], yet no reformation hath hitherto ensued . . . [Consequently,] the privileges liberties and franchises claimed by the foresaid merchants of the Steelyard shall from henceforth be and remain seized and resumed into the king's majesty's hands until the said merchants of the Steelyard shall declare and prove better and more substantial matter for their claim in the premises . . .[41]

The legal justification claimed for this decision was a mere pretext. The real reason was that the Duke of Northumberland needed the goodwill and support of London more than he feared either the Hanseatic League or the Emperor, whose subjects most of the German merchants were. It was a typically pragmatic move, because Charles was far too absorbed by his perpetual struggle with the French to take any military action in support of the League, and far too concerned for the prosperity of the Netherlands to resort to retaliatory embargoes. His agents grumbled about the wickedness of the English, but in the event the Hanse was left to defend its own interests as best it could. There was no question of closing the Steelyard, or prohibiting its merchants from trading; the decision simply meant that they would have to do so on the same terms as other aliens. The League immediately appealed, and kept up a barrage of representations for the rest of the reign. They managed to get privileged clearance for cargoes already loaded when the judgement was issued, but otherwise made no progress as long as Edward was alive and Northumberland was in charge.

The English council had taken a calculated risk, which was very much in line with its general policy. Having extracted the country from vastly expensive and increasingly pointless wars with France and Scotland in March 1550, Northumberland was concerned to avoid any similar entanglements in future, and to protect English interests without reference to traditional alliances or obligations. The Hanseatic League, particularly if it was supported by the King of Denmark, could still mount a powerful navy, but its constituent cities were increasingly at odds among themselves, and England was perfectly capable of looking after itself at sea. The chances of an effective Hanse response were slight, and the economic advantages to the Merchant Adventurers considerable. There may not have been any connection between the withdrawal of these privileges and the dramatic recovery of the English cloth trade in 1553/54, but if not, the coincidence is a striking one.

Protector Somerset had retained Henry VIII's navy and shore establishments more or less unchanged. After the large-scale acquisition of ships between 1544 and 1546, there was no need for further building or purchase, and about a dozen small rowbarges were discarded as being tactically unnecessary.[42] A fleet of some 65 ships, including 34 royal fighting ships, accompanied the Protector's successful invasion of Scotland in September 1547.[43] However, as the war turned to one of attrition in the following year, the fleet became less effective. In spite of having about 70 ships at sea in the summer of 1548, the English were unable to prevent a French fleet from landing about 6,000 seasoned troops at Leith on 12 June. These reinforcements turned the whole fortune of the war, and over the following year the Protector was forced to abandon the majority of the garrisons which he had established after his victory in 1547.[44] By the Treaty of Haddington, the Scots formally and finally abrogated the Treaty of Greenwich, and betrothed their young queen to the Dauphin. In August 1548 she sailed for France by the western route, and the English fleet was again unable to do anything about it. Somerset intended to redeem the position in the north with another Army Royal in the summer of 1549, but the troubled state of England finally deterred him, and he redeployed his forces against the rebels in Norfolk and Devon.

Henry II, seeing his chance amid these distractions, at last declared war in August 1549, and launched his army against Boulogne. The English, however, turned out to be more resolute than expected. Boulogne held out, and an English fleet commanded by William Winter inflicted a decisive defeat on the veteran galley commander Leo Strozzi off Jersey in the first month of the war.[45] During the two and a half years between the creation of the Protectorate in February 1547 and Somerset's overthrow in October 1549, he had spent approximately £165,000 on the navy, including the costs of victualling. Important establishments were maintained at Deptford, Gillingham and Portsmouth, and lesser operations at Woolwich, Harwich and Colne. This was only about 10 per cent of the cost of the war, and was money well-spent in spite of the failures of 1548. Because the English fleet managed to keep the sea, the garrison of Boulogne could be supplied and reinforced throughout the winter of 1549–50, and this brought Henry to the negotiating table in February 1550 with fewer cards in his hand than he had expected.[46]

The domestic crisis which brought about the end of the Protectorate, and which looms large in histories of the reign of Edward VI, eventually produced remarkably few changes. After about two months of uncertainty, the Earl of Warwick emerged as the new regent, although he never styled himself Protector; the policy of religious reform continued; and Warwick also resumed the office of Lord Admiral which he had surrendered to the Protector's brother Thomas Seymour in February 1547.[47] After a period of imprisonment and disgrace, the Duke of Somerset was released, pardoned, and eventually restored to the council. Warwick, however, shared none of the Protector's military illusions, and took the dire state of the exchanges and of the cloth trade very seriously indeed. He effectively abandoned the war in Scotland, and sold Boulogne back to the French for 400,000 crowns. This was a good deal more than Henry had wanted to pay, and turned a major financial burden to profitable account. The Treaty of Boulogne was not popular, and Warwick was denounced in some quarters for betraying England's honour, but it was undoubtedly necessary to protect the country from bankruptcy. Unfortunately he did not reverse his predecessor's fiscal policy with the same promptness. Although military expenditure sharply declined, he could not resist the temptation to go on milking the mint. A further issue of 6oz fine was made in the summer of 1550, which pushed the exchange rate into a further decline, and the government's debts continued to mount.[48] Because of the uncertain international situation, the garrisons of Berwick and Calais had to be maintained at full strength, and the navy could not be allowed to decline. Altogether the armed forces continued to absorb nearly £200,000 a year – very much less than the £700,000 which they were costing during the war, but a high level for peacetime, and more than could be easily afforded. The navy was taking nearly £25,000 of this, and the Council for Marine Causes continued to function efficiently. In 1550 a final brick was placed in this ediface when Edward Baeshe, who had been one of the main victualling contractors for a number of years, was appointed to the new office of Surveyor General of victuals, in which capacity he joined the council and completed its arc of responsibility.[49]

A survey of the navy, taken on 26 August 1552, listed 55 vessels with a combined displacement of over 10,000 tons.[50] Of these, 24 were described as fit for immediate service, three were in dock undergoing repairs, and another seven were to be 'docked and new dubbed'. Only four were marked for disposal. Regular patrols were being mounted, although the evidence is fragmentary. In March 1552 Benjamin Gonson, the Treasurer, was paid £3,000 to equip four ships for active service, and in June of the same year another squadron 'appointed for the Narrow Seas' was being fitted out at Gillingham.[51] Warships were now provided at the king's expense and on a regular basis to escort the Merchant Adventurers' fleet, and to protect the fishing fleet sailing to the Newfoundland banks.

Efforts were also made to tackle the perennial problem of piracy. At loggerheads with the Emperor, and by no means certain of the friendship of France, Northumberland could not afford to allow English seamen to provoke reprisals. In March 1552, according to the king's journal, a fleet of six royal ships – probably the ones which Gonson was paid to equip – was sent to sea 'for the defence of the merchants, which were daily before robbed'. Two pirates were quickly caught, but it is uncertain what further success may have been enjoyed.[52] The problem was intractable, because so many of the pirates were not full-time freebooters, who could at least be identified, but legitimate merchants working off a sense of grievance, real or imagined. The whole culture of reprisal was a consequence of the inadequacy of naval protection over the previous century, and escalated the problem to a level which even a significant improvement in naval activity could not solve. The best answer lay in a tightening up of Admiralty jurisdiction, so that more known offenders were called to account, and prevented from disposing of their booty. A step in that direction was taken on 27 August 1552 when William Thomas, one of the Clerks of the Council, was given a special commission to try piracy cases within the liberty of the Cinque Ports.[53] The Ports had a privileged Admiralty jurisdiction of their own, but it had become notoriously unwilling to discipline the men of the liberty; and the overriding of the franchise in this respect was undoubtedly justified. Whether it was effective is another matter. In spite of such efforts, there is little sign that Northumberland was getting the problem under control.

The duke, by his own admission, had little skill in financial matters. In spite of having the deficiencies of the previous fiscal policy pointed out to him, he still indulged in a final orgy of debasement in April 1551, when the worst coin of all (3oz fine) was issued.[54] It was in response to this misguided opportunism that the exchange rate bottomed out at 12s 9d in July. Thereafter he was persuaded to allow the Lord Treasurer, the Marquis of Winchester, to assume his proper responsibility for economic policy, and Winchester listened to the voices of the City. As we have seen, the currency was devalued in the summer of 1551, and the coin which was issued from October 1551 onward was 11oz fine.[55] In response to that recovery, the exchange rate leapt to 19s 2d in the same month. The problem was not solved. Inevitably the good coin was exported and the bad remained in circulation, because Winchester did not believe that a proper recoinage could be afforded. Nevertheless, Thomas Gresham was appointed as the king's agent in Antwerp, and he managed to keep the exchange rate at between 18s and 20s Flemish for the remainder of the reign. When Edward died in July, and Northumberland fell from power, very little had actually been achieved. Willoughby's small fleet was approaching the Lofoten Islands, and what it might accomplish was uncertain. The cloth trade was in the doldrums, and the coinage still struggling to recover confidence. However, the seeds of a more enterprising commercial culture had been sown, both in London and in Bristol; the need for new and more distant markets had been accepted; a means of mobilising capital for such activities had been devised; and the navy had emerged unscathed from what could easily have been a period of debilitating cost-cutting after March 1550.

Neither finance nor commercial policy were high on Mary's agenda in the opening weeks of her reign, but there was a legacy which quickly demanded attention. Northumberland had borrowed £40,000 from the Merchant Adventurers earlier in the summer, and for some reason which is not entirely clear, Mary asked them to take £15,000 of the repayment in Antwerp rather than in London.[56] They had little choice but to comply, but they were not pleased, and worse was to follow. Taking swift advantage of the new queen's totally different relationship with the Emperor, the merchants of the Steelyard were quick to resurrect their appeal against the council's decision of the previous year. Discussions were going on before the end of August, and on 24 October a new agreement was drawn up with the Hanse commissioners, restoring all the privileges which had been abrogated, and repeating the reciprocity clauses of the Treaty of Utrecht.[57] It is hardly surprising that the Merchant Adventurers regarded the new regime with a chilly hostility, because the council's decision does not seem to have rested on any economic considerations at all. Only one of the five English commissioners who signed this agreement (Sir William Petre) had any City connections, or any direct knowledge of the issues. A desire to please the Emperor, and a general conviction that anything which the previous government had done must be wrong, seem to have been the main prompters. In London the euphoria which had accompanied the end of the succession crisis at the beginning of August was short-lived. At about the same time as the Hanseatic privileges were restored, rumours began to circulate that the queen was to marry the Prince of Spain, and there were audible grumbles that the queen 'intended to enrich foreigners by opening the gates of the country to them, and to impoverish its unfortunate inhabitants'.[58]

The City authorities were suitably cautious. Although many merchants had had close connections with the discredited Northumberland and his circle, they had not suffered for it, and were in no mood for adventures. Moreover, there could be great advantages in the proposed Spanish match: not only smooth waters in Antwerp but also the possibility of trading lawfully with the rich Spanish colonies in the New World. The mayor and aldermen suppressed dissent, defended the City against the Wyatt rebellion in January 1554, and welcomed the terms of the marriage treaty, when these were proclaimed.[59]

The Merchant Adventurers, however, were not prepared to submit without protest, and attempted to demonstrate that the restoration of Hanseatic privilege had damaged the merchants of the Low Countries (who were also the Emperor's subjects) even more than it had damaged them. An anonymous memorandum drawn up in December 1554 was entitled 'A brief declaration of the discomoditie and hyndrance [to] this realme [and] the subvertion of the laudable trade and traphique of English merchants . . . by the usurped trade and trafick which the Easterlinges many yeres have used . . .'. The main thrusts of the argument were, firstly, that the privileges had cost the Exchequer nearly £10,000 in the year or so since their restoration, and secondly, that business worth over £150,000 had been taken out of the hands of English and Dutch merchants. 'Since the enlargement of the Easterlinges [the Dutch] have shipped never a cloth.'[60] It is not known whether this document was ever submitted to the council; if it was, it was ignored. Of course such representations were special pleading, but the sense of grievance was real, and may have contributed to the almost unprecedented refusal of the Adventurers to make the Crown a short-term loan in September 1554.

Nor did the benefits anticipated by the more optimistic follow from the marriage. Philip flatly refused his English subjects admission to the American trade, on the grounds that most of his other subjects were also excluded. Only Castilians were permitted to go to the Indies. This was disappointing, but did not affect any enterprise which was actually in being. More frustrating was the king's attitude towards English attempts to break into the West African trade, which were just beginning. There may have been earlier attempts which escaped the record, but the first known voyage to Guinea and Benin left Portsmouth on 12 August 1553. It consisted of three ships – the *Lion*, the *Primrose* and the *Moon* – all of London, under the overall command of Thomas Wyndham.[61] Wyndham was the Master of Naval Ordnance, but there is no suggestion that this voyage was officially sponsored. According to Renard, who later reported it, the inspirer had again been Cabot, but Richard Hakluyt named Antonio Pinteado, a Portuguese, as the 'first persuader'. The ships visited El Mina, but at some point 'lost their course'. Only one returned, and both Wyndham and Pinteado perished.[62] However, the attraction of both gold and slaves proved too strong to resist. A second voyage, set up by a City syndicate headed by Sir John Barnes and Sir John Yorke, set out in October 1554. This enjoyed better success, and William Towerson followed it up with three further voyages, in 1555, 1556 and 1557, each of which involved substantial investment.[63] The Portuguese regarded these voyages as piratical intrusions into their own territory, and appealed to Philip to stop them. In July 1555 he agreed, and ordered the English council to prohibit such activities.[64] The London merchants were extremely indignant, not least because they were Philip's subjects, while the Portuguese were not. This time the council sympathised with the merchants, and made no attempt to implement the king's orders until the following summer.

As Towerson's voyages demonstrate, the Londoners paid no attention to either the king or the council. By this time tension between the capital and the king was building up, and the council was caught in the middle. Perhaps as some compensation for being compelled to obey Philip's orders over West Africa, on 28 June 1556 they responded to a petition from the Merchant Adventurers by embargoing all cloth exports to the Low Countries until 1 November. Exactly why the Adventurers wanted this is not clear, but the Flemings immediately appealed to Philip, who weighed in on their side without a second thought.[65] The king had developed an understandable but somewhat unreflective dislike of the English, most of whom (and particularly the Londoners) he suspected of being heretics. Knowing this, the Flemings took the obvious step of accusing the Merchant Adventurers of using their privileged base in Antwerp to hatch treasonable conspiracies against the English government. The combination of this rather curious embargo with the activities of Towerson, Chancellor and others, seems to have convinced Philip that the English were determined to ruin Antwerp and take their trade elsewhere. On 17 October a member of the Council of Brabant presented a series of articles to the English council in the king's name:

> His Majesty findeth this to be the trewe way wholely to divert the
> said traphique from his said low countries and to transport it into some
> other place, and to separate the subjectes of both parts from all mutual
> traphique, communication and affection. A thing contrived by certyn privat
> persons of the said nacyon for their singular proffyt and convenyience . . .[66]

This time, however, the king overreached himself. The Adventurers were in a well nigh unassailable position because of the assistance which they were giving to the Lord Treasurer as he struggled to reduce the queen's debts, and the council rebutted Philip's charges with some firmness.[67] By the following year the king was beginning to think that he had acted precipitately, but by then the damage had been done and relations between Philip and London remained extremely cool.

Meanwhile, unaffected by domestic politics, Sir Hugh Willoughby and Richard Chancellor were working out their fate. The former, by a combination of misfortune and misjudgement, was forced to winter in Northern

Lapland, where he perished with his entire crew in the early weeks of 1554. Chancellor, who had become separated from his compatriot, was luckier. Having rounded the North Cape he reached Vardo, where he waited for some days before pressing on into the White Sea, a region totally unknown to western navigators. Reaching the small port and fishing village of Nenoska, at the mouth of the Dvina close to the present location of Archangel, he decided he had gone far enough for one year. The winter was closing in, and further progress would in any case have been impossible. Realising that he had reached the territories of the Grand Duke of Muscovy, and perhaps learning something of the impossibility of his original mission, when the spring came he decided to make the long overland journey to Moscow instead of taking to the sea again. His gamble was rewarded.[68] The Tsar (as the Grand Duke styled himself) Ivan IV was on the look-out for westward contacts, having no outlet either on the Baltic or the Black Sea. A regular trade with England via the North Cape provided a very acceptable alternative. He graciously received Chancellor's commendation from Edward VI (ignoring the fact that it was addressed to the Emperor of China), and sent him homeward with a courteous letter to the English king, welcoming the prospect of trade.

Chancellor returned to England in the summer of 1554. Both Edward and the Duke of Northumberland were dead, but Cabot and most of the shareholders were very much alive. Muscovy wasn't quite Cathay, but in the circumstances it would do very nicely, and had the immense advantage of not upsetting anybody, least of all the touchy Iberians. For that same reason neither Mary nor her council had any objections, and in February 1555 the charter which had originally been sought from Edward was finally granted.[69] Although normally called the Muscovy Company, the official title of this new body was (rather misleadingly) 'The Merchant Adventurers of England for the discovery of lands and territories unknown'. It was headed by the Lord Treasurer and eleven other Privy Councillors, and included Sir William Cecil, Henry Sidney and John Gresham as well as other aldermen and merchants to the number of 97. Sebastian Cabot was named as Governor for life 'in consideration that he has been the chief setter forth of this journey'; four consuls and 24 assistants were appointed to manage the company's affairs. Although the volume of trade which would be handled by this company remained small – and very small by comparison with the Low Countries trade – the symbolism of this new venture could hardly have been more important. The Privy Council presence was on an unprecedented scale, both in numbers and seniority, and indicated that in spite of his own demise, the Duke of Northumberland's efforts to persuade the City and the council to collaborate actively in pursuit of English interests had succeeded at least in one direction.

In the summer of 1555 Chancellor returned to Moscow by the same route, taking with him a number of merchants to remain in Russia as factors for the new trade. His instructions indicate that the company had by no means given up its original ambitions, which is perhaps why its official title made no mention of Muscovy. Chancellor was ordered 'to use all wayes and meanes possible to learne how men may passe from Russia either by land or sea to Cathaia'.[70] He reached the Russian capital in October 1555, and Ivan immediately gave him a generous charter of commercial privileges, arranging for a Russian envoy to accompany the Englishmen on their departure in the spring.[71] However, at that point Chancellor's luck began to run out. He embarked with four ships in July 1556. Two were lost on the Norwegian coast, and Chancellor himself was cast away off Aberdeenshire, having struggled against adverse weather until November. Miraculously the Russian ambassador who was accompanying him survived, and eventually made his way to London; and the fourth ship also returned, having been forced to winter in Trondheim. Thereafter the Russian trade, although not without its problems, was an established fact, and diplomatic contacts between the two countries also developed in consequence.

Meanwhile another enterprising Englishman had been poking around the Levant looking for legitimate sources of profit in resurrecting the almost defunct trade to Aleppo and the eastern Mediterranean. Anthony Jenkinson had left London in 1546, and had spent about seven or eight years wandering around the Ottoman Empire. In 1553 he secured an audience with the sultan, and Suleiman proved surprisingly willing to entertain the prospect of trade with distant England.[72] This may have been because he knew of the hostility between Edward's government and his arch-enemy Charles V, but if that was his motive it was doomed to frustration. When Jenkinson finally returned to England in 1555 or 1556, flourishing his promise of favourable trade with Turkey, he found the country ruled by Charles's son, who had no intention of encouraging such subversive contacts. Not to be defeated, Jenkinson threw in his lot with the new Adventurers, and when the next Muscovy fleet set out in May 1557, bearing a substantial cargo of broadcloths as well as the returning Russian ambassador, Anthony Jenkinson Esq. was in command.[73]

Jenkinson reached the White Sea in July and anchored on the 12th in approximately the same spot that Chancellor had reached three years earlier. He and his companions made their way by easy stages to Moscow, setting up trading posts *en route*, and were warmly entertained by the Tsar at Christmas. At that point Jenkinson detached himself from the main party, which went about its normal business, and obtained from the Tsar letters of commendation for a further journey into central Asia. Accompanied by two other Englishmen and an interpreter, he set out again in April 1558 and journeyed down the Volga to Astrakhan. Coasting round the northern shore of the Caspian sea, they then joined a large caravan of Tartar and Persian merchants on their way to Urjeni, on the old Oxus. Finally, on 23 December 1558 they arrived at Bokhara.[74] There they remained for over two months, trading such goods as they had, and gathering information. What they learned was not encouraging. The lands to the east and south were seriously disturbed by war; they were still nine months journey from Peking, and there was little or no demand for English cloth among the merchants who flocked to this communications centre. On 8 March 1559 they left with a caravan bound for the Caspian. Forced by further war to abandon a planned excursion into Persia, Jenkinson and his companions returned to Moscow, a journey which took them over six months. Finally, in the summer of 1560, they arrived in London to tell the tale of an epic adventure, but also to report that there was no future in Bokhara as an outpost of English trade. Although its outcome was in a sense negative, the importance of this journey was nevertheless great. It provided precise geographical knowledge of regions hitherto known only by repute, and whetted English appetites for tales of travel to strange and distant places.[75] The awakening of this curiosity, hitherto confined to a mere handful of individuals, in a large section of literate English society was not the least important outcome of these mid-century explorations.

The queen's contribution to these developments was slight – less than that of her brother, who was at least interested in ships. She was pleased enough to encourage enterprise which did not offend her husband, or her husband's other subjects, but her most positive action was to encourage her Lord Treasurer to get the Crown debts under control. At their worst, the debts of Edward's council had totalled over £250,000, but the tough policies eventually adopted by the Duke of Northumberland had reduced that figure to about £180,000 by the end of the reign.[76] Mary had at first made the situation worse by borrowing 300,000 ducats in Spain, and by forgoing about £50,000 of the last Edwardian subsidy. Both these were political decisions rather than fiscal ones, and by October 1554 the total debt was probably back to approximately where it had been in 1552.[77] However, at that point Winchester began to insist on economic priorities, and Gresham's talent for recycling loans and manipulating cloth credits began to get the situation under control. By June 1556 the exchange rate was up to 22s 6d and the Crown debts were down to about £150,000, of which approximately £110,000 was owed in Antwerp.[78] Rather surprisingly in view of the collapse of the exchange rate in 1551, the credit of the English Crown on the Bourse remained sound throughout this period. First Stephen Vaughan and then Gresham was able to borrow as much as the council needed at about 12 per cent, when both the Emperor and the King of France were having to pay three times as much. This was due to skilful debt management, because the English Crown never defaulted. Gresham in particular often had a desperate struggle to meet repayment dates, and was forced to recycle loans which he was unable to discharge. But he was always able to do so, and once he had managed to stagger the repayment dates, the problem eased.[79]

Unfortunately, in May 1557 England returned to war. Mary's council advised her as strongly as they could against such a course, but the decision did not rest with them and the queen considered it to be her duty to support her husband. Although Philip paid the full cost of the English expeditionary force which joined him in the Low Countries in the summer of 1557, military expenditure soared. The navy was returned to a full war footing, and Berwick had to be strengthened against a threatened Scottish invasion. Calais, however, was not strengthened, or not strengthened sufficiently, and fell to a surprise French attack in January 1558. These were hard times. The harvests had failed in 1555 and 1556, bringing food shortages, high prices and sickness. Throughout 1557 and the early part of 1558 an influenza epidemic raged.[80] This was not as lethal as the plague in terms of mortality, but widespread and prolonged illness, coupled with the general unpopularity of the war, inhibited mobilisation and made any counter-stroke against Calais impossible.

At the time the English felt the humiliation of losing the last fragment of their once great continental empire keenly. Mary, it is claimed, declared that it would be found written on her heart, and Elizabeth spent the first five years of her reign in futile attempts to recover it. However, it had become extremely expensive to garrison and maintain, and had ceased to serve any essential purpose. The wool staple, now no more than a shadow of its former self, was removed to Bruges, and a perpetual irritant in Anglo-French relations disappeared. The loss of Calais also symbolised the re-orientation of English priorities which was beginning to take place. Even in Henry VIII's reign, Calais had been an entry point for English incursions into France. Once she had burned her fingers at Le Havre in 1563, Elizabeth was no longer interested in continental adventures, except for very limited operations in the interest of English security.[81] It was not until the end of the seventeenth century, and in very different circumstances, that another Army Royal was to campaign in Europe. England no longer had a land frontier, except against Scotland, and the Channel became, for the first time, primarily a defensive moat. The metamorphosis of England from the military power which it had been in the early fifteenth century, to the naval power which it had become by the late sixteenth century, had taken another step forward. England also learned another lesson from this war (if it still needed learning): she could not afford to fight without some major changes in the fiscal system. Henry's last French war had dissipated the enormous capital assets gained from the religious houses; Somerset's Scottish war had ruined the coinage; and both had created substantial debts to plague successor regimes. Mary did the same. In spite of her conscience, she continued to sell monastic lands, but sensibly refrained from renewed debasement. As a result her debts mounted alarmingly. Having been reduced to about £100,000 on the eve of the war, they tripled in eighteen months, in spite of the fact that no significant land campaign was mounted, except at Philip's expense.[82] The warning could hardly have been starker.

The only part of England's 'war machine' which functioned with any credit was the navy. As we have seen, it had been well maintained after the end of the wars in 1550, although the replacement programme was at a modest level. Four pinnaces had been built instead of Henry's rowbarges. The *Mary Willoughby*, recovered from the Scots in 1547, was rebuilt in 1551, and the *Primrose*, a new 300 tonner, was launched by the king in the same year.[83] There were a number of personnel changes in the Admiralty: Benjamin Gonson succeeded Robert Legge as Treasurer in 1548, and Sir William Woodhouse became Vice Admiral in 1552. In spite of Northumberland's positive record as Admiral and patron, the navy had promptly declared for Mary in the crisis of 1553, and this had materially assisted her power in East Anglia.[84] The new queen did not show the same personal interest in the fleet that her brother had done, but the programme of maintenance, the regular patrols, and a modest level of activity against pirates were all maintained through the first year of her reign. Towards the end of 1554 there were 29 ships in commission. Fourteen others deemed to be older and less seaworthy were sold off in 1554 and 1555, the extremely modest price of £181 indicating their debilitated state.[85] Various scraps of evidence reflect the routine use of these vessels during the same years, but diplomatic sources also suggest that a new danger had arisen. Henry II had been seriously alarmed by the Anglo-Spanish marriage treaty. He had done his best to frustrate it by diplomatic means, and had toyed with the idea of supporting rebels. When the rebellion collapsed, a number of gentleman adventurers took refuge in France, and the king welcomed them. With his encouragement and active assistance, a number of them took to the sea and began to prey on English and Imperial trade. These pirates included some, like Sir Peter Carew, with little experience of the sea, but others were seasoned campaigners such as Henry Killigrew, whose activities long antedated any political pretext. By the summer of 1556 a fleet of six or eight of these marauders was causing havoc in the Channel, and a squadron of warships out of Portsmouth was sent against them. We do not know how large this fleet was, but it caught up with the pirates off Plymouth and defeated them comprehensively, capturing at least six ships, including one belonging to the King of France.[86] Philip considered the English fleet to be one of the few tangible assets which he had acquired through his marriage to Mary, and was incensed when the English council blandly declared in the autumn of 1555 that it did not have enough ships to meet his request for service.[87] In fact a modest replacement programme had already been decided upon, and it is extremely unlikely that the king's indignation had anything to do with that. The *Philip and Mary* of 500 tons was laid down, probably in September, and was launched the following summer. The *Lion*, also of 500 tons, was completed in 1557, and the smaller *Falcon* of 100 tons was rebuilt early in 1558.[88] Unlike the previous French war, the conflict of 1557–59 did not see any significant rise in ship acquisitions, and this is a strong indication that the English had no serious military ambitions. A fleet of 21 ships was at sea in the summer of 1557, and escorted the Earl of Pembroke's expeditionary force in July, but saw only desultory action as the French did not challenge at sea that summer.

Only a small squadron was retained in service during the winter, but it was the speed of the French advance rather than any lack of naval preparedness which prevented those ships from going to the rescue of Calais. In fact a fleet was at sea within days of the first warning (a remarkable feat at that time), but by the time it reached the harbour the controlling fort of Rysbank had already fallen and access was impossible. A couple of weeks later, as the same fleet awaited the mobilisation of the force commanded to recover the town, it was scattered and badly damaged by a winter gale, and that, combined with the difficulties which we have already noticed, caused the operation to be abandoned.[89] A major armada of some 140 ships was sent out from Portsmouth in June, but this seems to have been intended mainly to impress Philip with a display of willingness. It achieved little beyond some raiding of the Breton coast. There were other actions, such as John Malen's success at Gravelines and Sir John Clere's failure in Orkney, but no major sea battle.[90] More significant for the future than this rather lacklustre performance was probably the licensing of no fewer than 23 privateers in the summer of 1558. As we have seen, these were first sent out officially in 1544, but this represented an important increase in scale, and a precedent for one of the most distinctive contributions of the Elizabethan seamen.[91]

In the run up to the war, the naval administration was also given a major overhaul. The reasons for this are not particularly obvious from the surviving records, but it may have been felt that the Admiralty was becoming too independent, and perhaps not entirely reliable, as both Clinton and Winter had been under suspicion at different times. In January 1556 the Lord

Admiral was ordered to take 'secret musters' of the fleet, without the knowledge of the Council of Marine Causes, and this was followed up with further orders for stocktaking and audit.[92] Some kind of fraud or peculation seems to have been suspected, but if anything untoward was revealed, it was not recorded. The main consequence was that a year later the whole responsibility was taken out of the Lord Admiral's hands, and delivered to the Lord Treasurer. At the same time an 'ordinary' or regular budget of £14,000 a year was decreed, in two equal instalments, and the Treasurer and the Controller General of the Victuals were instructed to account separately.[93] Winchester seems to have thought that there was a backlog of maintenance work, because he was prepared to allow the Ordinary to drop to £12,000 in the long term. Part of the intention may well have been to use the direct labour forces already available at Deptford and Portsmouth, rather than putting repair work out to contract. Tighter budget control was obviously the overall aim, but nothing was actually achieved before the outbreak of war in the summer, and the implementation of these reforms had to await the return of peace in 1559. To put these figures in perspective, between 31 December 1556 and 31 December 1558, when the peacetime ordinary should have amounted to £28,000, Gonson actually received and disbursed £144,941 1s 6d.[94]

When Mary died in November 1558, she bequeathed to Elizabeth 39 ships in serviceable condition, six of which were actually at sea.[95] Peace negotiations had already commenced, but were suspended until the attitude of the new queen should be known. Threatened by France both in the north and the south, Elizabeth was in no position to fall out with Philip, and in fact was quick to admit 'how moche Hir Majestie hathe ben beholden to him her good brother in the late tyme of her sisters reigne'. This was nothing less than the truth. Although Philip had been anxious to marry her to his ally the Duke of Savoy, he had accepted defeat in that campaign with a good grace. Realising that he had no pretext in law to press his own claim to the succession, that he could not afford to fight a civil war in England, and that Mary's preferred choice, Margaret Douglas, was a non-starter, Philip had backed Elizabeth's claim with some enthusiasm.[96] He knew that she was popular in England, and that her most plausible rival, Mary Stuart, was in the pocket of the French.

At the time, some of the new queen's advisers lamented the precariousness of her position, but in fact it was stronger than it appeared. France was exhausted, and Scotland was in the early stages of a major aristocratic revolt. Philip's poor relations with London had not prevented a reasonable recovery by the London–Antwerp cloth trade, and it appeared that the new and restless energies of England's merchants had been successfully diverted to Russia and western Asia. Sebastian Cabot was no longer a bone of contention, and he had no obvious successor. Only the pertinacious attempts of some Londoners to penetrate the Guinea trade marred what could have been an amicable and fruitful collaboration. However, the world had changed a lot since 1547. The genie of English maritime enterprise, having first escaped from the bottle with official encouragement, could not now be forced back. Like her brother, Elizabeth was unconcerned about traditional friendships and obligations, except in so far as they served her interests. She almost immediately risked giving mortal offence to her 'good brother' by embracing a Protestant religious settlement. Equally to the point, the Duke of Northumberland's servant, Sir William Cecil, became her chief minister, and his son Robert Dudley became her personal favourite. Elizabeth was interested in anything which strengthened her position, and that of England in Europe. A well-equipped and well-organised navy was her strongest military card, and a restless band of merchants and adventurers an asset which she was quick to exploit. Where Mary had permitted activities (if they did not offend Philip), and made no attempt to stop her councillors from becoming involved, Elizabeth was prepared to be proactive, and Cecil was the foremost promoter of the 'enterprise culture'.

Notes

1. E.W. Ives, 'Henry VIII's will: a forensic conundrum', *Historical Journal*, 35, 1992, 779–804. R.A. Houlbrooke, 'Henry VIII's wills: a comment', *Historical Journal*, 37, 1994, 891–900. E.W. Ives, 'Henry VIII's will: the Protectorate provisions, 1546–7', *Historical Journal*, 37, 1994, 901–13.

2. Glyn Redworth, *In Defence of the Church Catholic: A Life of Stephen Gardiner* (Oxford, 1990). D. MacCulloch, *Thomas Cranmer* (London, 1996), 359–60.

3. MacCulloch, *Cranmer*, 351–409.

4. The traditionally accepted figure of approximately £800,000 was calculated by F.C. Dietz in 1921 (*English Government Finance, 1485–1558*, 137–43). It has recently been convincingly argued by Peter Cunich that this figure is too low. Cunich, 'The Dissolution of the Monasteries and the growth of royal patronage in England, 1536–1547' (Cambridge, Ph.D, 1989).

5. C.E. Challis, *The Tudor Coinage* (Manchester, 1978), 252–3.

6. J.D. Gould, *The Great Debasement* (London, 1970), 38–9; Challis, *Tudor Coinage*, 255; for a summary of the fineness, see Gould, *Great Debasement*, 11.

7. Challis, *Tudor Coinage*, 219–47, 307.

8. P.H. Ramsey, *The Price Revolution in Sixteenth-Century England* (London, 1971), 23–6.

9.   Gould, *Great Debasement*, 89.

10. Challis, *Tudor Coinage*, 232; Gould, *Great Debasement*, 11.

11. Ramsey, *Price Revolution*, 24; Gould, *Great Debasement*, 89.

12. Gould, *Great Debasement*, 173–7; D.C. Coleman, *The Economy of England, 1450–1750* (London, 1977), 64; Ralph Davis, *English Overseas Trade, 1500–1700* (London, 1973).

13. J.F. Larkin and P.L. Hughes *Tudor Royal Proclamations* (New Haven, 1964), I, 518, 520, 525. By giving advance warning, the council encouraged traders to enhance their prices in preparation, thus aggravating the situation in the short term. David Loades, *John Dudley, Duke of Northumberland* (Oxford, 1996), 171–2. Challis, *Tudor Coinage*, 105–11.

14. Gould, *Great Debasement*, 177.

15. Coleman, *Economy of England*, 64.

16. *Acts of the Privy Council (APC)*, ed. J.R. Dasent *et al.* (1890–1907), II, 137, 9 October 1547.

17. *Calendar of the Patent Rolls (Cal. Pat.), Edward VI*, ed. R.H. Brodie (London, 1924–29), I, 320.

18. *Calendar of State Papers, Spanish (Cal. Span.)*, ed. Royall Tyler *et al.* (London 1869–1954), IX, 381, van der Delft to the Emperor, 28 May 1549.

19. Ibid.

20. *Cal. Span.*, IX, 408–9, van der Delft to the Emperor, 19 July 1549.

21. *Cal. Span.*, IX, 430, van der Delft to the Emperor, 13 August 1549.

22. *APC*, II, 320, 2 September 1549.

23. *APC*, III, 55, 26 June 1550.

24. *Cal. Pat., Edward VI*, III, 324.

25. Richard Hakluyt, *The principall navigations, voiages and discoveries of the English nation* (London, 1589), 259–63.

26. Sir William Foster, *England's Quest of Eastern Trade* (London, 1933), 8.

27. Hakluyt, *Principall navigations*, 259–63.

28. John Stow, *The Annals of England Faithfully collected . . .* (London, 1592), 609. W.K. Jordan, *Edward VI: The Threshold of Power* (London, 1970), 492–3.

29. *Cal. Span.*, XI, 2, Jehan Scheyfve to the Bishop of Arras, 10 April 1553.

30. *Cal. Span.*, XI, 204–5, Ambassadors to the Emperor, 4 September 1553.

31. *Cal. Span.*, XI, 308, 19 October 1553.

32. *Cal. Span.*, XI, 261, Cabot to the Emperor, 15 November 1553. There is, as far as I am aware, no evidence of this plot in either French or English sources.

33. More accurately, Renard reported that Cabot had told him that the Chancellor had countermanded his permission. It need not be assumed that this was the truth. *Cal. Span.*, XI, 373.

34. *Cal. Pat., Philip and Mary* (London, 1936–39), II, 55–8; III, 33, 485.

35. *Cal. Span.*, X, 67.

36. D.R. Bisson, *The Merchant Adventurers of England: The Company and the Crown, 1474–1564* (London, 1993), 58.

37. P. Simpson, ed., *Danziger Inventar: Inventare Hansicher Archive des 16. Jahrhunderts* (Aalen, 1913), III, 147–8.

38. *Danziger Inventar*, III, 155; Jordan, *The Threshold of Power*, 486–7.

39. *Danziger Inventar*, III, 168–70; *APC*, III, 365.

40. Public Record Office (PRO) SP10/14, no. 11.

41. *APC*, III, 489.

42. T. Glasgow, 'A list of ships in the Royal Navy from 1539 to 1588', *Mariners Mirror*, 56, 1970, 299–307.

43. D. Loades, *The Tudor Navy* (Aldershot, 1992), 142.

44. M.L. Bush, *The Government Policy of Protector Somerset* (Manchester, 1975), 32–40.

45. Loades, *Tudor Navy*, 148.

46. The talks were opened through an intermediary, Antonio Guidotti; and because the English garrisons were actually being reinforced in December 1549, the English council was able to make it appear that the French had made the first move. *Cal. Span.*, IX, 469. British Library (BL) Harleian MS 284, no. 38, f. 56.

47. *APC*, II, 347.

48. Gould, *Great Debasement*, 11, 89.

49. Loades, *Tudor Navy*, 150.

50. BL Harleian MS 354, f. 9.

51. *APC*, III, 503.

52. W.K. Jordan, *The Chronicle and Political Papers of Edward VI* (London, 1966), 116.

53. PRO SP10/14/69.

54. Gould, *Great Debasement*, 11, 89.

55. Challis, *Tudor Coinage*, 306.

56. *Cal. Span.*, XI, 66, Scheyfve to the Emperor, 24 June 1553; *Calendar of State Papers, Foreign, Mary*, ed. W.B. Turnbull (London, 1861), 30.

57. *Cal. Span.*, XI, 315.

58. *Cal. Span.*, XI, 347, Renard to the Emperor, 8 November 1553.

59. David Loades, *The Reign of Mary Tudor* (London, 1991), 77–80.

60. PRO SP11/4/36.

61. Hakluyt, *Principall navigations*, I, 85.

62. Ibid., 87; *Cal. Span.*, XII, 291, Renard to the Emperor, 28 June 1554.

63. Hakluyt, *Principall navigations*, I, 98–125.

64. *Calendar of State Papers, Venetian*, ed. Rawdon Brown *et al.* (London, 1864–98), VI, 218.

65. BL Lansdowne MS 170, f. 129.

66. Ibid.

67. Ibid., f. 141.

68. Hakluyt, *Principall navigations*, I, 263–91. Chancellor's account of the voyage, both in Latin and English.

69. *Cal. Pat. Philip and Mary*, II, 55–8.

70. Foster, *England's Quest*, 12.

71. Hakluyt, *Principall navigations*, I, 297–303.

72. Foster, *England's Quest*, 14.

73. Ibid., 17.

74. Ibid., 17–19; based on Hakluyt.

75. For a discussion of this cultural development and its significance, see E.G.R. Taylor, *Tudor Geography, 1485–1583* (London, 1930); and Taylor, *The Haven Finding Art* (London, 1967).

76. This was in May 1552, and according to Edward's *Journal* (123). There have been many attempts to compute the true sum, ranging from £220,000 to £251,000. Dietz calculated that Mary inherited a debt of £180,000–185,000, a figure which roughly agrees with my own calculations.

77. Loades, *Reign of Mary*, 129–38.

78. PRO SP69/8/461.

79. Loades, *Reign of Mary*, 232–8.

80. F.J. Fisher, 'Influenza and inflation in Tudor England', *Economic History Review*, 2nd series, 18, 1965, 120–30.

81. For a summary of Elizabeth's foreign policy and its objectives, see R.B. Wernham, *The Making of Elizabethan Foreign Policy, 1558–1603* (London, 1980).

82. Loades, *Reign of Mary*, 340–61.

83. Jordan, *Chronicle of King Edward*, 70; N.A.M. Rodger, *The Safeguard of the Sea* (London, 1997), 478.

84. J.D. Alsop, 'A regime at sea: the navy and the 1553 succession crisis', *Albion*, 24, 1992, 577–90.

85. PRO E351/2195.

86. This was the notorious *Sacrette*, about which there was a long-running diplomatic battle. Loades, *Tudor Navy*, 164–5.

87. This was partly because a fleet had been raised to escort the Emperor back to Spain, and had not been needed; the council had no desire to be caught out twice. Loades, *Reign of Mary*, 180–1.

88. Rodger, *Safeguard*, 478.

89. PRO SP11/12, f. 35; C.S.L Davies, 'England and the French War, 1557–9', in J. Loach and R. Tittler, eds, *The Mid-Tudor Polity* (London, 1980).

90. T. Glasgow, 'The navy in Philip and Mary's war', *Mariners Mirror*, 53, 1967, 331–2.

91. Loades, *Tudor Navy*, 173–4.

92. *APC*, V, 220–1.

93. *APC*, VI, 39. For a discussion of these moves and their significance, see Loades, *Tudor Navy*, 167–8.

94. PRO E101/64/1.

95. Loades, *Tudor Navy*, 178–9.

96. Loades, *Reign of Mary Tudor*, 334, 336.

CHAPTER THREE

Trade, Privateering and New Priorities, 1558–1570

When Elizabeth succeeded to the throne in November 1558, many things changed. Normally the spotlight is on her religious settlement of 1559, which (as it transpired) brought the final acceptance of Protestant doctrine. The suggestion is that the young queen (she was 25) brought in new men, and proposed new solutions. For the most part, however, and particularly in respect of her religious settlement, that is not true. What Elizabeth did was to restore her brother's regime, which Mary had aborted. There was no Thomas Cranmer, no Nicholas Ridley, and no John Dudley, all victims of Mary's sense of justice, but the Dudley and Boleyn families (the queen's kindred on her mother's side) returned in strength to the court; and Sir William Cecil, her chief prop and adviser, was an old servant of both Somerset and Northumberland. Less than a quarter of Mary's council retained their places, but the replacements were men of equal, or greater, experience.[1] All significant offices were automatically vacated on the demise of the Crown, so there was no question of men being dismissed; the question was whether they would be reappointed. The most significant survivor was William Paulet, Marquis of Winchester, the Lord Treasurer, but he had originally been an Edwardian appointment. The most significant casualty was Lord Paget, the Lord Privy Seal, who was neither reappointed nor replaced, the office remaining vacant.[2] However, there was no spoils system in Renaissance England, and the great majority of office-holders at every level below the highest retained their places.

At court the Household proper was almost untouched by the change of ruler. The Lord Steward, the Earl of Arundel, retained both his office and his seat on the council. By contrast, both the Lord Chamberlain and the Vice Chamberlain (positions closer to the monarch's person) were replaced, and there was a moderate turnover of the regular Chamber staff.[3] It was the group closest to the queen, however, the Privy Chamber, which changed most dramatically. Not a single one of Mary's female familiars was retained. However cautiously Elizabeth might shuffle her political pack, when it came to unrestricted personal choice she had nothing at all in common with her predecessor.

Although he was not identified immediately as the queen's particular favourite, Robert Dudley became Master of the Horse within days of her accession, and quickly began to rebuild some parts of his father's clientage network.[4] It was Robert who brought to court, at some point before Christmas 1558, the enigmatic John Dee. Dee was a Cambridge graduate, who had taken his M.A. from Trinity College in 1548. Deeply interested in mathematics, he had visited the Low Countries as early as 1547, and had met the celebrated scholar and cosmographer Gemma Frisius. Immediately after taking his degree, he had returned to the Continent, where he spent the next two years in travel and study.[5] By the time that he returned he had already acquired a reputation, and in 1551 Sir John Cheke had brought him to the attention of Sir William Cecil, who in turn had introduced him to the king. Edward was sufficiently impressed to grant him an annuity of 100 marks, but he seems not to have entered the royal service. Briefly, in 1552, he was with the Earl of Pembroke, but later in that year transferred to the household of the Duke of Northumberland. It is said that he was tutor to the duke's sons, but they were all grown men by 1552, so that is unlikely.[6] He certainly formed a close friendship with the Earl of Warwick, who was about 24, and later expressed the warmest admiration for the young man's qualities. A friendship with Robert, who was nineteen, can be deduced, and it was probably to Dee that the later Earl of Leicester owed his interest in mathematics and navigation. Dee probably took Holy Orders at some point between 1550 and 1553, because he exchanged his annuity for the rectory of Upton-on-Severn in March 1553.[7] He may have been technically a chaplain to the duke, but his main employment seems to have been in connection with the voyages inspired by Cabot, for which he served as a technical adviser.

He was not troubled for his association with Northumberland after the latter's fall, but tempted providence in corresponding with several of Elizabeth's servants during her arrest in 1554. Moreover, there was also a sinister side to Dee's reputation. His mathematical studies had led him into astrology, and possibly also into alchemy. In 1555 he was arrested on suspicion of conspiring against the queen's life by poison or 'conjuring'.[8] His lodgings in London were searched and sealed, and he was interrogated a number of times, first by John Bourne, then by the whole council, and finally by the Chief Justice of Common Pleas. These enquiries apparently cleared him of any suspicion of treason, but there remained the question of his religious orthodoxy. He was brought before the council in Star Chamber, and on 20 August released into the custody of Edmund Bonner, Bishop of London.[9] Dee later described Bonner as his friend (a startling admission to make during Elizabeth's reign), but whether this friendship antedated his incarceration is not clear. In 1563 John Foxe described one of Bonner's chaplains as 'a Conjuror by repute', but did not name him. However, in another place he also referred to 'Master John Dee, a Bachelor of Divinity' (a degree which the cosmographer did not hold) as a chaplain. Foxe, who was working at speed, either believed that one of these men was the Dee he knew, or his nineteenth-century editor was jumping to conclusions.[10] The leap from imprisoned suspect to chaplain in less than a year is somewhat improbable, but it is unlikely that there were two John Dees, and the mathematician's friendship for the bishop must have sprung from this extraordinarily rapid rehabilitation. In 1558 it was precisely his reputation as a conjurer which brought him back to court. He was invited secretly to cast the queen's horoscope in order to identify a favourable date for her coronation. Robert Dudley and William Cecil were often at odds in the early years of the reign, but both were patrons of Dee, and listened with respect to his advice, whether astrological or scientific.[11]

The return of Cecil to office, and of Dee to a position of influence, helped to restore Edwardian priorities in matters other than religion. The position of the Crown in its relations with the City of London was not strong, and Elizabeth realised that perfectly well. The hectoring tone which Mary's council had sometimes adopted disappeared, and the policy of partnership, which had been severely strained by Philip's intervention, was unobtrusively restored. Cabot was gone, but the outward-looking strategy which he had advocated was being actively promoted by Stephen Borough, Richard Eden, and of course John Dee.[12] War in northern Europe and complete uncertainty over future relations with the Low Countries made the search for new markets a matter of survival rather than ambition. It is unlikely that the queen herself had any views about this, but as she struggled with a heavy legacy of war debts, the prosperity of the richest city in her kingdom was very much on her mind. If she wanted the Merchant Adventurers to help her out of the financial hole into which her sister's war had dropped her, she had to encourage them to make money in any way they could, whether by trading to Guinea and the West Indies in defiance of the Iberians, or to the Baltic in defiance of the Hanseatic League. This was at first less a policy than a gut reaction, but it was to have important consequences. At the same time the foreign Protestant congregations, which had been such a feature of Edwardian London, quickly re-established themselves.[13] Those who had survived the Marian blitz emerged from their cellars, and were joined by new refugees, quick to take advantage of the openings created by the establishment of so many of their friends in the restored church.[14] These congregations carried a political price tag, but the skills which their members brought with them, and the commercial networks which they represented, far outweighed the liabilities incurred.

It is often said that Elizabeth's position at the beginning of her reign, like England's position in Europe, was extremely weak. Some pessimistic contemporaries certainly saw it that way, but in fact the dangers were less than they supposed.[15] Once it was clear that Elizabeth was not going to be challenged at home (which could not have been taken for granted), her position had many advantages. Philip and Henry II were already negotiating for peace, both being virtually bankrupt.[16] In spite of her debts, Elizabeth's credit in Antwerp was better than either of theirs. Scotland, it is true, was virtually a French province, and Mary had a hereditary claim to the Crown of England, but not only did she have virtually no support in England, both Henry and Elizabeth knew that the one thing which would force Philip to forget his financial troubles would be the prospect of a Franco-Scottish takeover in England.[17] Whatever Henry might say, there was not the slightest chance of his trying to implement his daughter-in-law's claim. At the same time, however much he might dislike the return of heresy to England, Philip was dependent, as his father had been, on English friendship, or at least complaisance, to maintain his lines of communication between Spain and the Low Countries. Most of this did not depend upon England being rich or powerful, and in comparison with France or Spain she was neither, but if her strategic position was to provide any leverage, she had to be strong at sea. This did not require exceptional percipience to be observed. As Sir Nicholas Throgmorton wrote to Cecil:

> Bend your force, credit and device to maintain and increase your
> navy by all the means you can possible, for in this time, considering all
> circumstances, it is the flower of England's garland . . . your best and
> best cheap defence and most redoubted of your enemies and doubtful
> friends . . .[18]

Throgmorton had a talent for stating the obvious, and English kings had been bombarded with such advice since the 1430s, but at least he had an elegant turn of phrase.

As we have seen, when Mary died the navy was in good estate, and Lord Clinton, the Lord Admiral, was one of those officers who was reappointed to his position.[19] Six royal ships and seven armed merchantmen in the queen's service were actually at sea on 17 November.[20] A large new ship, provisionally called the *Peter*, but later the *Elizabeth Jonas*, was in building at Woolwich, and two older ships, the *Jennet* and the *Hare*, were being rebuilt at Portsmouth.[21] In March 1559 a survey was taken to assess the navy's capability. It listed 21 ships as fit for service, a further ten in need of repair, and 45 merchant ships available to be converted for fighting purposes; the second part of the same document listed seven royal ships and eight armed merchantmen at sea, which seems to have been the standard 'winter guard'; and the third part listed the work currently in hand at Deptford, Woolwich and Portsmouth.[22] This survey was shortly followed by a stategic plan, which envisaged a future navy of 24 warships, varying in size from 200 to 800 tons, four barks (60–80 tons) and two pinnaces (40 tons). It was also noted that it was significantly cheaper to keep ships on a care and main-tenance basis at Deptford than at Portsmouth, although the latter was the most convenient operational base in wartime.[23]

The thinking behind these documents is reasonably clear. The navy's job was to discharge the regular duties attendant upon coastal defence, the protection of commerce and fisheries, and such minor shows of force as might be called for. This was based upon a realistic assessment of what could be afforded, rather than what the defence of the realm would ideally require. Even low-key military operations would need the mobilisation of merchant ships, approximately on a 1:1 ratio. However, except in a dire emergency it was not wise to take too many of these ships at once, or for too long a period. London was the most available source both of ships and skilled mariners, but too heavy or too frequent a demand would strain cooperation to its limits. The plan thus outlined in 1559 was roughly ad-hered to, and until full-scale war with Spain broke out in 1585, the navy remained approximately half the size that it had been during Henry VIII's last French war.[24] The ships were repaired, rebuilt and replaced upon a regular basis; a core of master mariners, gunners, shipwrights and carpen-ters were retained in employment, and victualling was reorganised upon a contract basis in 1565.[25] Elizabeth gradually abandoned the ordinary budget decreed in 1557, preferring payment by occasional warrant as required, but this did not mean that she was squeezing the navy of necessary funds. By contemporary standards the Council for Marine Causes continued to be cheap and extraordinarily effective.

The constant availability of warships at relatively short notice was an underlying factor in the maritime developments of the 1560s. The war with France made little further demand upon English resources before peace was concluded at Câteau Cambrésis in April 1559; on the other hand, Elizabeth got relatively little out of the treaty. Henry II abandoned his daughter-in-law's claim to England, but as Queen of Scotland she refused to ratify the agreement. Calais, which Elizabeth made strenuous efforts to recover, remained in French hands.[26] No one expected Câteau Cambrésis to last longer than it took the ink to dry, and the queen prudently kept her fleet on a quasi-war footing. As it turned out, the pessimists were wrong, and there was no further major European conflict until 1618. France began to slide into civil war after 1560, the Holy Roman Empire ceased to be an aggressive power, and Philip II had his hands full, first with the Barbary corsairs, then with the Turks, and then with the Dutch revolt.

These circumstances created opportunities for Elizabeth which she was not slow to take. The rebellion of the Lords of the Congregation in Scotland against the French-dominated regency of the queen mother, Mary of Guise, is a case in point. Elizabeth was temperamentally averse to supporting rebels, and if Henry II had still been alive would have used her scruples as an excuse for inactivity. However, Henry's sudden death in the summer of 1559, and the troubles which were already afflicting his young successor, enabled her more aggressively minded advisers, such as Cecil, to persuade her of the advantages of intervention. In December 1559 William Winter took 34 ships to the Firth of Forth to cut communications between Scotland and France.[27] Aided by the winter weather, and his own skill in keeping station, he was completely successful. In January 1560 the French army operating against the rebels in Fife was forced to abandon its ordnance and retreat to Leith by way of Stirling. In February a French relief expedition was dispersed by storms without even reaching the Forth, and Elizabeth was emboldened to send an army into Scotland. Although the Anglo-Scottish siege of Leith in May was a fiasco, the death of the queen mother in the following month, and the continued effectiveness of the naval blockade, persuaded the French to negotiate. In July, unsure of further support from home, the expeditionary force effectively surrendered. Mary abandoned her claim to England (although not to the succession), the Lords of the Congregation formed a *de facto* government, and Winter shipped the French troops back to France.[28] Apart from the capture of two French galleys, there had been very little sea fighting; but nevertheless this was a naval victory. Winter's skill, and the effectiveness of the Marine Council in keeping him supported and victualled through a long, hard winter, marked an unobtrusive but significant advance in the whole art of sea warfare. It is no wonder that a delighted William Cecil could write 'of Mr. Winter all men speak so well that I need not mention him'.[29] Although there were to be many subsequent alarms, time was to show that this victory marked a definitive turning point in Anglo-Scottish relations, and the wars which had intermittently plagued the border since the thirteenth century were at an end.

By contrast, Elizabeth's attempts to exploit the divisions in France in order to recover Calais were a dismal failure. Throughout 1560 the queen had remained in a state of acute nervous apprehension. Even while her forces were being successful in Scotland she had a fleet of 20 ships in the Narrow Seas, and another 40 in the Western Approaches;[30] these large armaments were not at sea for very long, but for a part of the summer she must have had about 100 ships on active service. Only a quarter of these can have been her own, but the auxiliary mobilisation seems to have worked very well in spite of the absence of a major crisis. Elizabeth's fears were a measure of her reluctance to believe the sudden collapse of French will, and her eagerness to intervene in 1561 is a reflection of her conversion. What the Lords of the Congregation had accomplished in Scotland, perhaps the Huguenots could achieve in France. In September she signed an agreement, offering military support in return for the surrender of Calais. Le Havre was accepted as a garrison town until Calais should be available. However, this was not a war which could be won at sea. The navy kept open the lines of communication with Le Havre throughout the 20 months of the occupation, ensuring that the garrison was supplied and reinforced, but it could do little more. The Huguenots were defeated, and came to terms with the government in February 1563, ignoring their treaty with England.[31] The Earl of Warwick remained at Le Havre until plague and the collapse of his local support forced his surrender in July. Elizabeth had burned her fingers, and learned the lesson.

Some of her subjects also learned a lesson, because the Huguenot seamen were famous pirates, and the English operated in the same way out of Le Havre, constituting a menace to all shipping in the Channel. Officially the queen deplored and condemned their activities, but it seems likely that many of them held letters of marque either from the Huguenot governor or from Warwick, in spite of there being no official war. Francis Clarke is alleged to have fitted out three ships in this way, and accumulated booty worth over £50,000.[32] It was a life which was to prove increasingly appealing, and the skills which were acquired could always find a market – not least within the royal navy itself. This was not a new situation. Robert Reneger, Peter Killigrew, and a number of others had moved from piracy into the royal service, but it became increasingly important as Elizabeth sought for ways to keep up her naval guard without overcommitting her resources.

In a year which saw virtually no action (such as 1558–59), the navy cost about £25,000 to run and maintain. However, even a modestly active year, like 1559–60 which saw no large-scale campaigns, could cost £85,000 and a year of full war more than twice as much again.[33] Taxation was also an unpopular option, and although it was no longer considered improper for the monarch to ask for a subsidy in peacetime, Elizabeth was extremely reluctant to do so. Calais was no longer a burden on the Exchequer, but in spite of the improved situation in Scotland it would be a long time before the queen felt able to relax her vigilance at Berwick, and the need for a military presence in Ireland was increased rather than diminished as the plantation policy developed.[34] All this meant that the auxiliary navy, as it might be termed, came increasingly under scrutiny. No one believed that a royal navy of 30 ships would be sufficient, even for a very limited war. It represented the professional (and immediately available) core of a fleet which could be quickly expanded to four or five times that size. This was import-ant, because after 1559 it became increasingly difficult to say whether England was at peace or not. There had been a brief period in 1538–39 when Henry VIII had felt sufficiently threatened to place the country on a war footing without actually being at war, but normally the distinction between war and peace had been fairly clear-cut. In the 1560s that was no longer the case. As we have seen, neither the Scottish intervention of 1559–60 nor the French campaign of 1562–63 constituted official warfare; but both operations had to be paid for. For several years after the Treaty of Troyes in 1564, France remained low on the agenda, but relations with Spain became increasingly uneasy. In spite of his open professions of friend-ship – extending even as far as a proposal of marriage at one point – Philip quickly became the refuge of first resort for those who found the Protestant religious settlement intolerable.[35] For some time he did nothing to take advantage of this situation, even protecting Elizabeth from possible papal censures in 1561; but he allowed his ambassador in England, Alvaro de Quadra, to become a focus for Catholic disaffection and intrigue.[36] In 1563 the ambassador was ejected from the court, and almost expelled from the country, for involvement in Catholic plots. Philip coolly disavowed his ac-tivities and there was no open rupture, but he nevertheless listened to what de Quadra was saying: 'This woman desires to make use of religion in order to excite rebellion in the whole world . . . If she had the power today she would sow heresy broadcast in all your Majesty's dominions, and set them ablaze without compunction . . .'.[37]

The fact that Elizabeth's purposes were entirely defensive does not in-validate the ambassador's assessment. Her actions in Scotland and in France were already sufficient evidence; and when trouble flared up in the Nether-lands in 1566, she extended a warm welcome to the thousands of refugees who sought asylum in southern and eastern England. This was playing with fire, and some of her councillors were deeply disturbed by the course of events; but in truth she had little option. Once Mary's status as Queen of France had been ended by the death of her husband Francis II in Decem-ber 1560, and she had returned to Scotland in August 1561, Philip's inter-est in supporting Elizabeth began to wane. At first Mary made a fair success of ruling her turbulent subjects; she married her kinsman Henry Stewart, Lord Darnley, in July 1565, and bore his son in the following year. Mean-while Elizabeth's marriage negotiations had come to nothing, and she had to do her best to make sure that Philip was fully occupied in his own dominions.[38] Moreover, the refugees were skilled craftsmen, and their contribution to the economy, particularly of East Anglia, was substantial. However distasteful she may have found it, it made sense for her to encourage resistance to Spanish rule in the Netherlands, just as it made sense to encourage whoever was opposing the schemes of the Guises in France.

Because such involvement jeopardised the already shaky structures of traditional trade, the council's incentive to encourage alternatives increased. If England were to protect its interests, it needed more ocean-going merchantmen, more skilled mariners, and more men with experience of sea fighting. The queen's attitude to these adventurers, usually called pirates by their victims and (anachronistically) privateers by historians, was consistently ambivalent.[39] A lot depended upon who they chose to plunder. Those who preyed on the ships of other Englishmen, who were probably the majority given the casual nature of most piracy, were treated (if caught) as common criminals. Those who preyed on Scottish, Dutch or Flemish vessels were also more likely than not to suffer punishment, although that depended to some extent on the immediate circumstances. On the other hand if the victims were French, Spanish, Portuguese or Hanseatic, then official eyes were usually averted.[40]

By 1560 the Muscovy trade was established, and operating more or less under its own steam. Bypassing the Baltic, and avoiding established Iberian interests, it was also relatively uncontroversial. West Africa, however, was a different matter. A toehold in the rich trade in pepper, gold, ivory and palm oil had been established in the 1530s, but the London merchants' efforts to increase their stake in the 1550s had had to contend not only with the hostility of the Portuguese, but also that of their own king. After 1559 government attitudes changed, and what has been called the 'Navy Board circle' becomes visible for the first time. The officers of the navy, particularly William Winter and Benjamin Gonson, had close links with the London mercantile elite, and invested in the Guinea voyages sent out by William Garrard, William Chester and others in 1562 and 1563.[41] Because of Portuguese hostility, these fleets had to be adequately protected, and both ships and guns were made available by the navy. Whether these ships were hired by the merchants or represented a royal investment is not entirely clear. They were probably hired, which would have been in accordance with precedent going back at least to the previous century. Thomas Wyndham had done the same thing in the previous reign. Elizabeth, however, was far more willing to encourage her servants in this kind of enterprise, and a slight but significant change of policy was about to take place. This appears to have been occasioned by an extension of the West African enterprise. There had been slave trading on the Guinea coast for centuries, and the Portuguese had been involved since their first arrival. However, by about

1560 a new opportunity was opening up. A combination of short-sighted brutality and alien diseases had reduced the indigenous population of the Spanish West Indies to a fraction of what it had been 40 years before, occasioning an acute labour shortage. At the same time French ships, mainly Huguenots out of La Rochelle, had taken to attacking and plundering these vulnerable colonies, which Philip's overstretched resources were not adequate to defend.[42] This combination of circumstances suggested to an enterprising consortium of Englishmen the chance for a very large profit.

The moving spirit was John Hawkins, a son of that William Hawkins who had attempted to pioneer the Brazilian trade, and who had died in 1554. Hawkins was not only well established in the 'Navy Board circle', he also believed himself to be in favour with the King of Spain. The reasons for this conviction are unclear. Stories were subsequently told about how he had ingratiated himself with the king during the latter's voyage to England in 1554, but since Philip had travelled in a Spanish ship, that is unlikely.[43] For whatever reason, Hawkins believed that the king would allow him to trade legitimately in the West Indies, in spite of the fact that the English had been explicitly excluded from the Castilian monopoly in 1557. The plan therefore was to buy slaves in West Africa, where they were plentiful, and sell them in the West Indies, where they were desperately needed. John laid his plans carefully, exploiting the contacts which he already had with the Spanish mercantile community, and with those English merchants who had returned to Spain after the thaw in relations in 1553–54. His particular friend and collaborator was Pedro de Ponte of Tenerife, in the Canaries. It is possible that this man, who is named only in Spanish sources, was actually of English descent, and Michael Lewis suggested that he may have been related to Sir John Bridges, who is known to have had Spanish connections.[44]

The expedition itself, which was sent off in 1562, was modest in scale, consisting of two ships and a pinnace, and was probably intended as a trial run. It was financed partly by Hawkins himself and partly by a group of his London friends; there is no evidence of royal involvement or interest. Its fortunes have to be reconstructed from two equally unsatisfactory sources: the complaints made by the Portuguese at the time, and the account which Hawkins himself gave to Richard Hakluyt 26 years later.[45] The Portuguese claimed that he seized nearly 1,000 negroes and one ship by force; Hawkins declared that he purchased 300 slaves, scrupulously paid for, and said nothing about a ship. The truth is probably somewhere between. Hawkins's ships could have accommodated a cargo of 300, but not much more, and the chance to increase his payload would probably have been taken.[46] At the same time the Portuguese dealers, even if they had traded willingly and been properly paid, would have had to plead coercion in order to escape the wrath of their own government. Hawkins regarded himself as a legitimate merchant, because England did not recognise either of the monopolies claimed by the Iberians, based as they were upon a papal adjudication of their respective rights. The Portuguese described him as a pirate because he flouted their claims, irrespective of how he behaved.

Having acquired his cargo, by whatever means, Hawkins then sailed to Tenerife where he was welcomed by his friend, who provided him with a Spanish pilot to take him to Hispaniola, having earlier written to his friends there, urging them to trade. The colonists, however, were in the same position as their Portuguese counterparts. They wanted the slaves but were not, in theory, allowed to trade. A series of complicated charades were then played out: goods were traded on remote beaches; theoretical ransoms were paid; and written authorisations were issued in response to notional threats. Hawkins sold all his trade goods, human and otherwise, and loaded his ships with pearls, ginger, hides, and a little gold and sugar. By the time that he set out on the return journey he had acquired two additional ships; one was probably that which he was alleged to have stolen in West Africa, the other was purchased in the Indies. In spite of allegations to the contrary, it is reasonably certain that he traded honestly, not least because he sent his two acquired vessels to sell their cargoes in Lisbon and San Lucar.[47] Perhaps he trusted to his good relations with Philip; perhaps he did not take the histrionics of Spanish and Portuguese officialdom seriously. Whatever the reason, he lost both the ships and their contents, and with them a large slice of his profit. In spite of this, the voyage was adjudged to have been a success. All the three original ships returned safely, and their cargoes were more than sufficient to make a respectable return for the investors. Hawkins himself made a futile trip to Spain in an effort to recover his lost ships; but he returned instead with several valuable lessons. The first was that he enjoyed no special favour from Philip, whatever may have been said nine years before; another was that Spanish and Portuguese officials would be inflexible in enforcing the law as they saw it, and would in future have to be deliberately defied or circumvented.

Notwithstanding this, the syndicate which was formed to follow up this pioneering voyage in 1564 was not only much larger, it had a much higher political profile. The Earl of Pembroke, the Earl of Leicester, Lord Clinton and Sir William Cecil were all investors, along with the 'Navy Board group' and the usual City interests.[48] Most important of all, for the first recorded time, the queen herself was a partner. Her investment did not consist of cash, but of one large and rather elderly ship, the *Jesus of Lubeck*, together (probably) with some guns and victuals. At first sight the deployment of the *Jesus* does not appear to be particularly significant; royal ships had often been used for private trading voyages, sometimes on preferential terms through the good offices of the relevant officials. However, when that had happened the monarch was in no sense a party to the venture, merely the recipient of an agreed rental. In this case, however, Elizabeth was entitled to a (large) share of the profits, and her involvement altered the whole status of the expedition. Hawkins was entitled to describe himself as the captain of a royal ship, and as the queen's servant.[49] Although he held no commission, he hoisted the standard of England when it was expedient to do so, and no one challenged him. Whether for that reason or not, this second voyage was relatively trouble-free. The main English source was again written many years later for Hakluyt, only this time by John Sparke rather than Hawkins himself.[50] The other sources are mainly Spanish colonial records, and the stories they tell are broadly compatible.

The best tactic to secure slaves, and to avoid (as far as possible) upsetting the Portuguese authorities, was to participate on one side in one of the endless tribal wars of the region. Having used European weapons to secure victory for your allies, you then purchased (at a cut price) their prisoners of war. The first time he tried this in 1564, Hawkins nearly came to grief, and lost several of his men in an ambush. However, he was eventually able to load between 400 and 500 slaves, and shortly after new year 1565 he sailed to Dominica by way of Tenerife, as before. This time there were more obvious signs of hostility among the Spanish officials, but the colonists were as willing to trade as they had been before, and a similar set of charades ensued. Whether Hawkins's enhanced status was any help in this connection is not recorded, but as the orders of the Provincial Governor had become far more explicit since 1562, it is possible that it was. There could be much more legitimate excuse for not knowing quite how to deal with an emissary of the Queen of England! With rather more difficulty than on the first voyage, but with the same outcome, Hawkins exchanged his goods, and collected his affidavits from the colonies he visited. On the way back, and following instructions from London, he called at the French Huguenot colony in Florida. His brief was either to offer them assistance or to repatriate them, according to the circumstances he found.[51] The colonists were reduced and demoralised, but their leaders refused to contemplate giving up; so Hawkins left them a pinnace, and such supplies as he could spare. Within a year they had been wiped out by the Spaniards.[52]

Hawkins reached Padstow in September 1565. He had been away nearly a year, had lost barely a dozen men, and returned a profit of about 60 per cent on the voyage. This was not enormous by the standards of the time, but bringing back all his ships and almost all his men was a much more remarkable achievement, and greatly enhanced his growing reputation. Meanwhile the political situation in Europe was becoming even more confused, and the reports were contradictory. France was paralysed by civil war, the government headed by Catherine de' Medici in the name of her thirteen-year-old son, Charles IX. In Scotland Mary was at loggerheads with her husband, Lord Darnley, who was showing increasing signs of paranoia; and in the Low Countries the ending of the Franco-Habsburg wars had opened the way to Calvinist preachers who were busily capitalising upon the economic hardships caused by the war between Sweden and Denmark which had begun in 1563.[53] Philip's authority had not yet been openly challenged, but his chief minister Cardinal Granvelle had been forced to retire, and relations with his regent and half-sister, Margaret of Parma, were strained. A major Turkish assault on Malta had been repulsed in the summer of 1565, but Philip's financial resources were heavily overtaxed, and experts like Thomas Gresham believed that any further military adventure would be beyond him.[54] Gresham's views were known both to the council and to the City of London, and may have influenced John Hawkins to make a further attempt to gain Philip's goodwill. He now knew that the King of Spain felt no gratitude for whatever service he had previously rendered, but in his present hard-pressed condition might welcome the assistance of an experienced seaman. Using his political contacts, he approached the Spanish ambassador in London, Guzman da Silva. Hawkins's objective is reasonably clear. He wanted licence to trade legitimately in the West Indies, and other places within the Spanish 'sphere of influence'. In return he was prepared to serve Philip in arms, preferably against the Turks.[55] This would not have involved any disloyalty to Elizabeth, but we do not know whether either she or Cecil knew about the approach. Philip kept Hawkins waiting over a year for a response. Whether this was because he was seriously considering the offer or because it was low down his list of priorities we do not know, but the answer was negative. Either John must give up his carefully laid plans for transatlantic trade, or he must continue as before, by subterfuge and running the risk of conflict. He chose the latter alternative.

Meanwhile the Merchant Adventurers trade to Antwerp had suffered another blow. Having 'bottomed out' at about 53,000 cloths in 1562, it enjoyed one good year (a freakish 133,000 in 1563) before disaster struck again. The reason was largely political. The English made no secret of their sympathy with the city's resistance to Philip's proposed ecclesiastical reorganisation, and other threatened measures of centralisation. This led to a niggling exchange of restrictions, and finally an embargo imposed by Margaret of Parma in 1564.[56] The Merchant Adventurers were forced to move their staple to the welcoming but much less convenient location of Emden. This particular dispute was settled within a year, but the trade remained depressed and the average number of cloths exported was about 80,000 over the next five years.[57] Antwerp suffered more severely than London, and the hardship created by this disruption, coming on top of the loss of the Baltic grain trade, contributed substantially to the iconoclastic riots of 1566. By the end of that year it appeared that the regent had the situation under control, but Philip repudiated the concessions which she had been obliged to make, and in 1567 sent the Duke of Alba to replace her, with a powerful army.

Significantly, William Cecil opposed the continuance of the staple, on the grounds that more diversified trade offered the better future, but the Adventurers were not ready for so radical a doctrine, and it struggled on, buffeted from place to place by political winds.[58] If the Adventurers suffered in Antwerp, they made their rivals of the Hanseatic League suffer in London. Mary's restoration of the Steelyard privileges had been deeply unpopular, and no sooner was she dead than a vigorous campaign began to have them again withdrawn. William Garrard and William Chester, two of those most prominent in funding the Guinea voyages, led the charge.[59] In spite of this hostile political climate, the privileges remained, although somewhat reduced and hedged about with conditions, possibly because of the powerful advocacy of the Lord Treasurer, the Marquis of Winchester. The League did not honour its ancient pledge of reciprocity, but was allowed to trade on sufferance, possibly because of its steadily dwindling importance, until the Steelyard was finally closed in 1598.[60]

Attempts to spread the Muscovy trade into Persia were also resumed in 1564. Individual agents such as Thomas Alcock and Richard Johnson undertook extended and adventurous journeys, sometimes losing their lives in the process. Although those who returned brought back some profit and some optimistic reports, the quantity of trade in that direction remained insignificant.[61] Further probes around the north of Russia demonstrated the unlikelihood of progress in that direction, and the attention of hopeful explorers such as Humphrey Gilbert was already turning to the north-west as early as 1566, when a plan for such a voyage was quashed by the opposition of the Muscovy Company.[62]

Throughout the summer of 1566 John Hawkins awaited a reply from Spain. He even fitted out some ships at Plymouth, apparently expecting a call to serve in the Mediterranean. The call did not come, but the ships were ready and Hawkins was a disappointed man. Relations with Philip were in a delicate state, and da Silva may have anticipated trouble. On his insistence, the council sent for Hawkins and forbade him to take his ships to sea, under a recognisance of £500.[63] Whether any of them had contributed to the preparations is unclear, but probably not as Atlantic trade was not the original object. The scale of the operation was very similar to that of 1562. The small fleet set out, late in the year, under the command of one John Lovell, and without any royal or official cognisance.[64] In most respects its fortunes were unremarkable, but Lovell lacked Hawkins's diplomatic skills. In the course of securing his slaves he became embroiled in a fracas with the Portuguese which cost several lives, and he contrived to get himself cheated out of about a quarter of his cargo at Rio de la Hacha, apparently because he did not understand the sophisticated system of bluffs which Hawkins had developed with the local officials.[65] He returned to Plymouth in September 1567 with a modest profit and a major sense of grievance. It was becoming increasingly difficult for the Spanish settlers to ignore or evade the orders of their own authorities, and even Hawkins might have been repulsed, but one consequence of the voyage was that a young kins-man of Hawkins called Francis Drake came back with the abiding impres-sion that all Spaniards were liars. Drake had sailed on the 1564 expedition also, but in spite of its grander scale that seems to have left less impression on his mind. By the time that Lovell returned, the storm clouds which had been visible in the previous year were building up in earnest. The queen and Cecil watched with increasing apprehension as Alba strengthened his grip on the Low Countries, and the stream of refugees began to build up. In Scotland Lord Darnley was murdered in February, and Mary was defeated and captured at Carberry Hill in June.

Some time before Lovell returned, the council thought better of its em-bargo on Hawkins, and the syndicate which had financed his second voy-age began to lay fresh plans.[66] Two somewhat elusive Portuguese adventurers had turned up in London with stories of a fabulously rich gold mine some-where to the south of El Mina, and Elizabeth, to whom 'gold were as good as twenty orators', was persuaded to investigate. The original idea seems to have been for the syndicate to mount an expedition in search of this mine. No one, apart from the queen, really believed in its existence, but there were plenty of other ways in which such a fleet could be used when it came to the point. In the late summer of 1567 Hawkins began to assemble his ships at Plymouth. There were four of his own, and two of the queen's, the old *Jesus* and the *Minion*, totalling about 1,300 tons and manned by some 400 men.[67] Philip's agents inevitably knew about these preparations, and did not believe the stories about the African mine. Towards the end of August, when the fleet was almost ready to sail, and the Portuguese adven-turers had disappeared, taking the secret of their alleged mine with them, a curious incident occurred which illustrates the tense state of Anglo-Spanish relations. Seven armed ships flying the Spanish flag sailed into Plymouth Sound and approached Hawkins's vessels moored there, neglecting the cour-tesy of dipping their foresails, which was customary on entering someone else's water. Hawkins interpreted this as a hostile gesture, and opened fire. The intruders sustained some damage, and withdrew without returning fire.[68] The Flemish admiral, de Wachan, claimed that he was sheltering from the weather and had sustained an unprovoked assault. His real intention is impossible to recover, and Michael Lewis's statement that 'there really can be no doubt' of his purpose to destroy Hawkins's ships seems quite unjustified.[69] The action was probably one of calculated intimidation, which backfired because of the speed of Hawkins's reactions. In response to vociferous diplomatic protests, the queen publicly rebuked her captain, but she did not countermand the expedition, or relieve him of his command. The expedition eventually sailed on 2 October, and was very similar in its nature and purpose to that of 1564.

Elizabeth's motivation was never simple, let alone transparent. Her participation in 1564 can probably be attributed to a desire to encourage her seamen, coupled with the pleasure of a potentially profitable 'flutter'. The risk of serious diplomatic repercussions would have been slight. By 1567 Alba's activities in the Low Countries and de Wachan's curious incursion into Plymouth Sound had raised the temperature considerably. In 1566 the queen had forbidden Hawkins to sail; now, with the situation even more threatening, she encouraged him. One reason, of course, was her constant need for money, and it may be that her investment in these voyages was no more than a cheap option. If her ships had remained in harbour, they would still have had to be looked after. It was far easier to let Hawkins use them than to find a cash contribution of £5,000, and it entitled her to some 40 per cent of the profits. Hawkins was playing on his mistress's well-known cupidity when he wrote just before sailing: 'The voyage I pretend is to lade negroes in Guinea and sell them in the West Indies in truck of gold, pearls and emeralds, wherewith I doubt not but to bring home great abundance for the contentation of your Highness'.[70] However, by 1567 the risk was palpable. Philip's reaction to the Netherlanders had been unexpectedly emphatic, and English attempts to imitate the Rochellais in preying on Spanish shipping invited a military response. Elizabeth was certainly not resigned to conflict with Spain, and it may be that she was still calculating on Philip's dislike of Mary (reinforced by her entanglement with Bothwell) to protect her against extreme measures. It is also likely that Hawkins's schemes were supported by both Cecil and Dudley (although not necessarily in collusion), and that Elizabeth was convinced by this consensus between her rival advisers.

The expedition's first port of call was Santa Cruz in the Canaries, where Hawkins had the difficult and no doubt distasteful task of resolving a violent conflict between two of his gentlemen volunteers[71] The presence of such men was a mixed blessing. On the one hand they were brave fighters, and they represented the growing prestige of such enterprises among the English ruling class, which was a factor of crucial importance for the future. They also served at their own expense. On the other hand they were undisciplined, opinionated and often absurdly touchy. In this case the quarrel was resolved without bloodshed, but not all commanders were as fortunate, or as skilful. Communication with the Governor of Santa Cruz was polite without being at all cordial, and a suspicious watchfulness was maintained by both sides.

On reaching the Guinea coast Hawkins discovered that here, too, things had changed since 1564. Portuguese officials were both more alert and more in control of the situation than they had been, and his first approaches were repulsed rather as Lovell's had been. By January 1568 he had taken 150 slaves and suffered a number of casualties. Partly frustrated, he moved south to the region of modern Sierra Leone, and there resorted to the tried tactic of involvement in native war. In so doing he lost another dozen men, but came away with a further 320 captives, which gave him a full cargo.[72] In early February he set off for the West Indies without, apparently, calling at Tenerife. The weather was adverse and the passage took almost two months, although with his customary care he seems not to have lost many crewmen or slaves in the process. Among the colonists the situation had changed somewhat, but not dramatically. The planters still wanted the slaves, the officials were under strict orders to allow no trade, and it is often hard to tell whether the rituals of coercion which followed were real or contrived. The Spanish sources, naturally, make it appear that a spirited resistance was overcome by superior force, and English eyewitnesses give the same impression. But scraps of other evidence, together with the low casualty figures, suggest at least a degree of collusion.[73] At Rio de la Hacha where his old sparring partner Miguel de Castellanos was still in charge, a conflict which started by claiming a few lives ended with suspiciously effusive cordiality. A few miles along the coast at Santa Maria the ritual was transparent, but at Cartagena the resistance was genuine, and, having very little left to trade, after a brief reconnoitre Hawkins passed on.

So far, in spite of the difficulties, and more casualties than he would have liked, Hawkins's luck had held and the voyage had been successful. However, having passed Cartagena, fortune deserted him. The main problem was the unseaworthy condition of the old *Jesus of Lubeck*. If it had not been the queen's ship, he would probably have abandoned it, as there was adequate space in the other ships for his somewhat reduced crews and light but valuable cargo. He seems to have acquired and discarded three or four other vessels in the course of this voyage, for which he was not accountable to his shareholders.[74] However, whether on principle or as a result of calculating the royal reaction, he refused to discard the *Jesus*, which did at least have the merit of looking imposing. With this encumbrance, and adverse winds, he was forced into the Gulf of Mexico, looking for somewhere to land and carry out essential repairs, as well as to take on fresh victuals. There were very few suitable havens on that coast, and he was forced to head for the small anchorage of San Juan d'Ulloa, which was the outport for Mexico City. In spite of that apparently important function, it was little more than a shallow rocky bay, protected by a low shingle island. There was a small fort on the island, but the settlement itself was unfortified, and could have offered little resistance. Hawkins's intentions were not aggress- ive, but as he quickly discovered, the important 'flota' or treasure fleet was about to rendezvous there before beginning its regular crossing of the Atlantic.[75] There was little chance that he could complete his repairs and leave before that happened, so he had to seize and hold control of the harbour. The officers of the 'flota' were servants of the king and they would not dissemble or negotiate. The fort offered no resistance, and the local officials perforce agreed to his demands. However the 'flota' arrived the very next day, 16 September, and consisted of thirteen large ships, all well armed.

Hawkins was placed in an extreme dilemma. He could have risked trying to hold his position by force, keeping the flota in the inhospitable outer road. Although he later claimed to have been confident of his ability to do that, at the time he chose a more discreet course. On board the flota was the new Viceroy of Mexico himself, Don Martin Enriquez, and with him Hawkins negotiated a specific and careful agreement.[76] The English re- tained control of the island, agreeing to complete their work and depart as quickly as possible. The Spanish ships entered the harbour and moored as far off as possible in the confined space. Hostages were exchanged. For a couple of days work proceeded peacefully, but it appears that Enriquez never had any intention of honouring his agreement. From his point of view the English ships, royal standard or not, had no right to be on that coast in the first place. He probably did not know, and certainly did not care, that Hawkins was principally a trader, who had a subtle and on the whole amicable relationship with the colonial planters. The fact that the English were also heretics made it easier to break a given word with a clear conscience. Once he had completed his surreptitious preparations, the Vice- roy gave the order to attack. Unfortunately the only detailed description of the action comes from the English side, with much emphasis upon Spanish treachery and their own heroism.[77] In the confined space, the gunfire was unusually effective, and inflicted great damage and many casualties on both sides. It is quite probable that the Viceroy was taken aback by the fierceness of the resistance, but he had an overwhelming superiority in numbers, both of men and ships, and in the event the only issue was whether any of the English would manage to escape. There was no chance of extracting the *Jesus*, particularly once gun damage had added to her disabilities, but her guns had a devastating effect, and held up the assault sufficiently to enable the *Minion* and the *Judith* to get away.

Once clear of the harbour the two survivors separated in mysterious circumstance, and the 50-ton pinnace *Judith*, commanded by Francis Drake, sailed directly home.[78] It is possible that Drake, realising that he had rather more than his fair share of both goods and victuals, calculated that if he lingered it would be the death of both of them. Hawkins clearly felt that he had been deserted, and Drake never offered any explanation. The *Minion* had over 200 men on board, and virtually no supplies. As soon as he was clear of the Spanish settlements, Hawkins called a crisis meeting of his crew. About half believed that they would stand a better chance of survival if they went ashore and took their chance with the natives. The remainder opted to stay with the ship. In a sense both were right. Some of those who went ashore certainly survived, and told the tale;[79] while those who remained on board suffered from both disease and starvation. Buffeted by the weather, Hawkins's landfall in Europe could hardly have been less auspicious. He arrived at the end of December at Vigo, in northern Spain! Although the authorities knew perfectly well who he was, they allowed him to purchase food, and made no attempt to arrest him, as they had been ordered. His crew still further reduced by the abundant and unfamiliar diet, Hawkins reached Mount's Bay in the last stages of exhaustion on 25 January 1569. Da Silva reported that only fifteen men returned with him. A similar number seem to have survived from those left behind in America, and rather more had returned in the *Judith*, but altogether the expedition had cost over 300 lives and four ships. Probably the financial loss was less disastrous, because Hawkins had managed to transfer much of his goods from the *Jesus* to the *Minion* before the former was lost, and he was certainly not short of money when he reached Vigo. If anyone did the sums, they did not record the result.

Many other voyages were equally unfortunate, but this one made an unusual impression for a number of reasons. Hawkins took the unusual step of publishing a simplified and not very informative account within a few months, which blamed the whole sorry story on Enriquez. Philip became convinced that Elizabeth's professions of goodwill were meaningless, because she conferred both her ships and her authority upon marauders who invaded his territories and plundered his subjects.[80] Both Hawkins and Drake were now convinced of the perfidy of all Spaniards, particularly those in authority, and burning with a desire for revenge. This ambition, however, was temporarily allowed to mature, and the queen countenanced no further high-profile excursions to the Spanish Main for the time being. She had quite enough problems nearer home.

On 2 May 1568 Mary had escaped from Loch Leven castle. Within weeks her adherents had been defeated again at Langside, and the deposed queen had escaped south into England. Elizabeth's instinct was to welcome and assist her, but it did not take the council long to persuade her of the unwisdom of such a course.[81] Alternatively, she could have returned her as a prisoner to Scotland, which would almost certainly have meant her death; and that Elizabeth's conscience would not permit. So Mary was kept in more or less honourable confinement on the pretext that the charges which were being levied against her in Scotland needed to be properly investigated. This course avoided trouble with the Earl of Murray, the Scottish regent, and possibly with her Guise kindred, but it exposed Elizabeth to another danger, which was probably unexpected. Mary as a queen, implicated in murder and married to one of her Protestant nobles, was an unsavoury object to the pious King of Spain. However, Mary as an imprisoned and friendless fugitive, shorn of her power both in France and in Scotland, could be converted into a very plausible Catholic candidate for the Crown of England. Before the end of 1568 a complex and eventually tragic political conspiracy began which was to last for almost 20 years, and impose intolerable strains on Elizabeth's council, and others who were responsible for her security.

Part of the background to this conspiracy lay in France, never far from civil war, even during the negotiated interludes. Elizabeth was represented at the French court by Sir Henry Norris, who was convinced that the Guise party, in collusion with Philip, was planning a pre-emptive strike, either in Scotland or in England.[82] The English counter-measure was to enter into close but surreptitious relations with the Protestants of La Rochelle. In August 1568 the queen appeared to be threatening direct intervention, but the assistance eventually rendered was more subtle. Money and munitions were provided via the Merchant Adventurers, in return for wine and salt. Ostensibly this was private business, and neither the queen nor Cecil knew anything about it, although in practice the guns were conveyed by the efficient William Winter, using the queen's ships.[83] This somewhat transparent subterfuge satisfied honour on both sides, and there was no breakdown in diplomatic relations (nor any French Catholic raid on England). Paradoxically the deteriorating situation in the Netherlands, which so alarmed the English council, actually made Philip more willing to swallow the provocations offered by such men as John Hawkins. Although in fact increasingly irritated, in the early part of 1568 he was being studiously careful to be polite, not wishing to become embroiled in conflict with the islanders before the Low Countries had been thoroughly pacified – or suppressed.[84] The English involvement with La Rochelle, however, was a sore trial to his patience. Piracy had always been a profession to the Rochellais, and now they turned it into a vocation, with ships displaying letters of marque from the Huguenot princes creating a veritable reign of terror in the Western Approaches. Even their allies and co-religionists, the English, were not immune; and in spite of the alliance (or perhaps in order to avoid proclaiming it openly) English ships trading to Biscay were escorted by royal warships.[85]

This placed Philip in a serious dilemma. His naval forces were concentrated in the Mediterranean, and he had barely enough fighting ships in the Atlantic to protect the flota. At the same time his army in the Low Counties had to be paid. Even in its heyday 20 years before, the Antwerp market had imported much of its specie from Spain, and in the conditions of 1568 there was no way in which such a large sum could be raised in the Netherlands themselves. It would have been out of the question to send it across France, where the government could barely protect itself, let alone the assets of others. The obvious route was the so-called 'Spanish Road', over the Alps and down the Rhine; but some of the German princes were hostile, and Philip could not afford to despatch a large force to protect his treasure. Consequently he had to take the risk of sending it by sea, without adequate protection. The money had been taken up from the Genoese bankers who normally served the king, and was sent north in Italian galleys, perhaps in the hope that these would attract less hostile attention. The gamble failed, but not quite in the way which had been feared. Attacked but not taken, in the middle of November the Genoese ships took refuge in several havens of Devon and Cornwall, and the Spanish ambassador in London, now Guerau de Spes, asked the queen to provide escorts for the remainder of their journey.[86] This request Elizabeth apparently granted, pointing out that Winter's squadron had already rescued a number of beleaguered Spaniards.

What happened next is not quite clear. According to the Spanish version, the treasure was then unloaded from the ships against the protests of the Genoese captains. The English claimed that, on the contrary, the captains had asked to have the money taken ashore on learning that Winter was to depart immediately for France, presumably because they were not yet ready to accompany him.[87] Alba's payroll was therefore collected at Southampton during the first half of December. De Spes heard of this on the 18th, and immediately began to press the queen for an explanation. It would appear, however, that the quickness of the hand was deceiving the diplomatic eye. At some point in early December, Winter was told about the fiasco at San Juan d'Ulloa. Neither Hawkins nor Drake had yet returned, so his source of information is something of a mystery.[88] Hawkins did not even reach Vigo until later in the month, so the most likely explanation is that Drake, who seems to have made an easy and leisurely return, had contrived to send word ahead. However it came about, Winter passed the news on to Hawkins's brother, William, at Plymouth. William immediately began to agitate for the money then lying in harbour to be seized in reprisal, claiming that it was not, in any case, the legal property of the Spaniards until it reached its destination.[89] This helpful hint he received from Benedict Spinola, an Italian merchant resident in London. Cecil took rapid steps to verify this, and then decided to act. At Southampton itself,

Edward Horsey, acting on direct orders from the Secretary, persuaded the captain to land his cargo on the grounds that Winter's departure meant that his security from French depredations could not otherwise be guaranteed.[90] Further west, in the Devon ports Sir Arthur Chapernoun 'under cover of friendship' did the same, commenting: 'I am of the mind that anything taken from that wicked nation is both necessary and profitable to our commonwealth'.[91]

Consequently, although no force seems to have been used, the Spanish version of events is slightly closer to the truth. De Spes was fobbed off until 29 December, when the queen blandly informed him that a decision would be made within a few days. In fact the decision had been made a fortnight before, and the ambassador knew it. On 21 December, more than a week before his delayed audience, he had written to Alba, explaining what had happened, urging him to embargo all English trade, and to seize any English assets within reach.[92] The duke acted on this advice within a few days, in fact before the queen had admitted to making any decision. This surrendered the moral high ground, and Elizabeth displayed outrage. Not only was there now no question of releasing Alba's money, but all Spanish and Flemish assets were seized, along with any Spanish ships that the English could lay their hands on.[93]

For a while the crisis was intense. De Spes was placed under house arrest on the grounds that he had wilfully misled the duke and betrayed his master's legitimate interests. However, neither side was looking for a fight. Alba not only had his hands full with the Dutch, he also had an unpaid army to placate. The English made the most of the ambassador's indiscretions (of which there were several), but did not insist upon his recall.[94] This was probably a mistake, as de Spes not only became the advocate of all sorts of economic sanctions against England, but threw himself energetically into every plot, however insubstantial, for the destruction of the queen and Cecil. Meanwhile English involvement with the Rochellais had provoked a rather similar crisis in relations with France. In January 1569 Anglo-French trade was embargoed and English ships at Rouen were seized. It was not a good time to be trading into northern Europe; and after Hawkins's misfortune the prospects in the Caribbean did not look too bright either.

In fact, the situation looked worse than it was. By March 1569 both Alba and Philip had made clear that their range of sanctions against England did not include invasion, and they retained that position even when directly appealed to by the leaders of the rebellion which broke out in northern England later in the summer. Tension with France also eased after a virtual ultimatum from La Mothe Fenelon was skilfully evaded in March.[95] As with Spain, Charles IX had too many troubles at home to be keen on a war with

England, and England was not strong enough to confront either power, except at sea. Charles did not have the power to prevent English trade with the Protestant-controlled areas of the west and south, and Philip's orders were not always obeyed, even quite close to home, but the constraints were nevertheless becoming more severe. Embargoes were always relaxed eventually, but not before they had caused serious disruption and long-term uncertainty. By 1570 the traditional dependence of the Merchant Adventurers on the export of broadcloths from London to Antwerp was at an end. Northern Europe continued to be the main market, but various Dutch and North German ports were used as convenience dictated.[96] The decline of the Hanse also opened up the Baltic, and the Muscovy trade, although small in volume, was relatively high in value.

The political winds, which had brought so many dangers and disruptions, also brought gains. The French and Flemish refugees who settled in London, Norwich and Southampton brought not only unfamiliar skills in silkweaving and metal work, but also new ways of working with wool. It was thanks to them that the 'New Draperies' (worsteds and semi-worsteds) began to be produced in quantity in the late 1560s. This cloth was much more suitable for the southern markets than the heavier woollens, and created opportunities to re-enter the Mediterranean markets which had not been available during the tentative efforts of the previous decade.

The first ten years of Elizabeth's reign saw a major change in the political climate of Europe. Ideological warfare was a new phenomenon. Renaissance wars had been bloody, but they had been pragmatic, fought for dynastic or territorial gain, and alliances had shifted quickly and radically. Even the traditional dislike of the English for the French could not match the settled and violent animosities which developed after 1550. By choosing a Protestant settlement in 1559 Elizabeth had also chosen (whether she liked it or not) her place in this new scheme of things. By so doing, she had also imposed constraints upon the economic activities of her subjects. Trade with Catholic countries became increasingly vulnerable as the ecclesiastical authorities stepped up their campaign against heretics and heretical ideas. Horror stories about the treatment of English merchants and seamen by the Inquisition were matched by Spanish stories of desecrated churches and murdered priests.[97] Trade between England and the various domains of the King of Spain survived until 1585, but only just, as a result of long-established friendships and a willingness to dissemble on both sides. Quantitatively it became insignificant.

Philip did not dismiss the English as a nation of shopkeepers; he had more unflattering epithets at his disposal, but Elizabeth did take her merchants more seriously than any of her immediate predecessors. She listened to their vociferous complaints about the new book of customs rates, introduced earlier in 1558, and allowed them to evade charges which they ought to have paid.[98] The benefits of this in improved cooperation are hard to calculate. Military operations between 1558 and 1564 cost in excess of £750,000, but that was substantially less than Protector Somerset had spent in half the time. Parliament contributed about £200,000 of that, and various Antwerp bankers, via Thomas Gresham, contributed another £300,000.[99] It was probably in the prompt and relatively painless discharge and recycling of these loans that the goodwill of the city was most manifest. Direct loans in England were kept to a minumum (about £45,000), which was also appreciated by the mercantile community. A somewhat unexpected bonus was the profit of £97,000 made from the recoinage which commenced in 1561. It had been known for ten years that this was necessary, but both Northumberland and Mary had failed to grasp the nettle, expecting a heavy loss. Again Elizabeth listened to her City men, who persuaded her that the risk could no longer be evaded, and she was rewarded with a stabilised coinage, a temporary check to inflation, and a healthy profit.[100]

After 1564, with the scaling down of military operations, and an improvement in ordinary revenue occasioned partly by the new customs, partly by the resumption of ecclesiastical revenues, and partly by improved estate management, the ordinary account moved into surplus and the debts were gradually reduced. The financial situation, however, remained delicate and any major interruption to trade was bound to have unfavourable repercussions. In one sense the policy shaped by the queen and Cecil was orthodox enough, although it went a little beyond precedent. In 1566 the Marian patent of the Muscovy Company was confirmed by statute, and a similar company of 'Adventurers' was established in Bristol.[101] However, when she invested her own ships, and her own credit, in high-risk private voyages, Elizabeth was setting off in quite a new direction, just as she was when she allowed Cecil to lay hands on £85,000 which was destined for the Duke of Alba.

By 1569 the queen was sailing very close to the wind, apparently calculating on the practicalities of the wider political situation to protect her from the consequences of acts which were not individually very dramatic. Knowing that Philip did not want war, she allowed her seamen to seize ten Spanish vessels off Plymouth in February 1569, and encouraged intimacy with the Rochellais throughout the renewed civil war of 1568–70. English captains held letters of marque from Henry of Navarre, and Huguenot privateers disposed of their prizes in Devon and Cornwall with the full connivance of the authorities.[102] Every so often she took fright at her own effrontery, as when she expelled the Huguenots from English ports in December 1569, but the underlying thrust of her strategy remained the same. London's wealth depended upon trade, and England's security was on the sea. Elizabeth was not interested in Protestant crusading, nor in waging traditional wars for land or glory. But she had to protect herself, and for that she needed loyal subjects, rich merchants and skilled seafighters. Encouraging adventurers like Hawkins, and later Drake and Frobisher, contributed to each of these objectives. At the same time circumstances played into her hands by forcing even the most conservative merchants to realise that they could no longer make safe profits in the traditional ways. Some moved as little as possible, selling their broadcloths in Emden or Hamburg, but others responded (and contributed) to a heightened curiosity about the world and its potentialities. The sea was beginning to catch the English imagination, with everything from serious manuals on cosmography and navigation to colourful travellers tales, finding an increasingly eager market. English and Welsh navigators and cartographers were also beginning to be taken seriously by their French, Dutch and German counterparts, thanks largely to the expanding reputations of men like Dee, Humphrey Lhuyd and William Bourne.[103] English maritime science was rapidly catching up, and one of the great revolutions in English history was fairly launched.

Notes

1. Mary's council numbered about 45 at the time of her death, of whom ten were retained. David Loades, *The Reign of Mary Tudor* (London, 1991), 404–11; W. MacCaffrey, *The Shaping of the Elizabethan Regime* (London, 1969), 27–40.

2. Paget's exclusion is something of a mystery, because he had been one of Elizabeth's protectors in the dark days of 1554. However, he had been a principal architect of the Spanish marriage, and had become very much Philip's man. For a full discussion see S.R. Gammon, *Statesman and Schemer: William, First Lord Paget, Tudor Minister* (Newton Abbott, 1973). The post was not filled until Lord Howard of Effingham was appointed in 1572.

3. Sir Edward Hastings was replaced as Lord Chamberlain by Lord Howard of Effingham, and Sir Henry Bedingfield as Vice Chamberlain by Sir Edward Rogers. D. Loades, *The Tudor Court* (London, 1989), 57–8. Several of the departmental sergeants within the Household were also replaced, but these constituted only a small fraction of the total staff.

4. S. Adams, 'The Dudley clientele, 1553–1563', in G.W. Bernard, ed, *The Tudor Nobility* (Manchester, 1992).

5. P.J. French, *John Dee: The World of an Elizabethan Magus* (London, 1973).

6. Both French, *John Dee*, and *The Dictionary of National Biography* say this, but even Dudley's youngest son, Guildford, would have been about seventeen at

this time, so Dee's position could not have been that of a tutor in the ordinary sense.

7. *Calendar of the Patent Rolls, Edward VI*, ed. R.H. Brodie (London, 1924–29), V, 199. He does not seem to have exercised any ministry in this capacity, and later declared that he would not accept any preferment which involved the cure of souls.

8. *Dictionary of National Biography*.

9. Dee was arrested by order of the council on 28 May 1555, and examined along with three others over the following month 'touching conjuring or witchcraft'. In spite of his background he was not charged with heresy, and the Bishop of London may have spoken for him. *Acts of the Privy Council*, ed. J.R. Dasent *et al.* (1890–1907) V, 137, 143, 176.

10. J. Foxe, *Actes and Monuments of these latter and perillous dayes* (London, 1563), 1253 (examination of Robert Smith), 1414 (examination of John Philpot). Edited S. Cattley (1837–41), VII, 319n.

11. Derek Wilson, *Sweet Robin: A Biography of Robert Dudley, Earl of Leicester* (London, 1981), 16, 20, 85, 151.

12. Borough had sailed on Chancellor's first voyage to Russia in 1553, and made two subsequent attempts to find a north-east passage. In 1557 he visited the Casa de Contratacion in Seville at Philip's invitation, and endeavoured (unsuccessfully) to have himself appointed Pilot Major at the beginning of Elizabeth's reign. He subsequently assisted Frobisher and Gilbert when they turned their attentions to the north-west. Richard Eden translated Peter Martyr's *Decades of the New World* in 1555, and Martin Cortes's *Art of Navigation* in 1561. E.G.R. Taylor, *Tudor Geography, 1485–1583* (London, 1930).

13. A. Pettegree, *Foreign Protestant Communities in Sixteenth-Century London* (Oxford, 1986), 133–81.

14. B. Usher, ' "In a time of persecution": new light on the secret Protestant congregation in Marian London', in D. Loades, ed., *John Foxe and the English Reformation* (Aldershot, 1997).

15. The classic view was expressed by J.B. Black in *The Reign of Elizabeth* (Oxford, 1936), 1; but much more recent scholars such as Wallace MacCaffrey have not challenged it. It seems to have been based upon a jeremiad addressed to the queen in the early days of her reign, probably by Armigal Waad.

16. Negotiations had begun in October 1558, but Mary's death caused a suspension at the end of November until Elizabeth could accredit new representatives. Loades, *Reign of Mary*, 337–9.

17. M. Rodriguez Salgado, *The Changing Face of Empire: Charles V, Philip II and Habsburg Authority, 1551–1559* (Cambridge, 1988), 330, 332–3. Henry

endeavoured to embarrass Philip by inviting his support in Scotland in defence of the faith.

18. M. Oppenheim, ed., *The Naval Tracts of Sir William Monson* (Navy Records Society, London, 1902–14), I, 7.

19. Originally an Edwardian appointment, he had been removed by Mary in 1554, but restored on 10 February 1558. He served until his death in 1585.

20. British Library (BL) Add. MS 9294, f. 1.

21. T. Glasgow, 'A list of ships in the Royal Navy from 1539 to 1588', *Mariners' Mirror*, 56, 1970, 299–307. Glasgow, 'The navy in Philip and Mary's war', *Mariners' Mirror*, 53, 1967, 321–42.

22. Public Record Office (PRO) SP12/3/44, ff. 131r–134v.

23. D. Loades, *The Tudor Navy* (Aldershot, 1992), 181. Although no ship larger than 800 tons was envisaged in this plan, both the *Triumph* (1562) and the *White Bear* (1564) were about 1,000 tons.

24. N.A.M. Rodgers, *The Safeguard of the Sea* (London, 1997), 477–80.

25. PRO E351/2358; Bodleian Library MS Rawlinson C 846, ff. 132–3.

26. Rodgriguez Salgado, *Changing Face of Empire*, 317–21.

27. T. Glasgow, 'The navy in Elizabeth's first undeclared war, 1559–60', *Mariners' Mirror*, 54, 1968, 23–37. Winter's original instructions were to undertake this as though of his own initiative – an implausible assignment with a fleet that size. That aspect of his orders was quickly revoked. PRO SP12/7/169–71.

28. Rodgers, *Safeguard*, 197–8.

29. S. Haynes, ed., *Burghley Papers* (1740), 351–2.

30. PRO E351/2197. Loades, *Tudor Navy*, 212–13.

31. By the Pacification of Amboise, signed on 19 March. For the role of the navy, see T. Glasgow, 'The navy in the Le Havre campaign, 1562–4', *Mariners' Mirror*, 54, 1968, 281–96. Bodleian Library MS Rawlinson A.200.

32. Loades, *Tudor Navy*, 215.

33. PRO E351/2195–99. F.C. Dietz, *English Public Finance, 1558–1641* (New York, 1932), 9–11.

34. PRO E351/3472–3. S.G. Ellis, *Tudor Ireland* (London, 1985), 228–75.

35. J. MacConica, 'The Catholic experience in Tudor Oxford', in T.M. McCoog, SJ, ed., *The Reckoned Expense: Edmund Campion and the Early English Jesuits* (London, 1996). This discusses particularly the flight of Oxford fellows to Louvain after 1559, where many became Philip's pensioners.

36. MacCaffrey, *Shaping of the Elizabethan Regime*, 79–81.

37. Black, *Reign of Elizabeth*, 53.

38. Not only the Dudley negotiation, but a more serious and long-running one with the Archduke Charles, the Emperor's son. Susan Doran, *Monarchy and Matrimony* (Stroud, 1996), 13–98.

39. Rodgers, *Safeguard*, 198–201.

40. H. Kelsey, *Sir Francis Drake: The Queen's Pirate* (New Haven, 1998), 11–39.

41. Richard Hakluyt, *The principall navigations, voiages and discoveries of the English nation* (London, 1589), I, 130, 135. M. Lewis, *The Hawkins Dynasty* (London, 1969), 56.

42. B. Dietz, 'The Huguenot and English corsairs during the third civil war in France, 1568–70', *Proceedings of the Huguenot Society*, 19, 1952–58, 278–94.

43. Andres Muñoz, *Viaje de Felipe II a Inglaterra* (Zaragoza, 1554).

44. Lewis, *Hawkins Dynasty*, 78–9.

45. Ibid., 79–80.

46. Hawkins certainly acquired another ship in Africa (see below). There was a story about his having found it abandoned. The chances are that he paid for the slaves but stole the ship.

47. Lewis, *Hawkins Dynasty*, 84.

48. Hakluyt, *Principall navigations*, II, 523. Lewis, *Hawkins Dynasty*, 85–6.

49. Hakluyt, *Principall navigations*, II, 523–44.

50. Lewis, *Hawkins Dynasty*, 87. Sparke was, if anything, more widely travelled than Hawkins. He went to Novgorod in the service of the Muscovy Company in 1566.

51. Although called 'Florida' at the time, this settlement was actually at Battle Creek, South Carolina. It had been established by Jacques Ribaut (a man who had also had strong connections with the Duke of Northumberland) in 1562.

52. G.V. Scammell, *The World Encompassed: The First European Maritime Empires, c.800–1650* (London, 1981), 439.

53. For a full account of the background to the troubles in the Netherlands, see G. Parker, *The Dutch Revolt* (London, 1977), 41–67.

54. Black, *Reign of Elizabeth*, 45.

55. Lewis, *Hawkins Dynasty*, 94–100. Alvaro de Quadra had died in 1563.

56. D.R. Bisson, *The Merchant Adventurers of England: The Company and the Crown, 1474–1564* (London, 1993) 94–6. Haynes, ed., *Burghley Papers*, 409.

57. Bisson, *Merchant Adventurers*. A.G.R. Smith, *The Emergence of a Nation State, 1529–1660* (London, 1984), 438.

58. PRO SP12/35, f. 33. Bisson, *Merchant Adventurers*, 97–8.

59. Guildhall Record Office, Repertories of the Court of Aldermen, 14, ff. 42, 329. BL Add. MS 48010, f. 368. Bisson, *Merchant Adventurers*, 67–8.

60. Ibid., 68.

61. Sir William Foster, *England's Quest of Eastern Trade* (London, 1933), 31–2.

62. Ibid., 34–5.

63. Lewis, *Hawkins Dynasty*, 95.

64. Kelsey, *Francis Drake*, 21–5. According to Spanish sources, Lovell was a kinsman of Hawkins, but this seems not to have been the case.

65. According to one Spanish source, Lovell abandoned his cargo; according to another, there was an abortive, exchange of threats. Antonio Rumeu de Armas, *Los Viajes de John Hawkins a America, 1562–1595* (Seville, 1947), 416, 422–3. Kelsey, *Francis Drake*, 23 and ns.

66. Kelsey, *Francis Drake*, 27. For the gold mine, see BL Cotton MS Otho E VIII, f. 17.

67. Lewis, *Hawkins Dynasty*, 97–8.

68. Ibid., 98–9.

69. Ibid.

70. Ibid., 100. For Cecil's involvement, see *Historical Manuscripts Commission, Calendar of the Hatfield MSS*, I, 1139, Clinton to Cecil, 30 September 1567.

71. Edward Dudley and George Fitzwilliam. Dudley was sentenced to death, but pardoned.

72. Discourse by Miles Phillips in Hakluyt, *Principall navigations*, II, 563. Job Hortop, 'Travailes', in ibid, III, 487.

73. Kelsey, *Francis Drake*, 35–6. Rumeu de Armas, *Viajes*, 426.

74. Lewis, *Hawkins Dynasty*, 109.

75. BL Cotton MS Otho E VIII, ff. 39v–40. Kelsey, *Francis Drake*, 37.

76. Rumeu de Armas, *Viajes*, 287–8. C.R. Markham, *The Hawkins Voyages* (Hakluyt Society, London, 1879), 75.

77. By Hortop. Hakluyt, *Principall navigations*, III, 487.

78. But not very rapidly, since it arrived only a few days before Hawkins reached Vigo. No details of Drake's return journey survive.

79. Both Phillips and David Ingram; Hakluyt, *Principall navigations*, II, 557–60.

80. England was by no means central to Philip's concerns at this stage, and the extent of his irritation seems not to have been understood in London, where the Spanish ambassador tended to be treated as a loose cannon. MacCaffrey, *Shaping of the Elizabethan Regime*, 184–5. H. Kamen, *Philip of Spain* (London, 1997), 108–42.

81. MacCaffrey, *Shaping of the Elizabethan Regime*, 172–3.

82. Ibid., 182–3.

83. The French ambassador in London knew perfectly well what was going on. *Calendar of State Papers, Foreign*, 23 vols (London, 1863–1950), *1566–68*, 551, 561–2. PRO Baschet's Transcripts, 31 October 1568.

84. Parker, *Dutch Revolt*, 105–17.

85. Rodgers, *Safeguard*, 202–3. MacCaffrey, *Shaping of the Elizabethan Regime*, 189.

86. MacCaffrey, *Shaping of the Elizabethan Regime*, 189.

87. *Calendar of State Papers, Spanish (Cal. Span.)*, 4 vols (London, 1892–99), *1568–79*, 90, 91, 101, 102. Conyers Read, 'Queen Elizabeth's seizure of Alba's pay ships', *Journal of Modern History*, 5, 1933, 443–64.

88. Drake arrived at the end of December, and Hawkins on 25 January.

89. Read, 'Queen Elizabeth's seizure'.

90. PRO SP12/48/50, 62.

91. Ibid., 60.

92. *Cal. Span.*, 1568–79, 90.

93. MacCaffrey, *Shaping of the Elizabethan Regime*, 194. Read, 'Queen Elizabeth's seizure'.

94. *Cal. Span.*, 1568–79, 98. BL Cotton MS Galba C III.

95. A. Teulet, *Correspondance diplomatique de . . . de la Moth Fenelon* (Bannatyne Club, 1840), letter to Charles IX, 8 March 1569.

96. R. Davis, *English Overseas Trade, 1500–1700* (London, 1973), 17–18.

97. W.S. Maltby, *The Black Legend in England* (Durham NC, 1971).

98. F.C. Dietz, *English Government Finance, 1485–1558* (Urbana IL, 1921), 7.

99. Ibid., 16–19.

100. C.E. Challis, *The Tudor Coinage* (Manchester, 1978), 112–33.

101. 8 Elizabeth, c.17 (not printed in *Statutes of the Realm*).

102. MacCaffrey, *Shaping of the Elizabethan Regime*, 182–2. K.R. Andrews, *Trade, Plunder and Settlement: Maritime Enterprise and the Genesis of the British Empire, 1480–1630* (London, 1984).

103. E.G.R. Taylor, *Tudor Geography, 1485–1583* (London, 1930), 30–5.

CHAPTER FOUR

War and Colonial Initiatives, 1570–1604

The dangerous years from 1568 to 1572 also brought a new stability to English affairs. The threats presented by the Spaniards in the Netherlands and the Guise party in France increased the need for unity in England, and rallied the country behind the queen. Paradoxically, Elizabeth benefited considerably from the northern rebellion of 1569. The fall of the Percys (again), the Nevilles and the Dacres, and the reduction of their affinities, enabled the queen to complete the work that her father had begun after the Pilgrimage of Grace 30 years before.[1] The forfeited lands were redistributed among loyal supporters of the Crown, and in 1572 the Puritan Earl of Huntingdon began his 23 years stint as President of the Council of the North. By a stroke of good fortune the Earl of Cumberland (who had not been implicated in the rising) also died in 1570, leaving his son as a minor to be brought up in the south of England.[2]

At the same time Elizabeth's personal endorsement of William Cecil's handling of the Spanish treasure crisis put an end to years of backstairs intrigues against the influence of the powerful secretary. Successive Spanish ambassadors (and others) had been able to exercise leverage within the council by intriguing with Cecil's opponents, including the Earl of Leicester. One of these intrigues had been the promotion of a marriage between Mary Stuart and the Duke of Norfolk, to secure her recognition as heir. The queen's reaction to Cecil's adventure in December 1568, however, convinced Leicester that there was no future in continued attempts to undermine him. He revealed the Norfolk marriage plot to Elizabeth, and thereby preserved himself at the cost of precipitating the northern rising and ruining the Duke of Norfolk.[3]

The rebellion of the northern earls was a little like a stone cast into a pond. Its ripples not only washed away much of what was left of the traditional order of northern politics, they also eroded Elizabeth's religious ambiguity. For a decade the queen had attempted to lead a Protestant establishment without terminally alienating her many Catholic subjects. However, the more radical leaders of the rebellion had begged the Pope to aid their cause by declaring that no Catholic could owe allegiance to a heretical ruler. In February 1570, long after his action could have served its original purpose, Pius V obliged, excommunicating Elizabeth by the Bull *Regnans in Excelsis*, and absolving her subjects of their allegiance. This thunderbolt had little immediate impact, but it changed many things. There was no longer any point in the queen dissimulating in the interests of unity or foreign policy. On the other hand, those who continued to adhere to the traditional faith were caught in an impossible dilemma. If they accepted the Bull, they became actual or potential traitors; if they rejected it, they could not call themselves Catholics.[4] A minority became conscientious recusants, and received the missionary priests who soon began to arrive. Most of those who chose this course earnestly (and sincerely) denied treasonable intention, but the government, with good reason, did not believe them. The majority, however, drifted more or less reluctantly into conformity in order to preserve their status as good subjects and good Englishmen.

After 1570, for the first time patriotism became unequivocally Protestant, and the queen was forced to take sides in the ideological struggle that was increasingly preoccupying European politics. Although Philip had opposed Pius's action, he was unavoidably affected by it. He now had no excuse to turn a blind eye to the militant heresy of the English, or to treat them as ordinary political adversaries, but rather began to adopt the course which many of his servants and officials had been advocating for some time.[5] At the same time, the discovery of the messy and somewhat far-fetched Ridolfi plot accelerated English sentiments of 'la patrie en danger'. Ridolfi's intention was to use the Mary/Norfolk marriage as a lever to get rid of Elizabeth, using all those Catholics who were supposed to be committed to rebellion by the Pope's pronouncement, and a Spanish army from the Low Countries. As the Duke of Alba treated the whole proposal with contempt, and hardly any English Catholics were willing to get involved, the actual danger which Ridolfi represented was minimal. The main consequence was the ensnaring of Mary and Norfolk into a treasonable correspondence, bits of which were picked up all over Europe. Mary was revealed to be every bit as dangerous as her Protestant antagonists had been claiming, and Norfolk went to the block in 1572.

By that time, Elizabeth had been forced into a Protestant strategic policy, and the actions of her merchants and seamen became a part of that policy. Even the queen no longer pretended that Spain was not, at least potentially, the main enemy. This was the main reason for the *rapprochement* with France in April 1572.[6] As was long ago pointed out, this was not a diplomatic revolution so much as a tactical convenience. The enemy in France was not the government of Charles IX but the Spanish-backed Guise faction; so it made sense to strengthen the hand of the king, who was already looking to the Huguenots for support. In the short term that policy had no future. Fears that Huguenot influence would lead to war with Spain through entanglement in the Low Countries turned the king against them, and the St Bartholomew's Day massacre in August 1572 was effectively a Guise *coup*.[7] The Treaty of Blois was not abrogated, but it became for the time being inoperative. Elizabeth was saved from the possible consequences of this setback by the unintended results of her other actions. Philip had been more impressed than Alba by the Ridolfi plot, and was prepared to order his forces into action if the English end of the plot had made any progress. At the same time the exiled Dutch leader, William of Orange, was trying very hard to involve both Elizabeth and the French in his intended rising against Alba.[8] Anxious as always to avoid commitment for as long as possible, and under pressure from some of England's other trading partners, in March 1572 the queen expelled the so-called 'Sea Beggars' from their refuges in England. These were Dutch Calvinists, displaced by the Council of Blood, who for several years had been revenging themselves upon Spanish and Flemish shipping. On 1 April they seized control of the small port of Brill, and for a variety of reasons could not be dislodged.[9] This event, like the northern rising, turned out to be a stone in the pond, and marked the effective beginning of the military struggle for Dutch independence which was to last on and off until 1648.

In this increasingly dangerous situation, Elizabeth continued to be largely reactive; there was little political scope for any alternative. However, there were those among her advisers who were beginning to see positive strategic options. The immensely influential John Dee was in and out of the court, talking to Cecil, Leicester, Hatton and the queen herself. From the early 1560s, and particularly after 1570, he was propagating the notion of what he prophetically called the 'British Impire'. This did not bear much relation to the entity which was later to be known by that name, but was rather a control of the coasts and waters northwards to the Orkneys, and including the north-eastern seaboard of America – the former on the grounds that 'King Edgar enjoyed the unchallenged sovereignty of the seas around Britain' (which was true);[10] and the latter on the grounds of discovery by Madoc (which was not true). Dee's ideas were in most respects not very revolutionary. The queen should maintain a 'Petty Navy Royal' to protect the realm against invasion, protect the comings and goings of merchants against piracy, and to dissuade foreign princes from imposing harmful and capricious embargoes. The force necessary to achieve this he judged to be 'Three score tall ships (or more), but in no case fewer, and they to be very well appointed, thoroughly manned and sufficiently victualled'. Such a fleet would not only provide protection in the traditional sense, but also a training ground for the far larger numbers of men who might be needed in an emergency; 'So that, in time of great need, that expert and hardy crew of some thousands of sea-soldiers would be to this realm a treasure incomparable'.[11] There was also an expansionist agenda which began in a small way to break new ground, because when these ships were not required for defensive duties they could be otherwise deployed, 'Some towards new foreign discoveries making for Gods glory, the wealth public, and the honorable renown of this Island Empire'. This was remarkably close to what the queen was actually doing after 1564, and an agenda warmly embraced by the 'men of action': Hawkins, Drake, Frobisher and Gilbert particularly. Such a fleet, Dee calculated, would cost up to £200,000 a year, and this could be found by imposing an *ad valorem* tax of 10 per cent on all foreign fishermen operating in English waters.[12] The navy, in short, could be made to pay for itself.

   These ideas were published in 1577 under a thin veil of anonymity, as *General and rare memorials pertayning to the Perfect Arte of Navigation*, with a dedication to Sir Christopher Hatton.[13] They sail alongside reality in a very interesting way. The 'Petty Navy Royal' is just about twice the size of the fleet which Elizabeth actually possessed, and £200,000 a year more than four times what was normally spent, except at times of crisis. On the other hand, there was no way in which even a modest proportion of that sum could be raised in the manner proposed. There is no doubt that Dee was central to that ferment of ideas and speculation the practical result of which can be seen in the great voyages after 1570. He wrote far more than was published, but such works as 'De Nova Navigatione Ratione' and 'Synopsis Reipublicae Britannicae' circulated among his influential friends. He was close to Stephen Borough and to the mathematician Thomas Digges, and no doubt passed on some of their ideas as his own.[14] It was he, primarily, who kept the Cathay enterprise alive after Gilbert's and Jenkinson's plans were shelved in 1566, an initiative which was supported by his influential friend Mercator, who argued that it was the responsibility of the English to complete the exploration of northern Asia which they had begun – especially as no one else seemed keen to do it.[15] Dee's concept of Empire seems at this point to have been confined to a control of the seas. If he had any thoughts of establishing colonies in North America, for example, he does not seem to have written them down. The man who was having such thoughts was another friend, the elder Richard Hakluyt, who was busily collecting economic information about the region to support arguments of that nature. Dee's interest in North America was mainly stimulated by a desire to find the eastern end of the so-called 'Strait of Anian', which was believed to connect the Atlantic and Pacific oceans.

After 1572, Anglo-Spanish relations gradually improved. In spite of the crisis of 1568, and Philip's enthusiasm for Ridolfi, there had never been a formal rupture, and some English merchants had continued to trade in Spain. Their numbers were insignificant, but their fortunes are instructive. Henry Hawks, who was active in the Mexico trade out of Seville, was accused of heresy in 1570, and either escaped or was deported. He was back in England by 1572. Roger Bodenham, who was similarly occupied, married and settled in Spain. He also had a kinswoman in the service of the English-born Countess of Feria, whose husband was an enthusiastic sup-porter of Ridolfi.[16] It must be assumed that Bodenham was a good Catholic, but that did not prevent him from spending nearly two years in England about his business affairs from 1572 to 1574. John Frampton, also a Seville merchant, translated Monandes's *Joyful Newes out of the New Found World*, with a dedication to Edward Dyer, another friend of Dee's.[17] Frampton seems to have remained more closely in touch with the London circle than either of the others, but how long his Spanish connection survived we do not know.

In April 1573 agreement was reached in principle with the government in the Low Countries for the resumption of trade, and a treaty was finally signed at Bristol in August 1574. By that time Bernardino de Mendoza had also arrived as Philip's new ambassador in London, and had been well received. In March 1575 Don Luis de Requesens, who had replaced Alba as Governor, signed an agreement with the English merchants, readmitting them to the Antwerp mart, on the condition that they did not visit Flushing, which was in rebel hands.[18] London's cloth exports immediately recovered from 63,000 in 1571 to 110,000 in 1575, before falling back to 98,000 in the following year. Thereafter the figure remained stable at about 100,000 for the next decade, although Antwerp was virtually abandoned after its sack by unpaid Spanish troops in 1576. It had taken the London mercantile community almost a generation to come to terms with the increasing fragil-ity of the Antwerp market, but when it finally ceased to be available there had been enough rehersals to enable them to cope. The year 1576 proved a bad one for Philip. He was effectively bankrupt, and the Antwerp mutiny temporarily united the whole of the Low Countries against him. This took much of the pressure off Elizabeth, but it did not much effect the momentum of overseas exploration and enterprise which looked to her for support.

Francis Drake married in the summer of 1569, from which his latest biographer has deduced that he had managed to salvage a reasonable profit from the disaster of San Juan d'Ulloa.[19] He did not, however, settle down. On 25 November he was off again in the company of William Hawkins.

They carried trade goods to Guinea, which they presumably exchanged for slaves, because although Hawkins returned home from West Africa, Drake with two ships followed his previous route to the West Indies. There is no record of what he did there, which suggests that he had learned quite a lot about the art of surreptitious trading. It has also been suggested that he used the voyage for reconnaissance, and investigated both the successful activities of French corsairs in the region, and also the counter-measures which the Spanish were adopting. He must have been back in England by the late summer of 1570, because before the end of that year he had embarked upon a further venture, which had reached the Caribbean by February 1571.[20] This was an even more obscure enterprise. The fleet seems to have been organised and led by William and George Winter, both of whom were officials of the Admiralty, and to have consisted of three ships, of which Drake commanded the smallest. The identity of the investors, apart from Richard Dennys of Exeter, is not known but was probably the usual mixture of London and provincial merchants. The queen must have given her permission for the sailing, but seems not to have been otherwise involved, and may not have understood the real purpose of the voyage. This time there was no pretence of legitimate trade, and the English ships joined forces with the French in a campaign of plunder. It was at this time that Drake was first noticed as an unusually daring and successful pirate. The expedition was brief, because he was back in England by June 1571, but it was fully and colourfully chronicled by his victims in preparing their indignant claims for compensation.[21] Whatever his nominal position at the beginning of the voyage, it was Drake rather than his colleagues or French allies who was noticed and feared. Uncertain of his reception, Drake sent word of his return ahead to the council. He need not have worried. The state of Anglo-Spanish relations at that point, and plunder worth about £100,000, were sufficient to guarantee him a welcome.

By this time Drake and his friends seem to have declared a private war against the King of Spain. In May 1572 he set out again, this time accompanied by his brothers John and Joseph, using two small ships which may have been his own, purchased out of his share of the previous voyage. Again he must have been given permission to sail, but there is no evidence of investment by anyone other than himself. In contrast to his previous voyage, this one was protracted, and enjoyed very variable fortunes, including a completely fruitless attack on Nombre de Dios. In spite of suffering a number of casualties, it was Drake's determination to have something to show for his efforts which kept him in the Caribbean until the summer of 1573. Working in collaboration with a French captain called Le Testu, at the end of April he succeeded in ambushing a mule train of silver, and then having careened and repaired his ships, he came home, arriving in Plymouth on 9 August.[22] Both his brothers had died on the voyage. Although Drake was now a wealthy man, his restless energy was undiminished and he spent the next two and a half years serving under the Earl of Essex in Ireland, a venture in which he probably invested a substantial amount of his own money. Drake was now as well known in court circles as John Hawkins, and when plans for a new voyage began to be discussed in 1576, he seemed the obvious man to entrust it to. The idea may have originated with Walsingham, or Hatton, or even with the queen herself. There are a number of conflicting accounts, both as to its origin and its intended purpose. However, some important things are clear. Elizabeth was involved from the start, but did not wish this fact to be known; and trade was never any part of the plan. Exploration was probably the main agenda, but whether of the coast of South America, that Terra Australis which was thought to lie north and west from the Strait of Magellan, or of the westward end of the Strait of Anian, is not clear.[23] It is quite likely that 'annoying the King of Spain' was also an objective from the beginning, and that would help to explain the appointment of Drake to the command. Elizabeth's willingness to harass Philip by encouraging such a voyage had probably got less to do with some bold new departure in foreign policy than with her clear understanding that he would be far too preoccupied to respond to provocation upon such a comparatively modest scale.

The supporting 'team' was very similar to that which had backed Hawkins in 1568. The queen contributed her own ship, the *Swallow*, and the investors included the Lord Admiral, the Earl of Leicester, Sir Francis Walsingham, Sir Christopher Hatton, John Hawkins and the Winter brothers. Drake sailed in his own new ship called, on Elizabeth's insistence, the *Pelican*. The pelican in her piety was one of the queen's favourite symbols, and this gesture seems to have been another calculated signal of her approval.

The expedition, which eventually consisted of four ships and about 180 men, left Plymouth on 15 November 1577. There are many surviving accounts of this important voyage, each written for some different apologetic or propaganda purpose, and its events are too well known to be recounted here.[24] The complex and unedifying story of his feud with Thomas Doughty and its tragic outcome is also well known, but is worth remembering because of the light which it sheds upon the men who carried out these epic voyages. Drake lacked John Hawkins's capacity for tact and forbearance; but it was precisely because he was prepared to be ruthless, and even unscrupulous, that his men followed him with such courage and devotion. Although he went where no Englishman had been before, Drake's voyage did not add very much to the stock of geographical knowledge. A characteristic later embellishment described him as claiming Elizabeth Island in the Strait of Magellan, for the Queen of England.[25] What he actually did was to sail up the Pacific coast of South America, raiding the settlements and capturing small merchant ships. His appearance caused surprise and consternation, which is lavishly documented in the Spanish sources. The English reach had become long, and here there were no French privateers either to compete with or collaborate. Drake sailed as far north as Lower California, beyond the end of the Spanish settlements, but not beyond their explorations. Some thought, both at the time and since, that he was looking for the westward end of the 'Strait of Anian' as his way home, but if that was the case, then he changed his mind long before he could have expected to find it. Again it was later claimed that he landed in California and claimed it for his sovereign, but there is no contemporary evidence of such action.[26] From California he crossed the Pacific to the East Indies, and then the Indian Ocean to South Africa. By July 1580 had reached Sierra Leone, and on 26 September returned to Plymouth after a voyage of almost three years, bringing home one ship, and about half the men he had started out with.

The great significance of this circumnavigation was always symbolic. It was a superb feat of seamanship, courage and determination. In practical terms it made little difference to anyone, except Drake himself, who had again brought home a rich booty, and, catching the queen in a good mood, earned himself a knighthood. It opened no new lands, or routes to lands, and established no new trade. What it did, however, was to send out an unequivocal signal to other maritime powers that the English now had global aspirations, and the necessary knowledge and skills to make them real. This was a long step beyond what Hawkins had achieved in the previous decade, and greatly enhanced the spirit of self-confidence which had been building up in the seafaring community since the beginning of the reign. Even while Drake was away, Martin Frobisher, who had reached Baffin Island in 1576 and returned with some kidnapped esquimaux, set out to try his luck again.[27] He was confident that he had discovered the north-west passage, and also a source of mineable gold. A London consortium led by Michael Lok was set up to support him, and chartered as the Cathay Company. However, his 1578 voyage was a failure. His strait turned out to be a dead end, and his gold ore to be worthless. Frobisher himself was undeterred, but the Cathay Company went bankrupt. With Humphrey Gilbert's schemes still failing to find realisation, the news of Drake's success was a welcome relief.

By 1580 a number of important developments were taking place, as a direct result of this spirit of enterprise and self-confidence. As we have seen, courtiers and councillors had been involved in trade and discovery since the early 1550s, but by 1580 the gentry were becoming seriously interested. This was partly because of the development of the joint stock company. Within a regulated company, such as the Merchant Adventurers, each individual merchant handled his own business, and this did not, on the whole, attract participants from outside the mercantile community. However, a joint stock company simply required an investment of money to set up the stock which the professional merchants would then trade on behalf of the shareholders, paying them a dividend in proportion to their investments.[28] This was the kind of gamble which proved increasingly attractive to those with money to spare. At the same time the stories of derring-do were attracting gentlemen adventurers, and linking the exploits of seamen (and pirates) to a sense of patriotism and national identity. In a study written a generation ago, Theodore Rabb identified more than 30 companies which were established between 1575 and 1630.[29] Some, like the Baffin Company, had no more than eight shareholders; others, like the East India and Virginia companies, had well over a thousand. Altogether, he identified nearly 5,000 of these shareholders, many of them holding shares in several companies. Some 3,800 were merchants, and 1,177 either gentlemen or nobles – between 20 and 25 per cent of the total. Individual companies varied enormously in their composition. At one extreme, the Africa Company included only seven merchants among its 37 shareholders; while at the opposite end of the spectrum the Levant Company counted only nine aristocrats among its 529 members. The first great boom in company membership came in 1577 when 383 were admitted; 1581 was another good year with 307 admissions. The annual average was far below that until after the turn of the century, but the number of new companies grew faster than the failures, and that sector of the economy was expanding steadily.

The economic significance of these developments was not immediately very great. In 1604 woollen cloth was still by far the most important export commodity, and the great bulk of that trade was still directed by the Merchant Adventurers into northern Europe.[30] The troubles of the Netherlands after 1572 opened up the Baltic trade in a manner which the Hanse was now powerless to stop, and in 1580 two London merchants, Sir Edward Osborne and Richard Staper, obtained a *firman* from the Sultan Murad III granting full rights and privileges to English merchants within the Ottoman Empire.[31] The Levant Company quickly established depots at Aleppo, Damascus, Tunis, Alexandria, and a number of other places. A few years later the Venetian Company followed it into the eastern Mediterranean. Meanwhile John Newbury, a London merchant every bit as intrepid as Drake in his own way, travelled by way of Persia to India between 1579 and 1582, laying the foundations for that enterprise which was eventually to be the East India Company.[32] Individual fortunes were made, particularly in the Levant trade, and diplomatic relations were established with the Porte, but still these long-distance companies were handling no more than 20 or 25 per cent of England's exports. What mattered in the short term was not so much the size of the profits as the growing belief that England's trading future lay in these rich and exotic markets, and that the country had the expertise and the capital which was necessary to unlock the golden gates. Individual voyages failed, like that of Edward Fenton in 1582–83, and companies collapsed, as the Cathay Company did, but that no longer mattered. There was always someone else to try – and succeed.

As English confidence grew after 1570, colonisation first came onto the practical agenda. There were a number of reasons for this. Hakluyt seems to have seen colonies as captive markets for English produce, trading raw materials in return. Ideally gold and silver, of course, but failing that, iron, timber, furs, or whatever was appropriate to the latitude. Military strategists saw them as bases for operations against the similar colonies of Spain and (after 1580, when Philip acquired that Crown) Portugal. Sir William Monson later blamed Drake for not having left a garrison in the New World to harass the Spaniards after his Caribbean raid in 1586, ignoring the impracticability of such an idea.[33] However, the most powerful motivation was straightforward emulation. Sir Edwin Sandys was later to write:

> The Kingdoms and States of the Romish part are not only in riches . . . by greater opportunity to traffic to all parts of the world, by manifold degrees superior to their Northern adversaries, but also in fineness and subtlety of wit . . . Neither have the Northern people ever yet for all their multitude and strength, had the honour of being founders or possessors of any great Empire, so unequal is the combat between force and wit, in all matters of durable and grounded establishment.[34]

Consequently the main drivers of colonial ambition were not at first the merchants. They were quite content to have company agents based in established centres of population – a few families protected by the privileges granted by local rulers. It was the gentlemen adventurers who wanted to show the flag, and gain honour for themselves, their country and their faith, like new conquistadores. A military colony on the American mainland was first suggested to Elizabeth by Humphrey Gilbert in 1577, but she preferred the less hazardous and less expensive option of supporting Drake. When he returned to the subject the following year, she licensed him to occupy lands in North America not held by any other European power. Gilbert sold notional plots of this land to raise the necessary funds, and was warmly supported by both Dee and Hakluyt. After some reconnaissance, he eventually set out in 1583 with a miscellaneous company numbering about 260. He went first to St Johns, Newfoundland, where he found a few temporary fishing settlements already established, and then to Cape Breton. His plans seem never to have been clear, and after a perfunctory attempt to find gold, the entire company set out to return, and was lost when their ship foundered in a storm.[35]

In spite of this discouraging start, Gilbert's plan was picked up almost at once by his former associate Walter Raleigh. Raleigh believed that one of Gilbert's errors had been that, in his anxiety to respect the terms of his patent, he had gone too far north. Raleigh proposed to establish a settlement in a warmer climate, and closer to the Spanish treasure routes. The coast of what is now North Carolina had already been explored and mapped to some extent, and Raleigh picked on Roanoake as a suitable location, naming his prospective colony Virginia, in honour of the queen. The party which Raleigh sent out in 1585 contained all sorts of talent, but again there seems to have been no agreed plan. Some of the backers, particularly Hakluyt, thought that an agricultural settlement was intended, and that was certainly what was needed. However, when it came to the point no one was prepared to do the work.[36] The gentlemen saw themselves as soldiers, and the rest, who were mainly craftsmen and traders, showed no willingness to till the soil. Nor was the site a particularly good one for that purpose, having been selected for its strategic position rather than its fertility. For several months the colonists traded for food with the local Indians, and the leaders fell out over what to do next.

By the following year they had outstayed their welcome, and food supplies were no longer forthcoming. When Francis Drake arrived, on the way back from his Caribbean raid in July 1586, the Governor, Ralph Lane, asked him for supplies and a ship to enable his people to fend for themselves. Drake agreed, but the settlers' morale was so flimsy that a bad storm during his stay persuaded the whole community to abandon their enterprise and come home.[37] They reached Plymouth in Drake's ships at the end of July.

Undeterred by this second misadventure, Raleigh sent out a further group the following year. This time the agricultural purpose seems to have been agreed, and the party included both women and children, but they got off to a bad start. Intending to head for Chesapeake Bay, they were instead landed at the old site of Roanoake. The intention was to supply and reinforce them the following year, but the Armada crisis overrode all such intentions, and by the time the intended help arrived in 1590, the entire community had disappeared.[38] Further plans continued to be discussed. One was for the establishment of trading posts on the Gulf of St Lawrence, another was for a form of penal colony at some unnamed location, and a third was a refuge for disgruntled religious separatists. None came anywhere near realisation, but lessons had been learned. Garrisons would have no chance of survival without viable communities to support them, and such communities would have to be able to feed themselves as quickly as the cycle of the year permitted. Establishing a colony was not a happy patriotic adventure, but a matter of sustained hard work and determination. Between 1590 and 1604, with so much effort having, perforce, to go into the war with Spain, and with Spain's grip on the New World tightening, neither the will nor the resources were available for an effort on the scale which was now seen to be required.

The outbreak of war in 1585 intensified an existing situation rather than creating a new one. It made all pretence of trade with the New World unnecessary, and turned the freebooting forays of men like Drake into legitimate acts of war. There was now less danger that Elizabeth would disavow the actions of her seamen, but on the other hand she no longer had as much incentive to make her own ships available for voyages which could be represented as patriotic duties. Philip's councillors had for some time been urging him to strike at the English gadflies, and when the Marquis of Santa Cruz won a decisive victory over the Franco-Portuguese fleet of Dom Antonio at Terciera in 1583, it began to look as though he had the means to do so.[39] At the same time the assassination of William of Orange in 1584, and the total failure of the Duke of Anjou to assist the beleaguered Dutch rebels, forced Elizabeth to act. It was imperative for English security that Spain should not recover control of the deep-water ports of Holland and Zeeland, and as the queen struggled to make up her mind, Philip obligingly made it up for her by seizing all English ships and cargoes in Spanish ports.[40] At Nonsuch in August 1585 she agreed, with no very good grace, to assist the Estates General. Philip regarded this as tantamount to a declaration of war, but neither side issued any formal statement.

Meanwhile news of the Spanish action had reactivated plans, dormant since the previous year, for a new large-scale expedition under the command of Sir Francis Drake. The original intention had been a voyage to the Moluccas, and Drake himself, Leicester, Hawkins and Raleigh had been among the investors. More significantly, the queen had pledged £10,000 and two ships, making her by far the largest shareholder.[41] Even before she came to terms with the Dutch, Elizabeth decided to send Drake to sea. Instead of going to the Moluccas, he was to sail in the first instance to Vigo to negotiate (with a show of force) the release of the detained English ships. At that point his formal instructions end, and there is some doubt as to what orders for subsequent action he received, because these were from the queen herself, and were never put into writing. His latest biographer concludes that he was probably instructed to intercept the treasure fleet, and failing that to raid the West Indies.[42] However, the long delay between the issuing of the orders in July and the eventual departure of the fleet in September suggests that Elizabeth may have been hoping that Philip would release the ships which he had taken without the need for any hostile demonstration. However, a number of further incidents involving English ships and Spanish officials finally convinced her that there were no grounds for such optimism. Christopher Carliell was recalled from Ireland to command the soldiers, and Drake left Plymouth with a miscellaneous fleet of about 25 ships on 14 September 1585.

In some respects this voyage was very similar (except in scale) to that which had resulted in the circumnavigation. There was a similar degree of royal involvement, a similar list of 'establishment' backers, and a similar lack of defined objectives. However, in one very important respect it was different. Reluctant as Elizabeth may have been to admit it, this was an act of war, and as such it set the pattern for a number of similar campaigns over the next eighteen years. This expedition, the raid on Cadiz in 1587, the expedition to Lisbon in 1589, and the Islands voyage of 1597, were all examples of 'partnership' warfare. In each case some of the ships were from the royal navy, some belonged to individual nobles or gentlemen, and some to companies or groups of merchants; and the necessary capital was raised in the same way. The commanders were armed with royal commissions and official instructions, but they were plagued by conflicting priorities resulting from contracts with the participants.[43] This did not greatly hamper the voyage of 1585–86, because the military objectives were imprecise, and perfectly compatible with the profitable plunder for which most of the investors were looking. It did, however, affect the Armada, in spite of the absence of contracts in that operation, and both Drake and Howard allowed themselves to be temporarily distracted from the business in hand in order to secure rich prizes.[44] It also affected the raid on Cadiz, the military success of which might have been far more emphatic if Drake had not felt obliged to yield to pressure from the London captains to go booty hunting at the earliest possible opportunity. More seriously, both the Islands voyage and the Lisbon expedition were ruined by such conflicts.

In 1589 the queen's orders were specific. The fleet was to go to the Biscay ports of northern Spain and destroy the remnants of the Armada, which had taken refuge there.[45] Having accomplished that, it was free to attempt an interception of the treasure fleet. However, partly because of the complicating involvement of Dom Antonio, the pretender to the Portuguese throne, and partly because of the greed of the private investors, the expedition achieved nothing. Ignoring Elizabeth's orders entirely, the fleet sailed straight to La Coruna on a rumour of rich prizes to be taken. The rumour was false; the town was taken, but offered little, and the fortress held out. Then, instead of turning back to the Biscay ports, Dom Antonio succeeded in persuading the leaders, Francis Drake and John Norris, to attack Lisbon. His story was that the Portuguese were longing to rise up against Spanish tyranny, and that his appearance with a military force to back him would provoke a general and spontaneous rebellion. Once in possession of his crown, he would be generous, both with rewards to individuals and with trading privileges to merchants. Nothing of the kind transpired. The Portuguese showed no enthusiasm for the pretender, the English attack was repulsed, and Drake and Norris quarrelled. The expedition received many casualties, both from the fighting and disease, and returned with nothing to show for the effort and expenditure.[46] Not surprisingly, both the queen and the council were furious, and Drake's career was effectively ended.

Just as the queen was responsible for that royal involvement which boosted the earlier enterprises of Hawkins and Drake, so she was responsible for this flawed method of waging war. English monarchs had always requisitioned large numbers of privately owned ships when a 'navy royal' was required, but they had always paid the bills themselves, apart from the obsolete contributions of ship service. Consequently the commander appointed for that particular service had unquestioned authority. By inviting private investment in what were really military operations, and by leaving her commanders a good deal of discretion as to the details of their operations, Elizabeth confused and weakened the command structure. Her objective was obviously to fight as cheaply as possible, taking advantage of the consensus of opinion within the 'political nation' which supported the war. It also sprang partly from her whole style of government, which was based upon a partnership with the service nobility, the gentry who controlled the shires, and the mercantile community, particularly in London.[47] Elizabeth was notoriously reluctant to ask parliament for taxation, even when such a request was fully justified, and was extremely secretive about the real extent of her financial difficulties. After 1590 parliament was generous by its own standards, but warfare was hugely expensive, and before the end of her reign the queen was admitting that she lacked the capability to be generous to her servants, and resorting to surreptitious expedients such as monopolies to enable them to reward themselves. 'Partnership' government worked reasonably well, although it left a legacy of trouble for her successors. 'Partnership' warfare worked better than might have been expected, but it did have some major failures, and it is perhaps significant that the most successful of all the Elizabethan amphibious operations, the raid on Cadiz in 1596, was not conducted upon that basis.

In theory partnership operations were carried out in the queen's name and in obedience to her orders; but there were also other operations which were entirely independent, and conducted merely by the queen's licence. The men who waged war on this basis were known as 'voluntaries', and later as privateers, and they operated by virtue of letters of permission, also known as 'letters of marque'.[48] Some privateers were simply taking the law into their own hands, by virtue of the ancient custom of reprisal. A merchant whose goods had been unlawfully seized, either on the high seas or in a hostile port, was bound in the first instance to seek redress through the admiralty court of the country concerned. If (as was usually the case) he failed to obtain satisfaction, then he was entitled to obtain from the Lord Admiral a 'letter of reprisal', which authorised him to seize goods to the value of his losses from ships belonging to the offending port, or country.[49] Inevitably the issuing of such letters had a knock-on effect, and the reciprocal plunder could go on for years. Reprisals had nothing to do with any state of war which might exist between nations, and were chiefly a reflection of the inadequacies of international law. At the same time, others who belonged to this same general category saw themselves as waging war on their sovereign's behalf, and only operated when a state of hostilities had been acknowledged. These might be individual noblemen or gentlemen, or they might be groups of merchants deprived of their normal activities by the fortunes of war. In both cases the principal motivation was profit. They used their own ships, equipped and manned at their own expense, and except in special circumstances kept 80 per cent of the loot, the other 20 per cent going to the Crown. These privateers, of whom the most conspicuous was the Earl of Cumberland, were usually careful to operate within the terms of their licences, and were legitimate belligerents.[50] There were many others, however, mostly small operators, who were less scrupulous. As we have already seen, piracy was a well-established part-time profession within the maritime community, and there were hundreds of practitioners. Although these men also described themselves as voluntaries if challenged, and claimed to be 'going upon the queen's enemies', they often had no specific authorisation, and were not careful to distinguish the queen's friends from her foes. They did not normally disgorge their 20 per cent unless forced to do so, and were in fact simply pirates taking advantage of the muddying of the waters.

The first privateers of this war, mostly claiming letters of reprisal, were on the Spanish coast by July 1585, nearly two months before Drake sailed, but there is no doubt that it was his example which inspired the large-scale operation which followed. Following his instructions, Drake headed first for Vigo, where, after a show of force, he secured the release of those English ships which were detained there, and took on fresh supplies. The slow deliberation with which he went about the business of revictualling meant that he missed both the incoming treasure fleets, which happened that year to be unescorted because of the deteriorating international situation. Realising his error too late, Drake was forced to implement plan B, and set off for the Cape Verde Islands about the middle of October. For six months he then cruised in the Caribbean, and the detailed accounts of the voyage which survive make clear both his qualities and limitations as a commander.[51]

In one sense the expedition was a failure: the quantity of plunder taken did not cover the costs, and the investors lost money. On the other hand both militarily and psychologically it was an outstanding success. Places like Santo Domingo and Cartagena had been destroyed; fortifications had been reduced to rubble and many colonists to penury. Philip's prestige was badly dented, and he was forced to divert to the New World resources which he urgently needed in the Netherlands. Having picked up the Roanoake settlers, Drake reached Plymouth at the end of July 1586, and quickly became a national hero. Walter Bigges's *A summarie and true discourse of Sir Francis Drakes West Indian voyage*, which was published within a few months, and went through several editions in various languages over the next three years, elevated Drake to the status of Protestant Hero, battling against the tyranny and bigotry of Spain.[52]

This mythical triumph had just enough substance to be truly compelling, as well as being just what a beleaguered but aggressive England needed. John Hooker wrote that the news 'inflamed the whole country with a desire to adventure unto the seas, in hope of like good success, [so] that a great number prepared ships, mariners and soldiers, and travelled to any place where profit might be had'.[53] Over the next few years ports like Weymouth and Southampton became largely devoted to fitting out privateers and disposing of prizes. One contemporary, looking back on these exciting years a generation later, claimed that there had been 'never less than 200 sail of voluntaries and others upon [the Spanish] coasts' in any given year. This was probably an exaggeration, and a modern computation puts the figure at about half that, but the effect upon Spanish commerce was similar to that of a swarm of locusts upon a field of wheat.[54] Philip was not to be defeated by such means, and his treasure fleets continued to get through because of the priority which could be given to defending them. But ordinary seaborne trade was virtually destroyed, and many small commercial centres reduced to poverty. Whether the benefit to the English was as great as the damage to the Spanish remains a matter of doubt. Large-scale operators like Cumberland probably made little or nothing, because although they brought off the occasional spectacular *coup*, like the capture of the *Madre de Dios* in 1592, many of their expeditions were fruitless and they had high overheads. They persisted, partly in hope like inveterate gamblers, but partly also out of a sense of patriotic duty. The smaller privateers, who were much more numerous, must have persisted because it was worth their while, although statistics are hard to come by. No doubt as Spanish prey became hard to find they made do with others, but they had no incentive to make grand gestures, and could not have afforded to continue if the profits had not been reasonable.[55] However, the myth perpetuated by writers such as Hooker and Hagthorpe, that a sea war could not only be made to pay for itself, but could yield a handsome profit, was to haunt English public opinion for the next half century.

The line between legitimate reprisal and piracy had always been hard to draw. As we have seen, English seamen operated under letters of authorisation from Huguenot commanders throughout the civil wars in France. After 1572 others obtained similar authorisations from the Prince of Orange, and after 1580 from Dom Antonio. It was by no means clear whether a subject of the English queen was acting lawfully in receiving such instruments, and much depended upon how they were used. This required a certain sensitivity to contemporary politics. Before 1585, Elizabeth went through phases in which she actively discouraged attacks on Spanish ships, and it was not easy to tell a Catholic Frenchman from a Protestant, until it was too late. A freebooter operating in this way could easily fall victim to the need for a scapegoat, but the number that were proceeded against, let alone punished, was so small that the risk was clearly no deterrent.

It would be no exaggeration to say that the period from 1570 to 1604 changed the whole military culture of England. As recently as the French war of 1557–59 soldiers were still recruited via the noble retinue or the Commission of Array, and auxiliary fighting ships were taken up by the traditional methods. By 1585, however, troops were raised by county quotas, and the private warship, which had disappeared over a hundred years before, had made a striking comeback.[56] The longbowman had given way to the sea gunner, and the free company to the privateering fleet. An adventurous gentleman could still serve with the Earl of Leicester in the Low Countries, or the Earl of Essex in Ireland, but he was just as likely to take to the sea in his own ship or that of a kinsman. Private warfare, banned within the realm by the rigours of Tudor government, reappeared in these tough but ill-disciplined seamen. It was in such ships that the captains and gunners of the queen's navy learned their skills, because privateers were usually small, fast and heavily armed. They had to develop superior skills in order to keep the great carracks which pursued them at bay. It was not in the 60 tall ships of Dee's 'Petty Navy Royal' but in these swarms of 'voluntaries' that Elizabeth's fighting seamen learned their trade.

In military matters, as in civilian government, the secret of getting the best results lay in striking the right balance between public authority and private interest. Henry VIII, who had been forced to rely heavily on his nobles for troops, had made the navy very much a public and royal monopoly. Elizabeth, as she edged away from dependence upon noble retinues, equally opened the navy to private enterprise. The highwatermark of bureaucratic management had been the Marquis of Winchester's 'ordinary' of 1556. After 1560, Elizabeth had gradually returned to more *ad hoc* methods of funding, and in April 1565 had put the victualling out to contract.[57] This was not a question of inviting tenders in the modern manner, but was more akin to the established practice of 'farming' an office. Edward Baeshe, the Surveyor General, was allowed $4\frac{1}{2}$d a day for every man in harbour, and 5d a day for every man at sea. Out of that sum he was expected to provide victuals in accordance with an established schedule, and to pay his own fees and expenses. Baeshe was to operate on this basis for 22 years, and although inflation forced the council to raise the rates twice in that time, and he was constantly lamenting his difficulties, he did not die in poverty. Nor did the complaints about what he provided rise above the level of routine grumbling. His successor, James Quarles, may have been less efficient, or less honest, or both. Between taking office in 1587 and his death in 1595 he was in constant difficulties, and his provision was subject to a crescendo of abuse.[58]

Baeshe's contract was undoubtedly adjudged a success, and when Sir John Hawkins became Treasurer of the Navy on the death of his father-in-law Benjamin Gonson in 1577, he sought to extend the principle. In 1579 he entered into a contract with the Admiralty to maintain 25 ships to a specified standard, but not to repair them or provide shipkeepers, in return for £1,200 a year. At the same time Peter Pett and Mathew Baker, the queen's master shipwrights, entered into a similar contract to ground and grave the ships at fixed intervals, and to carry out certain types of repair, for £1,000 a year.[59] Royal ships had always been built on contract, so there was nothing revolutionary about this change, but it did not work. Edward Baeshe had a complete and autonomous responsibility, but to divide up the work of maintaining and repairing ships in this way was asking for trouble – the more so because the contracts did not cover the full range of work which was required. Inevitably officers without contracts complained that expensive jobs were being dropped on them in order to save the contractors' profits; and Pett and Baker complained that Hawkins was using his office to force work on them which he should have done himself.

By 1584 the mutual recriminations had become so disruptive that a commission of inquiry was instituted, and all existing contracts were abrogated. The commissioners identified the root of the trouble, not in any of the alleged malfeasance, but in the limited scope of the contracts. Hawkins was then offered, and accepted, a new contract for the whole range of service, repair and provision which had been covered by the old ordinary, for £4,000 a year.[60] In real terms this was less than a quarter of the 1556 allocation, and almost certainly much less than was really needed. Pett and Baker immediately began to accuse Hawkins of default and negligence on a heroic scale, and the atmosphere became worse rather than better. In fact Hawkins seems to have done what he undertook efficiently, but he certainly cheated by shifting a lot of work onto extraordinary accounts, and paying for it by special warrants. The navy did not suffer greatly from this fracas, but neither did the queen benefit, because the overall expenditure levels remained about the same. Hawkins surrendered his contract in December 1587, because of the steadily rising pressure of work, and the system was abandoned.[61] Hawkins was efficient, and reasonably honest in spite of the storm of criticism which he endured, but after his death in 1595 the situation deteriorated. This was not because of 'privatisation', but because of the queen's increasingly neurotic unwillingness to spend money. She set her officers to check up on each other, and positively encouraged complaint and misrepresentation. Marmaduke Darrell, who succeeded Quarles as Surveyor General of the Victuals, was subjected to a perpetual barrage of denunciation from one of his subordinates who wanted his job and claimed to be able to do it more cheaply. Instead of silencing such irresponsible criticism, Elizabeth encouraged it.[62] As Hawkins had written in 1590, 'the matters in thoffice growe infenyte and chargeable beyond all measure and soche as hardly any man can gyve a reason of the innumerable busynesses that dayly growe; yet the mistrust is more troblesome and grievous than all the rest'.[63] As an institution, the Admiralty had come of age, and could cope with the burden of a war being fought largely at sea, but the queen's constant attempts to find someone else to pay her bills was seriously undermining morale by 1600.

Elizabeth's continued enthusiasm for privateering of course sprang from the same root. In 1590 Dr Julius Ceasar, the Admiralty Judge (who was in a good position to know), claimed that 'her majesty hath gotten and saved by these reprisals since they began above £200,000' – that is, about £40,000 a year, about two-thirds of the cost of running the navy.[64] The English were accused with justice of making up the laws of contraband as they went along, and Ceasar was besieged with complaints from Danish, Dutch, Italian and French merchants who protested that their goods had been seized on the specious pretext that they were bound for some Spanish-controlled port. Elizabeth ignored the diplomatic flak, and pressed her claims to a share of the loot with indecent zeal. In 1592, for example, she insisted on taking far more from the declared value of the *Madre de Dios* than the part played by her ships in its capture would have justified.[65] That this caused no more than muffled complaint may be attributed to the fact that no more than 60 per cent of the value had been declared. In the same year it was felt necessary to reiterate that all prizes had to be declared to the Lord Admiral on pain of being declared pirate goods, but the queen's acquisitiveness guaranteed that much continued to evade the searchers. Ceasar knew that the Admiralty Court was in urgent need of reform, and demonstrated by a memorandum written in 1601 that he knew how to do it, but the continuing need to maintain the goodwill of those who profited from its deficiencies ensured that nothing was done.[66] It was precisely because their operations were so conspicuous that large-scale privateers like the Earl of Cumberland so often failed to return a profit. In 1598 Cumberland led a fleet of eighteen ships to the Indies, headed by his own *Scourge of Malice*, which at 900 tons was as large as any of the queen's warships. As an act of war his expedition was a great success, but it cost the earl a lot of money, not least because it would have been impossible to smuggle the proceeds of such a venture ashore.[67]

It has been calculated that privateers supplied about 50 per cent of the war effort between 1585 and 1604, making it possible for a country with a totally inadequate financial infrastructure to sustain one of the longest wars in its history, and to confront a power whose resources were in every way superior. However, the navy proper should not be deprived of its share of the credit. It was the queen's ships which 'kept the seas' – the essential but unglamorous work of patrolling the Channel and the North Sea at all seasons of the year, while the privateers went chasing prizes, often in warmer climates.[68] Service in the navy proper was reasonably (if not always reliably) paid, and the food was no worse than usual; but the work was hard, the discipline severe, and the opportunities for occasional windfalls very rare indeed. It is not surprising that, as the war went on, naval service became increasingly unpopular, while private ships, where both the risks and the rewards were very much greater, had no difficulties in recruiting.[69] In partnership ventures the naval rules on prizes were unofficially bent, but never enough to satisfy the seamen, for whom the perils of life at sea were never adequately rewarded. In Drake's 1585–86 expedition, his flagship the *Bonaventure* (600 tons) and the 250-ton *Aid* represented the navy, a rather larger share than might appear, because although six of the private ships were also over 200 tons, the remaining fourteen were all small. Moreover the firepower of the flagship was a major factor in all military operations.

By the time that Drake returned it was clear that Philip, now provoked beyond all endurance, had decided to strike a massive blow against England. Aware of these preparations, Elizabeth accelerated the navy's building and replacement programme so that about a dozen ships joined the fleet in 1586 and 1587. The *Gran Armada* was never intended to conquer England, but it was intended to launch an invasion which would knock England out of the war, and hopefully get rid of Elizabeth. The real aim was the reconquest of the Netherlands, but that could not be accomplished while England stood in the way.[70] In spite of the damage which he had suffered, Philip did not see England as a rival empire, and in the short term he was right. The plan, as the king eventually settled it, was to ship some 18,000 men directly from Spain, and by rendezvousing with the Duke of Parma, his commander in the Low Countries, to escort another 30,000 men across the Channel. For this purpose about 150 ships would be required. Unfortunately for Philip, Spain did not have the administrative infrastructure to manage such a mobilisation. Ships were summoned, and many did not arrive; the crews of those that did arrive consumed victuals as fast as they could be collected; there were not enough guns, and the ones which could be found varied so greatly that matching shot to them was a major task in itself.[71] Philip's veteran sea commander, the Marquis of Santa Cruz, proved to be an incompetent manager, and Elizabeth had no intention of allowing this chaos to resolve itself undisturbed. In March 1587 Drake (now a demon of almost mythological proportions in Spain) completed his preparations for a visit to the Spanish coast. He had sixteen ships and seven pinnaces: four of the ships and two of the pinnaces represented the navy, while seven ships and three pinnaces came from London; the remainder were privately owned, some by Drake himself. The contract which set up this enterprise specified that any plunder was to be divided equally between the Crown and the investors, but at this stage there was no dispute that the aims of the expedition were military.[72]

Leaving Plymouth on 27 March, Drake reached Cadiz on 19 April. The Armada itself was not there, but the harbour was full of supply vessels and support ships of various kinds. The surprise was complete, and the destruction immense. At least two dozen ships were burned, and huge quantities of naval stores destroyed. At the same time it was demonstrated beyond dispute that the royal galleys which attempted to defend the anchorage were no match for heavily armed galleons, even when the wind conditions seemed to favour them. Having completed his main mission, Drake was then mindful of his shareholders, and raided both Lagos and Sagres. Staying at the latter base for about a month, he took some 30 small ships, before setting off at the end of May for the Azores in search of bigger fish. By this time the weakness of the partnership system was beginning to show and some of the London ships, simply ignoring his orders, sailed home.[73] Fortunately for Drake, the Azores venture was quickly successful, and on 8 June he captured the *San Felipe*, inward bound from the East Indies with a rich cargo. Having satisfied all reasonable expectations, he returned to Plymouth with his prize on 26 June. For those with eyes to see, like Lord Burghley, the weaknesses of partnership operations were sufficiently obvious, but this time Drake had got away with it, and the queen liked it for reasons which we have already seen.

The Armada campaign itself was not a partnership in the same sense, because although more than two-thirds of the fleet was contributed by private or corporate owners, it was not upon a contractual basis, and no plunder was expected. The details of the action in 1588 do not need to concern us here. Although much of the Spanish failure can be put down to poor planning and overstretched resources, it was nevertheless the largest, as well as the most important action that the royal navy had ever fought.[74] The campaign cost Philip the equivalent of over £2 million and almost bankrupted him. The English response cost £200,000, and was covered, although with great difficulty. The difference was partly in the efficiency of the English Admiralty, and partly in the intangible spirit of cooperation which partnership had fostered. The psychological effects of the victory were immense. God had spoken decisively in England's favour. The Catholic threat, diminished by the execution of Mary Stuart in 1587, was further blunted by the defeat of its champion, while Puritan critics of the queen's half-hearted Protestantism also began to lose credibility. In fact the danger had not gone away, and Philip was to launch two further armadas, which were frustrated more by the weather than by English vigilance.[75] However, that only fortified the myth. Even if the queen was getting old and tired, God was still watchful. The English council was probably not deceived, even when it promoted this sort of propaganda. The failure of the Lisbon expedition in 1589 was enough to deflate any official complacency, and although there were successes over the next few years, the balance of power at sea swung back in Philip's favour by about 1592, as was demonstrated by the failure and death of both Hawkins and Drake in 1595. This was the largest partnership venture so far; the queen provided six ships and £30,000, the investors 21 ships and £60,000. In military terms it was not a disaster, but it failed to inflict the damage that might have been expected of such a large venture, and conspicuously failed to cover its costs.[76] However, Philip failed to carry the war to his enemy. Although there were small-scale raids on Cornwall, and an intervention in Ireland, English commerce with countries other than Spain was not seriously damaged, and there was no success to compare with Essex's devastating capture of Cadiz in 1596.

Strictly speaking, Essex commanded only the soldiers. The fleet was led by the Lord Admiral, Lord Howard. He had under him 18 royal warships, 68 auxiliaries 'taken up' in the old way, and a squadron of 24 Dutch warships commanded by Jan van Duijvenvoorde, the Admiral of Holland.[77] They were instructed to 'annoy' the King of Spain 'by burning of [his] ships of war in his havens before they should come forth to the seas, and therewith also destroying his magazines of victuals and his munitions for the arming of his navy'.[78] Unlike the instructions of 1589, these orders were faithfully observed. As in 1587, the English arrival on 21 June took the city by surprise, and this time the consequences were far more severe. Cadiz itself was captured in a few hours of brisk fighting, and the garrison was ransomed for £180,000, but Howard refused to ransom the shipping in the harbour. In two days of concentrated violence he destroyed fifteen men of war, eleven Indiamen, and a large number of miscellaneous smaller merchantmen, as well as removing 1,200 pieces of ordnance. The total loss to Spain was calculated at 20 million ducats — a staggering £5 million sterling, or 20 times the ordinary annual revenue of the English Crown.[79] Essex wished to remain in Cadiz, but more prudent councils prevailed and the English left on 5 July, having razed the fortifications and many of the principal buildings. 'It is plainly', wrote the Duke of Medina Sidonia in an echo of the English propaganda, 'a chastisement from the Lord, and his will alone.'[80] On the English side the only person not pleased was the Earl of Essex, who felt that he could have achieved much more.

In spite of such a victory, the English did not win the war. What did happen was that England came of age as a naval power, and gave substance to the aspirations of its maritime community. By 1600 Englishmen were no longer in awe of Iberian achievements, but seeking to emulate or surpass them. A few years later Sir Robert Cecil was presented with a memorandum, outlining an ambitious strategy:

> First, and principally, we must keep employed two main fleets upon the coast of Spain eight months in the year, that is from March to November. Every fleet to consist of forty five ships to be divided into three squadrons; one to lie off the Rock [Cape Roca] to intercept all traders of Lisbon; the second at the South Cape [St Vincent], to stop all intercourse to San Lucar and Cadiz, and to and from the Indies; the third to the Islands [Canaries], lest they should there stop and put their goods ashore, having intelligence of our being upon the coast of Spain . . . Perhaps the number of these ships will exceed the proportion her majesty is willing to employ. But if Holland will be drawn from the trade of Spain and join with us the number may be easily raised by them and our maritime towns in England, so that her Majesty need but employ six ships of her own in each fleet, to serve for the Admiral and Vice-Admiral of every squadron . . .[81]

This was a little bit like Dee's Petty Navy Royal, plausible but not really practicable. However, what it does represent is not only supreme confidence, but also the kind of strategic imagination which would be guiding the Royal Navy in its great wars two centuries later. By 1600 English galleons were as good as those built anywhere in Europe; English cartography and navigational skills were matched only by the Dutch, and English sea gunnery was the best in the world.[82] A long war, which had exhausted the queen and stretched her resources beyond their limit, had created all manner of opportunities for her subjects, who emerged from the experience richer, tougher, and more ambitious.

Notes

1. Penry Williams, *The Later Tudors, 1547–1603* (Oxford, 1995), 258. The Percys soon regained the Northumberland title, but were permanently exiled to the south.

2. This was George Clifford, the third earl, who subsequently became the noted privateer. Richard T. Spence, *The Privateering Earl: George Clifford, Earl of Cumberland* (Stroud, 1995), 20–1.

3. Derek Wilson, *Sweet Robin: A Biography of Robert Dudley, Earl of Leicester, 1533–1588* (London, 1981), 211–12.

4. The propaganda argument resulting from this situation was vigorously conducted on both sides, neither with complete honesty. For the government Cecil argued that Catholics were not being punished for their faith, but for treason, to which William Allen responded that this was hypocritical, since the government had first made Catholicism treason. Although the penal laws were enacted by statute, it could equally be argued that it was the papacy, and not the English government, which had made Catholicism treasonable. William Cecil, *The Execution of Justice in England* (1583), ed. R. Kingdon (London, 1965); William Allen, *A True, Sincere and Modest Defence of the English Catholics* (1584), ed. R. Kingdon (London, 1965).

5. Cardinal Granvelle had warned Philip against the heresies and commercial ambitions of the English as early as 1562. Henry Kamen, *Philip of Spain* (London, 1997), 93.

6. J.B. Black, *The Reign of Elizabeth* (Oxford, 1959), 154.

7. N.M. Sutherland, *The Massacre of St Bartholomew and the European Conflict, 1559–1572* (Oxford, 1973).

8. Geoffrey Parker, *The Dutch Revolt* (London, 1977), 122–3.

9. The main reason was that Alba's main force was deployed in the south against a French intervention which never came. Parker, *The Dutch Revolt*, 132–3.

10. John Dee, *General and rare memorials* (London, 1577), 60. N.A.M. Rodger, *The Safeguard of the Sea* (London, 1997), 19–20.

11. Dee, *General and rare memorials*, 6.

12. Ibid., 19.

13. Short-Title Catalogue (STC) 6459.

14. E.G.R. Taylor, *Tudor Geography, 1485–1583* (London, 1930), 103–24.

15. Ibid.

16. Ibid. The Countess of Feria was Jane Dormer, a Lady of Queen Mary's privy chamber, who had met the count during his stay in England with Philip. A number of English Catholics took service in her household after 1559.

17. STC 18005.

18. An adjudication of claims at the same time put Spanish losses (from piracy and seizure) at £89,076 and English losses (almost entirely from seizure) at £68,076. The balance seems not to have been paid. Black, *Reign of Elizabeth*, 164.

19. Harry Kelsey, *Francis Drake: The Queen's Pirate* (New Haven, 1998), 44.

20. Ibid., 46.

21. For example, Archivo de Indias, Seville; Panama 32, no. 15, ff. 3v–7; interrogatory, 15 May 1571. Kelsey, *Francis Drake*, 49.

22. Philip Nichols, *Sir Francis Drake Revived* (1626) (STC 18455), 78–80.

23. It is quite possible that no specific orders were given, and that Drake was merely instructed to do what time and weather permitted. Terra Australis turned out to be a long way from where it was thought to be.

24. Walter Bigges, *A summarie and true discourse of Sir Francis Drake's West Indian voyage* (London, 1586) (STC 3056); *The World Encompassed by Sir Francis Drake* (London, 1628) (STC 7161); Richard Hakluyt, *The principall navigations, voiages and discoveries of the English nation* (London, 1589) (STC 12625). For the latest discussion of the Doughty incident, see Kelsey, *Francis Drake*, 106–9.

25. *World Encompassed*, 35–6.

26. The earliest reference to a landfall in California occurs in John Drake's testimony to the Spanish authorities in 1584. Specific references to the claim seem to have been motivated by later political considerations.

27. G.V. Scammell, *The World Encompassed: The First European Maritime Empires, c.800–1650* (London, 1981), 473.

28. W.R. Scott, *Joint Stock Companies: The Constitution and Finance of English, Scottish and Irish Joint Stock Companies to 1720* (London, 1910–12).

29. T.K. Rabb, *Enterprise and Empire, 1575–1630* (New Haven, 1967), 104.

30. Ralph Davis, *English Overseas Trade, 1500–1700* (London, 1973), 53.

31. Sir William Foster, *England's Quest of the Eastern Trade* (London, 1933), 69. The actual negotiator was William Harborne, who had to overcome the constant attempts of the French (who had a long-established link with the Ottoman Empire) to undermine this new development. Harborne remained as ambassador until 1588. Although the volume of this trade was not great, individual cargoes could be of immense value. In 1587 the freighting of the *Hercules* was valued at £70,000.

32. Samuel Purchas, *Hakluytus posthumus or Purchas his pilgrimes* (London, 1625; Hakluyt Society, Glasgow, 1905–07), VIII, 449 et seq.

33. M. Oppenheim, ed., *The Naval Tracts of Sir William Monson* (Navy Records Society, London, 1902–14), I, 123.

34. Sir Edwin Sandys, *Four Paradoxes or Politique Discourses* (London, 1604), 79. T.K. Rabb, *Jacobean Gentleman: Sir Edwin Sandys, 1561–1629* (London, 1998), 323.

35. D.B. Quinn, *The Voyages and Colonising Enterprises of Sir Humphrey Gilbert* (Hakluyt Society, London, 1940). Scammell, *World Encompassed*, 482.

36. 'Discourse of the first colony', in D.B. Quinn, *The Roanoake Voyages, 1584–90* (Hakluyt Society, London, 1955), 272–3.

37. Bigges, *Summarie and true discourse*, 34–6. For a consideration of some of the achievements of this abortive venture, see Paul Hulton, 'Images of the New World: Jacques Le Moyne and John White', in K.R. Andrews, N.P. Canny and Paul Hair, eds, *The Westward Enterprise* (Liverpool, 1978), 195–214.

38. Scammell, *World Encompassed*, 483.

39. Kamen, *Philip of Spain*, 252. Santa Cruz was strongly urging such a strike.

40. S. Adams, 'The outbreak of the Elizabethan naval war against the Spanish Empire, and the embargo of May 1585', in S. Adams and M-J. Rodriguez Salgado, *England, Spain and the Gran Armada, 1585–1604* (London, 1991).

41. Kelsey, *Francis Drake*, 240.

42. Ibid., 241.

43. Wallace MacCaffrey, *Elizabeth I* (London, 1993), 243–9, 275–6.

44. Geoffrey Parker and Colin Martin, *The Spanish Armada* (London, 1988), 167.

45. 'Before you attempt anything either in Portugal or in the said islands [Azores] our express pleasure and commandment is that you first distress the ships of war in Guipuzcoa, Biscay, Galicia, and any other places that appertain either to the King of Spain or his subjects . . .' R.B. Wernham, *The Expedition of Sir John Norris and Sir Francis Drake to Spain and Portugal* (1589) (Navy Records Society, London, 1988), xxix.

46. Wernham, *The Expedition*, passim.

47. D. Loades, *Politics and the Nation, 1450–1650*, 5th edn (London, 1999), 255–60.

48. K.R. Andrews, *Elizabethan Privateering, 1585–1603* (London, 1964), 2–5.

49. F.E. Dyer, 'Reprisals in the sixteenth century', *Mariners Mirror*, 21, 1935, 187–97.

50. Andrews, *Elizabethan Privateering*, 5–6; Spence, *The Privateering Earl*, 84–113.

51. Kelsey, *Francis Drake*, 250–5.

52. STC 3056.

53. W.J. Harte, *Gleanings from the Commonplace Book of John Hooker* (Exeter, 1926), 39.

54. John Hagthorpe, *England's Exchequer, or a Discourse of the Sea and Navigation* (London, 1625) (STC 12603), 25.

55. C.L. Kingsford, 'The taking of the Madre de Dios, 1592', *Naval Miscellany*, 2, 1912, 85–121; E.W. Bovill, 'The Madre de Dios', *Mariners Mirror* 54, 1968, 129–52; C.R. Boxer, 'The taking of the Madre de Dios, 1592', *Mariners Mirror* 67, 1981, 82–4.

56. C.G. Cruikshank, *Elizabeth's Army* (Oxford, 1966); D. Loades, *The Tudor Navy* (Aldershot, 1992).

57. Public Record Office (PRO) E351/2358; Loades, *Tudor Navy*, 203.

58. M. Oppenheim, *The History of the Administration of the Royal Navy, 1509–1660* (London, 1896, rep. 1988), 142.

59. PRO SP12/132/88–91. S. Adams, 'New light on the "Reformation" of John Hawkins: the Ellesmere naval survey of January 1584', *English Historical Review*, 105, 1991, 97–111.

60. Oppenheim, *Administration*, 162–3.

61. Loades, *Tudor Navy*, 185.

62. Ibid., 278. If Darrell was guilty of malpractice, his accounts conceal it very effectively. Bodleian Library MS Rawlinson C.340, ff. 84–8.

63. PRO SP12/231/83.

64. British Library (BL) Lansdowne MS 157, f. 434. Ceasar to Howard, 18 December 1590.

65. See above, n. 55.

66. For a full consideration of this problem, see Andrews, *Elizabethan Privateering*, 22–31.

67. Spence, *The Privateering Earl*, 157–75.

68. Loades, *Tudor Navy*, 267–8.

69. Sir William Monson testified to this problem, even in the early days of his service, in the 1580s. Loades, *Tudor Navy*, 199.

70. Kamen, *Philip of Spain*, 270–2. 'The English are masters of the sea, and hold it at their discretion', as Ambassador Lippomano reported to the Doge and Senate in May 1587. *Calendar of State Papers, Venetian*, ed. Rawdon Brown *et al.* (London, 1864–98), VIII, 277.

71. Parker and Martin, *The Spanish Armada.*

72. BL Lansdowne MS 56, no. 52, f. 175. Kelsey, *Francis Drake*, 287.

73. Kelsey, *Francis Drake*, 298–9.

74. I.A.A. Thompson, 'The invincible Armada', in *Royal Armada* (London, 1988), 172.

75. In 1596 and 1597; there were also rumours in 1594. Loades, *Tudor Navy*, 269.

76. Kelsey, *Francis Drake*, 377–91.

77. Loades, *Tudor Navy*, 263.

78. BL Cotton MS Otho E IX f. 313. The fullest account of this campaign is in S. and E. Usherwood, *The Counter Armada, 1596* (London, 1983).

79. Usherwood, *Counter Armada*, 84–6.

80. Ibid., 94.

81. 'A project how to make war upon Spain, written in the Queen's time and presented to Sir Robert Cecil, by her Majesty's appointment'; *The Naval Tracts of Sir William Monson*, V, 53–6.

82. For the alleged 'invention' of the galleon by Sir John Hawkins, and the development of this type of ship in England, see Peter Kirsch, *The Galleon* (London, 1990), 3–35. E.G.R. Taylor, *Later Tudor and Early Stuart Geography* (London, 1934).

CHAPTER FIVE

The City of London, the New World and the Navy, 1604–1650

In 1600 the only English experience of establishing successful colonies had been in Ireland. In a sense the English presence in Ireland had always been colonial, but the same could be said of Wales and by the sixteenth century that did not mean very much. In the Dublin Pale, the port towns of the south, and the lordships such as Meath and Limerick, the English had been so long established that it is proper to speak of an Anglo-Irish community. In the same way originally English boroughs in Wales, like Caernarfon and Conway, and areas of English settlement like Montgomeryshire, were not politically distinct by the Elizabethan period. However, there was one major difference. Large parts of Ireland were virtually untouched by English influence, and although in theory Elizabethan Ireland was a single kingdom under the English Crown, in fact the queen's writ did not run in the tribal territories, whereas the whole of Wales was under effective royal government.[1]

As England and Wales moved steadily towards more stable and central-ised administration, from the 1530s onward, feuds and rebellions became endemic in Ireland. Ireland became, like Scotland, a fruitful soil for the generation of conspiracies by England's European enemies. After 1560 Anglo-Scottish relations improved, and although there were occasional scares induced by the chronic instability of Scotland's domestic politics, there was no return to the suspicion and hostility which had dominated the first half of the century. Scotland ceased to be a threat, and the Scottish navy, which had been formidable under James IV, virtually disappeared.[2] Ireland, on the other hand, became progressively more dangerous, and the harder the English tried to make their government effective, the more disaffected the Irish became.[3]

Although the Spanish intervention at Smerwick in 1579 came to nothing, English strategists became increasingly paranoid. Edmund Spenser even went so far as to advocate what we would now call 'ethnic cleansing'.[4] Such a solution would never have been practicable, but a fresh wave of colonisation was attempted. This began in 1555 and 1556 with King's County and Queen's County, designed to protect the Pale from tribal incursions, but most took place during Elizabeth's reign. The Earl of Essex projected an enormous plantation in Antrim in 1572–73, but the eventual settlements were much more modest in scale. As the English government attempted to expand the county system into the tribal lands, indigenous politics became even more violent and fragmented. Lacking the resources to impose a solution by force, the Lord Deputy and his officers attempted to play one chief off against another, but the cooperation which resulted was usually unstable and short-lived. Every unsuccessful rebellion in the tribal lands brought fresh confiscations and dispossessions, and the lands were redistributed, some to Anglo-Irish landlords, and some to 'new' English, who mostly remained absentees.[5] When this was done the Irish tenants normally remained in place, and sensitive estate policies could be made to work reasonably well. In Monaghan in 1592 a sizeable 'native plantation' was created by expelling a rebellious Irish community, and introducing a more tractable one in its place. That also enjoyed some success. However, such moderate courses did not please the more radical on either side, and the very large Munster plantations which began in 1584 were conceived to place over 8,000 English settlers in 20 seignories. Needless to say this grandiose scheme did not work out as intended, and by 1590 there were only approximately 2,000 settlers, who were far more mingled with remaining Irish tenants than had been envisaged.[6] At the same time such large-scale dispossession helped the Earl of Tyrone to rally the forces with which he attempted to fight a war of independence after 1594.

This was the extent of England's colonial experience – a very much larger venture than the 100 who had gone to Roanoke, and very different in its circumstances and context. Although some English writers described the Irish as savages, they were not alien in the same sense as the Amerindians.[7] Irish resentment was probably just as strong, but the English settlers were both more numerous and better protected than the pioneers in the New World, and so were not subject to the same casual depredations. Moreover, the Englishmen who took up tenements in Munster (although not the gentlemen who took up lordships) expected to till the land themselves, and knew how to do it. Politically, the English colonies in Ireland were a mistake, and sowed the seeds of long-term trouble, but economically they worked well, and it was the system of plantation grants used in Munster and in Ulster which was adapted to set up the first colonies in Virginia and Bermuda when these were finally established in 1607 and 1612.[8]

Although the long war with Spain had encouraged thoughts of permanent settlements, they had been the wrong sort of thoughts, and had attracted the wrong type of person. However, a lesson had been learned. Freebooters, whose main aim is to prey on others, do not make good colonists. Nor do hastily contrived adventures take root. After 1604 the enterprise and the capital that for nearly 20 years had been channelled into privateering became available for new activities. The easiest option was ordinary piracy, and many small operators shifted their bases to southern Ireland, and worked out of minor havens like Kinsale and Baltimore, preying on legitimate trade without regard to nationality.[9] However, there was also a more positive spirit abroad. Although the bulk of England's overseas trade, and that which made the great commercial fortunes characteristic of early seventeenth-century London, continued to run into Europe along more or less traditional routes, there was a much greater willingness to risk money in speculative ventures than there had been in the nervous 1570s and 1580s. Then the Crown and Privy Councillors had led and prodded, and a relatively small number of their City friends had responded. After 1604 the Crown was no longer prodding, but that did not matter as the commercial community, backed by an increasingly large number of gentlemen and noblemen, had developed an entrepreneurial momentum of its own. Elizabethan courtiers had become a penurious breed by 1603, but James was a generous master. This caused him all sorts of problems in the long run, but one of the first things it did was to create a new group of rich men, many of them with a gambler's instinct in their makeup. Some of their money went into industrial and mining activity. Coal output increased, new methods were developed for smelting iron, and all sorts of consumer goods were produced: stockings, buttons, pins, nails, salt, starch, tobacco pipes.[10] Growing towns (particularly London) attracted market gardening, and the end of the war also encouraged a revival of established trades, leading to a boom in shipbuilding and its ancillary crafts.

There were, as we have seen, many new companies launched in this period, but even more enterprises operated below that level of organisation, and their collective impact is impossible to quantify. The biggest and most successful operations were conducted by the Levant Company and the East India Company. The former, already well established by 1604, depended largely on the goodwill of the Ottoman authorities, and was therefore adversely affected by political instability. It also had to cope with increasingly ferocious and well-organised piracy from the so-called 'corsair states' of North Africa.[11] In a sense this worked in the company's favour, because although it was expensive to arm and man ships to the level necessary for self-defence, the well-equipped company convoys were much more likely to get through than the individual ships of the interlopers, who might otherwise have constituted formidable competition. The East India Company operated in a much more competitive environment, but showed a capacity for pragmatic adjustment which was unusual among English merchants. Portuguese control over the trade of the Indian Ocean (effectively Spanish control from 1580 to 1640) was waning rapidly, and the main beneficiaries were the Dutch, who established a number of trading posts throughout the East Indies, and a permanent headquarters and fort at Batavia in Indonesia. The English share of this enormous market remained small by comparison, but thirteen voyages between 1601 and 1617 deployed about £500,000 in capital, and brought in a profit which was probably in excess of 100 per cent.[12] Thereafter the margins tightened. The first decade of joint stock (1613–23) deployed £400,000 at a profit of about 87 per cent, and the second decade less again because of the need for increased military activity. However, fresh agreements continued to be negotiated with local rulers, and new trading posts established. These were not colonies in the same sense as Goa or Batavia, and did not represent imperial ambition, but they did represent a commitment which had to be defended. Like the Levant Company, the East India Company traded partly in the 'new draperies', and partly in consumer goods; but it also purchased part of its extremely valuable importation in cash. Although this increased the profit margin rather than diminishing it, it was anathema to the economic purists of the period, and the company was subject to heavy criticism.

The fortunes of England's European trade fluctuated. Legitimate trade with Spain revived strongly, while that with France also benefited from the new stability of that country. With the virtual demise of the Hanse, the traditional cloth trade of the Merchant Adventurers now went mainly to Middleburg and Hamburg. The export of unfinished shortcloths went up from 125,000 to about 144,000 between 1604 and 1614.[13] However, this development was virtually sabotaged in the latter year, when the king was persuaded to forbid the export of unfinished cloth in the interest of building up the English finishing industry. A new company, the King's Merchant Venturers, was set up to handle this trade. The scheme collapsed within three years, partly because there was little demand for finished English shortcloth, and partly because of the powerful resentment of the dispossessed Merchant Adventurers.[14] By 1620 the traditional trade had been re-established, but the export figure for that year was 95,000, and the boom level of 1614 was never recovered.[15] The future of the English textile trade did not lie with shortcloths, finished or unfinished, but with finished kerseys and other lighter cloths, the export figures for which went up by some 250 per cent during James's reign. The Muscovy and Eastland companies saw a sharp downturn after 1610, largely because of political instability in Russia, and there was a general 'decay of trade' over much of western Europe between 1620 and 1625, on account of the return to war. The Dutch defied this general trend, in spite of their direct involvement in hostilities, because the Estates General, unlike James I, or Louis XIII, or Philip III, understood the economies of warfare.[16] The English parliament did succeed in 1624 in compelling James to acknowledge the error of his ways, and to withdraw some of his interventionist policies, but parliament had only a negative voice in the shaping of policy, and England's own involvement in the war soon after checked a number of promising developments.

In spite of crises, misconceived policies, and the growing threat of the Dutch, English commerce grew significantly during James's reign, and thanks largely to success in the Mediterranean and the Far East, merchant shipping increased both in number and in size. At the same time the first true colonies stuttered into uncertain life. The object of the Virginia Company, founded in 1606, was profit. The original idea was to establish a settlement within reach of the Spanish colonies, not for the purposes of plunder, but of trade, particularly in sugar and tobacco. It was also believed that such a settlement would absorb at least a part of England's surplus and unemployed population. Both expectations proved false.[17] Spain was as determined to keep foreign traders out of the Caribbean and Central America as it had been during the war, and by 1607 had successfully suppressed the tobacco trade from New Granada. Similar trade from Trinidad continued for a while, but by 1612 that had gone as well, so almost as soon as Jamestown was founded in 1607 its *raison d'être* disappeared. Chesapeake Bay was not particularly healthy, and the 144 original colonists were no better prepared than their predecessors at Roanoke. They traded for food with the local Indians, and began in a rather haphazard way to look for gold. Within a year three-quarters of them were dead.[18]

Two things saved Jamestown from rapid extinction. The first was the existence in London of a parent company which was determined to succeed and had considerable resources, and the second was their choice of the right man to take over the settlement. Captain John Smith took the first and most essential step to survival when he compelled all the colonists, whatever their status, to work the land and grow food.[19] Despite the continuing attrition of accident and disease, this survival strategy worked, thanks to the willingness (and ability) of the company to keep up a steady stream of new settlers, including a sensible proportion of women. As the settlement expanded, relations with the neighbouring Algonquin tribes deteriorated, and an Indian war in 1622 cost 300 lives.[20] Thereafter the colonists were not only more careful of their defences, they also felt entitled to expropriate as much Algonquin land as they wanted by right of conquest. By that time they had also found a cash crop profitable enough to make them self-sufficient. Although Spain was again allowing a limited tobacco trade, there were obvious advantages in encouraging Virginian production, and imports from the Spanish lands were subjected to quota. This did not come in time to save the Virginia Company, which collapsed in insolvency in 1624, but it did persuade James and his council to continue the now modestly thriving colony, which was placed under Crown control, with a royal governor and a popular assembly.[21]

In 1625 the population of Virginia was about 1,200. Even in the improved conditions after the Indian war, some 5,000 of the 7,000 who had gone out from England had died. However, by 1630 the corner had been turned. The remaining Algonquin were expelled from the area between the James and York rivers, and by 1642 the population had reached somewhere between 8,000 and 10,000, including a first generation born in the colony.[22] Some grants of land were made to favoured courtiers or soldiers, in the same way as in Ireland, but the major expansion was caused by the establishment of tobacco syndicates which undertook to settle a given acreage. A large proportion of the second wave of colonists came out as indentured servants to work on these estates, sometimes induced by promises, sometimes virtually kidnapped, and sometimes to escape from even less promising circumstances at home.[23] Tobacco continued to be the economic mainstay of the colony, but subsistence farming also developed, together with local crafts and industries, although most manufactured goods continued to be imported from England. With the removal of the Indian threat, isolated farms and small hamlets spread, although not all the outlying settlements survived for a variety of reasons. A separate colony established by the Virginia Company on Bermuda in 1612 was also taken over by the Crown in 1624, and survived by the cultivation of tobacco.[24] Another Jamestown, established by a different company on St Kitts in 1628, also remained, but attempts in Guyana and further south on the Amazon came to nothing.

Virginia and Bermuda had both been established primarily for economic reasons, but other colonies also appeared during this period quite differently motivated. Maryland, just to the north of Virginia, was a proprietary colony, granted in 1632 to Sir George Calvert, Lord Baltimore. Calvert was a Catholic convert who intended the colony to be a refuge for his disadvantaged co-religionists. Some did indeed go, but within about 20 years the social and economic composition of the colony was very similar to that of Virginia; however it remained much smaller, numbering less than 1,000 in 1640.[25] By contrast, the New England colonies were distinctive from the beginning. The New England Company, which was chartered in 1620, was an offshoot of the Virginia Company, and was empowered to colonise any land between the Atlantic and the Pacific which lay between the latitudes of 40 and 48 degrees north. The company itself soon became nothing more than an agency for the leasing of concessions, and that may have been the intention behind it.[26] Its first concessionaries, however, were the so-called Pilgrim Fathers: 102 men, women and children who made their landfall at Cape Cod, and established a settlement at New Plymouth, in what was later to be Massachusetts, before the end of 1620. These people, who originated from Lincolnshire and East Anglia, were separatists who had broken away from the Church of England in the last decade of the sixteenth century. In 1607 they had migrated to the Low Countries to escape the attentions of the ecclesiastical authorities, and their intention was to establish a free and Godly commonwealth in the wilderness of North America.[27] Even the Godly need money, and the 1620 voyage was funded, to the tune of about £7,000, by sympathetic merchants and bankers of London, to be repaid out of the profits of fur trading and fishing.[28] Almost half of the original settlers died in the first winter, but the survivors were tough, and strongly motivated. They were prepared to do whatever they had to do to realise their vision, and they were joined by a steady trickle of like-minded volunteers. They were also fortunate in one important respect. The indigenous population in the immediate neighbourhood of the settlement had cleared much of the forest, and then conveniently died of the plague, leaving their clearings to be used, and no one to dispute the right to the land. By 1622 they had created a self-supporting village of about 300 people, centred on the church, and capably led by William Bradford.

In that year they were visited by John Pory, the former secretary of the Virginia Company, who knew both settlements, and his description in a letter to the Earl of Southampton is illuminating:

the harbour is not only pleasant for air and prospect, but most sure for shipping, both small and great, being land locked on all sides. The town is seated on the ascent of a hill . . . such is the wholesomeness of the place (as the Governor told me) that for the space of one whole year of the two wherein they had been there, died not one man, woman nor child. The healthfulness is accompanied with much plenty both of fish and fowl every day of the year, as I know no place in the world that can match it . . . From the beginning of September until the end of March their bay in a manner is covered with all sorts of water fowl . . . Touching their fruit, I will not speak of their meaner sort, as of rasps, cherries, gooseberries, strawberries, delicate plums and others, but they have commonly through the country five sorts of grapes, some whereof I tasted, being fairer and larger than any I saw in the South Colony [Virginia] . . . So much of the wholesomeness and plenty of the country. Now as concerning the quality of the people, how happy were it for our people in the Southern Colony if they were as free from wickedness and vice as these are in this place. And their industry as well appeareth by their building, as by a substantial palisade about their [town] of 2700 foot in compass, stronger than any I have seen in Virginia, and lastly by a blockhouse which they have erected in the highest place of the town to mount their ordnance upon, from whence they command all the harbour . . .[29]

Few communities can have received a warmer testimonial, but without either royal or aristocratic patronage, it grew only slowly. However, the example it had set was influential. A similar group from the West of England settled what was later to be Salem in the 1620s,[30] and in 1629 the Massachusetts Bay Company was formed. This was very much a symptom of the times, because it had the support of aristocrats, gentry and lawyers as well as merchants. These men were Puritans, not in the sense of being radical separatists like the New Plymouth colonists, but in the sense of being on what we might now call the 'left wing' of the established church. Ten years earlier they would have seen no need to promote a refuge on the other side of the Atlantic, but Charles I, who had succeeded his father in 1625, was moving the political and religious goal posts. Having fallen out with his parliament, he had dissolved it in 1629, firmly resolved not to call it again. He was also patronising and promoting within the church those clergy misleadingly called 'Arminians', whose ambition was the restoration of sacramental theology, and their own authority.[31] Charles was not a crypto-Catholic, but he allowed himself to be represented as one, and he had married a French Catholic wife whose missionary zeal he regarded with indulgence.

The appeal of a Godly commonwealth spread from the separatists to earnest mainstream Protestants, who had very much more social and financial clout. Boston was founded in 1630, and like New Plymouth survived the difficult early months by self-discipline and tenacity of purpose. Thereafter, however, its fortunes reflected the very much wider constituency from which it was drawn. By 1635 8,000 had joined the colony. Most paid their own passages, and many, by subscribing to the company, obtained 200-acre grants similar to those enjoyed by the more substantial recruits to Virginia.[32] As at New Plymouth the indigenous population had been much weakened by disease, and the survivors were either conciliated or driven away. John Winthrop, the first Governor, was as able and determined as William Bradford, and created a similarly disciplined, God-fearing community. Only it was on a vastly greater scale, well organised for its own defence, and commercially aggressive almost from the start. By 1642 it numbered over 15,000, which made it larger than Virginia and Maryland combined, and it greatly exceeded both political and economic development.

On the eve of the civil war in England, there were some 50,000 English colonists in North America. James had approved a plan in 1621 for a

Scottish colony in what was later to be Nova Scotia, and after preliminary reconnaissance in the 1620s, some settlements were established there by 1640.[33] Apart from these, only small French trading settlements around Quebec and a Dutch outpost at New Amsterdam challenged what was rapidly becoming an English dominance. Massachusetts was the pace setter in every way. Unlike either Maryland or Virginia, its settlers arrived mainly in family groups, and although there were a few gentry and indentured servants, the great majority were yeomen or substantial craftsmen by status. They had no interest in seeking either gold or conquest, but were intensely concerned to run their own affairs without outside interference. The literacy and educational levels were higher than in any other colony, and this was reflected in the foundation of Harvard College, the first institution of higher education in North America, in 1636. Not surprisingly, such rapid expansion produced tensions, and minor differences of opinion over church government produced breakaway settlements in Connecticut and Rhode Island between 1636 and 1639.[34] At the same time the government of Charles I began to wake up to the nature of England's rapidly growing offspring, and to realise that it had virtually no control. Both Maryland and Virginia were amenable to government agents, but not Massachusetts. In 1638 it was ordered to submit its charter for scrutiny, and refused. When the charter was condemned by the Privy Council in the same year, the decision was ignored, and Charles was contemplating the use of force against the recalcitrant colonists when more immediate crises engulfed him.[35]

Unlike Virginia, Massachusetts had no dominant cash crop which it could trade in European markets. Nor did it produce raw materials which were in demand. On the other hand, it could produce more than enough food for its own needs, and began to export to Virginia and Maryland. It exported cattle to the West Indies, and corn to New Plymouth in return for fish. There were virtually no ties of dependence to the mother country, but by 1640 something more than individual congregations and village assemblies was needed by way of government, and the twin pillars upon which the new polity were built were Protestantism and the common law. Whereas both Virginia and Maryland had imported something akin to an English social structure, and were dominated by gentry families, some of whom had acquired that status only in America, Massachusetts, true to it origins, was dominated by the Godly. So dominant were the ministers, and so seriously did they take their regiment, that full political rights were restricted to those of whom they approved. The success and rapid expansion of the colony between 1630 and 1640 had attracted many who acquiesced in the theocracy of the ministers rather than supporting it, and such were not admitted to the franchise, which embraced no more than 20 per cent of the adult men – rather less than 10 per cent of the total adult population.[36] All the magistrates and public officers of every kind were drawn from this small minority, which had relatively little difficulty in retaining either its unity or its ascendancy.

The civil war was not transported across the Atlantic, and there was no fighting in the New World. Bermuda, which was the smallest colony, imposed a strict neutrality upon its members, fining anyone who attempted to proselytise for either party. Virginia and Maryland, particularly the latter, were royalist in sentiment, but only a handful returned to fight for the king, and no attempt was made in the colonies to reject the parliamentary victory. The New England colonies, predictably, took the other side, and a significant number returned to take part. Some of these had always seen Massachusetts as a temporary expedient, and when there was a Godly party to fight for at home, they saw that as their proper place. Several of the most radical Independent officers and preachers had matured their convictions in America, and were not at ease with the relative conservatism of the Protectorate.[37] In spite of the defeat of Charles I, England did not become the New Jerusalem, and many of them had returned to Massachusetts well before the Restoration.

The return of Europe to large-scale war after 1618 benefited English commerce in several ways. Although never as successful as the Dutch, English ships were able to pick up part of the carrying trade between belligerents, and this was particularly true in the Mediterranean where the large and well-armed ships of the Levant Company offered almost the only security against the depredations of the corsairs. The East India Company developed a profitable sideline in carrying Spanish and Portuguese goods from the Far East, and even Spanish goods and bullion to Europe from the New World.[38] The English merchant marine, which had totalled about 70,000 tons on the eve of the war with Spain, in 1585, had risen by some 75 per cent to 115,000 tons by 1629, and was still increasing.[39] English shipwrights never equalled the Dutch *fluyt* for economic bulk carrying in European waters, but were producing warships and large armed merchantmen which were as good as, or better than, those of their rivals.[40] Also the re-export trade, which was to become so important later in the century, was beginning to become significant. Spices and tobacco, in particular, were being redistributed from London in significant quantities on the eve of the civil war, and although London could not compete with Amsterdam in Far Eastern goods, she actually did more trade in tobacco, thanks to the growing productivity of the plantations in Virginia. The peaceful 20 years or so which followed 1604 also encouraged the Newfoundland fisheries, where the English ascendancy of the early sixteenth century had long since been overtaken by the French. However, after the end of the war there were again more than 300 ships making the hazardous crossing to the Newfoundland banks every year, and large quantities of cod, usually dried or salted, were being passed on to the Mediterranean, where the dietary rules of the Catholic Church continued to be a blessing to Protestant fishermen.

The chief beneficiary of these changes was the City of London. Although London had always been the greatest city in England, and a powerful financial centre, in the first half of the sixteenth century it had been no more in international terms than a major satellite of Antwerp. The decline of Antwerp after 1550, and particularly after 1576, created new opportunities, and the two main beneficiaries were Amsterdam and London.[41] In the early seventeenth century Amsterdam was doing better, thanks to the extraordinary success of the Dutch East India Company (the Verenigde Oost-Indische Compagnie, or VOC) and thanks also to the fact that it was a newcomer to the 'Premier League', which was unusually free to adapt to new opportunities.[42] London found this harder because of the entrenched power of the Merchant Adventurers. Although some Adventurers were prepared to invest in speculative enterprises, most of the money for the new companies came from merchants of other companies, or from outside the commercial community altogether. As we have seen, as late as 1602 north-western Europe was still taking about 75 per cent of England's exports, and providing nearly 70 per cent of its imports; and that meant mainly the Merchant Adventurers. However, the crisis of 1614–17, artificial as it was, broke this mould to the city's lasting advantage. By 1635 only 35 per cent of London's imports was coming from north-western Europe, while 44 per cent was coming from the eastern Mediterranean, 11 per cent from the Far East and 5 per cent from North America.[43] Although the corresponding export figures did not match these exactly, they were in approximately the same proportion.

By the 1630s the big fortunes were being made in the Levant and East India companies. The Merchant Adventurers recovered their traditional monopoly in 1634, but by then the textile trade had fragmented, and those parts of it which came outside the Adventurers' control were more thriving than those which it covered. Between 1600 and 1625 about 25 per cent of the new Aldermen elected were Merchant Adventurers. By 1640 some 50 per cent were members of the Levant and East India companies, although some of these were Merchant Adventurers as well. Only about 10 per cent were exclusively traders into northern Europe.[44] This shift of commercial orientation had a major impact on the East London shipbuilders. In the 1560s the greatest fleet operating out of the Thames was that of the Merchant Adventurers, which numbered about 30 ships, all under 100 tons. Bigger ships were built, of course, but mainly on the Medway and the south coast. But the demands first of privateering and then of long-distance trade changed this situation dramatically. Between 1591 and 1619 over 300 ships exceeding 100 tons were built on the Thames, a total of over 90,000 tons, and by far the largest element in the overall increase of merchant tonnage.[45] East Indiamen, particularly, needed to be large and sturdy – updated versions of the great carracks which had served the Portuguese so well. At first this imitation was taken too literally, and the enormous *Trades Increase* of 1,000 tons, built at Deptford in 1605, sank on its maiden voyage. Thereafter these large galleons averaged a rather less ambitious 500 tons, which was perfectly adequate for their purpose.

The expansion of England's trade between 1604 and 1650 was very much against the odds. For ten years the circumstances were favourable, but then came the disruptions resulting from Sir William Cockayne's attempt to foster the English cloth-finishing industry, the outbreak of European war, and the collapse of the Virginia Company. From 1625 to 1629 England was herself at war, and both James and Charles tried to extract extra revenue from customs and other levies. By 1638 there was rebellion in Scotland, and from 1642 to 1649 full-scale civil war in all the three kingdoms of Britain. Both in the European carrying trade and in the Far East the English were trailing far behind the Dutch, and yet it was a successful period, during which the volume and the value of overseas trade grew significantly. The main reason for this was the shift of emphasis from northern Europe, where all trade was seriously disrupted, to the Levant, the Far East and America. Failure to compete with the Dutch in the orient was relative. Some factories had to close for that reason, and there were even armed clashes which ended in defeat, but the region was enormous and very diverse. Unable to make an impression in one place, the company moved on somewhere else, and its profits were never less than 60 or 70 per cent per voyage.[46] The Dutch were the commercial giants of the early seventeenth century, and after 1621 were driven by the need to fund their renewed war of independence. Trade with Persia, which failed to operate through the Muscovy Company, was able to go in through the Levant or the Indian Ocean. American trade, at first mainly in tobacco, became increasingly diversified as the colonies grew, and although the West African trade remained small-scale, it was largely uninterrupted by the conflicts in Europe.[47] The diversification of trade, which had been the subject of half a century of thought and experimentation, actually happened during this period on a significant scale, and that left England second only to Holland as a commercial power when it emerged from the political upheavals of the 1640s.

At the same time, and somewhat paradoxically, English power at sea conspicuously failed to develop. The warning signs were already there by 1600, but they were not obvious to the world at large. As late as 1599 the Admiralty, alarmed by Spanish mobilisation in the Low Countries, rigged, fitted out and victualled eighteen warships in twelve days. Such a feat was regarded with amazement. 'The Queen', wrote Sir William Monson, 'was never more dreaded abroad for anything she ever did.'[48] Nevertheless, all was not well with the Navy Board. Part of the problem lay in Elizabeth's pathological reluctance to spend money, and her willingness to embrace unsound schemes which promised economies. The officers' salaries and expenses had not been increased since the Board was formed 60 years before, a period which had seen inflation of at least 100 per cent, and seamen's wages had been raised only once, in 1585.

A second problem was the patronage system. Until the 1580s the queen had determined admiralty appointments herself, or accepted the advice of Lord Burghley. However, by the time Burghley died in 1598, Lord Admiral Howard, who had become Earl of Nottingham in 1597, had engrossed the whole system. 'The Lord Admiral', wrote Sir John Coke, 'hath drawn into his hands not only the appointments of captains and commanders, but of all clerks of the cheque, masters, boatswains, pursers, stewards, cooks, smiths, joiners, carpenters, sailmakers and all manner of workmen.'[49] Nottingham was not personally corrupt, but he did allow his kinsman Sir Robert Mansell, who became Treasurer in 1604, a free hand. Mansell and Sir John Trevor, the Surveyor since 1598, exploited the control over appointments which Nottingham allowed them, exclusively for financial gain.[50] Every position was sold at a going rate (£20 for a boatswain, £30 for a cook, £100 for a purser etc.) without regard to the suitability of the candidate. This did not necessarily mean that the navy became full of well-off incompetents. What it did tend to mean was that the grantee, who would be a friend or dependant of one of the officers, would then sell on the appointment he had purchased at a slightly enhanced rate to the man who actually wanted to do the job. This in turn meant that practically everyone who held a position above that of ordinary sailor was trying to recover his outlay, and turn his appointment to profit, over and above the pay which he would legitimately receive.

The impact of this can be seen in a number of ways. Everyone who purchased supplies, whether it was Mansell and Trevor buying timber in bulk, or a sailmaker buying extra thread and needles, charged double what he had paid, and falsified the invoices.[51] Services were similarly overcharged. Every officer who went to sea paid himself at an admiral's rate; every clerk who hired a horse or a boat in the course of his duties doubled his outlay. Phineas Pett, the Chief Shipwright, was hand in glove with Trevor and Mansell. In 1605, with their connivance, he built and fitted out a vessel called the *Resistance* at the king's expense, and then leased it to the Crown as his own ship![52] Such practices also spread down the line. Boatswains cut lengths of cable and sold them, so that cables which were recorded as being of 90 fathoms were in fact only 60. Old junks were sold instead of being turned into oakum, so that the ships were not properly caulked; green timber was purchased as mature, and sometimes used as such. Nor was it only the Exchequer which suffered. 'Dead pays', whereby officers claimed wages for non-existent men as a perquisite for themselves, was an ancient and, up to a point, legitimate practice. It was, however, subject to a fixed and recognised percentage. To exceed that meant either falsifying the muster rolls to return men as paid who were not present and never had been, or simply to withold payment from men who had actually worked, particularly if they were sick and in no condition to protest. The *Answer* was at sea in 1605 with only 70 of the 100 men on her muster roll, which meant a profit of 17s 6d a month to her officers in victuals alone.[53] Fraud over pay at the expense of ordinary seamen or workmen was nothing new, but by the early seventeenth century it was reaching an unprecedented level, and adding hugely to the difficulty of manning the king's ships. Victualling was similarly vulnerable to malpractice. It had long since been complained that tubs of salt beef turned out to be one-third brine, but now it was alleged that victuallers, pursers, and even cooks, were selling good provisions, and feeding the men with rotten or reject stock which they had picked up for next to nothing. It is not surprising that seamen fell sick, deserted, or swore that they would be hanged rather than serve in the navy. 'Everyone practiseth to accomplish his own end of profit, not caring how he hath it as long as he may come by it.'[54]

It was claimed that fraud cost the Admiralty over £39,000 between 1605 and 1608, and nobody could quantify the decline in efficiency and morale. However, neither unrestrained greed nor the negligence and complaisance of the Admiral explain entirely this deplorable situation. During the war the queen had exploited the patriotism of her subjects. Not only had men like the Earl of Cumberland spent far more than they recovered in privateering operations, but regular service was paid late, and in many cases not at all. In 1625 Sir Thomas Button was still owed £3,615 for services which he had performed under Elizabeth.[55] Perhaps it is not surprising that Button was one of the most shamelessly corrupt sea officers of James's reign.

Neither the king nor Robert Cecil, Earl of Salisbury from 1605 and chief minister until his death in 1612, cared very much about the navy. It had cost about £55,000 a year during the last decade of the war, which was remarkably cheap for a service still in good working order, and those charges should have been about halved by the return of peace. However, for reasons which we have seen, that did not happen. After coming down briefly to about £40,000 a year, by 1610 the costs were again amounting to over £50,000, and that was not cheap for peacetime, particularly for a service which was not in good order. There should have been, and were, honest naval officers who complained bitterly about the state of affairs. Unfortunately the action which was taken was not disinterested, and its failure was therefore predictable. Henry Howard, Earl of Northampton, a kinsman and political enemy of the Lord Admiral, saw in these well-founded grievances a golden opportunity to discredit Nottingham. He secured two separate but related commissions of enquiry, one into the navy as a whole, and one specifically into the circumstances of the building of a new great ship which Phineas Pett had in hand, and which had been the subject of particular complaint.[56] Both commissions sat in 1608, and produced damning reports. Mansell, it was concluded, had made an illicit profit of £12,000 in four years from the sale of stores, and had embezzled £1,000 in a single year from the wages account.[57] Other officers were equally culpable, although not on such a grand scale, and the evidence recorded makes absolutely convincing reading. At the same time Pett's professional activities were similarly exposed: fraud in the purchase of timber, shoddy workmanship, false accounting, and so on. James, however, had no will to act. In spite of the reports, he was convinced that the attacks were motivated principally by political malice, and chose to support Nottingham rather than Northampton. He gave Mansell and Trevor a mild lecture on the merits of honesty, and went down to Deptford in person to name Pett's new creation the *Prince Royal*.[58] All three carried on as before, and it was not long before the strictures upon Pett's workmanship began to be justified.[59]

Northampton died in 1614, and by then the political landscape at court was changing. Both Salisbury and Prince Henry had died in 1612, and the king's financial affairs were declining from difficulty into disaster. The parliament of 1614 refused any support, except at a political price which James was not willing to pay, and some policy of retrenchment became unavoidable. Lionel Cranfield, an astute London businessman and financier who had been appointed Master of Requests in 1616, showed the way with a thorough overhaul of the royal household, and in 1618 the king's new favourite, George Villiers, Marquis of Buckinghham, joined the reforming party. Buckingham's motives were not much more disinterested than Northampton's had been – he was an enemy of the Howards – but he was in a much better position to be effective.[60] A new commission was appointed, headed by Cranfield and including men of integrity with specialist knowledge, such as Sir John Coke. Both the evidence and the conclusions were very similar to those of ten years before:

And which of all is the most inconvenient, they are the warrants and vouchers for the issuing of all his Majesty's monies and stores, who are most interested in the greatness of his expense; and therefore the business ever was and is still so carried, that neither due survey is taken of ought that cometh in, nor orderly warrant given for most that goeth out . . .[61]

The blame was laid, not on the aged Nottingham, who had long since retreated from any direct involvement, but upon those whom he had appointed to office. This time, however, the commission's recommendations went far beyond the reform of corrupt procedures, or the dismissal of individuals. Repeating the exercise of 1559, a new establishment was suggested of 30 ships: four 'ships royal' of 900–1,200 tons, fourteen 'great ships' of 600–800 tons, six 'middling ships' of about 450 tons, two small ships of 350 tons and four pinnaces.[62] This fleet would be smaller in the number of ships than Elizabeth's navy (or Henry VIII's) at its largest, but would be greater in tonnage and firepower. Sweeping changes of management were also recommended, on the grounds that the traditional structure had fallen apart, and that the old distinctions of function no longer applied. Mansell had already resigned as Treasurer, and in November 1618 the Privy Council summoned all the remaining officers and asked whether they were prepared to accept the commission's recommendations. Since this would have involved accepting a complete indictment of their own conduct, it is not surprising that they refused.[63] Sir Richard Bingley the Surveyor and Sir Guildford Slingsby the Controller were then suspended on full pay and the Admiralty was put into commission. In January 1619 Nottingham retired as Lord Admiral, and was replaced by Buckingham.

The new commissioners consisted, for the most part, of those who had conducted the investigation, so they knew what they were taking on. A new Treasurer was appointed in the person of Sir William Russell, a London banker and shipowner, but the leader and driving force of the new team was Sir John Coke.[64] The support of Cranfield and Buckingham ensured that adequate funds were forthcoming from the Exchequer, and the overall cost was reduced from £53,000 in 1618 to £30,000 in 1624, in spite of pay rises for the officers, and an increase in the seamen's rate from 10s a month to 14s.[65] Shipbuilding was concentrated at Deptford, where eleven new launches took place between 1619 and 1623, nine of them of ships exceeding 400 tons. In 1618 there had been 23 serviceable and 10 unserviceable ships on the books, and in 1624 there were 35, all fit for the sea.[66] By the time that James died in 1624 his navy was ostensibly more effective and better administered than at any time since his accession. However, the appearance was deceptive. The only operation of any significance to be conducted during the reign, a campaign against the Algerian corsairs in 1620–21, was an expensive failure, largely because men with the relevant skill and experience either to prepare or to lead such an expedition were no longer available. For all their conscientiousness and (relative) honesty, the new commissioners did not have these qualities, and the partner groups which Elizabeth might have called upon to supply the navy's deficiencies were either preoccupied with their own affairs, or unavailable for some other reason.[67] Consequently, although Charles inherited a fleet which was much more powerful in ships and guns than that of 1603, it was actually less powerful in relative terms, because both France and Holland had made immense strides over the previous 20 years. It was also largely untested as an instrument of war.

Between 1625 and 1630 its limitations were cruelly exposed, partly by war and partly by the increasing depredations of North African raiders. In 1625 'Turkish' pirates captured prizes within Plymouth Sound, and over 1,000 fishermen from Devon and Cornwall were carried off into slavery. The village of East Looe lost 80 men in ten days in 1626, and although that was an extreme case, it was not untypical.[68] The carefully nurtured royal navy seemed to be incapable of doing anything about it, and it is interesting to speculate what John Hawkins or Francis Drake would have said! In spite of this, by 1625 the English were suffering from delusions of grandeur. They not only believed that they had won the last sea war against Spain, but that they had made a profit out of it. Here, therefore, was the perfect way to help the beleaguered Protestant cause in Europe, and to force the Habsburgs to restore the Palatinate to Frederick V. Moreover, it was a way which could give the king no possible excuse to demand the extravagant financial support which he was always seeking. Such naivety may well have convinced the king and his ministers that they were dealing with a bunch of country bumpkins, but unfortunately the members of the House of Commons who were urging this policy upon him were not only powerful men in their own communities, they were also the same men who were making such a success of investing in the Levant and East India companies, and busying themselves in the American colonies. In 1625 both Charles and parliament wanted war, but there was complete disagreement about how much it would cost, and how the money was to be found.[69]

In the event, it was decided to attack Cadiz by sea, perhaps for no better reason than that the two previous attacks, in 1587 and 1596, had been successful. The result was military failure and logistical disaster. The commander, Viscount Wimbledon, was a competent soldier with no seafaring experience. His battle orders show some tactical intelligence, but no gift for command. Most of his officers were both inexperienced and inept, owing their promotions to their courtly connections with Buckingham rather than any capacity to do the job required.[70] Experienced seamen were available, but were kept in subordinate positions. At the same time the sudden demands of large-scale mobilisation blew apart the fragile victualling and supply systems, which were no more than adequate in peacetime. Food arrived late, in insufficient quantities and poor condition; clothing did not arrive at all. Before the expedition was half over the commander was at loggerheads with his rebellious captains, and those men who had not had the energy or initiative to desert were naked and starving.[71] The ships arrived at Cadiz in no fit state to fight, and retreated ignominiously. It was almost irrelevant that the ships themselves were well found, and their guns in excellent condition. Buckingham had either forgotten, or had never known, that victories at sea are not won only by good weapons and heroics. Without trained captains and efficient support services, even the best of fleets can achieve nothing. The Cadiz expedition cost thousands of lives, almost entirely by starvation and disease, and something approaching £500,000 in cash. In spite of having voted over £400,000 in 1624 and 1625, in 1626 parliament was informed that the war debt stood at over £1 million, of which £313,000 was still owed for the Cadiz expedition.[72]

Characteristically, Buckingham blamed everybody but himself, and the man who in the early 1620s had looked like the saviour of the navy by 1626 was looking suspiciously like its nemesis. Early in 1627 the Huguenot revolt in France, in which the English had become ambiguously embroiled, resulted in an open rupture with that country, and Charles found himself in the unprecedented situation of being at war with France and Spain at the same time. In both 1627 and 1628 the main efforts were focused on the relief of the Huguenot stronghold of La Rochelle. In July English troops were landed on the Ile de Rhé, but they accomplished nothing, and were withdrawn in October.[73] In spite of the lessons of Cadiz, many of the same mistakes were repeated with similar, if less extreme, results, and another £500,000 was spent to no purpose. In May and September 1628 further relief expeditions were sent out, but failed to penetrate the blockade, and in October 1628 the fortress fell, thus virtually ending the Huguenot revolt, and opening the way for a negotiated peace, which was achieved in 1630.

English fleets did operate during these years in other contexts, and held their own in what might be termed strategic deployment, but by 1628 they had conclusively proved themselves incapable of carrying out a major military operation successfully. Not since the fifteenth century had the English navy been so consistently humiliated. The Lord Admiral, however, did not live either to extricate himself from this mess, or to redeem it. He was assassinated in August 1628, a fact which probably saved him from impeachment, but did nothing to relieve tension between the king and the House of Commons. The Commons refused to be convinced that their own parsimony had been partly responsible for the fiascos, and rightly pointed to the sheer lack of professionalism which afflicted the navy at all levels. Men like Benjamin Gonson, William Winter and John Hawkins, who had moved amphibiously between the navy and private seafaring ventures, no longer served Charles I in the way they had served Elizabeth. Civil servants could keep a peacetime navy in being, and even service it to a respectable standard, but they could not turn it into an efficient fighting arm, and the whole patronage system which Buckingham had controlled had militated against the appointment of competent officers. They were not corrupt in the sense that Nottingham and Mansell's appointments had been corrupt 20 years before, but they were untrained, inexperienced, and often temperamentally unsuited for their responsibilities.[74]

Buckingham's death, and Charles's decision in 1629 to break off diplomatic relations with his parliament, spelt further change for the navy. The duke himself had realised that his reformed administration could not cope with active service. Even a fleet sent on an ordinary winter patrol in 1626 had been inadequately equipped and provisioned. A further commission had been instituted, but abandoned in 1627 and the old Navy Board reconstituted in February 1628.[75] The situation had been further complicated by the ill-defined relationship between the Lord Admiral and the navy commissioners on the one hand and the Council of War, which was a committee of the Privy Council, on the other. This had caused confusion and acrimony, but had been saved from worse consequences by the appointment of Sir John Coke as a Secretary of State in 1625, because he was able to ensure that the right hand knew what the left hand was doing.[76] For a few months after Buckingham's death the office of Lord Admiral was in commission, until the appointment of Lord Weston in September. Neither Weston nor his successors (there were four admirals in a decade) were of much significance. The Navy Board became in effect a Privy Council committee, and Charles, who was much more interested in the navy than his father had been, made the important decisions himself. Bitterly as he mourned his friend, Buckingham's death was a benefit to the king in many ways. Most importantly, it spelt the end of that personal patronage system which had dominated so much office-holding since 1603. Charles was not impervious to influence, but he had no more personal favourites. Like Elizabeth, he made important appointments himself, and although he did not always make good ones he did at least make them for valid reasons. He also ensured that his officers were properly accountable, and after 1630 that corruption which had tainted every aspect of public life for a generation largely disappeared.[77]

However, corruption and patronage had not been the only troubles to afflict the Stuart navy. Even when it was honestly administered, as it was mainly after 1618, there was never enough money. Sir Alan Apsley, who took over the victualling contract in 1613, and who was allowed $7\frac{1}{2}$d per man in harbour and 8d at sea, was always struggling even in peacetime. In 1625 he needed £45,000 in advance ('prest') to victual Wimbledon's fleet. He did not get it, and had to improvise as best he could. When the sailing was delayed by other considerations, the victuals deteriorated, with the consequences we have seen. By the end of 1627 the Crown owed him

£41,000, and £100,000 by the time he died in 1630.[78] Apsley was not corrupt, and he was not incompetent, but victualling was a disaster area throughout the war. Sir James Bagg, Apsley's deputy at Plymouth, was corrupt, at least to the extent of not keeping proper accounts, but even he was owed about £25,000 at the same time. Attempts were made both in 1627 and 1628 to raise money by special levies, but both had to be abandoned in the face of opposition from a parliament which obstinately refused to understand how much an effective navy must cost. With the return of peace, the situation improved. Local agreements were negotiated with particular ports to provide naval protection in return for victuals and men. Another projected expedition against the Barbary corsairs was abandoned in 1633 for lack of means, but in the same year the shipbuilding programme was re-started, and there were eleven new launches in nine years, including the massive and revolutionary *Sovereign of the Seas* of 1,500 tons, in 1637.[79] Ship Money, which was officially a levy in lieu of service rather than a tax, raised £800,000 between 1634 and 1640, and funded much of this building programme. The money was paid direct to the Treasurer of the Navy, and accounted separately from the normal income.[80]

The king did his best to make his navy impressive, because it was the only instrument of foreign policy which he could afford, even with the new revenue. Ambitiously, he attempted to revive the ancient doctrine of the *mare clausum*, and attempted to demand recognition, at least within the Narrow Seas.[81] Sometimes this wish was respected when the other party was in a complacent frame of mind, and Charles was probably led to believe that his policy was more successful than it was. Confrontations with the Dutch in 1636 and 1637 failed to impose licence fees on Dutch fishermen in English waters, and the depredations both of the North Africans and of the Dunkirkers continued unchecked. The imposing great ships which made up the summer fleets might suggest (as they were intended to) that England was back in business as a naval power. Unfortunately the reality was rather different. Although the navy possessed a few fast pinnaces, capable of matching the raiders if they were in the vicinity, they were seldom in the right place at the right time, and the commercial community, apart from the great companies which could look after themselves, believed that they were paying through the nose for the king's futile posturings.[82] The only success of this period was, significantly, an old-fashioned partnership operation against the pirate base of Sallee (now Rabat). Two naval ships and two armed merchantmen, with a few small support ships under the command of William Rainsborough, sailed in 1637. Rainsborough was an experienced seaman (who would later have been called a 'tarpaulin'), and by making intelligent use of the hostility between Sallee and its overlord, the Emperor of Morocco, was completely successful in smoking out that troublesome nest.[83]

Although a real achievement, this was an isolated and rather anachronistic success. Not only were 'tarpaulin' officers very rare in Charles I's navy, the expedition stands in marked contrast to the almost total lack of privateering enthusiasm which had marked the Spanish war of 1625–30. Partnership operations had had their drawbacks, as had uncontrolled entrepreneurs, but when both were lacking the war effort was conspicuously impoverished.

By 1639 the political storm signals in England and Scotland were fluttering vigorously. The king's inept attempt to impose a religious settlement on Scotland had provoked a revolt known as the 'Bishops' War', and his lack of a competent army had forced him to back down. The fleet had sailed to the Firth of Forth, but had not become engaged.[84] At the same time the Dutch pursued their hostilities against Spain without regard to English representations, and in October defeated a Spanish fleet at the Battle of the Downs, within sight of the English coast, a humiliation which was all the more effective for being totally accidental. In November 1640 the Long Parliament met, and all attempts to find a political solution to the resulting deadlock failed. By the summer of 1642 Charles had alienated the great majority of the political nation, and effectively destroyed that 'partnership in government' which the Tudors had built up and which James had (more or less) preserved. There were many reasons for this: fear of the king's absolutist pretensions; fears for the security of property and the common law; and deep distrust of his religious policy, which was largely misunderstood. London was divided. The leaders of the great monopoly companies, which had done well out of royal protection, favoured the king, particularly as many of them were his creditors. Other merchants, including many who were involved in the new trades or the colonies, opposed him, and in late 1641 this latter group gained control of the Common Council, and thus of the effective government of the City.[85] In January 1642 Charles abandoned an increasingly hostile London, and parliament assumed control of all the established machinery of government, including the Navy and Ordnance Boards. A parliamentary committee vetted the list of officers, removing the gentlemen and replacing them with 'tarpaulins', most of them friends and associates of William Rainsborough, and men who had commanded Levant or East India company ships during the previous decade. What little privateering experience had been created by the last wars was largely confined to this group. The Earl of Warwick was appointed to command this fleet in the name of the parliament, and simply ignored the king's attempt in July 1642 to recover control.[86] In August Charles formally declared a state of war, but he had lost his navy.

This was not at first decisive, because Charles commanded too many ports in the north and west, and too much shipping, to be denied access to the sea, but it did mean that he could not interfere with the trade of

London, which rapidly resumed after the crisis and which drove the whole parliamentary war machine. However, without the navy the parliament could not have outflanked the king's main positions, and by the end of 1642 it controlled not only Hull, Yarmouth and Dover, but also Portsmouth, Dartmouth, Plymouth and Bristol.[87] Over the next year the struggle was finely poised. The king's forces were successful in Ireland, and in the summer of 1643 he recovered both Bristol and Exeter; meanwhile the parliament was short of money and naval wages and maintenance fell into arrears, which could have had serious consequences. Privateers were commissioned by both sides, but it was men like Rainsborough who represented the authentic Elizabethan tradition, and this sense of *déjà vu* was increased in the autumn of 1642 when, in spite of many other preoccupations, a squadron of seven ships was sent to raid the Caribbean, and briefly captured Jamaica.[88] Unfortunately the Elizabethan delusion that a war fleet could support itself also survived, and it was not until November 1643 that John Pym finally grasped the financial nettle. The excise which he then imposed for the support of the navy was deeply unpopular, but absolutely necessary. Warwick was appointed Lord Admiral on parliament's authority in December, and civilian interference with the navy reduced. Thereafter the deployment of the navy was determined by the strategic needs of fighting the royalists.

Charles did not have a navy; what he did have was a fleet of about 50–70 privateers, operating mainly out of Irish and Welsh havens.[89] These were effective up to a point, but difficult to control and of uncertain allegiance. To counter this threat the parliament laid up most of Charles's great ships – what has been called his 'foreign policy' navy – and instead purchased and hired smaller and handier ships to operate in the Irish Sea, where most of the fighting took place.[90] Some local campaigns, particularly in South Wales, were greatly influenced by the fluctuations of sea power, but once it was clear that the navy as a whole could be properly paid and maintained (and that ships were consequently unlikely to desert), it did not feature largely in the military calculations. The war was won in such decisive battles as Marston Moor (1644) and Naseby (1645), not at sea. When the Self Denying Ordinance forced Warwick to surrender his office in April 1645, he was replaced by another parliamentary committee, but the lesson of 1642 had been learned and he remained in operational command until 1649 when the Council of State assumed full responsibility.

The story of the navy during the first half of the seventeenth century was by no means one of unrelieved gloom. Below the obvious activities of fleets and officers and royal commissions, the infrastructure continued to develop. New docks were built, Chatham was developed as a base, and the permanent workforce was increased. By 1640 these docks and the facilities which serviced them constituted England's largest industrial complexes.[91] The navy absorbed most of the £2.5 million which was spent on the wars of 1625–30, and needed quite a lot more. After 1620 the building and repair programme was properly maintained, and the new ships were of the latest design, seaworthy and well-armed.[92] The Ship Money fleet would have been able to give a good account of itself, if it had been called upon to do so.

The reasons why England was not a respected sea power in 1640 in the same sense that it had been in 1600 lay deeper and were more subtle. The professional skills of the seafaring community, which had served the Tudors so well, were not available to their successors. One of the reasons for that was that the need for such skills was simply not understood by the courtiers and favourites who stood closest to the Stuart kings. The 'sea dogs', with their close links to councillors and nobles, were things of the past. When court and country began to drift apart, particularly after 1620, the maritime community went with the country. It was no coincidence that Sir Edwin Sandys, one of the most persistent and obstreperous critics of royal policy in the parliaments of James's reign, was also a leading member of the Virginia and East India companies, or that one of the organisations which held the leaders of the House of Commons together during the eleven years without parliament was the Providence Island Company.[93] This estrangement was not entirely the king's fault. Paradoxically, it was partly the result of the flourishing state of civilian maritime enterprise during these years. In the 1580s there had been no North American colonies, no East Indies fleets, and Levanters had been few and far between. The maritime community was of limited size, and there were simply far more things for its members to do. However, having said that, when these men were again required for naval service, they were available, as witness the appointments which were made in 1642.

The fortunes of the early Stuart navy were determined mainly by political considerations. Its offices, even down to the humblest, were treated as profitable pieces of patronage, without much regard to how the duties were performed. This was of a piece with the whole fabric of public life, and the navy was not singled out for special treatment. In peacetime a modicum of responsible supervision was sufficient to preserve a respectable appearance, but active service required skill, and above all experience, and that was what the commanders and administrators in 1621, 1625 and 1627 had lacked so disastrously. The fact that the navy almost unanimously accepted parliamentary authority in 1642, in spite of the great efforts which the king had made over the previous decade, tells its own story. By 1649 it was not at the top of anyone's agenda. It was adequately funded, well serviced and professionally officered, but it had not been an instrument of frontline policy for several years, and only half a dozen medium-sized ships had been built since 1642.[94] However, once the country's new masters had burned their political boats by executing the king, they had to assume the full responsibilities of government, and that meant finding a foreign policy to face a hostile world.

Notes

1. N.P. Canny, *The Formation of an Old English Elite in Ireland* (Dublin, 1975); N.P. Canny, *The Elizabethan Conquest of Ireland: A Pattern Established, 1565–1576* (London, 1976); S.G. Ellis, *Tudor Ireland* (London, 1985); G. Williams, *Recovery, Reorientation and Reformation: Wales 1415–1642* (Oxford, 1987).

2. The Scots navy was a victim of the weakness and factional strife which followed the death of James V in 1542. It had never been large, and had required a major effort on the part of the king to maintain it. N.A.M. Rodger, *The Safeguard of the Sea* (London, 1997), 239. See also N. MacDougall, *James IV* (Edinburgh, 1989) and MacDougall, '"The greatest scheip that ewer saillit in Ingland or France", James IV's Great Michael', in *Scotland and War, AD 79–1918* (Edinburgh, 1991).

3. Ellis, *Tudor Ireland*, 278–312.

4. 'I would have them first unarmed utterly, and stripped quite of their warlike weapons, and then these conditions set down and made known unto them, that they shall be brought and removed with such creet as they have into Leinster, where they shall be placed . . .', *A View of the Present State of Ireland* (1596), ed. W.R. Renwick (1970), 123.

5. Cyril Falls, *Elizabeth's Irish Wars* (London, 1950). John McGurk, *The Elizabethan Conquest of Ireland: The 1590s Crisis* (London, 1997).

6. D.B. Quinn, 'The Munster Plantation, problems and opportunities', *Cork Historical and Archaeological Society Journal*, 71, 1966, 19–40.

7. N. Canny, 'The permissive frontier: social control in English settlements in Ireland and Virginia, 1550–1650', in K.R. Andrews, N.P. Canny and P.E.H. Hair, eds, *The Westward Euterprise* (Liverpool, 1978); L.E. Pennington, 'The Amerindian in English promotional literature, 1575–1625', in ibid.; H.C. Porter, *The Inconstant Savage: England and the North American Indian, 1500–1660* (Cambridge, 1979).

8. D.B. Quinn and A.N. Ryan, *England's Sea Empire* (Liverpool, 1983), 167–70.

9. *The Life and Works of Sir Henry Mainwaring*, ed. G.E. Mainwaring and W.G. Perrin (Navy Records Society, London, 1920–22), II, 18–19.

10. Barry Supple, *Commercial Crisis and Change in England, 1600–1642* (London, 1959) 120–31; Quinn and Ryan, *England's Sea Empire*, 184.

11.	Many of these pirates were British, Irish or Dutch renegades. Men such as Peter Easton and Richard Bishop commanded up to 20 ships, and were a match for any force likely to be sent against them. Christopher Lloyd, *English Corsairs on the Barbary Coast* (London, 1981); C.M. Senior, *A Nation of Pirates: English Piracy in its Heyday* (London, 1976).

12.	Quinn and Ryan, *England's Sea Empire*, 158–9.

13.	Ralph Davis, *English Overseas Trade, 1500–1700* (London, 1973), 53. J.D. Gould, 'Cloth exports 1600–1640', *Economic History Review*, 2nd series, 24, 1971, 249–52.

14.	A. Friis, *Alderman Cockayne's Project: The Commercial Policy of England in its Main Aspects* (London, 1927); B. Coward, *The Stuart Age* (London, 1994), 27–8.

15.	Davis, *Overseas Trade*, 53.

16.	There are many studies of the Dutch economy in the early seventeenth century, and of the wars of independence, but the best remain Geoffrey Parker, *The Dutch Revolt* (London, 1977) and C.R. Boxer, *The Dutch Seaborne Empire, 1600–1800* (London, 1965). See also M. Bogucka, 'Amsterdam and the Baltic in the first half of the seventeenth century', *Economic History Review*, 26, 1973, 433–47.

17.	Roy Strong, *Henry, Prince of Wales and England's Lost Renaissance* (London, 1986), 61–2; T.K. Rabb, *Jacobean Gentleman: Sir Edwin Sandys, 1561–1629* (London, 1998), 319–33; W.F. Craven, *The Dissolution of the Virginia Company: The Failure of a Colonial Experiment* (New York, 1932).

18.	Edmund S. Morgan, 'The labor problem at Jamestown, 1607–1618', *American Historical Review*, 76, 1971, 595–611; Karen Kupperman, 'Apathy and death in early Jamestown', *Journal of American History*, 66, 1979, 24–40.

19.	R.L. Morton, *Colonial Virginia* (Williamsburg, 1960); G.V. Scammell, *The World Encompassed: The First European Maritime Empires, c.800–1650* (London, 1981), 485. L. Barbour, *The Three Worlds of Captain John Smith* (Boston, 1964).

20.	Susan M. Kingsbury, *The Records of the Virginia Company of London* (London, 1906–35), III, 550–1.

21.	Craven, *Dissolution*, 318.

22.	Quinn and Ryan, *England's Sea Empire*, 195.

23.	Morton, *Colonial Virginia*.

24.	There were also colonies on Barbados, Nevis, Montserrat and Antigua, the total population of which had reached about 10,000 by 1640. R. Dunn, *Sugar and Slaves: The Rise of the Planter Class in the English West Indies, 1624–1713* (London, 1974), 55; C. Bridenbaugh, *Vexed and Troubled Englishmen* (Cambridge MA, 1974), 427–8.

25.	Quinn and Ryan, *England's Sea Empire*, 196–7; W.F. Craven, *The Southern Colonies in the Seventeenth Century* (New York, 1949).

26. C.M. Andrews, *The Colonial Period of American History* (New Haven, 1934), I, 371.

27. Bridenbaugh, *Vexed and Troubled Englishmen*; K.G. Davies, *The North Atlantic World in the Seventeenth Century* (London, 1974); Scammell, *World Encompassed*, 489–90; R.S. Dunn, 'Experiments holy and unholy', in Andrews, Canny and Hair, eds, *The Westward Enterprise*, 271–89.

28. The money was repaid in a little over a decade. D.B. Rutnam, *Winthrop's Boston* (1965); Quinn and Ryan, *England's Sea Empire*, 174.

29. Quinn and Ryan, *England's Sea Empire*, 174–5.

30. Dunn, 'Experiments holy and unholy', 279–81.

31. Jacob Arminius was a Dutch theologian who had challenged the orthodox Calvinist doctrine of double predestination, claiming a degree of freewill. The English High Church party did not follow Arminius in this, but they did challenge Calvinist teaching in other ways, hence the description. N. Tyacke, *Anti-Calvinists: The Rise of English Arminianism, 1590–1640* (Oxford, 1987); P. Lake, 'The impact of early modern Protestantism', *Journal of British Studies*, 28, 1989, 293–303.

32. Scammell, *World Encompassed*, 489–90.

33. Ibid., 492.

34. Edward Johnson, *Wonderworking Providence* (1651), ed. J.F. Jameson (1910). Quinn and Ryan, *England's Sea Empire*, 208–9.

35. Quinn and Ryan, *England's Sea Empire*, 203.

36. Rutman, *Winthrop's Boston*.

37. Andrews, *The Colonial Period*; Sean Kelsey, *Inventing a Republic: The Political Culture of the English Commonwealth, 1649–1653* (London, 1997).

38. K.R. Andrews, *The Spanish Caribbean: Trade and Plunder, 1530–1630* (London, 1978). A Spanish Company was set up in 1604 to take advantage of these new opportunities, but its monopoly was terminated by statute in 1607, opening the trade to all comers. Rabb, *Jacobean Gentleman*, 133.

39. Boxer, *Dutch Seaborne Empire*, 179–89.

40. P. Kirsch, *The Galleon* (London, 1990), 21–35.

41. For a more specific evalution of these changes, see E.E. Rich and Charles Wilson, eds, *The Cambridge Economic History of Europe. IV: The Economy of Expanding Europe in the Sixteenth and Seventeenth Centuries* (Cambridge, 1967).

42. The Verenigde Oost-Indische Compaignie was formed in 1602 out of a number of smaller companies. It was floated with an initial capital of 6,500,000 florins, raised by the sale of shares at 3,000 florins each (£1,085,000 and £500). By comparison, the English East India Company, set up in 1600, had an initial capital of £72,000, put up by 125 shareholders. Individual shares

thus cost about the same, but the numbers involved in the Dutch venture were vastly greater.

43. F.J. Fisher, 'London as an "engine of economic growth"', in P. Clark, ed., *The Early Modern Town: A Reader* (London, 1976), 210–11. The most recent, and by far the most thorough exposition of this 'engine of growth' theory is set out by Robert Brenner in *Merchants and Revolution; commercial change, political conflict and London's overseas traders, 1550–1653* (Cambridge, 1993).

44. Stephen Inwood, *A History of London* (London, 1998), 181–4. Brenner, *Merchants and Revolution*, 183–95.

45. R. Davis, *The Rise of the English Shipping Industry in the Seventeenth and Eighteenth Centuries* (London, 1962), 259–62; B. Dietz, 'Overseas trade and metropolitan growth', in A.L. Beier and R. Finlay, eds, *London, 1500–1700* (London, 1986), 127–9.

46. K.N. Chaudhuri, *The English East India Company* (Cambridge, 1965).

47. Supple, *Commercial Crisis and Change*; G.D. Ramsay, *English Overseas Trade in the Centuries of Emergence* (London, 1957).

48. Cited in W. Laird Clowes, *The Royal Navy: A History from the Earliest Times* (London, 1897), I, 528.

49. Cited by M.B. Young, *Servility and Service: The Life and Work of Sir John Coke* (London, 1986), 20.

50. A.P. McGowan, *The Jacobean Commissions of Enquiry, 1608 and 1618* (Navy Records Society, London, 1971), 201; Rodger, *Safeguard*, 364–5.

51. McGowan, *Jacobean Commissions*, 36–48, 57–9, 79–83, 241–2, 267–9.

52. Rodger, *Safeguard*, 365; W.G. Perrin, ed., *The Autobiography of Phineas Pett* (Navy Records Society, London, 1918), lviii–lxi.

53. McGowan, *Jacobean Commissions*, 60.

54. N. Clayton, 'Naval administration, 1603–1628' (University of Leeds Ph.D., 1935), 225; Rodger, *Safeguard*, 366.

55. R.T. Spence, *The Privateering Earl: George Clifford, Earl of Cumberland* (Stroud, 1995), 125–40; A.D. Thrush, 'The navy under Charles I' (University of London Ph.D., 1991), 154–6.

56. Rodger, *Safeguard*, 367–8.

57. McGowan, *Jacobean Commissions*; Rodger, *Safeguard*, 367.

58. James appears to have regarded the report of the commission as an infringement upon his right to choose his own servants. Menna Prestwich, *Cranfield: Politics and Profits under the Early Stuarts: The Career of Lionel Cranfield, Earl of Middlesex* (Oxford, 1966), 212; Linda Peck, 'Problems in Jacobean administration; was Henry Howard, Earl of Northampton, a reformer?', *Historical Journal*, 19, 1976, 831–58; Howell Lloyd, 'Corruption and Sir John Trevor', *Transactions of the Honourable Society of Cymmrodorian*, 1974–5, 77–102.

59. Although Pett claimed the credit for the *Prince Royal*, and was certainly responsible for the chicanery, it was actually built by a young Scotsman named David Balfour, as an almost exact copy of Danish flagship *Te Kroner*. McGowan, *Jacobean Commissions*, 230–2; W. Salisbury, 'A draught of a Jacobean three decker. The Prince Royal?' *Mariners Mirror*, 47, 1961, 170–7; Thomas Riis, *Should auld Acquaintance be Forgot . . . Scottish-Danish relations, c.1450–1707* (Odense, 1988), I, 108, II, 54.

60. Roger Lockyer, *Buckingham* (London, 1981).

61. McGowan, *Jacobean Commissions*, 273–4.

62. Ibid., 287.

63. Rodger, *Safeguard*, 369–70.

64. Thrush, 'Navy under Charles I', 189; Clayton, 'Naval administration, 1603–1628', 27–8.

65. Young, *Servility and Service*, 79–80.

66. McGowan, *Jacobean Commissions*, 287; Rodger, *Safeguard*, 370–1.

67. The substantial increase in long-distance trade, and the increasing suspicion with which Charles and his government were regarded, were both contributory causes. Also English ships had not been built for privateering since the 1590s, and could not match either the Dutch or the Dunkirkers for speed and manoeuvrability. K.R. Andrews, *Ships, Money and Politics: Seafaring and Naval Enterprise in the Reign of Charles I* (London, 1991).

68. Todd Gray, 'Turkish piracy and early Stuart Devon', *Transactions of the Devonshire Association*, 121, 1989, 159–71; Gray, 'Turks, Moors and Cornish fishermen: piracy in the early seventeenth century', *Journal of the Royal Institution of Cornwall*, new series, 10, 1987–90, 457–75.

69. Barry Coward, *The Stuart Age* (London, 1994), 158–65.

70. J.S. Corbett, *Fighting Instructions, 1530–1816* (Navy Records Society, London, 1905), 63–72; C. Dalton, *The Life and Times of Sir Edward Cecil, Viscount Wimbledon* (London, 1885), II, 143, 249; Rodger, *Safeguard*, 357–60.

71. Rodger, *Safeguard*, 357–60.

72. Lockyer, *Buckingham*, 339; Conrad Russell, *Parliament and English Politics, 1621–1629* (Oxford, 1979), 284–5, 290.

73. Lockyer, *Buckingham*, 420–37; Charles de La Roncière, *Histoire de la Marine Française* (Paris, 1899–1932), IV, 537–47; Rodger, *Safeguard*, 360–2.

74. Lockyer, *Buckingham*; Andrews, *Ships, Money and Politics*.

75. Rodger, *Safeguard*, 372.

76. *Historical Manuscripts Commission Reports*, 23: The Manuscripts of Earl Cowper, I, 164. Letter from Coke to Buckingham about the Council of War and its responsibilities.

77. Charles Carlton, *Charles I: The Personal Monarch* (London, 1995).

78. Thrush, 'Navy under Charles I', 139, 178; Rodger, *Safeguard*, 373–4.

79. Rodger, *Safeguard*, 482–3.

80. Kevin Sharpe, *The Personal Rule of Charles I* (London, 1992), 588–93; F.C. Dietz, *English Public Finance, 1558–1640* (New York, 1932), 279–80.

81. T.W. Fulton, *The Sovereignty of the Sea* (London, 1911), 15–20, 209–12; Brian Quintrell, 'Charles I and his navy in the 1630s', *The Seventeenth Century*, 3, 1988, 159–79.

82. Rodger, *Safeguard*, 381–2.

83. Andrews, *Ships, Money and Politics*, 165–83; D.D. Hebb, *Piracy and the English Government, 1616–1642* (Aldershot, 1994), 237–63.

84. Peter Donald, *An Uncounselled King: Charles I and the Scottish Troubles, 1637–1641* (Cambridge, 1990).

85. V. Pearl, *London and the Outbreak of the Puritan Revolution* (Oxford, 1961); Inwood, *History of London*, 217–19. Brenner, *Merchants and Revolution*, 393–400.

86. Rodger, *Safeguard*, 413–17. M.L. Baumber, 'Parliamentary naval politics, 1641–9', *Mariners Mirror*, 75, 1989, 255–68.

87. Coward, *Stuart Age*, 204–14. R. Hutton, *The Royalist War Effort, 1642–46* (London, 1982).

88. V.T. Harlow, ed., *The Voyages of Captain William Jackson, 1642–1645* (Camden Miscellany, 13, London, 1924).

89. Warwick estimated the royalist threat at 250 ships, but this is now thought to have been wildly exaggerated. Rodger, *Safeguard*, 420–1.

90. In 1642 Charles's navy consisted of 42 ships. Between 1643 and 1645 about 160 ships operated under the flag of parliament, most of them purchased, and less than 200 tons burthen. A further 120 merchantmen of similar size were hired, reflecting a complete transformation in the navy's perceived function. J.S. Wheeler, 'Navy finance, 1649–60', *Historical Journal*, 39, 1996, 457–66.

91. Rodger, *Safeguard*, 375–7. PRO E351/2241–2.

92. S.J. Stearns, 'The Caroline military system, 1625–1627' (University of California, Berkeley, Ph.D., 1967), 314–15. By 1625 the navy was at the same strength in terms of ships and weapons as it had been under Elizabeth, but the strategic threats which it faced were much greater because of the developments in Holland and France, and it lacked the pool of skilled manpower which had been available before 1604.

93. J.H. Hexter, *The Reign of King Pym* (Cambridge MA, 1941).

94. Rodger, *Safeguard*, 482–3.

CHAPTER SIX

The Commercial and Naval Policies of the Commonwealth, 1650–1660

From about 1512 to 1642 the royal navy of England had evolved. Although there had been significant steps in that evolution, some of them backwards, there had been no dramatic revolution. Expenditure had increased steadily through Henry VIII's reign, but since the middle of the sixteenth century, in spite of inflation (and corruption), there had been remarkably little change. In the early 1550s, and again in the relatively peaceful 1570s, the navy had cost about £25,000 a year. After the reforms of 1618, the peacetime expenditure was no more than £30,000. Only after the advent of the Ship Money fleet in 1635 did routine spending rise significantly, to about £100,000 a year by 1640.[1] War had become considerably more expensive, but not by much more than the rate of inflation. In the Anglo-French war of 1557–59 the navy had cost rather more than £100,000 a year, and in the war of 1625–30 about £350,000 a year. A major expedition like that to the Ile de Rhé could cost £500,000 in a few months, but that level of expenditure was not sustained. From 1553 until the eve of the Armada, the queen had deployed between 35 and 45 ships, and, as we have seen, the Jacobean commissioners had recommended an establishment of about 30. In 1640 Charles had 42 ships, totalling 23,000 tons, an average displacement of 550 tons, which was about 200 tons more than had been the case in 1560.[2]

It was the civil war which moved the foundations. As we have seen, the navy declared (almost) solidly for parliament, but it was the wrong kind of fleet for what was required in a domestic conflict. The great warships were laid up, and large numbers of smaller vessels purchased and hired to patrol the Irish coast, chase royalist privateers, and support army campaigns against seaports and maritime counties. The cost of this 'new' navy was about £200,000 a year, midway between a wartime and a peacetime level. On the whole the navy mirrored the successes of the army, but victory brought its own problems, with the one as with the other. In the context of the second civil war of 1648, a part of the Channel fleet went over to the king, and activity by royalist privateers and their allies actually increased after Charles's execution in 1649.[3] Moreover once the civil war was over, the Rump, as the new government of the state, had to confront the international situation. It had no friends, and the Peace of Westphalia had recently seen Europe's most powerful naval country, the Netherlands, emerge victorious from its long war of independence. Fortunately Spain and France were still fighting, and France was also wracked by those internal troubles known as the Frondes, so there was little immediate danger of an attack from that quarter. Nevertheless, it was imperative to move back towards a 'foreign policy' navy. At the beginning of 1649 the establishment was again 50 warships, and five more were built during the year.[4] At the same time the navy was 'politicised', to bring it into line with the New Model Army, and ensure that there was no repetition of the defections of 1648. Because the parliament had made a consistent point of employing 'tarpaulin' officers since 1642, this produced comparatively little change, and impaired the navy's efficiency hardly at all.[5]

In the summer of 1649 it must have looked as though the Rump had simply picked up the naval policy which Charles had laid down in 1642, and modified it to suit its own requirements. The 'summer guard' and the 'winter guard' ran continuously from 1643 to 1649, with little change of scale or duration.[6] However, it soon became apparent that much more sweeping changes were in prospect. In the eleven years from 1649 to 1660 £7.52 million was spent on the navy, an average of nearly £684,000 a year.[7] This was, admittedly, a period of war – briefly in 1650 against Portugal, from 1652 to 1654 against the Dutch, and from 1655 to 1660 against Spain. There were also campaigns against Ireland, the Channel Islands and in the Caribbean which required sea power. However, the whole scale of naval operations was transformed from the wars which had finished in 1630. Over the same eleven years 218 ships were added to the navy, of which 110 were prizes. A number of the prizes were sold, and about 20 ships were lost, but when the republic came to an end in 1660, the navy counted 154 ships, of which 132 were warships of varying sizes.[8] Of the fleet which had sailed against the Armada, only about 20 per cent had been the queen's ships, and as late as the Ile de Rhé campaign more than 60 of the 90 ships involved had been merchant auxiliaries. Some continued to be used after 1649, and contracts survive from 1651–52, but merchant auxiliaries were considered to be both politically and militarily unreliable. The defeat at Dungeness in 1652 was attributed to their failings, and after that date they disappear. Bounties had been discontinued in 1618, and 35 years later the navy had become a wholly professional and state-owned service.[9]

167

This transformation was also reflected in the design of the ships, which became increasingly standardised. No two Elizabethan warships had been exactly alike, and although they were loosely grouped by tonnage, there was no system of classification. Ratings begin to be mentioned in the 1630s, and by 1649 all warships were described in six classes, according to tonnage and number of guns.[10] The big East Indiamen and Levanters which were being built at the same time were certainly armed, but they were primarily designed as cargo carriers, and were not rated. The whole culture of seafighting had changed since 1604, and the private warship, which had staged such a comeback in the Spanish war of Elizabeth, had again vanished. This was partly because privateering had long since lost its attractions, and partly because it was not necessary. When Kenelm Digby had led such an expedition to Scanderoon in 1627, the merchants had complained bitterly of the damage to their trade. With the vast increase in the size of the navy after 1649, the state could use its own ships to attack enemy commerce – and keep the profits. At the same time, in the context of a civil war, the parliament needed to keep a tight control over the ships which were operating in its name. It neither needed nor wanted private enterprise. The overall tonnage of the merchant fleet increased significantly between 1625 and 1660, from approximately 110,000 to 180,000, but 71,000 tons of the latter figure were contributed by colliers plying between Newcastle and London, so too much should not be made of these figures.[11] There was still a shortage of merchant shipping capacity, but the changing relationship between the merchant marine and the navy was a question of policy, not necessity.

This policy was, of course, largely a question of resources. Elizabeth had used auxiliaries because she could not afford a navy large enough for all the tasks it had to perform. James I and Charles I had done the same, although with less conviction and success. But the Rump had the will, and the means, to raise the money, and was prepared to commit to the navy the resources necessary to turn it into a fighting force suitable for the late seventeenth century. At first this was done with relative ease. The bloody suppression of Ireland late in 1649, and victory over the Scots at Dunbar in September 1650, meant that there was little challenge to army control thereafter, and no resistance to levels of taxation which neither Elizabeth nor Charles could have contemplated. For example, on 1 April 1651 a duty of up to 2s a chalder was imposed upon the rapidly growing coastwise traffic in coal, and the commissioners for customs were directed to hand the proceeds directly to the Treasurer of the Navy.[12]

At the same time a government which knew that an unpaid army (or navy) was hugely dangerous, also knew that the most flexible and available source of wealth was commerce. Most of the restraints which Charles had imposed for fiscal reasons, or in order to bolster the authority of the London oligarchy, were removed. The broadcloth trade, although it remained substantial, never recovered its old ascendancy, but commerce with the Far East, the Mediterranean, Africa, and above all America continued to grow healthily. Income from the deeply unpopular excise duties (first levied in 1643) varied from £162,000 to £238,000 a year between 1653 and 1658, and customs revenue, which had produced no more than £140,000 in 1643, had risen to more than £500,000 (including the coal duty) by 1659.[13] Some of this increase was due to increased efficiency of collection, but most to the increase of trade. When in 1650 Prince Rupert, having been driven from his bases in southern Ireland, began to operate out of Lisbon, a visit from the English navy not only persuaded the Portuguese to expel him, but also to open up the trade of their still extensive overseas empire to English merchants, a move which they would not have contemplated without persuasion. Nevertheless the huge increase in the navy budget, which began in 1650, eventually got the government into difficulties. The naval debt, which had stood at £208,000 in 1648, and had actually come down to £129,000 by 1651, thereafter rose inexorably. By 1654 it was £466,000, and by 1660 over £1 million, accounting for about 50 per cent of the whole state debt.[14]

From 1651 onwards the Army Council, headed by Oliver Cromwell, was looking for a constitutional settlement which would institutionalise the developments of the English revolution. This inevitably meant compromise with the 'political nation', which had not gone away and could not be overawed indefinitely. As one result, taxation had to be reduced, and the yield of the assessment came down from £1.4 million a year to about £360,000. It was this principally which scuppered the Admiralty. By 1658 the purveyors were refusing to supply victuals except for cash, because in 1655 only about one in twelve of their bills had been met.[15] The situation improved slightly over the next two years (to about one in ten), but that was not enough to avert a crisis. The victuallers suffered, of course, because it was less dangerous to leave them unpaid than to fail to cover the wages of officers and seamen. Even so by 1659 only 27 of the 87 ships in commission were paid up to date.[16] Some 41 were unpaid for two years, and two for more than four years. All were described as 'foul . . . out of victuals and want repairs'. In the optimistic days of 1649 the rates of pay had been significantly increased. A captain's had gone up from 6s 8d a day to 10s, a gunner's from 1s 1d a day to 1s 8d, and an ordinary sailor's from 15s to 19s a month. At the same time a new Prize Commission had been instituted, and the rules drastically changed to give the crew 50 per cent of the value of every prize.[17] These changes, combined with the virtual disappearance of privateering as an alternative, seem to have eased the navy's recruitment problems, but they left the Admiralty with an even bigger headache when the taxation revenue declined. Men continued to be pressed, not only because word of these problems got around, but also because the demand for men had increased so greatly. Whereas the navy proper had needed only 4,000 men in 1627, by 1653 as many as 20,000 could be required when all the ships were engaged.[18] This also meant that in sixteen years the wages bill had increased by some 600 per cent.

Such problems contributed significantly to the fact that the navy played an important part in the restoration of the Rump in 1659, and finally in the return to monarchy in 1660, but they did not affect the operational efficiency of the fleet as long as the republic lasted. By 1652 the English navy was numerically superior to any of its rivals. The Dutch could muster about 50 warships, but continued to use converted merchantmen very effectively. The French fleet, by contrast, was in full decline from the efficiency which Richelieu had given it, and numbered only about 20 warships by 1659.[19] These statistics might suggest that the English should have been masters of the sea, and that was not the case, but the navy was more successful in action than at any time since the 1590s.

Politicisation had meant not only the promotion of tarpaulins, but also the introduction (or reintroduction) of experienced soldiers to positions of command, and practical merchants into the administration. The re-vamped Admiralty Commission was comprised mainly of the latter, selected from those with an Independent allegiance. The Treasurer, Richard Hutchinson, was a returned New Englander, as were some of the captains, notably Robert Moulton and Nehemiah Bourne, a pedigree which virtually guaranteed religious radicalism.[20] Specialist committees were set up to deal with such matters as ordnance and victuals, and the new Prize Commission worked much more efficiently than the old Admiralty Court. Most important, however, was the appointment of 'Generals at Sea' in 1649, particularly Robert Blake and Richard Deane. Both had served with distinction as soldiers during the civil war, and converted to naval command with equal success. The Independents may have been no more numerous in the population at large than the gentlemen and courtiers whom they replaced, and were much less heirs to traditional authority, but their level of commitment and their willingness to learn the professional skills required by their callings more than compensated for their lack of established status. Even the names of the ships reflected a revolutionary enthusiasm. New builds were called *Naseby* or *Dunbar*, while the *Charles* was (not surprisingly) re-christened the *Liberty*.[21] It would have astonished William Monson, or even Francis Drake, to find his seamen indulging in 'several days of fasting and humiliation' to put them in the right frame of mind for the Lord's work, but Robert Blake successfully led such an exercise in 1652.

Until the end of 1651 the navy was mainly occupied with mopping up royalist outposts like the Scilly Isles, and hounding Rupert's privateers into virtual oblivion, but relations with the Dutch were steadily deteriorating, and open war broke out in 1652. This conflict between the only two Protestant republics in Europe used to be attributed to commercial rivalry, and that view certainly has some contemporary support. Dutch carriers were both cheaper and more efficient, and one commentator wrote: 'merchants daily refuse to ship their goods with us, and chose rather to ship them in Dutch bottoms, whom they say have a constant convoy and can set sail at a day . . . so that thereby the Dutch have engrossed all the trade from the English, to the great prejudice of this nation'.[22]

In an attempt to rectify this situation, a Navigation Act was passed in August 1650, 'for the advancing and regulating of the trade of this commonwealth', and another in 1651, specifically aimed at taking the carrying trade out of Dutch hands.[23] However, such acts had been passed at intervals since the fifteenth century, and although they certainly indicated a serious interest on the part of government, they had never yet altered the patterns of commerce. Nor did these, and although the Dutch were annoyed, they did not go to war for that reason. Indeed recent research has suggested that the mercantile communities on both sides opposed the war, which did them nothing but harm. The real issues were political and ideological.[24] First the Rump, and even more the Nominated parliament which succeeded it in 1653, were deeply suspicious of the Godliness of the Dutch. No church which was as tolerant of dissent as that of the Netherlands could possibly be of the Elect; and, of course, if they were not Elect they must be Reprobate, and covert servants of Antichrist. Secondly in the internal politics of the Netherlands, the supporters of the House of Orange were at that point in the ascendant, and the Houses of Orange and Stuart were connected by marriage and sympathy. English royalists, including Charles II, had taken refuge there, and royalist privateers operated out of some Dutch ports. There was also the irritant of the *mare clausum*. The republican government of England was just as insistent as Charles I had been on the deference due to the English flag within the Narrow Seas, and in a far better position to enforce it.[25] Early in 1652, while English and Dutch politicians were trying to negotiate a settlement, the seamen were squaring up for a fight.

On 19 May Blake and Van Tromp faced each other in the Downs, and the English demand for the expected salute was met with a broadside. The resulting exchanges were inconclusive as a battle, but decisive as a political event. It soon transpired that the Dutch were not so much refusing a symbolic courtesy to England, as refusing to recognise the legitimacy of the regicide government. Van Tromp was a well-known Orangist, but he also

171

had the full support of the Estates General in declaring that all previous contracts and agreements had been made with the Crown of England, and were consequently null and void in the new circumstances. This and other similar statements raised the stakes considerably, but the English Council of State did not wish to admit that its legitimacy had been challenged. It therefore accused the Dutch of seeking to command the seas and destroy English commerce:

> [They] have laid it as their settled design to obtain to themselves the dominion and sovereignty of those seas ... thereby not only [to] give what rules of commerce they please, but to destroy the trade and shipping of this Commonwealth, as inconsistent (in their apprehension) with absoluteness and command at sea which they aspire after.'[26]

War did not follow immediately, but the press on both sides of the North Sea was assiduous in stirring up popular hatred and animosity, and the final breakdown came about the middle of June. The English were at first handicapped by having to provide against a number of eventualities. The Irish Sea and the Western Approaches could not be left undefended. Scotland might take advantage of English troubles to raise the flag of Charles II again. Consequently the fleet with which Blake again confronted Van Tromp off Dungeness on 30 November was understrength, and was soundly beaten. For a time Van Tromp claimed to be (and was) 'master of the Narrow Sea'. There was talk of a blockade of the Thames estuary, and some observers thought that the English must sue for peace. However, such defeatism was premature. In February 1653 Blake turned the tables on his old rival off Portland Bill, and then the talk was of completing God's work, and vindicating the honour of England.[27] The Dutch were also having second thoughts about their support for Charles, and in this new climate tentative negotiations for peace could commence. The dissolution of the Rump in April 1653 and the appearance of the Nominated (or Barebones) parliament in July did not greatly affect the direction of English foreign policy, which was (and continued to be) dominated by Oliver Cromwell and his fellow officers. Although there was by this time some will towards peace on both sides, progress was slow. On 2–3 June Blake inflicted another and more decisive defeat upon Van Tromp at the Battle of the Gabbard, a victory which cost the life of his colleague Richard Deane. Eleven Dutch ships were captured and nine destroyed at no loss to the English, who now clearly had the upper hand. This concentrated the minds of the Dutch negotiators, but the English radicals had the bit between their teeth and were proving hard to bring to terms. In this respect the self-destruction of the Barebones parliament in December 1653, and Cromwell's institution as Lord Protector proved decisive. Cromwell had much sympathy with radical positions and intentions, but was more pragmatic. The pleas of the London merchants, and the fact that the Dutch were moving away from their former royalism, weighed heavily with him, and peace was concluded in April 1654.

The balance of power between the two republics at this time was fairly even. Militarily the English had the edge, but commercially the Dutch were superior. Not only did the VOC have by far the greatest share of the lucrative oriental trade, but the Dutch *fluyt* still reigned supreme as the European cargo carrier.[28] A negotiated agreement between England and Portugal in 1654 somewhat strengthened the English position in Brazil and the Portuguese East Indies, but the strongest growth areas were North America and the Mediterranean. The Barbary corsairs had preyed on the latter trade for years, and had humiliated Charles I's government with raids on southern Ireland. The English had never been strong enough to challenge them in their own waters – until now. On 4 April 1655 24 English warships commanded by Robert Blake appeared off Tunis demanding restitution and compensation. When the Bey refused, Blake attacked Porto Farina, one of the Tunisian bases, destroying nine corsair ships and inflicting extensive damage.[29] This did not put an end to corsair activity, or even seriously diminish it, but it did inhibit attacks on English ships, which strengthened England's competitive position in the trade.

As we have seen, the civil wars did not lead to any fighting in the New World, but they did affect the position there. Just as ardent Puritans returned from New England to fight for the Godly Commonwealth, so royalist refugees fled to the southern colonies, particularly Virginia and Barbados. The whole period from 1640 to 1660 has been characterised as one of 'salutary neglect' in respect of the New World colonies.[30] All were sufficiently well established and prosperous to need nothing from England except by way of normal trade. Oliver Cromwell, who effectively ruled Britain throughout the Rump, the Nominated parliament and the Protectorate, had no interest in interfering with the government of the colonies, provided they acknowledged his ultimate authority. At first Virginia, Barbados, Bermuda and Antigua all rejected this, and in October 1650 the Rump declared the defiant colonists to be traitors.[31] Governor Berkeley and the Virginia assembly reaffirmed their position in 1651, but when the English navy arrived in 1652 bearing soldiers and parliamentary commissioners, a stand-off ensued. In March 1652 the colony submitted without resistance, and in April a new assembly appointed Richard Bennett as Governor with the commissioners' approval.[32] The other and smaller dissidents followed Virginia's lead.

There were those who thought this policy too slack in view of the number of 'undesirables' of one sort or another who had taken, and were still taking, refuge across the Atlantic. Colonies, it was declared, 'are and ought to be subordinate to and dependent upon' the mother country. No one disputed that in theory, by the meaning of 'dependent' was unclear. The proprietary colonies had appointed governors, and the others elected, but these officers had no soldiers at their disposal, and relatively little power.[33] The idea that North America should be brought to 'a more certaine and civill way of governmente' did not commend itself to a Protector who had many more urgent things to think about.

What really concerned the inhabitants of all the colonies, apart from growing and selling their crops, was the development of their own institutions, broadly conceived in the English tradition. The common law was adopted everywhere, and the court systems based on the leet, hundred and county courts rather than on assizes or commissions of the peace which would have required authorisation from Westminster.[34] The popular assemblies were based on settlement constituencies, usually with a householder franchise similar to that used in English towns, the representatives at first being known as 'burgesses'. In theory these assemblies were empowered only to make by-laws, again on the model of the English town council, but in practice they legislated on any matter of public concern which required regulation. No attempt was made to collect taxation voted by the English parliament, although in theory the colonies (unlike the Channel Islands) were subjected to English statute. Local taxes were devised and spent on the spot. Ecclesiastical organisation varied greatly. All the New England colonies were broadly congregational, such overall control as there was being vested in representative meetings. Virginia and the West Indian colonies used the Prayer Book and followed the parochial structure of the Church of England. In 1634 colonial commissioners had been empowered to provide endowments for the churches in the plantations by means of tithes or land grants, and this was generally done where the communities desired it.[35] Each colony formed what was effectively a self-governing Deanery under the nominal jurisdiction of commissaries of the Bishop of London, but because Anglican clergy had to be episcopally ordained, these churches were rather less independent than those of New England.[36] Puritan nonconformity was outlawed in Virginia in 1643, and factors of time and distance meant that the Commonwealth religious legislation never became effective. In spite of having a Catholic proprietor, the population of Maryland always had a Protestant majority, and in 1649 the second Lord Baltimore realistically levelled the playing field by pursuading the assembly to pass a law of religious toleration. Unfortunately events in England encouraged the Puritan wing of the Protestants to press for more, and alone among the New World colonies, Maryland saw religious strife in the 1650s.[37] In the short term the Puritans were victorious, and endeavoured to set up a system modelled on New England, but ironically Cromwell, who was more pragmatic abroad than he was at home, backed Lord Baltimore and the Catholic magnates to get the toleration law restored.

Economically there were two main developments across the Atlantic. The growth of trade with England and Scotland, particularly the steady expansion of tobacco exports, was unspectacular but important for both parties. Rising population and increasing prosperity made the colonies valuable markets. More dramatic was the rapid expansion of sugar cultivation in the West Indies after about 1650, which created a new plantation economy. Slaves began to be imported from Africa in large numbers, and the concentration on cash crops meant an increased need for imports.[38] The English, French and Dutch islands all shared in this boom, but the English had an advantage because the thriving mainland colonies were close. Sugar and other tropical produce was energetically traded for grain, timber, fish and other temperate produce, enhancing the prosperity of both parties. Large quantities of sugar also began to be sent to England, and like the tobacco crop, much of this was re-exported to Europe, turning what had been in 1640 a small-scale trade into a major component of the commercial life of London and Bristol.[39] The European powers began to eye each other's small but rich islands jealously, and to make provision to garrison and defend them. Consequently colonies like Barbados and St Kitts never developed the kind of robust autonomy which is most evident in New England, but which also developed rather later in Virginia and Maryland. When in 1653 the Danes, who were sympathetic to the Dutch, closed the Sound for over a year to English ships, the value of New England as a source of essential naval supplies was seriously tested for the first time.[40] In fact the Danes overreached themselves, because subsequent English naval victories not only forced them to change their minds, but caused England to back the Swedes when war broke out between the neighbours in 1657. The Danes were heavily defeated in 1659, and lost control of the eastern shore of the Sound in 1660. They continued to levy tolls, but their position was heavily undermined and they were compelled to purchase some English support by reducing the tolls for English ships in 1661.

There was nothing new about a close relationship between foreign policy and trade, but traditionally European monarchs had not allowed the pleas of their merchants much weight when it came to making decisions of war and peace. That began to change after 1650, particularly in England. The Council of State had no dynastic affiliations to distract it, and no personal honour to uphold. Committees such as those of the Navy and Customs, or Trade and Plantations, were pragmatic bodies, dominated by men who knew their business. The Navigation Acts of 1650 and 1651 were not original in concept, but in the circumstances they represented a shift in official priorities, not least because they were government measures.[41] In the past commercial legislation had almost invariably been the result of lobbying by the relevant interest group, and measures passed in one parliament were not infrequently repealed in the next as a result of counter-lobbying. Now, however, the Council of State was moving to impose its own overall control, and it becomes realistic to speak of an 'economic policy'. Instructions issued to the newly established Council of Trade in 1650 represent an altogether new level of ambition.[42] One of the reasons for this seems to have been the desire of some more politically radical merchants to abolish monopolistic companies, and replace them with a unified system of state control which would have regularised the position of erstwhile interlopers, and broadened the basis of trade by enabling small independent operators to enjoy official protection. This did not eventually happen, partly because the vested interest of the great companies had moved adroitly to endorse the new political situation, and partly because of Cromwell's inherent conservatism in all secular matters. A somewhat jaundiced retrospect upon the Navigation Act suggested that this was so much the case that little had changed: 'Some few persons interested in the highest degree in the East Indies and in the New Plantations of this nation have such credit with his highness and the Council that it is believed that they have the principal voice in the making of the said enactment'.[43]

However, Cromwell was not 'his highness' in 1651 and the council does not seem to have been motivated by any particular interest group. When the East India Company obtained a new charter in 1657, perhaps the charge may have had more substance. Nevertheless the relationship between commerce and public policy became steadily closer. Cromwell's decision to end the Dutch war in 1654 is one example of this new pragmatism. Another is the establishment of a public and national postal service in 1657, to replace the multiplicity of *ad hoc* private arrangements.[44] A General Post Office was set up, a Postmaster General appointed, and a uniform scale of charges laid down.

The navy was the prime instrument of this new state mercantilism. Hitherto English naval strategy had been almost exclusively defensive, with the possible exception of the French wars of Henry VIII. Aggressive tactics, such as the raid on Cadiz in 1596 or the expedition to the Ile de Rhé in 1627, should not disguise essentially defensive intentions. Similarly the navy had always been on the defensive against pirates and privateers, and only occasionally successful. England had become a sea power by defending itself successfully, whether against the French in 1545, or against the Armada in 1588. Maritime expansion had involved royal ships, royal servants and royal money (up to a point), but not the navy itself. However in the 1650s the navy became a weapon in the hands of an aggressive state.

This aggression was partly designed to enforce recognition from hostile neighbours (and could thus be represented as a form of defence), but it was also directed to the securing of commercial and maritime supremacy – something like the 'British Empire' envisaged by John Dee almost a century before. This aggression began before the first Dutch war. Eleven Dutch ships were seized for illegal trading with Barbados in 1651, in contravention of the Navigation Act, to indicate that the government was serious in its intentions.[45] During the war an aggressive policy of search and confiscation was applied to neutral shipping, in spite of the outcry raised, and when the council's Admiralty Committee was felt to be failing in December 1652, it was swept away and replaced by six Admiralty commissioners, directly responsible to parliament.[46] At this point the driving force was not Cromwell, but Sir Henry Vane, one of the council's most ideologically committed members. A total of over 1,500 Dutch prizes were taken during the war, and whereas in the past such captures would have benefited mainly the privateer captains who made them, now the profits were divided between the state and the crews of the successful ships.[47] At the same time the burden of losses sustained had to be borne by the merchant community without any real prospect of reprisals. The only compensating factor was the thought that the more successful the navy became, the fewer the losses would be; and the 'balance of trade' in this war, like the eventual outcome, favoured the English.

The victory of 1654 was not overwhelming, but it was, for the time being, decisive. Cromwell, moreover, was unlike any previous English ruler. At the end of a war even Henry VIII, the most aggressive King of England since Henry V, had needed time to retrench and recover. Neither Elizabeth nor Charles I could really afford to wage war at all, but Cromwell had a large army and navy which needed to be kept occupied. As one contemporary noted, 'since the peace with Holland, most men cry up war with Spain, saying that the fleet and the army must be kept in employment, and no place worth their attempting like the West Indies'.[48]

Cromwell, whose ostensible motivation was religious, did not mind which Catholic power he attacked, either France or Spain. Neither was as powerful as it had been, and each might have been glad to buy off English hostility. The price under discussion was about £400,000, but when it came to the point France would not, and Spain could not, pay the ransom. That left the Lord Protector with his options open, and he chose to attack Spain. Some thought at the time, and it has been argued since, that he made this decision because his prejudices were rooted in the 1590s, and he still regarded Philip IV as though he had been Philip II.[49] However, France, with a very limited merchant marine and hardly any colonies worth speaking of, was not particularly vulnerable to naval attack. By contrast Spain had many rich colonies, made vulnerable by her own naval decline, and still depended heavily upon the plate fleet bringing in South American silver.

In December 1654, without any formal declaration of hostilities, or even a propaganda smokescreen, the Protector launched his 'Western Design'. Some 38 ships and 3,000 soldiers set out from England, commanded by William Penn as General at Sea and Robert Venables as Colonel.[50] The expedition recruited a further 5,500 men in Barbados and St Kitts – a remarkable testimony to the development of those colonies – and launched itself against San Domingo in Hispaniola. To the surprise and chagrin of the commanders, it was repulsed with substantial losses. The navy appears not to have done very much wrong, but the soldiers were not up to the job. Those recruited in the West Indies were untrained and of little use, while those sent out from England were suspiciously ineffective. It is possible that they were undermined by tropical diseases to which the locals would have developed some immunity, but equally likely that someone had seen fit to get rid of potential troublemakers by sending them on a Caribbean cruise.[51] The capture of Jamaica, which was then poor and sparsely populated, seemed a poor consolation at the time, although it was later made to appear significant. A small garrison was left on the island, and the fleet, with the remnants of the English force, returned in June 1655. Penn and Venables faced a rigorous inquisition, and neither commanded again during Cromwell's lifetime. Cromwell was annoyed, and doubly so because Penn had also missed the plate fleet, but quite unrepentant. Rather belatedly, Spain declared war in March 1656.

Philip's official war effort was derisory. His fleet remained in port, unable or unwilling to face the English. Meanwhile Sir Richard Stagner captured the plate fleet on 8 September. Its value turned out to be seriously disappointing for so long awaited an event – about £250,000 – but its loss was both a measure and a cause of Spain's sad condition.[52] In the following April Robert Blake attacked and destroyed another such fleet in the Canaries, without even troubling to attempt its capture. More significantly Blake's fleet had maintained a blockade of the Spanish coast throughout the winter of 1656–57, the first time that such a feat had ever been accomplished.[53] Sir William Monson had projected the exploit nearly half a century before, and English strategists had long believed it to be possible, but Blake was the first to achieve it. Unfortunately, he died at sea on the voyage home, and was not adequately replaced for many years. The Spanish counter-attack was indirect, but remarkably effective. While Philip's warships remained in harbour, the privateers of Flanders and Dunkirk launched themselves against English commerce. Some 150 ships were lost in 1656 alone, and about 1,200 during the whole war. Most were small, but the loss was severe and caused a storm of anguish.[54] Convoys were slow and inefficient, and even the relatively small sixth-rate warships were not nimble enough to catch the predators. It was an old problem, but the commonwealth came nearer to finding an answer than any previous regime. After his failure in the West Indies, and the relative success of Blake's 'gunboat diplomacy' in the Mediterranean, which had frustrated a French invasion of Naples as well as battering Porto Farina, Cromwell had come to terms with France in October 1655.[55] One result of this had been the expulsion of the Stuarts; another was the Anglo-French attack on Dunkirk, which resulted in the capture of the town in June 1658. This was the New Model Army's only taste of European war, and it acquitted itself well, while the fleet bombarded the sea defences. Dunkirk was handed over to the English, and one of the most menacing privateer bases was thus extinguished.[56] At the same time Ostend was blockaded, and although some privateers continued to get to sea, the danger was under control by the time Cromwell died in September of that year.

In the West Indies there was little action on either side after the capture of Jamaica. A small English fleet was kept in the area, commanded first by William Goodson and later by Christopher Myngs, which protected Jamaica and carried out small-scale raids, but it was not powerful enough for any major operation, and seems to have been constantly undermined by diseases for which neither immunity nor remedy was available. Having been compelled to accept English terms by the seizure of his Brazil fleet in 1654, John IV of Portugal tried to take advantage of the Anglo-Spanish war to renege on his agreement, but another visit from Blake in the summer of 1656 forced him to ratify the treaty, and he died in November before witnessing the rigours of the English blockade. Once access to the Baltic had been restored in 1654, English merchants enjoyed parity with those of the Netherlands, but relations between the two countries remained hostile, which is why Cromwell cultivated good relations with the Swedes. After the Treaty of Roskilde transferred Scania to Sweden in 1658, English access was secured, and neither Denmark nor Sweden was in a position to challenge the English navy. After the fall of Richard Cromwell in May 1659 the restored Rump was committed to peace, being totally preoccupied with its own domestic problems. A new fleet was sent to the Mediterranean, but the merchants were strongly opposed to any renewal of hostilities, and plans to establish a naval base to replace a rather insecure reliance upon the free port of Leghorn came to nothing.[57] However, the mere presence of the fleet was sufficient to curb the activities of the Barbary pirates, and English commerce continued to grow under that protection.

Unlike the army, the navy accepted Richard Cromwell as his father's successor without demur. Relations with the military had been strained before, when the seamen suspected that the soldiers were using their political power to secure their own pay and perquisites ahead of the navy's, and during the troubled months from May 1659 to the summer of 1660 the two forces pursued entirely separate and sometimes conflicting courses. Radicals, both Levellers and Anabaptists, denounced the new regime, but neither group had much influence in the fleet, which duly sent addresses of loyal greeting. So did most units of the army, but the officers were not happy. Oliver Cromwell had been both Head of State and Commander in Chief, but Richard was a civilian, and a petition was presented for Charles Fleetwood to command the army. Prayer meetings and political discussions among the officers, which had not featured much since 1653, began again with ominous significance.[58] The new Protector acted with tact and discretion, accepting that a professional soldier should command the army, and mobilising the support of the Grandees against rank-and-file agitation. However, the council was also divided, and the decision to convene a new parliament on a modified version of the ancient franchise was a victory for the civilians, about which the soldiers for the time being reserved judgement.

Richard Cromwell opened the new session on 27 January 1659 with a sober speech emphasising the need for unity, and a strong navy to maintain England's interests abroad, particularly in the Baltic and against Dutch competition.[59] Neither the army nor the radicals were impressed. Only a minority of the new assembly were committed to the Protectorate as such; most would probably have preferred a return to the traditional order if they had been offered that option, and the most vocal, like Arthur Haselrigg, wanted a 'purer' form of republicanism. Every decision which was reached as a result of the long and confused debates was grudging and tentative – the endorsement of the Protectorate, the recognition of Scottish and Irish representation, the endorsement of a nominated Upper House.[60] Meanwhile neither the army nor the navy was being properly paid, and army discipline began to break down. Factions developed among the senior officers, some supporting Richard, others, particularly Fleetwood and his Wallingford House group, seeking the return of more or less disguised military rule.[61] Edward Montague, who was a strong supporter of the Protector, managed to prevent similar dissensions in the navy, and for the time being it remained quiescent.

A crisis was reached in April, when the Protector ordered an end to the officers' political meetings, and a return to their regiments. The parliament supported him strongly with a series of resolutions, but Fleetwood refused to back down, and called a general rendezvous of the army at St James on the 21st. When the majority of the available regiments obeyed his summons, the Protector's credibility was destroyed.[62] He lingered as a shadowy figure for several weeks, and then faded back into private life. The parliament, denounced as a 'plaything of courtiers and royalists', was swept away, but so bankrupt were the victorious officers of positive ideas that they could think of no better option than the recall of the Rump, which had last met six years earlier. On 7 May Speaker Lenthall and about 40 members reconvened at Westminster, and immediately declared for a reinstated republic, with no king, single person or second chamber.[63] The army was placed under the control of a commission consisting of Fleetwood and the members of his victorious faction. In May the administration of the navy was remodelled, Montague was dismissed from his command, and replaced by John Lawson, a staunch republican. Lawson did his best to reassure his officers and men about their pay and conditions (which overrode all other considerations at this time), and because he was a respected and experienced officer, he managed to retain control for the time being. Unlike the army, the naval officers were not divided into obvious factions, and a significant part of the fleet was at sea, in the Mediterranean, Caribbean and North Sea, for much of the year.[64]

About 120 members attended the various meetings of the revived Rump, but their power was much less substantial than they believed it to be. They made the same mistake that Charles I had made in 1648, believing that their recall indicated that their indispensability to lawful government had been recognised. Whatever the private agendas of Fleetwood and Lambert, the army as a whole was by this time totally preoccupied with the issues of indemnity and money. Aware of the fact that it could not afford to pay the army off, the Rump ducked both issues. An Act of Indemnity was passed, but was full of holes and exemptions, satisfying nobody.[65] Adequate taxation to resolve the problems of both the army and the navy was a political impossibility, and as early as June bets were being laid that the Rump would not last another fortnight. That might have been the case if anyone had known what to do next, but even the royalists were divided, substantial conservatives wishing to impose conditions for a restoration which were unacceptable to Charles himself. Then in August Sir George Booth raised about 4,000 men in Cheshire, declaring for a free parliament and tax reductions. Popular as such a platform may have been, all Booth succeeded in doing was reuniting the army to his own destruction.[66] Convinced that they were now the only prop of the Godly cause, in September the soldiers presented another list of grievances and demands, which the Rump denounced as insolent and illegal pressure. Identifying Lambert as the main promoter and originator of this petition, the house expelled him and ordered his arrest. In reply, Lambert appealed directly to force, as Cromwell had done in 1653, and in October the Rump was again excluded, and replaced with a 'Committee of Safety' of 23 members.[67] Apart from Lambert and his friends, nobody had any confidence in the new government, but equally nobody knew what to do about it. However, in November a part of the fleet at Portsmouth mutinied, and was joined by the garrison of the town, and by a second force which was sent down against them.[68] The rebel demand were commonplace enough – food, pay and indemnity – but they demonstrated that they had no more confidence in Lambert to provide these necessaries than they had in the Rump, or anyone else. Partly motivated by this demonstration, which included a rather vague demand for a free parliament, and partly by his own dislike of Lambert and the Grandees, John Lawson moved the bulk of his fleet to the Thames estuary in December and threatened to blockade London if the Committee of Safety did not stand down.[69]

Although again a negative move, Lawson's action proved decisive. George Monck, who had an army under firm control and had been playing a covert political game since October, was still far away in Scotland, and his intentions were unclear. Sir Thomas Fairfax by similar means had secured the far north of England, but he was waiting for Monck to declare his hand.[70] It was Lawson who restored the Rump again at Westminster on 26 December, more as a gesture of commitment to civilian rule than with any particular programme in mind. Nobody regarded this as a long-term solution, but for the time being it was acceptable to the civic authorities of London, who, although they were helpless against a united army, were bound to be powerful players in the new situation as the army disintegrated. As Monck advanced south during January, the Rump did practically nothing. Its members had no enthusiasm for what might happen when he arrived, and no more grasp of political reality than they had shown before. Lambert's failure to confront Monck owed nothing to the actions of the Rump, however hostile it may have been to him. Lawson kept his ships on station, supported by credit from the city, which he protected as well as threatened, but equally did nothing. When Monck finally arrived on 3 February 1660 he was warmly welcomed by the citizens, but faced a stand-off with the Rumpers, who were incapable of learning political lessons.[71] The closer Monck's relations became with London, the more hostile the parliament grew, even attempting to relieve him of his command. His answer to this move was just as decisive as that of Lambert, or Cromwell, but quite different. On 21 February he readmitted all those who had been excluded since 1648, on the understanding that they would vote a dissolution and provide for a new parliament.[72] This could have provoked a confrontation with Lawson, whose commitment was to the Rump rather than to parliament as such, and whose force was just as effective as Monck's, although in a different element. The admiral, however, made no move, and his tacit acceptance of the initiative was as decisive in its way as the initiative itself. Although Monck had made no declaration of intent, and seems to have been following his nose, he must have known that a new parliament on the old franchise would be dominated by the old political nation, even if active royalists were still officially excluded.

Lawson was not the only prominent man to be unhappy with this prospect, but Monck's authority was now unassailable. He refused to make any undertaking against a royal restoration, but insisted that he would obey the will of the new parliament, and that all his officers would do likewise. If Lawson was inclined to demur, he did not say so, but accepted the situation like everyone else, because it offered, in truth, the only possible way out of the morass that the republic had become. On 16 March the Long parliament finally dissolved itself, and new elections were held. As everyone must have anticipated, the radicals and republicans were destroyed at the hustings. Only sixteen members of the old Rump reappeared. There were a fair number of Presbyterians, but the religious climate of the Convention parliament (as it came to be known) was predominantly Anglican. The House of Lords was partially restored in two stages, not by the Commons but by Monck. On 25 April, the opening day, those peers who had declared against the king in 1642 resumed their seats, and two days later the heirs of those who had since died.[73] Neither the bishops nor the survivors of those who had fought for the king were to be admitted for the time being. The Convention promptly relieved John Lawson of his command, and recalled Edward Montague, the former Cromwellian who had made clear his willingness to accept a restored monarchy. The fleet accepted this decision, just as it had accepted Lawson's authority when he was in office. Perhaps warned by the army's example, the navy did not have a political programme in 1660, and consequently retained both its unity and its discipline. With the naval debt at £1.2 million and the victuallers on strike, the only possible solution was to establish a stable civilian government as quickly as possible. When the king had been proclaimed on 8 May, he was escorted from the Low Countries by his loyal navy (or at least a fair part of it).

Although the army had been so much more important than the navy in the domestic politics of the civil war and Interregnum, and the role of the mercantile community had been low-key, it was in those two areas that the most positive achievements of the Commonwealth lay. The triumph of independency left a legacy of bitter distrust against religious radicals, and fuelled an intolerant Anglicanism which lasted almost two centuries. The triumph of the army left a similar distrust of political soldiers which is still with us. The experience of a republic stifled republican ambitions until at least the middle of the nineteenth century, but the active involvement of the state in the promotion of trade, the willingness to allow commercial interests a dominant say in foreign policy, and a benevolent indulgence towards the development of colonies, were equally important legacies of a far more positive nature. Above all, the transformation in the scale and resourcing of the navy, and its use as a major instrument of aggressive and expansionist policies, transformed England from a second-rate power with occasional strategic importance into a first-rate power which was soon to dominate the sea lanes of the world in a way which John Dee and Francis Drake could only have dreamed about.

Notes

1. F.C. Dietz, *English Public Finance, 1558–1640* (New York, 1932), 279–80; J.R. Powell, *The Navy in the English Civil War* (London, 1962), 193. F.E. Dyer, 'The Ship Money fleet', *Mariners Mirror*, 23, 1937, 187–97.

2. J.R. Powell and E.K. Timings, *Documents Relating to the Civil War, 1642–1648* (Navy Records Society, London, 1963), 69–72.

3. Bernard Capp, *Cromwell's Navy* (Oxford, 1989), 35–50. D.E. Kennedy, 'The English naval revolt of 1648', *English Historical Review*, 77, 1962, 247–56.

4. Capp, *Cromwell's Navy*, 73–5.

5. W.N. Hammond, 'The administration of the English Navy, 1649–1660' (University of Columbia Ph.D., 1973). H-C. Junge, *Flottenpolitik und Revolution: Die Enstehung der englischen Seemacht wahrend der Herrschaft Cromwells* (Stuttgart, 1980), 110.

6. Junge, *Flottenpolitik*, 133.

7. Capp, *Cromwell's Navy*; M. Oppenheim, *A History of the Administration of the Royal Navy, 1509–1660* (London, 1896, rep. 1988), 321–5. The accounts of Vane and Hutchinson as Treasurers of the Navy from 13 May 1649 to 7 July 1660 remain in Public Record Office (PRO) E351/2288–96.

8. Capp, *Cromwell's Navy*; Hammond, 'The administration of the English navy'.

9. Norman Clayton, 'Naval administration, 1603–1628' (University of Leeds Ph.D., 1935). J.S. Wheeler, 'Navy finance, 1649–1660', *Historical Journal*, 39, 1996, 457–66.

10. Oppenheim, *Administration of the Royal Navy*; A.D. Thrush, 'The navy of Charles I, 1625–1640' (London University Ph.D., 1991).

11. C.H. Wilson, *England's Apprenticeship, 1603–1763* (London, 1965), 38–9.

12. Ibid.

13. Lewis Roberts in *The Treasure of Traffike* (1641) had also expressed the connection between trade and imperial ambition: 'It is not our conquests, but our commerce; it is not our swords but our sayls that first spread the English name in Barbary, and thence come into Turkey, Armenia, Moscovia, Arabia,

Persia, India, China and indeed over and about the world'. For the relative decline of the broadcloth trade, see B.E. Supple, *Commercial Crisis and Change in England, 1600–1642* (Cambridge, 1959), 266. For customs and excise revenue, Wilson, *England's Apprenticeship*, 130.

14. Wheeler, 'Navy finance, 1649–1660'.

15. Ibid. See also Bodleian Library MS Rawlinson A208, 'Account Books of the Treasurer of the War, 1653–5'.

16. Junge, *Flottenpolitik*, 325.

17. Capp, *Cromwell's Navy*.

18. Ibid. K.R. Andrews, *Ship Money and Politics: Seafaring and Naval Enterprise in the Reign of Charles I* (London, 1991).

19. Capp, *Cromwell's Navy*, 73–5.

20. M.J. Braddick, 'An English military revolution?', *Historical Journal*, 36, 1993, 965–75. Capp, *Cromwell's Navy*. S.C.A. Pincus, *Protestantism and Patriotism: Ideologies and The Making of English Foreign Policy, 1650–1668* (Cambridge, 1996), 77.

21. Hammond, 'The administration of the English navy'; Oppenheim, *Administration*, 330–7.

22. Cited by Junge, *Flottenpolitik*, 133.

23. C.H. Firth and R.S. Rait, *Acts and Ordinances of the Interregnum, 1642–1660* (London, 1911), 403–6. J. Thirsk and J.P. Cooper, *Seventeenth-Century Economic Documents* (Oxford, 1972), 502–3. G.N. Clark, 'The Navigation Act of 1651', *History*, 7, 1972, 285.

24. Pincus, *Protestantism and Patriotism*, passim.

25. Ibid., 70.

26. PRO SP105/144, f. 47, Council of State to the Levant Company, 23 July 1652.

27. Capp, *Cromwell's Navy*; Pincus, *Protestantism and Patriotism*, 102, 103–4.

28. C.R. Boxer, *The Dutch Seaborne Empire, 1600–1800* (London, 1965) contains a full analysis of the commercial strengths of the Low Countries.

29. J.R. Powell, *Robert Blake* (London, 1972). Capp, *Cromwell's Navy*, 87. This exploit made a major impression because it was the first time that ships had been taken out from under the guns of a shore battery.

30. By H.S. Commager, but see more particularly R.L. Morton, *Colonial Virginia* (Williamsburg, 1960).

31. Morton, *Colonial Virginia*, 168.

32. Ibid.

33. G.V. Scammell, *The First Imperial Age* (London, 1989), 160–3; for a fuller discussion, see J.J. McCusker and R.R. Menard, *The Economy of British America, 1607–1789* (Chapel Hill, 1985); for military aspects of power, see S.S. Webb, *The Governor General: The English Army and the Definition of the Empire, 1569–1681* (Chapel Hill, 1979).

34. This was the theory. In practice the authority of the English government in the colonies was always sketchy, and governors seem to have issued judicial commissions which were not challenged. Scammell, *First Imperial Age*, 164–6; Morton, *Colonial Virginia*.

35. Felix Makower, *The Constitutional History and Constitution of the Church of England* (Berlin, 1895), 141–2.

36. Ibid.

37. Aubery C. Land, *Colonial Maryland: A History* (New York, 1981).

38. R.S. Dunn, *Sugar and Slaves: The Rise of the Planter Class in the English West Indies, 1624–1713* (London, 1973).

39. G.D. Ramsay, *England's Overseas Trade in the Centuries of Emergence* (London, 1957).

40. Junge, *Flottenpolitik*, 175. Ramsay, *England's Overseas Trade*, 114.

41. Clark, 'The Navigation Act of 1651'.

42. Thirsk and Cooper, *Seventeenth-Century Economic Documents*, 501. C.M. Andrews, *British Committees, Commissions and Councils of Trade and Plantations, 1622–1675* (Baltimore, 1908).

43. Cited by Junge, *Flottenpolitik*, 151.

44. Thirsk and Cooper, *Seventeenth-Century Economic Documents*, 367.

45. Capp, *Cromwell's Navy*, 73.

46. Ibid., 75.

47. Ibid., 77.

48. Ibid., 87.

49. Christopher Hill, *God's Englishman* (Oxford, 1970); B. Coward, *Oliver Cromwell* (London, 1991).

50. J.F. Battick, 'Cromwell's diplomatic blunder: the relationship between the Western Design of 1654–5 and the French alliance of 1657', *Albion*, 5, 1973, 280. Capp, *Cromwell's Navy*, 87–9.

51. Capp, *Cromwell's Navy*, 87–9.

52. Ibid., 98.

53. J.R. Powell, *Robert Blake*; J.S. Corbett, *Successors of Drake* (London, 1900), 396–7; N.A.M. Rodger, *The Safeguard of the Sea* (London, 1997), 292–4.

54. Capp, *Cromwell's Navy*, 101–2.

55. Ramsay, *England's Overseas Trade*; Battick, 'Cromwell's diplomatic blunder'.

56. Capp, *Cromwell's Navy*, 104.

57. Ramsay, *England's Overseas Trade*; R. Davis, 'England and the Mediterranean, 1570–1670', in F.J. Fisher, ed., *Essays in the Economic and Social History of Tudor and Stuart England* (London, 1961).

58. A. Woolrych, 'The Good Old Cause and the fall of the Protectorate', *Historical Journal*, 13, 1957, 133–61; Woolrych, 'Last quests for a settlement, 1657–60', in G.E. Aylmer, ed., *The Interregnum: The Quest for a Settlement, 1646–1660* (London, 1972).

59. Ivan Roots, *The Great Rebellion, 1642–1660* (London, 1966), 232–4.

60. J.T. Rutt, ed., *The Diary of Thomas Burton, Esq. (1656–59)* (London, 1828), III, 268–9.

61. C.H. Firth, ed., *The Clarke Papers* (Camden Society, London, 1891–1901), III, 187; Root, *Great Rebellion*, 238.

62. R.W. Ramsey, *Richard Cromwell, Protector of England* (London, 1935); Sir Richard Baker, *A Chronicle of the Kings of England* (London, 1696), 641; *Clarke Papers*, III, 193, 209–17.

63. Roots, *Great Rebellion*, 241.

64. Capp, *Cromwell's Navy*; Junge, *Flottenpolitik*, 325.

65. C.H. Firth, *The Memoirs of Edmund Ludlow* (Oxford, 1894), II, 100. G.F. Warner, *The Nicholas Papers* (Camden Society, London, 1886–1920), IV, 152.

66. R. Petty, 'The rebellion of Sir George Booth, August 1659', *Journal of the Chester and North Wales Archaeological and Historical Society*, new series, 33, 1939, 119–37.

67. G. Davies, *The Restoration of Charles II* (Oxford, 1955), 156.

68. Roots, *Great Rebellion*, 249–50; Capp, *Cromwell's Navy*; Junge, *Flottenpolitik*, 324–6.

69. Junge, *Flottenpolitik*, 324–6.

70. Roots, *Great Rebellion*, 251–2; John Price, *The mystery and method of his majesty's happy restoration* (1680), in F.B. Maseres, *Select Tracts Relating to the Civil Wars in England* (London, 1815).

71. Roots, *Great Rebellion*, 252–4.

72. Maseres, *Tracts*, II, 774.

73. *The Parliamentary or Constitutional History of England* (London, 1751–62), XXII, 231.

CHAPTER SEVEN

The Navy as an Instrument of Policy, 1660–1690

Although in some respects the Restoration settlement was an explicit repudiation of what had happened in England over the previous eighteen years, in other ways it represented almost unbroken continuity. The royal court resumed its social and political importance, ignoring the somewhat palid imitation which Oliver Cromwell had created in his later years. The Church of England, although riddled with apprehension, was not only able to restore its material fabric and structure, but also to pick up the intransigent high churchmanship of William Laud where he had been forced to lay in down in 1644.[1] The parliaments of Scotland and Ireland returned, and the dreaded army was disbanded, leaving a legacy of antipathy which was to last well into the following century. Even the courts of common law reverted from English to 'law French' – to the benefit of no one except a few legal clerks.

However, Charles had no option but to start his foreign policy from the point he was at. He had not been restored by foreign intervention, either military or financial, and although he was in different ways indebted to both the Dutch and the French, he was not under any obligation to either. John Thurloe, the last Commonwealth Secretary of State, drew up a series of memoranda explaining the existing situation, but in terms of practical experience the king's new servants were left to find their feet as best they could. The war with Spain had been purely notional for the previous eighteen months, and the Spaniards were eager for a settlement, so that represented a very simple first step. The contentious issue of Jamaica was dealt with by ignoring it. Spain maintained its claim but England remained in possession, thus satisfying both honour and interest. For the time being England also retained Dunkirk, but it required a permanent garrison, which had not only become abhorrent in principle, but was also vastly expensive, costing in the region of £100,000 a year. In 1662 Charles cut his losses and sold it back to the French for £400,000.[2] In the long run this was not a clever move, because when Anglo-French relations later deteriorated the Dunkirkers resumed the occupation for which their grandfathers and greatgrandfathers had been notorious, and plundered English shipping. Like Cromwell, Charles saw the fulcrum of European politics in the rivalry of France and Spain, and chose the French side. However, since the effective defeat of Spain at the peace of the Pyrenees in 1659, that was an out-of-date perception, which obscured the view taken by both the king and his advisers of the rivalry which did now matter, that between France and the United Provinces.

Just as 1660 saw no dramatic change in English foreign policy, so it also witnessed continuity in both naval and commercial affairs. Although there were many short-term fluctuations in the state of the navy, sometimes caused by politics but more often by money, the fleet was maintained at or above the Commonwealth level for the whole reigns of Charles II and James II.[3] The largest total number of ships on the payroll during this period was 218 in 1666, and the smallest 142 in 1674. The number of warships peaked at 135 in 1665, and dropped to 90 in 1668, 1669, 1672 and 1674. The annual average over the 25 years was 164 and 111 respectively, about three times the size of Charles I's fleet at its strongest. Some 161 individual warships and 86 others were in service at one time or another during these years, of which 82 were warships of first to third rate, that is carrying between 50 and 100 guns.[4] Some of these larger ships enjoyed extraordinarily long careers. In 1660 fifteen of the first and second raters had been built before the civil war, and one of the first raters, the *Prince Royal*, had been launched in 1610. It had been extensively rebuilt in 1621 and 1641, and was to be repaired again in 1663 before being lost in the Four Day battle of 1666. Of less antiquity, but even more imposing, was the *Royal Sovereign*, which had been built as the *Sovereign of the Seas* in 1637, a massive 100-gun prestige ship which had originally cost almost £40,000. The *Sovereign* was refitted in 1651, 1659–60 and 1673, before being finally lost in 1696.[5] These had both been given 'politically correct' names during the Commonwealth, and were among the 27 naval vessels which Charles felt it necessary to redesignate at the beginning of his reign.

The expansion which had taken place in dockyard facilities since 1640 was likewise maintained. The yards at Chatham, Woolwich, Portsmouth and Deptford covered many acres and included dry and wet docks, barracks, warehouses, ropewalks, storage spaces for timber, mast ponds and sawpits. Although some ships continued to be built on contract in private yards, there was an increasing tendency to use direct labour in the royal yards, and the permanent workforce numbered many hundreds in each place: shipwrights, caulkers, carpenters, sawyers, rope makers and many others, under the watchful eyes of the master craftsmen, storekeepers and Clerks of the Check.[6] In 1664 a new yard was opened at Harwich, specifically to deal with the increased activity in the North Sea. Royal ships had been intermittently based at Harwich since the reign of Henry VIII, and there had been a small establishment there early in Elizabeth's reign, but as the danger had come increasingly from the west, it had been abandoned.[7] The main operational bases were at Chatham and Portsmouth, with an outlying anchorage at Plymouth. Plymouth was very convenient for operations in the Western Approaches, but had always presented difficulties for victualling, and these had not been overcome in the later seventeenth century.[8] The main Admiralty offices were beside the Tower of London, and in Whitehall.

Since about 1650 the Admiralty had been one of the chief spending departments of the state, both in war and in peace, and that continued to be the case after the Restoration. The total naval issues between 1660 and 1690 came to some £16 million, averaging about £550,000 a year, between 25 and 35 per cent of the total expenditure of the state.[9] The funding of the navy was consequently a recurring political issue. The Convention parliament had been persuaded to grant a supply which was intended to be sufficient to pay off the army, and discharge such other debts as the king was willing to acknowledge. These included sums owed on the naval accounts, but they were so large that they could not all be paid at once, even while parliament was in a giving mood. Consequently a part of the naval debt was carried over into the new reign, and remained a fluctuating but ever-present factor; £800,000 was provided, but because of the slowness with which it was collected, the army was not finally discharged until February 1661, at a cost of nearly £450,000. By that time the various naval debts came to £1.2 million, as we have seen, and only some £350,000 was available to discharge them.[10] All debts going back before 14 March 1658 were then written off, but that still left £637,000 to be carried on the normal budget. This problem was addressed during the years of peace which followed. Between midsummer 1660 and Michaelmas 1664 £1.65 million was spent on the navy, over and above the special allocation, and that reduced the ongoing debt to about £320,000 before the outbreak of the second Dutch war altered the situation again.[11] In 1664/65, and again in the following year, naval expenditure topped £1 million, which seems to have been sufficient to prevent the debt from getting worse, but insufficient to make any further progress in discharging it. At length in 1667 the customs farmers were persuaded to advance a further £300,000 which was specifically allocated to the naval debt, and the problem was thus reduced to manageable proportions, at least for the time being. Although the second

Dutch war could hardly be described as victorious, it had actually produced nearly £500,000 in prize profits, which had covered about 20 per cent of the costs of the fighting.[12]

Until about 1670, opposition to Charles's government came largely from adherents of the 'good old cause', who can be seen with hindsight to have been much less formidable than they appeared at the time. However, after that date, as the king's admiration for things French became increasingly apparent, a new kind of opposition began to materialise. Charles was suspected of popish and absolutist tendencies, and parliament became difficult about voting supply. In 1668 the Triple Alliance was a popular foreign policy, and the king had little difficulty in raising an extra £310,000 for the navy on the customs and excise. Even in 1670 when he asked for £800,000 for a 'precautionary fleet', it was forthcoming, albeit by the somewhat unusual expedient of a new subsidy.[13] However, by 1673 the climate had changed. The conversion of the Duke of York, the king's brother and Lord High Admiral, to Catholicism, which had taken place at some time during the previous two years, put the navy in the political front line. Although the Test Act was extended to the navy, and James was forced to resign his office, his influence remained extremely strong, and this was well known. Parliament was in a cleft stick. To weaken the navy meant undermining the country's security, and depriving it of the means to influence world affairs, to say nothing of damaging trade. On the other hand to strengthen the navy meant strengthening the Duke of York. Samuel Pepys, the Clerk of the Acts, upon whom we are dependent for so much of our detailed knowledge of naval affairs, was deeply enmeshed in the political conflict.[14] As early as 1673 he was attacked as a dependant of the duke (which was true) and as a crypto-Catholic (which was not).

The third Dutch war (1672–74) was not popular. It was seen as being fought for the benefit of the French, who were now a greater menace to the security of England than the Dutch were to her trade. By 1674 there was acute anxiety about France's growing strength at sea, but it was matched by a strong desire to economise on the navy and to undermine the Duke of York's position. The tension between these incompatible objectives surfaced frequently in parliament. In April 1675 Pepys, who was a member of the House of Commons, requested money for the rebuilding of the fleet. He was supported by Henry Coventry, who declared: 'The French increasing at this rate in shipping, as you are told, 'tis high time to lay your hands upon your hearts and purses . . . the King of France's great fleet is not built to take Vienna'.[15] However, the members were keenly aware that the navy had cost them £2.75 million between 1671 and 1675, out of a total war expenditure of a little over £5 million, and were in no mood to respond to such appeals. The whole peacetime military establishment was intended (by parliament) to cost no more than £610,000 per annum, but this total was always exceeded, and suspicion grew in consequence.

On 5 March 1677 Pepys's persistence was at last rewarded. Fear of the French temporarily triumphed over suspicion of the duke, and £600,000 was voted for the building of 30 new ships.[16] In 1678, in two very close votes, the Commons further approved an allocation of £109,000 a month to 'set forth' 90 ships during the summer. However, before the end of the same year the Franco-Dutch war was over and the mood had changed again: £200,000 was granted for the disbandment of the army, and a similar sum for the reduction of the fleet. Because of this unpredictable seesaw, which must have made forward planning almost impossible, by March 1679 the naval debt had risen again to nearly £900,000, and the total owed in military debts and anticipations was approaching £3 million. The Popish Plot was also injecting a large dose of paranoia into an already tense and unstable political situation. 'There is not a man in the fleet', declared Sir John Bennett in a debate on the militia in April 1679, 'that has served in the fleet since the king came in, but was made by the Duke of York.'[17] The resulting situation defied logic. Pepys's analysis of the dangers from both France and the Netherlands were accepted as accurate, but the secretary himself was committed to the Tower as a suspected papist, and the entire Admiralty Commission was dismissed. The oath required by the Test Act was administered to all naval officers and officials in the winter of 1678–79, and taken without demur by almost everyone, but the panic did not subside. It seems that Titus Oates had a particular grudge against the naval establishment, which had dismissed him from his position as a fleet chaplain in 1675 on the ground of sodomy. The witch hunt was not to be deterred by the fact that only a handful had refused the Test Oath. Foreign officers were hounded out, as were Irishmen, and indeed any gentleman who had the slightest connection with the Duke of York. This was not all loss, because the preference of the king and the duke for gentleman officers had blocked the promotion of many competent tarpaulins, who now came to the fore.[18] In fact the Whig leaders during the Exclusion Crisis soon recognised that they could not afford to starve the navy in order to victimise James's 'creatures'. By 1681 the mood of the country was hawkish, and the motto was 'strike the French king at sea'. The Popish Plot produced its own reasons, not for withholding supply, but for building up the navy to new strength.

> T'ensure the plot, France must her legions send
> Rome to restore and to enthrone Rome's friend
> Tis in return James doth our fleet betray
> That fleet whose thunder made the world obey.

Ships, once our safety and our glorious might
Are doomed with worms and rottenness to fight.
Whilst France rides sov'reign o'er the British main . . .[19]

With the sublime effrontery of the political propagandist, the writer turned to blame the Duke of York for the fact that Exclusionist members of parliament had forced the removal of a competent naval administration, and compelled its successor to cope without adequate funds.

The Admiralty Commission which functioned from 1679 to 1684 has had a bad press, but that is largely due to the fact that the best-known description of its activities was written by one of its chief victims, Samuel Pepys.[20] Pepys, who enjoyed the full confidence of the king, returned to office as soon as Charles felt strong enough to dispense with the relics of the Exclusion Crisis. He was then given the title 'Secretary for the Affairs of the Admiralty', and his influence over naval policy was much increased. On 31 December 1684 he submitted to the king a report on 'The state of the Royal Navy of England at the dissolution of the late commission of the Admiralty, May 1684', and it is upon that report, and upon Pepys's miscellaneous papers, that the reputation of the commission has largely rested.[21] In fact the commission had come into existence under the most adverse possible circumstances. The build up of 1678 had been aborted, and by April 1679 the Admiralty owed £327,000 on wages alone. Instead of confronting this situation, members of parliament refused money and attacked the Admiralty. Charles had no option but to dismiss the officers in whom he had full confidence, and replace them with commissioners who were more or less foisted on him by parliament.

Strenuous retrenchment became the order of the day. Most of the fleet was paid off; Harwich was abandoned and the staff in the dockyards reduced. It is against this background that Pepys's accusations of incompetence have to be seen. Very little new building could be undertaken beyond what what was already in hand, and the maintenance programme had fallen into arrears. The commissioners warned the Treasury in 1680 of the dire consequences of parliament's attitude, but nothing improved. By 1683 the immediate requirement was estimated at over £1 million, of which £120,000 was required for urgent repairs and £35,000 for dockyard wages.[22] Discipline had deteriorated, and no constructive policy was possible. However, the main reasons for this did not lie in simple inefficiency. The £425,000 per annum which parliament allocated to the navy from 1681 to 1684 was not sufficient to cover expenditure which needed at least £500,000. Moreover the king himself was largely responsible for the decline of discipline, because he clung obstinately to his preference for gentlemen officers, while his opponents campaigned with equal tenacity to remove them. In fact the number of warships in service significantly increased under the much-maligned commission, averaging 121 a year from 1679 to 1684, as opposed to 96 over the previous decade. Thomas Hayter, who served as secretary for most of the commission's existence, was every bit as competent as Pepys himself, a fact which the latter could not afford to admit, and it was only when Hayter was succeeded by John Brisbane that the standard of administration began to decline.[23] Moreover a new dock had been constructed at Chatham, and when the commission wound up its affairs in 1684, the debt was no more than £385,000. Apart from shortage of money, the real problem arose not from incompetence but from factiousness. This centred on the abrasive personality of Daniel Finch, Earl of Nottingham, the ranking commissioner, who had a talent for crossing wires with his colleagues and falling over his own feet. This situation was exacerbated by the fact that it had only been the political circumstances of the Popish Plot and the Exclusion Crisis which had called the commission into existence at all.

When James succeeded his brother in February 1685, there was an upsurge of loyal enthusiasm, which was quickly reflected in the parliament when it convened on 19 May.[24] Exclusion having been defeated, few kings can have come to the throne in a more supportive political climate. James's enthusiasm for the navy was undiminished, and parliament was easily persuaded to vote additional customs duties on wine, vinegar, tobacco and sugar, which were intended to produce £2.2 million over eight years to pay off the naval debt. In fact the actual sum raised fell far short of that total, but the assistance to the naval budget was nevertheless significant. Over the four years of his reign, James's ordinary revenue averaged £1.6 million, an increase of some 30 per cent over that which Charles had enjoyed, and taxation for special purposes (such as the navy) was also relatively easy.[25] However, neither the Francophobia nor the anti-Catholicism of five years earlier had gone away, and the king misconstrued the helpfulness of parliament, with fatal consequences for himself. It was the loyalism of this parliament which solved Pepys's problems for him. Not only was money voted, but the affairs of the navy were investigated by a special commission which accepted his version of events, so that the commission of 1679–84 became the scapegoat for a situation which in fact it had done its level best to address. When in the very different political climate of 1691–92 a second parliamentary commission took the same view, Samuel Pepys's victory over his supplanters became permanently enshrined in the history of the navy.[26]

In a way the care which James had lavished on the navy for over 20 years was poorly rewarded when the crisis of his own reign came in 1688, but the king had only himself to blame for that situation. With a clumsiness which is hard to understand, James did exactly what his political opponents had claimed that he would do during the Exclusion Crisis, and began a many-faceted campaign to force his personal Catholicism upon the country.[27] His enemies were outraged, the Pope was alarmed, and even the most zealous English Catholics became apprehensive as he ignored the increasingly obvious warning signs. No one knew at the time that James had made a secret approach to Louis XIV for money as soon as he came to the throne, but his partiality for a French alliance was soon apparent. However, he had no desire to get involved in Louis's wars, and renewed the 1678 treaty with the Low Countries in June 1687. At that point James's heir was his elder daughter, Mary, a Protestant born to his first marriage with Anne Hyde, who was also the wife of William of Orange, Stadholder of Holland. This meant that in the event of his death or removal, William, who was one of Louis's most implacable enemies, would obtain the Crown Matrimonial of England. Louis was perfectly well aware of this, and regarded James's reckless course during 1686 and 1687 with mounting alarm. If the king pushed his notoriously volatile subjects too far, France could soon be facing William as King of England. He did his best to restrain his ally, but he could hardly warn him openly against promoting the interests of Holy Church, and his influence had no effect.

There were many in England who saw the same situation, and debated furiously what they should do when a lawful king, such as James, pursued policies which were inimical to the established church, and to most of the political nation. The Anglo-Dutch treaty of 1687 had not only improved relations generally, it had established links between the navies of the two powers. By the terms of the agreement England was bound to provide 20 ships for combined operations against the Algerians, who continued to threaten the trade of both countries. The Dutch may have asked for these as early as August 1687, and in May and June 1688 they were being fitted out at Chatham.[28] William began to mobilise his own fleet, ostensibly for the same purpose, in January 1688, and at the same time sent a squadron to the West Indies commanded by Charles Mordaunt, Earl of Peterborough. William's purpose in doing that is not clear, but Mordaunt took the opportunity to sound out the English colonies in that area about their attitude to events in England, and such may have been the main intention.[29] In June 1688 a crisis was reached. James's queen, Mary of Modena, had been pregnant for months, but this had happened before and in fifteen years of marriage they had not succeeded in producing a live child. However, the prince who was born on 10 June was not only alive, but showed every sign of staying that way. At the same time Archbishop Sancroft and six diocesan bishops who had been prosecuted for sedition because they refused to endorse the second Declaration of Indulgence, were acquitted.[30] If the first event was an unexpected triumph for the king, the second was a defeat with enormous implications. James's opponents deemed that the birth of an heir made it imperative to act, and judged that the mood of the country offered every chance of success. They invited William to intervene, and the invitation was carried to The Hague by Admiral Arthur Herbert. Herbert was already out of favour with the king, but he was enormously popular in the fleet, and there are numerous signs that his action was supported by his colleagues.[31]

It did not, however, lead to an immediate test of allegiance. Although Louis hastened to offer James the support of sixteen French warships, the offer was declined, and a part of the fleet was stationed in the Downs to monitor Dutch preparations. The commander of this squadron was Sir Roger Strickland, who was a Catholic and unpopular with the men, but the king was well received when he visited the fleet in July, and nobody was in a position to know what would happen next. William, meanwhile, had diverted the Dutch Indies fleet round the north of Scotland to avoid a confrontation. By the time that he received fresh orders on 22 August, Strickland had 26 ships, but the largest was a single third rate and he would have been in no position to offer battle. On 2 September the Dutch were reported to be moving, but their purpose was unclear. On 9 September a second offer of French assistance was received and accepted, but a few days later Louis launched his armies against the Elector Palatine on the middle Rhine, thus making it clear that he had no serious intention of deterring William from intervening in England by keeping him occupied at home. It appears that the French king seriously misjudged both the mood of England and the determination of the Dutch. An open offer of support which was never likely to mean more than a few warships was counter-productive. At the end of September the English council ordered the impressment of seamen, and Lord Dartmouth took over the sea command from Strickland.[32] Dartmouth was a reliable Protestant loyalist, and popular in the fleet. It began to look as though James was preparing to strike against the Dutch, who had still not made their intentions clear.

On 1 October Dartmouth was alerted for action, and on the 19th William's armada finally set sail: 49 warships, 10 fireships and over 200 transports. Arthur Herbert sailed with the Dutch fleet, but his intention seems to have been to create a diversion rather than to accompany the main expedition. In spite of the odds, Dartmouth was perfectly willing to intercept, but his intelligence was defective and he had no idea of where the Dutch were going. Consequently the 'Protestant wind' took William around Dartmouth's groping scouts, and he landed unopposed at Torbay on 7 November. Some of the king's supporters cast aspersions on the admiral's loyalty, but this seems to have been unjustified, and James never accepted it.[33] However, fortune continued to favour William. He reached Exeter unopposed on 19 November, and already had the support of many leading

English politicians, but the outcome of his bid was still in the balance. Meanwhile Dartmouth's fleet, which had set out on the 16th with every intention of attacking the Dutch ships which had remained at Torbay, was driven back by adverse weather, and having received no further instructions, the admiral decided to wait on events. The decisive events of the next few days took place inside James's head, and the full truth is never likely to be known. Convinced that he was surrounded by treachery, the king decided to get his wife and son to a place of safety, and on 2 December broke his silence to instruct Dartmouth to get young James out of the country. The admiral objected strongly, arguing that such a move would be interpreted as a surrender; his officers seem to have been divided, but again their views were not put to the test. No further word came from James, but on 11 December the news arrived that not only had the prince been evacuated by other means, but that the king had followed him. When an approach was received from William the following day, there was no sensible course but to accept it.[34] There seemed little point in attempting to defend a cause which the principal had given up. On 13 December the fleet council concurred, and the crisis which never came to a head was over. In the event the world's most powerful navy had acted in one of the crucial events of English history like the dog in the night time; it had done nothing.

This was not because the fleet was underfunded, unprepared, or badly led. Mobilisation had been a bit slow, but 35 further warships were ready to join Dartmouth if he had gone into action in October or November. They were victualled and armed, and morale appears to have been good. Had James decided to fight, the navy might have divided. Herbert's presence in the Dutch camp means that such a development cannot be ruled out, but most evidence suggests that it would have stood by its lawful king, who had also for so long been its Lord Admiral and patron. At the outbreak of the civil war, and again at the Restoration, the navy had been an active political player, with an important influence upon events, but it would be hard to argue that in 1688. This was partly because it had become both more professional and better maintained.[35] There were few corrosive grievances in 1688 – no starvation, no intolerable arrears of pay. Nor were the officers ambitious politicians. Had James called upon his navy to fight, it would probably have done so, but the fact that the call never came makes the issue academic. Once William had consolidated his constitutional position in 1689, England's involvement in his perennial struggle against the French became inevitable, and the navy resumed its role as a major instrument of state policy. William did not neglect the navy – he could not afford to – but his perspective on the wars was inevitably more Dutch than English, and for the first time since 1660 the army challenged the Admiralty for resources and attention.[36]

Paradoxically, the Glorious Revolution meant that a navy which had seen most of its active service since 1660 fighting the Dutch, was taken over by a Dutch king to serve his continental purposes. Such an outcome could hardly have been foreseen. At the time of Charles II's restoration, the French threat hardly existed, and the king's first concern in foreign policy was to support the Portuguese who had reasserted their independence in 1640, but still felt threatened by their more powerful neighbour.

It was this concern which led in May 1662 to his marriage with Catherine of Braganza. In recommending the match his council was probably more influenced by the dowry of £800,000 which was on offer than by any more profound political consideration, but it had immediate and far-reaching consequences.[37] In addition to a very large sum of money, Catherine also brought with her the port towns of Bombay and Tangier. It has been argued that this was a shrewd move by the Iberians, because at the price of sacrificing small parts of their empire, which they were increasingly unable to defend, they enlisted the protection of the English navy for the rest. However, for the time being the king's imperial ambitions did not extend to the Far East. He handed Bombay over to the East India Company in 1668, and its future importance was commercial rather than military.

Tangier was a different proposition. When he had leisure to devote to such matters, Oliver Cromwell had very much wanted to strengthen England's military presence in the Mediterranean. Blake had operated against the Algerians with some success, but the Protector's great ambition had been to secure control of Gibraltar, and hence of the strait of that name. No opportunity had presented itself, and the English fleet had been recalled in the summer of 1659. However, the marriage treaty with Portugal reactivated these ambitions. In the summer of 1661 a new expedition took possession of Tangier, and plans began to be drawn up to convert it into a fortified naval base which could act as a permanent curb upon the corsairs.[38] Louis XIV encouraged such an ambition, partly because it would serve his own interests, and partly to deter any renewal of Spanish pretensions in the area. The Anglo-French deal over Dunkirk may have been another aspect of the same common strategic purpose. The Dutch were less enthusiastic, although it did not affect them directly. They were bound by treaty to collaborate in operations against the Algerians, and in June 1661 de Ruyter and the Earl of Sandwich mounted a joint campaign against the city, which achieved little. The Dutch viewed any Anglo-French understanding with suspicion, and Louis's enthusiasm for an English presence in Tangier caused them to move into a pro-Spanish stance, although for the time being their efforts were confined to diplomacy.[39]

In 1662 the Earl of Sandwich took over in Tangier, and quickly secured treaties with both Algiers and Tunis. The undertakings of such rulers were again demonstrated to be worthless, but a French campaign against the corsairs in the winter of 1662/63 was equally futile, and the case for a strong interventionist presence in the region seemed to have been greatly reinforced. In 1663 Sandwich was succeeded by Lord Rutherford, who secured from the Treasury the substantial sum of £30,000 for the construction of a mole at Tangier, and seems to have been given whatever he asked for to defend the town.[40] His concerns were well founded, because although the Spaniards were not willing to risk a renewed war by campaigning directly against the English enclave, they were perfectly willing to encourage the local Moorish emirates to hostilities, and in the course of one such campaign in 1664, Lord Rutherford was killed. Perhaps thinking that Rutherford's death would encourage the corsairs to renewed depredations, or perhaps merely anxious to make their own presence felt, the French planned to establish a similar enclave at Gigeri, but the scheme came to nothing. At the beginning of the second Anglo-Dutch war in 1665, Tangier was blockaded, but the defences held firm and the campaign was not pressed.

Once the war was over, the value of such a North African base for the protection of trade was soon demonstrated. Algiers was attacked again in 1669, and a blockade established which was taken over by another Mediterranean fleet under Sir Edward Spragge in September 1670.[41] Soon after the acquisition of Tangier, the English government seems to have determined to fight the corsairs on their own terms, and two galleys were ordered, one to be built at Genoa and the other at Leghorn. The former was never delivered, and it proved so difficult and expensive to obtain oarsmen for the other that by 1680 it had been declared useless, and replaced with two galley frigates built in England.[42] Even attempts to sell the galley failed, and the last slaves were disposed of in 1681.

In the short term the results of all these efforts were inconclusive, but the constant pressure was occasionally effective. In an attack on the Algerian outpost of Bougie in May 1671 the English destroyed an entire Algerian squadron, which triggered a revolt among the corsair captains. The Bey was murdered and his successor was compelled to make peace. By 1673 the mole at Tangier was complete, and a naval establishment was set up there, which was not disturbed during the second Anglo-Dutch war. After 1677 there was more danger that it might fall to the French, but English merchants regarded it as essential for the safeguard of their business, and the Admiralty took a similar view. However, the dismissal of the Admiralty Board, which resulted in 1679 from the Exclusion Crisis, and the drastic retrenchment which followed, caused even the most strenuous commercial representations to be ignored. In defiance of all well-informed advice in 1683 the navy was pulled out of Tangier, and the harbour destroyed.[43]

For about 20 years, until the capture of Gibraltar in 1704 finally realised Cromwell's vision, the English navy was without a base in the Mediterranean.

Naval activity in what might by this time be termed the English Empire was loosely associated with the Anglo-Dutch wars. The Dutch seized Cape Coast Castle in West Africa in 1663, and the English retaliated by sending a squadron in 1664, which captured all the Dutch settlements on the Guinea coast, except El Mina.[44] They were not retained, however, and there seems to have been no intention of doing so. The most important of these unplanned skirmishes was probably the capture of New Amsterdam in 1664, because that was retained at the Treaty of Breda three years later, and consolidated the English hold on the east coast of North America.[45] In the Far East the East India Company was in no position to challenge the VOC, but the possession of Bombay was eventually useful in expanding the number of English bases, although the English Crown had little interest in developing it. In the West Indies events were even more detached from European politics, and although naval ships were involved, it was more on the initiative of the colonial governors than of the Admiralty. Captain Myngs, for example, who had first been sent to the Caribbean in October 1654, and had been involved in both the permanent capture of Jamaica in 1655 and the temporary seizure of Rio de la Hacha in 1656, returned to the area in 1662 in command of the *Centurion*. There had been an official cessation of hostilities following the peace of 1661, but certain Spanish towns, notably St Iago in Hispaniola, Puerto Rico and San Domingo, refused to trade with the English in spite of the terms of the treaty. The Council of Jamaica ordered an attack upon St Iago in consequence, and that was carried out by Myngs in September 1662.[46]

Even more characteristic of the ambiguities of the region was the career of Henry Morgan. Morgan first appears as the leader of a band of buccaneers, or freebooters, in Jamaica at about the time of Myng's exploit. In 1671 at the head of what was virtually a private army, he captured both Porto Bello and Panama, seizing a large booty. Under orders to placate an outraged Spanish government, the Governor of Jamaica succeeded in arresting him and sending him back to England. However, like Drake a hundred years earlier, the line between criminal activity and royal service was a fine one. Impressed by his record, both as a soldier and a seaman, Charles II knighted him and sent him back to Jamaica as Deputy Governor![47] Unsurprisingly, his relations with successive governors were uneasy, but as a poacher turned gamekeeper he was an outstanding success. The period from 1670 to about 1720 was the most active period of buccaneering. Men (and a few women) of all nationalities were involved, but the small British naval force deployed in the West Indies, and under Morgan's inspired leadership until his death in 1688, did more than anything else to keep this menace under control.

However, the main story of the navy between the Restoration and the Glorious Revolution is the story of the two Anglo-Dutch wars of 1665–67 and 1672–74. These are the wars in which the so-called 'military revolution' is supposed to have come to the navy. The first aspect of this revolution was the question of scale.[48] The armies of the seventeenth century were rapidly growing in size, from tens of thousands in the early years of the Thirty Years War to hundreds of thousands by the War of the Spanish Succession. The demands of such vast numbers completely changed the financial systems of the states which deployed them, the victualling arrangements, and all other aspects of logistics. England never attempted to form such an army; even the New Model at its height numbered no more than 70,000, but it did pioneer the same revolution at sea. As we have seen, the number of fighting ships increased threefold between 1640 and 1660, including a proportionate increase in large warships, and we have already seen what a financial strain that imposed. In terms of deployment, however, we have to look carefully at the figures in order to understand their true significance. Medieval fleets occasionally numbered hundreds of ships, and even in the Armada campaign each side had mustered about 150. The greatest battles of the Anglo-Dutch wars did not approach such figures. On the other hand, if we count only the specialised fighting ships which belonged to the Crown (or the state), the picture looks rather different. Setting aside the question of galleys, which were used only in small numbers in northern waters, the great fleets of the early sixteenth century included no more than 30–40 specialised warships, and the same was true at the time of the Armada. However, at the Battle of Lowestoft in June 1665 each fleet numbered about 100 first to sixth raters, deploying a firepower which would have been unimaginable 80 years before.[49] The revolution was not simply a question of numbers; it was a question of ownership, state control, and professionalism of management.

In so far as there was a tactical revolution, it concerned the use of the line-ahead formation. Medieval sea battles had been mêlées, conducted on a ship-to-ship basis; and that had continued to be the case for a while after the introduction of heavy guns in the early sixteenth century. However, by the 1540s Spanish tacticians were taking advantage of the superior sailing qualities of contemporary ships to fight in formations, which increased the effectiveness of their gunnery. That development had been followed by Lord Lisle in his battle orders of 1545. Mid-sixteenth-century battle squadrons seem to have advanced in line abreast, with their guns canted as far forward as possible, and reverted to broadside firing once the enemy line had been broached.[50] The first use of line-ahead is disputed, and was probably unrecorded, but it was regarded as an innovation when the English used it against the Armada in 1588. The circumstances of that battle were unusual, in that the English were passing and repassing a closely packed formation which had no intention of allowing itself to be disrupted. When the more general battle developed at Gravelines, it is not clear that it was used. By the middle of the seventeenth century the sailing qualities of warships had further improved, and their guns were both heavier and more numerous. It was also possible to fire synchronised broadsides, which greatly increased their impact, and in these circumstances the use of line-ahead as a normal battle tactic became increasingly attractive. The traditional division of the fleet into van, centre and rear squadrons was retained, but they were now called the Red, White and Blue.[51] The great problem with line-ahead was that it stretched a fleet across many miles of open sea, and made communication extremely difficult. However, this problem could be reduced by division into squadrons, which also made the battle options more flexible.

This system had been firmly adopted by the English when the fleets met off Lowestoft in the first battle of the second Anglo-Dutch war in June 1665.[52] This encounter, in which the Dutch lost no fewer than 32 of the 100 ships they deployed, was not only a decisive English victory, it was also a conclusive demonstration of the superiority of the line-ahead tactic, which the Dutch thereafter followed. The wisdom of this decision was clearly demonstrated when the battle fleets again engaged almost exactly a year later. At the Four Day battle of June 1666 the English were understrength, and were severely mauled, losing seventeen ships to the Dutch four.[53] The Battle of Orfordness just over a month later was much more even, and the English claimed it as a great victory, on the grounds that the Dutch lost 20 ships out of 88, and the English only one. However, by the end of 1666 English enthusiasm for the war was waning fast, and the generosity of parliament had run into the sands. So great was the shortage of money that a main battlefleet could not be deployed at all in 1667. When the Dutch attacked the Medway anchorage on 12 June they were virtually unchallenged,[54] and Charles was forced to conclude a disadvantageous peace.

The reasons for this war, like those of the first Anglo-Dutch war, lay less in commercial rivalry (although that was real enough) than in the state of domestic English politics. Just as the first war of 1652–54 was largely caused by fears that the Dutch Orangists would support the Stuarts, the second war was caused by fears that the Dutch republic would seek to revive the 'good old cause'.[55] For the first two years of his reign, both Charles and his parliament lived in mortal dread that the Cromwellian army would reconstitute itself. This fear drew them close together, and inspired the Anglo-Dutch treaty of 1662. There were indeed plots and threats of plots, but by

1663 their failure was beginning to inspire the government with a new confidence. This was reflected partly in an outbreak of bickering within the House of Commons, and partly in a desire to confront the Dutch rather than appease them. Late in 1663 a new plot was discovered, intending a rising in the north of England, to be followed by a general mobilisation of the disaffected.[56] The panic was general, and Dutch involvement universally suspected, with good reason. Just as in the 1630s, the Godly were emigrating, partly to New England and partly to Holland, and those who followed the latter course were not without an intention of stirring up their hosts against the government which they believed to be oppressing them. When the English council demanded that such of the 1663 plotters as had taken refuge in the Netherlands should be surrendered, the Estates General refused. 'The false perfidious Hollander', declared one pamphleteer in 1664, 'takes all occasion and advantage to do what mischief they can to the King and his subjects . . .'.[57] When parliament reassembled in March 1664, the bickering of the previous year had subsided, and there was a loyalist clamour for war.

It was obvious that this would again be a sea war. Parliament had already (and for the first time) legislated in 1661 a set of articles of war for the navy,[58] and there had been casual fighting in West Africa and North America. On 21 April 1664 the House of Commons passed a resolution declaring

> that the several and respective wrongs, dishonours and indignities done
> to his Majesty by the subjects of the United Provinces, by invading his
> rights in India, Africa and elsewhere; and the damages, affronts and injuries
> done by them to our merchants are the greatest obstructions of foreign
> trade . . . for the prevention of the like in future, and in prosecution thereof
> this House doth resolve, they will with their lives and fortunes, assist his
> Majesty against all opposition whatsoever.[59]

This so-called 'Trade Resolution' may have been genuinely motivated by City interests, but is much more likely to have been an expression of that bellicose Anglican loyalism which was the prevailing climate of the moment. The November session perhaps expressed itself more openly by passing the Triennial Act and the Conventicle Act. However, the English once again suspected that the Dutch were using economic weapons to achieve the political goal of 'universal monarchy' (or more properly, authority, since the United Provinces were a republic), a fear which had motivated them in 1652, as well as throughout their long conflict with Spain.[60]

'To pretend to universal monarchy without fleets was long since looked upon as a politick chimera', wrote John Evelyn '. . . for whosoever commands the ocean commands the trade of the world, commands the riches of the world, and whosoever is master of that commands the world itself . . .'. In February 1665 the parliament finally gave substance to its opinions by putting its hand in the nation's pocket, and voted £2.5 million, to be raised by assessment. Thus armed, the king went to war.

The actual fighting was inconclusive from the start. English victory off Lowestoft was followed in August by defeat off Bergen, and the complete failure of an attempt to capture the main Dutch Indies fleet.[61] London was decimated by plague, which temporarily paralysed its economic activity, and although in October parliament voted another £1.2 million for the war, it accompanied the grant with a declaration appropriating it to the payment of the Crown's existing creditors. In April 1666 England's only ally, the Bishop of Munster, withdrew from the war, and both the French and the Danes came in on the Dutch side. Louis's motives had nothing to do with helping the Dutch, and not much to do with damaging England, but soon turned out to be a cover for the seizure of the Spanish Netherlands. The French fleet was being rapidly built up at this point, but it was not deployed. Denmark, on the other hand, was a real threat, because she still had the main control of the Sound, and consequently access to the Baltic. The navy did reasonably well in the summer of 1666, defeat in June being followed not only by victory in July, but also by a successful raid on the Vlie in August which resulted in the destruction of over a hundred Dutch merchantmen.[62] However, in September London was again paralysed, this time by a devastating fire, and the parliament which assembled at the same time, although it granted another £1.8 million, was extremely critical of the naval administration.

By 1667 disillusionment with the war was becoming general. The public mood seems to have been disproportionally influenced by the Great Fire, and the absence of any clear-cut war aims became increasingly apparent. If the real intention had been to prevent the Dutch from meddling in internal English politics, that could have been achieved without war. If, on the other hand, the purpose had been to seize control of a large part of the Provinces' commercial empire, that would have required a much more complete naval victory than was ever likely to be possible between two such evenly matched antagonists. In January parliament set up a commission to examine the public accounts, and the Admiralty (not for the first time) began to protest that without further large-scale supply it would not be possible to send a battle fleet to sea in the summer.

In a sense each party was the victim of its own propaganda. Those in parliament who were becoming suspicious of Charles's style of government, and thought that he was using the war to promote his own (and his brother's) personal authority, were reluctant to give more money. The king could probably have found the money necessary for one summer's campaign without resorting to parliament, but chose not to do so because he wished to confront his opponents with the full consequences of their own obstructiveness. The Admiralty could also have done more than it did, but only at the cost of disproving its own jeremiads, and reducing its credibility for the future. Consequently, nothing was done.[63] There was probably a will to end the war on both sides, but it was the English who were suffering from political paralysis. On 12 June a Dutch fleet commanded by Cornelius de Witt broke the boom on the Medway and captured or destroyed fifteen of the king's ships. The humiliation was more serious than the actual losses, although they were bad enough. As a result of retrenchment, capped by this destructive raid, the number of warships declined from 124 in 1666 to 90 in 1668, and the lamentations could be heard throughout the land. In the circumstance a rapid settlement was unavoidable, and the Treaty of Breda brought the war to an end the following month. Although it could be described as a national disaster, the terms of the treaty were mild. The Dutch were wise enough to know that a rival who was down today could well be up again tomorrow, and were not interested in imposing punitive terms. Moreover the Dutch government and the English parliament both had a wary eye on Louis XIV, whose power and ambitions were growing visibly from year to year. It would not be wise for either of the two powers which could realistically oppose him to be too severely weakened. In England the chief victim or scapegoat was the Earl of Clarendon, who in October was forced to flee the country to avoid impeachment.[64] However, the positive and popular consequence was the formation in January 1668 of the Triple Alliance of England, Sweden and the United Provinces to curb the ambitions of France.

Louis took the threat implied by this alliance seriously, and immediately set out to break it down. In order to have a free hand for his own acquisitive schemes, he needed to isolate the Dutch. They were likely to be his most implacable rivals, because they were not only rich and powerful, but also vulnerable to attack in a way which neither the Swedes nor the English were. Between 1668 and 1670 French diplomacy was highly skilful, and almost completely successful. The Swedes were easily persuaded that they had no real interest in opposing a policy which posed no threat to their own security; and Charles, whose private attitudes were seriously at odds with those of his ministers, was enveigled into the secret treaty of Dover. By the terms of this agreement the king agreed to become a Catholic, and to announce his conversion when that should become practicable. In return he was to receive a French subsidy of about £124,000 a year, intended to reduce his dependence upon an unsympathetic parliament.[65] That Charles should be willing to give such a hostage to fortune suggests that his grasp upon reality was no stronger than his father's, but in the event he turned out to be far more astute in escaping the consequences. The so-called 'camouflage', or open treaty with France entered into a few months later, was much less dramatic, but that also signalled the end of the Triple Alliance. Popular sentiment was now more anti-French than anti-Dutch, but it was not difficult to re-open old wounds, and to imply that the time was coming to revenge the humiliation of the Medway. The declared policy of Charles's ministers was to use the support of France to secure a decisive victory over the Dutch which would leave England as the supreme commercial, colonial and naval power.[66] Once that was achieved, it was apparently thought, England would have little to fear from France, and France, supreme on the European mainland, would have no interest in challenging her. However, such optimism also assumed that England would continue to be Protestant, and to be governed in accordance with its own constitutional principles; both assumptions seemed to be fundamentally threatened by the king's secret undertakings.

Early in 1672 the English cynically provoked hostilities. 'Our business is to break with them, and yet to lay the breache at their door', as one official admitted. Salutes to the flag were demanded in situations where they were bound to be refused, and in March Sir Robert Holmes launched an unprovoked attack upon the Smyrna fleet. The attack was a failure, but it made the formal declaration of war a few days later almost redundant. By the end of March the Dutch were fighting on two fronts, against a French invasion and against a combined Anglo-French fleet at sea. In theory the allied fleet was stronger, with some 172 ships (of which 92 were English) and 5,000 guns, against 130 ships and 4,500 guns.[67] But in practice the allies were reluctant and suspicious of each other, and the Dutch, under the able leadership of de Ruyter, had the best of the fighting at sea. By the terms of the Anglo-French treaty, England should also have participated in the land war, and received as its reward the island of Walcheren, which had been coveted since at least the mid-sixteenth century. De Ruyter's priority was defensive, and he was more concerned to keep his fleet in being than to win spectacular victories, so large sea battles were few. One took place off Southwold in May 1672, which saw heavy casualties on both sides, but no decisive result. The Dutch pulled back in good order and English plans for an invasion force were seriously delayed, so the advantage was to de Ruyter. A month later the French captured Utrecht, an event which precipitated the fall of the de Witts and the appointment of William of Orange as Stadholder of the whole United Provinces.[68] After that the invaders made little further progress, and de Ruyter retained control of the inshore waters, making amphibious operations impossible. Bad weather frustrated all naval operations in the latter part of the year, so no English seaborne attack came, and the Dutch were frustrated in an attempt against Brest.

At the same time in England the political fall-out began. The terms of the secret treaty of Dover were not fully revealed until 1682, but by early 1673 the substance was pretty well known. Parliament did not meet from April 1671 to January 1673, and both the timing and the manner of the outbreak of war had been determined by the king. No one denied that war and peace were prerogative matters, but this time, unlike the second Dutch war, Charles did not have his subjects behind him. Two days before the formal commencement of hostilities, he had issued a Declaration of Indulgence. This was also a prerogative action, an exercise of his 'supreme power in ecclesiastical matters'. It provided for Protestant dissenters to use licensed places of worship, and Roman Catholics to use approved private houses.[69] In principle it was a sensible attempt to damp down religious controversy and unite the nation in time of war, and that was no doubt the significance of the timing. However, it was not generally seen that way. Fighting alongside the French against fellow Protestants, and extending even the most limited indulgence to the hated Catholics, were the thin end of a wedge which would eventually introduce popery and arbitary government to England. Parliament knew what it had to do. In return for a modest war subsidy of £1.2 million over three years, it forced Charles to cancel his Indulgence, and instead passed the Test Act, requiring every office-holder, both civil and military, to take communion in accordance with the Anglican rite. The Duke of York, in spite of years of devoted (and at times distinguished) service, was forced to resign as Lord Admiral.

The campaigning season of 1673 saw the Dutch navy at sea first, the result not so much of greater efficiency as of a stronger sense of purpose. Nevertheless de Ruyter's plan to raid the Thames estuary again was frustrated by an English squadron under the veteran Prince Rupert, and by May the Anglo-French fleet was able to advance on the Dutch coast with the intention of seeking a decisive battle.[70] They were not disappointed, but off the Schoonveld Banks on 28 May de Ruyter attacked first, driving the allies back. This was not decisive, but a week later in the same area the fleets clashed again, and this time the English broke off and returned to their own coast. Having failed in their original purpose to destroy or seriously weaken the Dutch at sea, the allies now had to risk carrying out their main invasion plan in the face of powerful naval opposition. This they did in August, advancing on the Dutch coast with a large armada. At the same time the Dutch Indies fleet was approaching up the Channel, and the last thing that de Ruyter needed was for that vital argosy (without which the war could not be financed) to sail into the middle of a destructive naval battle. He therefore made haste to attack on 11 August at Texel, and a desperate battle ensued. De Ruyter's gamble was successful, not so much because of superior tactics or firepower as because of misunderstandings between the English and the French and (the English claimed) a lack of commitment on the part of the latter.[71] The manner of this defeat further soured relations between the allies, and made it unlikely that the English would take any further part in the land war. It also ensured the safety of the Indies fleet, and reopened those Dutch ports which the allies had been endeavouring to blockade. At about the same time, across the Atlantic, a Dutch squadron under Admiral Evertsen recaptured New York.

By November, Charles's government, known as the Cabal from the initials of its members, had collapsed.[72] Henry Bennet, Earl of Arlington, and Lord Thomas Clifford were forced out by the Test Act, and Anthony Ashley, Earl of Shaftesbury, was dismissed. Shaftesbury, unlike the others, came from a dissenting background and was an enthusiastic supporter of the Declaration of Indulgence for that reason. He had also supported the Dutch war, not out of any sympathy for France, but out of a zeal for what can only be described as commercial imperialism. By the beginning of 1674 he had become a leading opponent of royal policy, and was to be heavily involved in both the Popish Plot and the Exclusion Crisis. By February 1674 Charles had been forced to accept that there was no point in attempting to persist with the Dutch war and the French alliance. It was obviously in William's interest to make a separate peace, and that he did at the Treaty of Westminster on the 19th. Insofar as any concessions were made, William made them, because although in the limited terms of the naval war he had been (more or less) victorious, he urgently needed to free himself for the main struggle against France. He confirmed the willingness of his fleet to observe the courtesies demanded at sea, relaxed the traditionally strict Dutch interpretation of neutrality, and paid a small indemnity of £180,000. More importantly, as it turned out, he returned New Amsterdam, which became once again New York.[73]

For England the next fourteen years were to be a period of managed neutrality. Thomas Osborne, Earl of Danby, who became Lord Treasurer after the removal of Clifford in June 1673, was probably the ablest financial manager of the reign. Aided by the strong trade revival which followed the war, he repaired most of the damage wrought by the Cabal, which had included the bankruptcies following the stop of the Exchequer in January 1672. Danby, who remained in office until 1679, was anti-French, and his influence in parliament worried Louis XIV. Louis did not particularly mind losing England as an ally, but he was very anxious that she should not become an enemy. For several years he proclaimed the idea that Charles should broker a general peace, and at the same time worked to reduce the king's dependence upon parliament. In 1675 he tried a variation on the secret Treaty of Dover. If parliament tried to insist on war with France, then Charles would dissolve it and receive £100,000 a year from Louis.[74]

The outcome was undramatic, but significant. Members of the House of Commons tried to insist that English troops who were serving as mercenaries in the French army should be recalled, and Charles prorogued the assembly from November 1675 to February 1677. This was not a dissolution, but the king got his money anyway.

However, by the time that parliament reconvened, the success of the French armies in Europe was generating strong pro-Dutch sentiments in England, and it was that sentiment which came to Pepys's assistance when it came to getting £600,000 for the navy in March 1677. The Commons made it clear that they wanted war with France, but beyond the earmarked grant for the navy they were not prepared to trust Charles with the money. The king in turn refused to make any binding commitment until a grant had been voted. This deadlock produced another secret agreement, this time for a prorogation until May 1678 in return for £166,000, but neither side honoured the bargain.[75]

In November 1677 Charles agreed to a marriage between his niece, Mary, and William of Orange. The king's motive seems to have been an urgent desire to reduce the hostility which was building up against his brother, and James may simply have had no interest in preventing his Protestant daughter by his first marriage from marrying a Protestant champion. Louis was understandably annoyed, seeing this as evidence of an impending Anglo-Dutch alliance. Basking in unaccustomed parliamentary approval, Charles asked for money to raise 30,000 men and equip 90 ships, but a tentative treaty with the Dutch was never ratified, and many of the men were not mobilised.[76] When the king again approached Louis in March 1678, offering to stand down his preparations and broker a peace in return for £1.5 million over three years, the latter told him politely that he could do without his services. Finally, on 26 July, an Anglo-Dutch treaty was signed and some troops were sent to Flanders. However, the threatened war was never waged, because two weeks later the Treaty of Nymegen brought the Franco-Dutch conflict to an end. Louis had won his war, but William was not destroyed, and his links with England had been much strengthened. In October 1678 the Popish Plot erupted, and for a decade thereafter English politics was turned in on itself.

Traditionally the navy had expanded in wartime, and contracted in peacetime, but the complex politics of the Restoration period almost reversed that situation. During the second Dutch war and the anti-French posturings which followed it, fewer than 100 warships were in commission. Whereas the years of peace and financial difficulty from 1679 to 1685 saw an average of 120 warships in service. The explanation for this apparent paradox can be found in the distinction between 'in commission' and 'actively deployed'.[77] The navy was by far the largest industrial organisation of the period, and the scale of its operation did not vary much between war and peace, except when a particular economy such as the closure of Harwich was undertaken. Ships had to be maintained, serviced and repaired whether they were in active use or not, and even when there was peace in Europe squadrons had to be sent to the West Indies, West Africa or the Mediterranean. The highest costs were incurred when a war fleet had to be prepared for European waters, or when such a fleet had to be paid off.

The rhythms of naval finance and administration were no longer determined only by war and peace in Europe. The Admiralty was a major political institution, and was in the front line of the party battles which particularly characterised the period from 1670 to 1690. Its financial position thus depended far more directly upon the state of the parties than upon its actual level of need. At some times when expenditure was particularly high, supply was curtailed and debts mounted; conversely, when the climate changed, the debts could be reduced. Although parliamentary votes were often linked to particular situations, by the time the money arrived, it had either been overspent or the need had disappeared. Moreover, warships were a constant factor in the competitive displays in which governments indulged, and which sometimes took the place of war. A capacity for rapid and large-scale mobilisation had to be maintained, and by 1690 Great Britain's credibility as a European power depended upon its navy. 'It is upon the navy', Charles II is alleged to have said, 'under the good providence of God, that the health, wealth and strength of this kingdom do chiefly depend.' His opponents did not disagree, but when they were pulling in opposite directions, it was now the navy which bore the brunt of the conflict.

Notes

1. The failure of attempts to accommodate the Presbyterians, who had played a significant part in the Restoration discussions, can be largely attributed to the attitude of the House of Commons in the Cavalier parliament. For general discussions of this see P. Seaward, *The Cavalier Parliament and the Reconstruction of the Old Regime, 1661–1667* (Cambridge, 1989), J. Spurr, *The Restoration Church of England, 1646–1689* (New Haven, 1991), and R.S. Bosher, *The Making of the Restoration Settlement: The Influence of the Laudians* (London, 1951).

2. C.L. Grose, 'England and Dunkirk', *American Historical Review*, 39, 1933, 1–27; and Grose, 'The Dunkirk money', *Journal of Modern History*, 5, 1933, 1–18.

3. Frank Fox, *Great Ships: The Battlefleet of King Charles II* (London, 1980), which provides a year by year breakdown of the number and types of ship in commission.

4. Ibid. Fox also points out that the appearance of these ships is well known thanks to the thousands of drawings and hundreds of paintings left by the Van der Veldes, father and son, who began drawing English ships in 1648, and were based in England after 1673. The younger Van der Velde lived until 1707.

5. Alan R. Young, *His Majesty's Royal Ship* (New York, 1990).

6. Fox, *Great Ships*, 35–50.

7. Bodleian Library, MSS Rawlinson A 200, 201, 202, 203, 206.

8. Harry Kelsey, *Sir Francis Drake: The Queen's Pirate* (New Haven, 1998), 227–30. Plymouth was remote from the main sources of supply, and the prevailing wind was against vessels travelling from east to west.

9. C.D. Chandaman, *English Public Revenue, 1660–1688* (Oxford, 1975), 267ff.

10. Ibid., 196–9.

11. Ibid., 219.

12. Ibid., 223. Fox, *Great Ships*, lists 123 prizes taken between 1660 and 1685, most of them from the Dutch.

13. Sir Henry Richmond, *The Navy as an Instrument of Policy, 1558–1727*, ed. E.A. Hughes (Cambridge, 1953), 168.

14. J.D. Davies, 'Pepys and the Admiralty Commission of 1679–1684', *Historical Research*, 62, 1989, 34–53.

15. Cited by J.D. Davies, 'The navy, parliament and political crisis in the reign of Charles II', *Historical Journal*, 36, 1993, 271–88.

16. Chandaman, *Public Revenue*, 151.

17. Davies, 'The navy, parliament and political crisis'.

18. J.D. Davies, *Gentleman and Tarpaulins* (London, 1991).

19. Davies, 'The navy, parliament and political crisis'.

20. Davies, 'Pepys and the Admiralty Commission'.

21. Samuel Pepys, *Memoires relating to the state of the royal navy of England, 1679–1688*, ed. J.R. Tanner (Oxford, 1906); Tanner, ed., *Private Correspondence and Miscellaneous Papers of Samuel Pepys, 1679–1703* (London, 1926).

22. Davies, 'Pepys and the Admiralty Commission'.

23. Ibid.

24. J.R. Western, *Monarchy and Revolution: The English State in the 1680s* (London, 1972) provides a good summary of the situation at this time.

25. Chandaman, *Public Revenue*, 260.

26. Davies, 'Pepys and the Admiralty Commission'.

27. For James's actions, and the nature of his motivation, see J. Miller, *James II: A Study in Kingship* (Brighton, 1978).

28. E.B. Powley, *The English Navy in the Revolution of 1688* (Cambridge, 1928), 11.

29. Ibid., 9.

30. The bishops had protested against the declaration on the ground that the dispensing power upon which it was based was illegal, thus raising the constitutional issue of limitation upon the prerogative.

31. Powley, *English Navy*, 12.

32. Ibid., 24.

33. Ibid., 100.

34. For a clear exposition of the developments of these days, see W.A. Speck, *Reluctant Revolutionaries: Englishmen and the Revolution of 1688* (London, 1988).

35. The provision which James had made for the navy since 1685 is set out in Appendix 1 to Powley, *English Navy*.

36. For a consideration of this issue, and its effects on British politics, see J.H. Plumb, *The Growth of Political Stability in England, 1675–1725* (Cambridge, 1967).

37. C.L. Grose, 'Anglo-Portuguese marriage of 1662', *Hispanic American History Review*, 10, 1930, 313–52.

38. J.S. Corbett, *England in the Mediterranean, 1603–1713* (Navy Records Society, London, 1904), 17–23.

39. Ibid., 28–30. For a full discussion of the English position in Tangier, see E.M.G. Routh, *Tangier: England's Lost Atlantic Outpost* (London, 1912).

40. Corbett, *England in the Mediterranean*, 37.

41. Ibid., 70.

42. Alan Jamieson, 'The Tangier galleys and the wars against the Mediterranean corsairs', *The American Neptune*, 23, 1963, 95–112. G.E. Aylmer, 'Slavery under Charles II: the Mediterranean and Tangier', *English Historical Review*, 114, 1999, 378–88.

43. W.B.T. Abbey, *Tangier under British Rule, 1661–84* (Jersey, 1940); Corbett, *England in the Mediterranean*, 124.

44. Richmond, *The Navy as an Instrument of Policy*, 143–4.

45. G.N. Clark, *The Later Stuarts, 1660–1714* (Oxford, 1949), 65–6; C.M. Andrews, *The Colonial Period of American History* (New Haven, 1934–38).

46. C.H. Firth, 'The capture of St Iago by Capt. Myngs, 1662', *English Historical Review*, 14, 1899, 536–40.

47. E.A. Cruikshank, *The Life of Sir Henry Morgan; With an Account of the English Settlement on the Island of Jamaica, 1655–1688* (London, 1935).

48. M.A.J. Palmer, 'The "military revolution" afloat: the era of the Anglo-Dutch wars', *War in History*, 4, 1997, 123–49.

49. Ibid.

50. N.A.M. Rodger, 'The development of broadside gunnery, 1450–1650', *Mariners Mirror*, 82, 1996, 301–24.

51. Palmer, 'The "military revolution" afloat'.

52. Ibid.

53. The English deployed only 54 warships, as against 84.

54. There are many accounts of this action, the best-known being by Samuel Pepys, *Diary . . . 1660–1669*, ed. H.B. Wheatley (London, 1893–9), VIII, 344–6. See also S.C.A. Pincus, *Protestantism and Patriotism: Ideologies and the Making of English Foreign Policy, 1650–1668* (Cambridge, 1996), 272–3.

55. Pincus, *Protestantism and Patriotism*, 222–68.

56. The so-called 'Derwentdale Plot'. H. Gee, 'The Derwentdale Plot, 1663', *Transactions of the Royal Historical Society*, 3rd series, 11, 1971, 125–42.

57. For a full discussion of the propaganda barrage of this period, see Pincus, *Protestantism and Patriotism*, 256–68.

58. Davies, 'The navy, parliament and political crisis'.

59. Reported in *The Newes*, 5 May 1664, 289–90. S.C.A. Pincus, 'Popery, trade and universal monarchy: the ideological context of the outbreak of the second Anglo-Dutch war', *English Historical Review*, 107, 1992, 1–29.

60. John Evelyn, *Navigation and Commerce: Their Original and Progress* (London, 1674), 15–17.

61. Pincus, *Protestantism and Patriotism*, 283. These successes were enthusiastically celebrated in Holland.

62. Ibid., 287. The raid was directed by Captain Van Hemskerke, a disaffected Orangist.

63. Chandaman, *Public Revenue*, 219–21.

64. For a full discussion of the circumstances of Clarendon's dismissal, see David Ogg, *England in the Reign of Charles II*, 2nd edn (Oxford, 1955).

65. E.S. de Beer, 'The secret treaty of Dover', *English Historical Review*, 39, 1924, 86–9. R. Hutton, 'The making of the secret treaty of Dover', *Historical Journal*, 29, 1986, 297–318.

66. Barry Coward, *The Stuart Age* (London, 1994), 308–9.

67. Palmer, 'The "military revolution" afloat'.

68. E.H. Kossman, 'The Dutch Republic', in *The Ascendency of France, 1648–1688*, New Cambridge Modern History V (Cambridge, 1961), 291–2.

69. Coward, *The Stuart Age*, 307–12.

70. Fox, *Great Ships*; Palmer, 'The "military revolution" afloat'.

71. Palmer, 'The "military revolution" afloat'.

72. Sir Thomas Clifford, the Earl of Arlington, the Duke of Buckingham, Lord Ashley and the Earl of Lauderdale. Geoffrey Holmes, *The Making of a Great Power, 1660–1722* (London, 1993), 110–11.

73. Ibid., 115; Chandaman, *Public Revenue*, 228–30.

74. Clark, *Later Stuarts*, 82–4.

75. Ibid.

76. Chandaman, *Public Revenue*, 241.

77. The former practice of decommissioning ships not required for immediate service had been discontinued. All ships on the register were maintained, and could be mobilised and deployed at short notice.

CHAPTER EIGHT

Colonial and Commercial Expansion, 1660–1690

This period has been described as that of England's 'commercial revolution', but it would be more accurate to see it as the culmination of over a century of evolutionary development. As we have seen, it was the seamen and adventurers of the second half of the sixteenth century who began the move towards long-distance trade, who set up the first joint stock companies, and who developed the navigational skills needed for regular oceanic traffic. The first half of the seventeenth century saw the emphasis begin to shift off traditional textiles, and significant developments in Levantine and Far Eastern trade. From the 1590s to the 1640s there was a modest growth in the mercantile marine, and in the overall value of commodities traded, but the main change was the establishment of colonies in North America and the Caribbean. By 1650 these colonies were populous, and already beginning to develop trading patterns of their own. During the civil wars the trade of 'front line' ports, such as Bristol, suffered serious disruption, but London, under firm parliamentary control, continued to grow and played a crucial part in funding the parliamentary war effort. Keenly aware of this, and influenced by strong commercial lobbies, the governments of the Interregnum swept away much of the early Stuart control system, and introduced a new partnership between the City and the central government. For the first time the state became a proactive authority in commercial matters, and it became appropriate to speak of a national economic policy.

In the late 1650s trade was in the doldrums. This had nothing to do with government policy; it was part of a European-wide depression following over 30 years of war.[1] There had been several such depressions since 1600, and they did not indicate any particular inadequacy in English methods or commodities, but James and Charles had always taken the view that such slumps were acts of God, and had not felt obliged to intervene. The

Commonwealth Navigation Acts of 1650 and 1651, on the other hand, had been deliberate attempts to give the weight of state authority to aggressive and expansionst policies. There had been Navigation Acts before, but they had either been in response to particular merchant lobbies, or designed to make more seamen available for royal service. The Commonwealth Acts had helped to foment war against the Netherlands in 1652, and it was not clear that they had had their intended positive effect. On the other hand, without the support which they represented, the recession of the late 1650s might have been much worse.

In 1660 there was a large question mark over the future of these Acts, and the policy which they represented, because they automatically lost their legal force with the assembly of the Convention parliament in May 1660. However, the Restoration government was sensible enough to listen to the London consensus. Indeed, it could be argued that Charles and Clarendon had little option, given the part that the City had played in bringing about the Restoration. In September 1660 a new Navigation Act was passed, with the same aims as its predecessors, that is to take the English carrying trade out of the hands of the Dutch, and to build up the strength of the English merchant marine.[2] It also declared that no goods were to be traded to any colony or dependency except in English or Irish ships; that no alien might practice as a factor in any colony or dependency; and that imports to England from the colonies must be brought in English or colonial ships. More complex regulations controlled the transportation of naval stores, sugar, oils, wines, and some other named commodities, upon which penal 'alien' tariffs were imposed unless they were shipped either in English bottoms, or those of the country of origin. This was followed up in 1663 with the so-called Staple Act, which laid down that (with certain listed exceptions) all goods moving from Europe to the colonies must pass through England, and be subjected to the existing carrying restrictions.[3]

The architect of these Acts was not actually a City man, but Sir George Downing, the MP for Carlisle, who was also an official of the Exchequer. Downing had been brought up in Massachusetts, had returned to England during the Interregnum, and served as English Resident at The Hague from 1658 to 1660. He was considered uncouth, and was generally unpopular, but he had an extremely shrewd economic brain and did not let his New England background stand in the way of an accommodation with the restored monarchy.[4] Downing's most important insight was to realise that England had a balance of payments problem caused mainly by inadequate shipping resources. The Navigation Acts could not be enforced if there were not enough English ships to do all that the Acts required them to do. On the other hand, there was no incentive for English shipbuilders to expand their operations if merchants were to continue to evade the Acts whenever they could. It was to get around these problems that the 1660 Act was made more comprehensive, but also more flexible than its predecessors. At the same time, by virtually abandoning the shrinking textile markets of northern Europe, and concentrating on the Mediterranean, the Far East and North America, the demand for large ocean-going merchantmen was further increased. Over a period of about 25 years this policy was to be spectacularly successful. Between 1660 and 1686 the merchant tonnage more than doubled, from 162,000 to 340,000, and the half-concealed obstacle which had been hindering English commercial expansion was removed.[5] Although the Irish markets were treated as being of secondary importance, Irish ships were admitted to many benefits under the Navigation Acts. However, these benefits did not extend to Scotland, which was treated (correctly) as being autonomous. In the short term this did not matter, as Scottish merchants continued to exploit their own European markets, and early attempts at Scottish colonisation were not successful. However by 1690, with its European trade in serious recession, Scotland's exclusion from the colonial trades began to rankle, and admission on equal terms was an important inducement which could be held out in 1707 in support of the Act of Union.[6]

England's economic position was not transformed overnight by the Navigation Act. It represented an increased level of intervention rather than a major change of direction, and an enhanced understanding of what was needed rather than a new concept of policy. Neither the second nor the third Dutch war were anything like as successful as the first in respect of the seizure of Dutch shipping, or damage to main commercial interests.[7] On the other hand, by borrowing Dutch ideas, and by mobilising the greater political muscle of the state, the English were gradually able to gain the ascendancy in the competition for international trade.

The real advance did not begin until the second war ended in 1667, and it was then fuelled partly by a fresh burst of colonisation, and partly by a 'consumer revolution' at home. Carolina was first settled in 1663, Delaware in 1664. New York and New Jersey were taken from the Dutch in 1664 and 1665, and the foundations of Pennsylvania laid in 1681. In the West Indies the Cayman Islands were added piecemeal between 1655 and 1670, the Virgin Islands in 1666 and the Bahamas in 1670.[8] All this activity created larger colonial markets, and a greater diversity of both products and requirements.

At the same time the inflation of the sixteenth and early seventeenth centuries had run its course. Grain harvests, particularly from 1665 to 1672, were good, and the price of wheat first stabilised and then declined.[9] Real incomes began to increase, not just for some favoured groups, but generally for the first time for about 200 years. This not only stimulated domestic industry, it also created an increased, or new, demand for many exotic products, such as tobacco, sugar, coffee, tea, calico and silk. This trade defied mercantilist orthodoxy, in that it was led by imports rather than exports, the balance of trade with France remained consistently unfavourable, and many imports from India had to be paid for in bullion. So great was the demand for fine linen by the end of the century that it was being imported from Holland and Germany at a cost of nearly £1 million a year.[10] In 1694 it was estimated that the deficit with France came to £1.6 million a year, a fact which prompted the observer to comment, in a manner worthy of an earlier age, 'our gold and silver was exported to fetch from thence strong drink and fripperies, to the debauching and emasculating our bodies and minds'.[11] However, the effects of such emasculation were not very evident, either economically or militarily, and the fact is that such self-indulgence could be sustained on the back of an enormous growth in re-exports, particularly of colonial and Far Eastern produce. This trade, which had accounted for no more than 3–4 per cent of all exports in 1640, had risen to 22 per cent by 1669, and 31 per cent, valued at £2.9 million, by the end of the century.[12]

Trade with southern Europe, particularly Italy, was much more acceptable to the purists, because it was export-led. The key commodities were textiles, as had earlier been the case in the north, but not the traditional broadcloths. Mediterranean demand was for 'new draperies', particularly the serges and bays made in East Anglia and Devon. This trade went back to the 1570s, but had at first been small in scale. In 1600 only about 10 per cent of England's cloth exports had been going south of the Alps and the Pyrenees. By 1640 that figure had reached 30 per cent, and by 1669 almost 60 per cent, at which figure it remained for the rest of the century.[13] In 1635 the Levant Company had shipped about 6,000 cloths; by 1670 that figure had reached 13,500, and it peaked at 20,000 in 1677 before dropping back slightly to 19,000 by 1690.[14] Return cargoes included wine and fruit (particularly dried fruit such as figs, raisins and sultanas), but consisted mostly of silk, dyestuffs and cotton from Turkey. Although for reasons which we have seen the Mediterranean became somewhat less dangerous after 1650, the bulk of this trade continued to be handled by the London-based Levant Company, which maintained factors in Spain, Italy, Greece, the Aegean islands and the Ottoman Empire. Most of the imports of this trade were absorbed by the home market, and the Lancashire cotton industry, producing mostly 'Manchester small wares', was established at this time, although its scale remained small until the following century.

Although periodically obstructed by the effects of war, the Baltic and Scandinavian trades also grew rapidly, Their organisation, however, changed. Neither the Merchant Adventurers nor the Eastland Company were flourishing in the later seventeenth century. The latter was abolished in 1673, and the former in 1689.[15] This was not on account of any principled aversion to chartered companies, which were still being established for trade with other parts of the world, but simply because they were no longer necessary. At the same time cloth, although it continued to be the most important export, was by no means the only one, and the company mono- polies had related to exports rather than imports. The north-eastern coalfields, which had been producing about 65,000 tons a year in 1660, had expanded to 1.2 million tons by 1690, and much of this was being exported.[16] The staple imports continued to be flax, hemp, iron and timber, much of which was eventually consumed by the growing shipbuilding industry. The oldest of all the chartered companies, the Muscovy Com- pany, went the same way as the others in 1699 because its traditional com- modity control was no longer appropriate for an expanding and diversifying market.

It was in the trades beyond Europe, however, that the most spectacular changes took place. Some of them can be roughly quantified. The East India Company, for example, imported a variety of luxury goods, from spices to jewellery and brocades, but its staple was Indian textiles. Between 1631 and 1640 under 10,000 pieces a year had been brought in; by 1675 that figure had reached 540,000, and it peaked at 1.2 million ten years later before dropping back to about 900,000 at the end of the century.[17] The East India Company was virtually a London monopoly, and huge fortunes were being made in the City out of this trade, fortunes which were being distributed in numerous investments, commercial, industrial and political. Similarly in 1615 some 50,000 lb of tobacco was being imported, mainly from the Spanish and Portuguese colonies in America, as significant Vir- ginian production did not begin until the following decade. By 1672 the equivalent figure was 17.6 million lb, rising to 33 million lb by 1700, almost entirely from England's own colonies.[18] The whole of England could have kippered itself with this quantity, but tobacco was a prime re-export com- modity, and most of it went to feed the enormous market which was grow- ing up across Europe. A similar illustration can be provided by West Indian sugar. There was virtually none until Barbados was planted in the 1640s, but by 1670 about 200,000 cwt a year was arriving, rising to 370,000 cwt by 1700.[19] Most of this was also coming into London, whose share of the value at the end of the century was reckoned to be £526,000 out of £630,000, and although the capital was developing a sweet tooth, much of the sugar was also re-exported. Imports from Asia and the Americas into London, which had accounted for 16.6 per cent of all imports in 1634, accounted on average for 34.7 per cent between 1669 and 1700. The corresponding figure for all English ports for the same period is 31.8 per cent, so the tendency was nationwide, although (as in most respects) London was the market leader.[20]

Many other trades, which were clearly profitable, cannot be quantified in the same way. Although the English had pioneered the 'slave triangle' with West Africa and the Caribbean in the sixteenth century, by 1640 most of it was in the hands of the Dutch. Both sugar and cotton plantations were hungry consumers of slaves, and one of the most significant effects of the Navigation Acts was to regain control of this traffic insofar as it related to English colonies. It has been estimated that as many as 175,000 slaves may have been transported to the British West Indies alone between 1675 and 1700.[21] Much of this trade was conducted by the Royal Africa Company, which was formed in 1663 and reconstituted in 1672, but the levels of profit are elusive. The same company also traded in ivory and gold, but its main efforts went into slaving, and although it was London-based much of its business was actually conducted from Bristol. Similarly imports of tea and coffee, from China and Arabia respectively, were socially significant and were in time to make major city fortunes, but were in their early beginnings at this time. The rapid growth of the northern colonies in America, and the implementation of the Navigational Acts in respect of colonial trade, also created a sizeable market for English industrial products other than cloth, and for the first time an export trade in metalwork, hats, clothes, pottery, paper and leather goods developed.[22] In time the colonies were able to supply most of these needs for themselves, but during the late seventeenth century they still relied largely on the home country, and the value of this trade is thought to have doubled between 1670 and 1700. Apart from the Royal Africa, the only major new company to be founded in this period was the Hudson's Bay Company in 1670. There may have been some expectation of being able to exploit a way through to the west, if one could be found (and the efforts continued), but the real business of this organisation lay in a network of trading posts, receiving furs and pelts from the Canadian trappers in return for weapons and trade goods of all descriptions. The Hudson's Bay Company did a great deal towards opening up the northern wilderness, and its success may not have been unconnected with the demise of the Muscovy Company nearly 30 years later.[23]

The government's direct imput into the management of the economy fluctated with circumstances and personalities, being frequently based upon the priorities of particular ministers. In 1660 the Privy Council, keenly aware of its obligations to London, set up two advisory councils, one for trade and the other for the foreign plantations. These were partly composed of councillors, including the Secretaries of State, partly of experienced colonial officers, and partly of London merchants. The intention seems to have been to create an interface between those with the power and those with the relevant knowledge.[24] A number of men sat on both councils. By 1665, however, they had ceased to meet; not, it would seem, as a result of any disagreements, but perhaps because it was felt that there was insufficient business to justify them. For about three years thereafter the Privy Council followed a policy of establishing standing committees, similarly composed, to deal with specific issues, and called together *ad hoc* groups when more general advice was required. This had the advantage of being more flexible, and of being easier to target on particular problems, but these smaller groups inevitably lacked the overall competence of the earlier councils. This was likewise felt to be unsatisfactory, and in 1668 the council for trade was reconstituted, followed in 1670 by a new council for the plantations.[25] The cycle then repeated itself, with one important difference; from 1672 to 1675, in what looks like a deliberate experiment, the two councils were combined, reduced in numbers, and converted into a professional body. At the time this experiment was not persisted with, and by 1676 the informal system which had been used between 1665 and 1668 had been reinstated. It was, however, remembered. Twenty years later, in 1696, when the parliament was dissatisfied with the degree of security provided for merchants during the war, it proposed to set up its own committee for trade, with executive powers. William III, sensitive to the need but unwilling to permit such an encroachment on what was left of his prerogative, instead set up his own Board of Trade.[26] This consisted of eight full-time professional councillors, with the nominal membership of the principal officers of state, and a staff which effectively established it as a government department. It was set up by letters patent on 15 May 1696, and continued in operation until July 1782, when it was replaced by a new committee which was the lineal ancestor of the present Board of Trade.[27] Its first president was the Earl of Bridgewater.

In spite of these institutional fluctuations, the policy which was implemented remained remarkably consistent in all essentials. Starting in 1650, successive English governments, prompted by a solid London consensus, were protectionist. Whereas Tudor and early Stuart monarchs had used intervention for their own political or fiscal purposes, after 1650 the power of the state was used to foster and promote trade itself. The tactics were opportunist, and led to a complex tangle of regulations which sometimes became unenforceable, but the strategy was clear. English trade was to be encouraged, both negatively by the imposition of duties and prohibitions, and positively by bounties and preferential tariffs. Manufactures were to be encouraged and (what soon became a mercantilist shibboleth) a favourable balance of trade obtained. Goods which could be produced at home, such as shoes or woollen clothes, were subject to heavy import duties. Agriculture was protected by Corn Laws; the importation of cattle and dairy produce was discouraged, and the ancient export trade in raw wool was finally consigned to history.[28] As we have seen, some of the most prosperous trades, such as that with India, did not fit comfortably into this pattern, because re-exportation, which generated most of the profit, did not fit into any mercantilist category. Special trade treaties, such as that with Portugal in 1661, produced an exchange of benefits, but did not breach protectionist principles because the trade encouraged was always in congruent products, never competing ones.

The colonies were part of this system. All trade between England and its dependencies was to be carried in English or colonial ships, and a longish list of 'enumerated commodities' could be exported only to England. At the same time all imports of European origin had to be laded in England. The colonists could trade in other commodities where they chose, and import freely from outside Europe, which encouraged the colonies to trade with each other. However, the home country was the main beneficiary, except in one very important respect. North American shipbuilding, where the skills were available and the raw material abundant, developed significantly.[29] Until the end of the century colonial manufacturing was also promoted, and it was not until 1699 that the first restraints were placed on attempts at self-sufficiency, significantly by inhibiting the manufacture of woollen cloth.

England, however, needed imports, and not only from the colonies. Pamphleteers might moan about 'fripperies', but Oliver Goldsmith was a voice crying in the wilderness when he wrote in the early eighteenth century:

> While trade's proud Empire hastens to decay,
> As ocean sweeps the laboured mole away,
> The self-sufficient state can time defy,
> As rocks resist the billows and the sky.[30]

Wine or silk might be classed as luxuries, but not cotton, sulphur, saltpetre, tar, hemp or timber. Only some of these things could be even partly obtained from colonial sources. Similarly spices were still needed, as they always had been, to preserve meat, and to disguise that which had not been quite preserved. The East India Company could not obtain these, which came from Indonesia and Malaysia via the VOC, and they were traded exclusively through Amsterdam. So England's protectionism was part of a system which covered the whole of Europe. Everybody needed trade, and that need made the tough web of restrictions, privileges and exemptions mutually tolerable. England's tough new stance after 1660 eventually made substantial inroads into the commercial supremacy of the Netherlands, and created favourable conditions for trade with Spain, Portugal and Italy, but it made little impression upon the French. Only later did the wider range and greater volume of English trade give her the edge over her ancient rival, and offset the latter's greater inherent resources and population. Between 1663 and 1700 the total volume of English trade rose by about 35 per cent: imports from £4.4 million to £5.8 million, and exports from £4.1 million to £6.4 million,[31] and this was achieved not by free trade, but by the toughest of state controls. Political and commercial power fostered each other, and political power meant primarily sea power.

London was the focus of this commercial strength. Before the civil war it had handled about 70 per cent of the country's trade, and by 1700 that proportion had risen to 75 per cent. Only the short haul trade with Ireland was not dominated by the capital. Such a vast concentration of wealth could not be idle, and the demand for financial services was at least equal to the supply. London had been a major banking centre since the collapse of Antwerp in the later sixteenth century, but it had been unable to match Amsterdam while Dutch commercial supremacy lasted. The City and its major companies had a long history of lending money to the Crown, and since at least the middle of the sixteenth century had been investing in trading companies, exploration and privateering, as well as speculative plantations in Ireland. The foundation of the Royal Exchange in 1577 had marked London's coming of age as a banking centre, and the availability of credit attracted not only other merchants and adventurers with projects to fund, but also landowners needing ready capital on the security of their rent rolls. By 1650 goldsmith/bankers proliferated, and even Oliver Cromwell had an account at Hoare's.[32] The foundation of this developing system was the inland bill of exchange. These bills were 'running cash notes', or bank notes, in varying denominations, the amounts on them being 'written off' as encashments were made. They probably began to be issued about 1650, although the oldest example to have survived dates from 1665.[33] Of course credit notes had been used much earlier on an *ad hoc* basis, Italian examples surviving from the late fourteenth century, but these had really been notifications of transactions completed and awaiting settlement. The London system was to issue notes as negotiable instruments, against the security of deposits or other capital. It could be a risky business, because the bankers issued notes far in excess of their reserves, sometimes to an aggregate face value ten times their capital. On the other hand, their confidence inspired a similar confidence in depositors, and investment grew rapidly. The money supply could greatly exceed the real cash or bullion upon which it was based, but this was to everyone's advantage as long as confidence could be maintained.[34] These bankers also accepted written assignment instructions, orders to pay, or three party bills, probably starting before 1660, although again the oldest surviving example dates from the 1670s.

Some bankers also acted as fiscal agents of the Crown, farming customs, excise and other taxes in repayment for loans, and making payments for the Exchequer directly from these revenues. They also loaned directly, both to the government and to the monarch personally. Edmund Backwell and Gilbert Whitehall were leading providers in this respect, and also acted as 'bankers' bankers', holding deposits both for other London goldsmiths and also for provincial bankers, because the system was not confined to London.[35] Families like the Gurneys in Norwich and the Oakes in Bury St Edmunds were yarnmasters as well as bankers. In Newcastle upon Tyne it was the coal merchants, such as the Andersons, who supplied the role. As a recent study has pointed out:

> Country bankers like these dealt in inland bills of exchange, discounted
> bills on London for clothiers and others, took deposits, worked on
> fractional reserve systems, allowed overdrafts, issued bank notes, remitted
> funds, collected rents and taxes and returned them to London if and when
> required, ran insurance agencies, and supplied all financial services in their
> localities . . .[36]

Such a sophisticated and widespread network was not established over-night, and the country was behind the city, but it was well established by the 1690s, when the Bank of England (modelled allegedly on Backwell's 'Unicorn' Bank) was added as the highest tier of the structure. London banks fell into two groups, roughly by location. Those in the City itself, around Lombard Street and the Royal Exchange, tended to concentrate on discounting *bona fide* trade bills. They left the negotiation of bills of exchange to the merchants themselves, and acted as agents, bankers and lenders of last resort to country bankers. In the West End, around the Strand and in Westminster, a second group grew up to serve landowners, lawyers and members of parliament. These bankers received rents, acted as interme-diaries and brokers for mortgages, and lent on bonds to creditworthy cus-tomers. They bought and sold stocks and shares, and issued travellers cheques, but seldom discounted bills, except as a special favour.[37] By com-parison with the City banks, the West End banks held large deposits, and because they needed only small reserves to meet withdrawals, were able to invest heavily in City enterprises, including the Bank of England itself, when that was established.

This flourishing and rapidly growing system was severely shaken by the stop of the Exchequer in 1672, when a hard-pressed Charles II suspended payment on all government debts.[38] In 1660 Exchequer tallies had for the first time been authorised to bear interest, and they were then invariably accompanied by repayment orders which were assignable by endorsement, which made them effectively negotiable instruments. However, between 1667 and 1671 so-called repayment orders were issued which were not tied to specific sources of revenue, but merely in anticipation of hoped-for revenues. In other words they were nothing but unsupported paper. The stop suspended repayment on all such instruments for five years, which virtually bankrupted the Crown's chief creditors, notably Backwell and Whitehall. Most bankers were not royal creditors, and confidence in the commercial financial system was not seriously undermined, but private banks would no longer lend to the Crown. After the Revolution, with William's commitment to large-scale foreign wars, this lack of a major credit facility became unacceptable, and in the changed political climate a major consortium was put together, which put up £1.2 million, mainly in sealed bills and running cash notes.[39] This expedient was formalised and perpetuated by the creation of the Bank of England by statute in April 1694. Once the Bank was chartered, shares were sold, not only to London businessmen, but to the king and queen, the dukes of Marlborough and Leeds, a number of other noblemen, both Dutch and English, and to corporate bodies in Utrecht, Geneva and Berne. It became a financial expression of the Protestant alliance, and although not intended to be a permenant institution, it soon became one.[40]

Even the early history of the Bank of England takes us beyond our proper ground, but it should be emphasised that, although it was a new institution, and nothing quite like it existed anywhere else in Europe, it was only doing more comprehensively and efficiently what private banks had done before. The Bank of England saw to it that the troops besieging Namur in 1695 were paid, but Edmund Backwell had paid the garrison of Calais on much the same terms in 1657. The Bank shouldered much of the Crown's domestic financial business, for example discounting Exchequer bills and tallies, but it was doing no more than the private banks had done before 1672. The private banking system in London developed mainly between 1650 and 1670, and the provincial system followed between 1660 and 1690, but it was the stop of the Exchequer, and the collapse of confidence which followed it, which made the creation of the Bank of England necessary. The commercial community of London had always commanded a lot of money, but thanks to the major commercial developments of the late seventeenth century, its resources had become vastly augmented. The question for William and Mary was the same as it had been for Charles II, or indeed for his father and grandfather: how to mobilise those resources for the purposes of state policy. One method was to persuade parliament to vote taxes, which usually meant adjusting, or at the very least explaining, the intended political objectives. The alternative was to tap straight into the sources of wealth through an investment arrangement such as the Bank. At the end of the day the Bank was no substitute for adequate sources of revenue, but it solved the cash flow problems of government in an unprecedented manner, and in a manner which no other economy in Europe could match.[41] By 1690 the English were not only rich, they had devised a system to make that wealth count, without sacrificing the ultimate control of accountability. This was the foundation of Britain's great power status in the eighteenth century.

So a financial revolution was begotten by the commercial revolution, but in neither case is the term entirely appropriate, given the deep roots from which they sprang. There was, however, a new relationship between commerce and politics, or rather a number of relationships, because they varied from one part of the world to another. In India the East India Company had from the start built its business upon treaties with the territorial princes, and in 1660 did not own or control any territory, unlike the Portuguese in Goa, or the Dutch at Batavia.[42] It held all its factories as tenancies, and relied upon the Moghul emperors to provide the peace and security which it needed. Its main factory was at Surat, the principal city on the west coast, where it operated alongside the Dutch, and after 1668, the French. On the east coast there were factories at Masulipatam, Balasore, Hughli, and various places on the Coromandel coast. There were also outlying stations at Basra on the Persian Gulf, Mokha on the Red Sea, Bantam in Java, Bencoolen in Sumatra, and on the west coast of Africa as staging posts.[43] The company also claimed the island of Pulo Run under the 1654 treaty with Holland, but never obtained possession. Outside India itself, its position was fragile. Both Bantam and Bencoolen were eventually lost to the Dutch, the claim to Pulo Run was surrendered in 1667, and Basra was simply abandoned.

On the other hand, the cession of Bombay by Portugal in 1661 opened a new phase, because the town was Portuguese territory, which had been obtained by conquest. Charles II had no idea what to do with it, and in 1668 handed it over to the East India Company, which thus for the first time obtained an independent territorial base.[44] As the protective shield of the Moghul emperors declined in effectiveness, the security offered by Bombay became increasingly attractive, and the city flourished. In 1687 the 'presidency' of the west coast was transferred there from Surat. The Anglo-Dutch wars saw little fighting in the Far East, but by 1674 it was clear that there was no future for the English in Malaysia or Indonesia, which encouraged the company to concentrate its efforts in the subcontinent. There was a little sporadic trading with China, and in 1673 the company obtained the island of St Helena.[45] After 1674 the English got on with trading, and left hostilities to the Dutch and the French, who eventually weakened each other to England's advantage.

Apart from the possession of Bombay, it was the decline of Moghul power which mainly sucked the company into Indian politics. As early as 1664 a Maratha raid had sacked Surat, but the English factory, which was fortified and defended, remained unscathed. There were further threats from the same quarter in 1670 and 1677, and the unavoidable conclusion was that the company must provide for its own protection. The whole of India was sliding into a similar disorder, and every factor had to make similar provision, which required not only skills in which the factors were not trained, but also resources. Communications with London were slow, and the directors were reluctant to face up to this responsibility. In 1679 the garrison at Bombay was commanded by Richard Keigwin, and when another attack threatened he took the initiative, attacking and scattering the Maratha fleet, which outnumbered his ships by about ten to one. Instead of thanks for this resolute action, Keigwin was recalled and an order was sent to reduce the garrison.[46] However, neither decision was implemented, and in 1683 he led what was, from the company's point of view, a garrison mutiny. Keigwin wrote to the king, complaining that the company's pusillanimous policy would result shortly in the loss of this important possession. Charles was not prepared to intervene, but by the time the matter came to a head in England, the validity of Keigwin's arguments was beginning to be appreciated. A naval frigate was sent to Bombay along with the company's own ships, and the commander was displaced. However, he was not punished, and continued with his naval career, while the policy which he had advocated was effectively implemented.[47] The company had already been granted supplementary charters in 1660 and 1683, giving it the right to coin money, to exercise civil and criminal jurisdiction over English subjects, and to enter into alliances with Indian rulers, even to the extent of peace and war. By 1688 the company was, as the directors admitted, 'in the condition of a sovereign state in India', although such sovereignty at this time extended only to Bombay. Deteriorating security, and Keigwin's timely defiance, had changed the attitude of the directors completely in less than a decade.

In 1687, in an instruction to the president of Surat, the company opened the door to the acquisition of further Indian territory in full sovereignty. He was urged to 'establish such a politie of civil and military power, and create and secure such a large revenue . . . as may be the foundation of a large, well grounded sure English dominion in India for all time to come'.[48] This was an unequivocal imperial ambition of a kind which had not been expressed before. For the time being it was over-ambitious, and the commitment of large resources to a military campaign for the capture of Chittagong in 1686 led to disaster, and the loss of all the English factories in Bengal.[49] The war dragged on until 1690, wreaking havoc with the company's revenues, until it cut its losses and made an unsuccessful peace. Significantly, however, this setback did not cause the directors to revert to their earlier policy. The forward momentum, and the ambition which it represented, remained. Even the unsuccessful war resulted in the foundation of Calcutta. A fishing village until 1690, after the peace it became a flourishing trading town, and eventually the greatest city in India.

After the Revolution of 1689 there were further storms ahead for the company, not in India but at home. Close cooperation with the Crown, particularly under James II, had beaten off the numerous interlopers who were always trying to infringe its lucrative monopoly, but in 1693, under pressure from an unsympathetic parliament, it made the mistake of resorting to bribery to obtain a new charter.[50] The scandal was uncovered, several politicians were dismissed or impeached, and the company's reputation was severely damaged. Seizing their opportunity, a powerful London-based group of former interlopers indulged in their own form of bribery by lending the Crown £2 million towards the war effort. As a reward, they were formed into a General Society, which was then allowed to spawn a new joint stock company to trade to the Far East. This New East India Company came into existence in 1698, and continued to trade alongside the old company until the two were sensibly merged in 1709. In India the disruption was considerable, because the new company tried to arouse the suspicions of the Indian rulers against the imperial ambitions of the old company, and succeeded in getting the factory at Surat closed down. However, its agents lacked the skills to establish a profitable trade for themselves, and its finances were crippled by its initial loan to the government. By 1702 it was only a question of when, and on what terms, the old company would absorb it.[51] The result was an organisation 'which rested on self interest so enlightened that it resembled public spirit', but its eventual success lies well outside the terms of this study.

By comparison, West Africa, where the East India Company took over some of the forts for its own purposes, was a small-scale and extremely confused field of operation. The European bases resembled most of those in India, in that they were fortified trading stations rather than colonies, but the politics of the surrounding tribes was even more volatile than that of the Indian princes, and temporary understandings had to take the place of treaties. The main trade was the supply of slaves to the West Indies and America, and these were obtained from the coastal tribes, who in turn obtained them from the perpetually warring tribes of the interior.[52] There was no incentive, and few opportunities, for Europeans to explore the great rivers, and the climate was lethal. It is doubtful how profitable the slave trade was in itself, but it formed one leg of the lucrative triangle which ended by bringing West Indian and American produce to Europe. For this reason, as we have seen, it was fiercely contested by the English and the Dutch. The Elizabethan Guinea Company had long since deceased, but in pursuit of the protectionist policy of the 1650s and 1660s, a new Africa Company was founded in 1663, and the factory at Cormantine, near Cape Coast Castle, was taken back from the East India Company.[53]

Over the next decade the Anglo-Dutch struggle in West Africa, which embraced two full-scale wars, is poorly documented and hard to trace in detail. The Treaty of Breda confirmed Cape Coast Castle to England, but in 1672 the Africa Company went bankrupt and surrendered its charter. However, by this time the trade had acquired a strategic dimension, and the deceased organisation was immediately followed by a Royal Africa Company, on even more expansive terms.[54] For a while this became extremely prosperous, as conflict with the Dutch waned, and the old enemies joined forces against the French, who were trying to build up a power base in the Gambia. The Royal Africa Company established altogether six factories in what is now Ghana, and its success probably peaked at about the time of the Revolution. Thereafter the struggle with France sapped its energy. In 1697 parliament ended its monopoly, and in 1708 it became insolvent.[55] The slave trade itself continued energetically for most of the next century, but mainly in the hands of private operators. That trade did not really need the luxury of expensive factories when the supply was plentiful, and *ad hoc* deals could always be struck with the suppliers. Slaves could not conveniently be kept in store awaiting the arrival of the next ship, and the other trades which were carried on were not on a large enough scale to justify the infrastructure.

At the other end of the slave route, the West Indies were still very much a frontier zone in 1660. Spain held the mainland coast from Mexico to Venezuela, and most of the principal islands, but the claim that the whole area was *mare clausum* and under Spanish sovereignty no longer bore any relation to reality. The French, the English and latterly the Dutch had been raiding and settling for years. The English were firmly established in Barbados and in several of the Leeward Islands, and had recently acquired Jamaica, whence the last Spanish forces were ousted in 1660.[56] There were also irregular settlements, under no particular government, on the Bay of Honduras and in Surinam. The French held Martinique, Guadeloupe, and a number of other islands in both the Windward and the Leeward groups. There were also Dutch trading posts at St Eustatius and Curaçao. No colonial government had any authority beyond its immediate boundaries, and often not very much within them. Intervention from Europe was sporadic, and sometimes at odds with the interests of the colonists. Also, in true frontier fashion, there were powerful and lawless groups who pursued no interests but their own. These were the buccaneers, originally so called from the gangs who hunted the wild cattle of Hispaniola, and traded *boucan*, or dried meat, with the settlers.[57] Although a few of their leaders claimed commissions as privateers, by 1670 these gangs had taken to the sea as pirates, and established a number of bases, the chief of which was the island of Tortuga. They were drawn from all nationalities, and robbed without discrimination, but their normal targets were the Spanish settlements, and they were often in loose alliance with the governors of the English and French colonies, who otherwise did not have adequate military resources for their own protection.

Formal hostilities during the second Dutch war, however, exposed the limitations of this policy. The Dutch attacked Barbados in 1665, and the Governor was forced to call upon the buccaneers to help beat them off, but the same assistance turned out to be useless when the English tried to take the French half of St Kitts in 1666, and the 8,000 English settlers were expelled.[58] The French followed up this success by capturing a number of other islands, until the appearance of an English fleet turned the tide, and the *status quo* was restored by the Treaty of Breda. The Dutch acquisition of Surinam was recognised, and the English half of St Kitts restored. Far away in the north, France gained Acadia, or Nova Scotia. This disposition was to last until the wars of the mid-eighteenth century. Both the English and the French gained, but the Dutch presence became little more than nominal. The losers by this process of stablisation were the buccaneers, who flourished on a state of semi-official conflict. As the colonial governments became stronger and more settled they acquired the resources to suppress these bands, and the settlers who had previously bought their plunder without asking questions now had too much to lose. The Anglo-Spanish treaty of 1680 finally brought peace 'beyond the line', and put an end to the exploits of men like Morgan, who in 1670–71 had led 36 ships and 1,800 men to the capture and sack of Porto Bello. When a similar but smaller party returned from a foray in 1682 they found themselves treated as pirates.[59] The English and French authorities, although growing in mutual hostility, and to be in open conflict after 1689, were agreed about one thing: the private enterprise warfare of the buccaneers could no longer be tolerated. After about 1700 they were reduced to scattered bands of pirates, and although these continued to be a nuisance, they were no longer a threat.

Although there was a steady flow of emigration to the West Indies, the white population did not grow very dramatically. This was on account of changes in the economies of the islands. As general agriculture declined, and sugar planting became more important, there was less call for indentured labour, and the old system, under which poor emigrants had come out on semi-servile terms, was gradually abandoned. At the same time the number of small independent farms declined as the plantations grew. The planter aristocracy became richer and more powerful, and preferred slave labour, which, as we have seen, was imported in large quantities. By 1690 there were probably about 50,000 white settlers in the islands, and some 120,000 blacks.[60] Only Jamaica provided an exception to this trend, continuing to grow most of its own food, and other cash crops such as indigo, tobacco and cotton. The white population there continued to grow, while that of the other islands declined.

Constitutionally all the West Indian colonies were originally proprietary, that is to say that an individual or a syndicate held them under the Crown on a form of feudal tenure. However, the need to coordinate defensive measures, to enforce the provisions of the Navigation Acts, and to combat lawlessness led to the abandonment of this system, and by 1690 all the islands were royal provinces, with governors appointed by the Crown. Each governor was supported by a council, and by some sort of assembly, but the importance of the latter varied greatly from place to place. Only Jamaica, with its increasing English population, had an assembly which resembled those of the mainland colonies.[61] Elsewhere they tended to represent only the interests of the planters. The island governors varied similarly in effectiveness. Some were born colonials, and some were absentee aristocrats, but most tended to be English gentleman, often with a military or naval background, and their record of service, sometimes in difficult circumstances, was good. Because of distance, and the low priority frequently accorded to their efforts, they were poorly supported except in emergencies, and their salaries were often years in arrears. Friction between the governors and the colonists was unusual, particularly once the buccaneer problem had been solved, and the lynching of General Parke, the Governor of the Leeward Islands, by a mob in 1710 was altogether exceptional.[62]

On the mainland, all the colonies were chartered, and some of them, like the West Indian islands, were proprietary. Virginia had become a Crown colony long before, but Maryland was still proprietary at the Restoration, and the new colonies created during Charles II's reign were all of that type: Carolina, New York, New Jersey, Pennsylvania and Delaware. The others, Massachusetts, Plymouth, Connecticut and Rhode Island, were what was called 'corporate'. The corporate colonies elected their own governors, and appointed their executives under the terms of their charters. In the proprietary colonies the governors and executives were appointed by the individual patron or company. However, the commercial policies represented by the Navigation Acts required a stronger measure of royal control, and by 1690 only Rhode Island and Connecticut retained a corporate government, while only Maryland and Pennsylvania remained proprietary.[63] Massachusetts, Plymouth, Carolina, New York, New Jersey and Delaware had all followed the same course as Virginia, and were subjected to royally appointed governors. As in the islands, these officers were usually resident, competent, and poorly supported from London, but both their councils and their assemblies were larger, stronger and more self-confident. The former consisted of anything from 10 to 28 leading colonists, elected in the corporate colonies, but appointed by the Crown or the proprietor in the others. The council was both an advisory body to assist the governor, and also the upper house of the Assembly.[64] The lower houses of the assemblies were elected representative bodies, usually based on territorial constituencies, and were small-scale versions of the English House of Commons. They were distinctive to the English colonies, and were locally powerful bodies, particularly in the corporate (or formerly corporate) colonies. The assembly was the legislative body for each colony, and worked approximately like the home parliament.

During this period the English parliament concerned itself very little with colonial matters, and the Crown dealt directly with the assemblies.[65] Sporadic attempts were made to increase executive control. For example in 1677–79 plans were drawn up to bring Virginia and Jamaica into a new constitutional relationship, under which colonial legislation would have to be confirmed by the English parliament before it became valid – a situation similar to that which appertained in Ireland. Jamaica rejected the plan outright, and it proved to be unworkable in Virginia because of the distances involved and the lack of up-to-date information in London.[66] More successful were *quo warranto* proceedings against proprietors. Direct control over Barbados was obtained in this way early in Charles's reign, and in 1682 the Somers Island Company was dissolved by the same device. Massachusetts had been almost from the start the most stubbornly autonomous of all the colonies, and before 1660 the government had been forced to accept this situation. However, the fact that the colonial assembly was virtually ignoring the Navigation Act, encouraging evasion and defiance at every level, eventually compelled Charles II to take action. After careful legal scrutiny, the colony's charter was revoked in 1683 and it became a royal province, analogous to Virginia.[67] However, the effect of this was less significant than might have been expected, as the independent spirit of the colonists was not dampened in the slightest.

Encouraged by this apparent success, between 1684 and 1689 the ministers of the Crown drew up a scheme for the complete reorganisation of the New England colonies. This would have placed them all under a single executive authority, answerable directly to the monarch, and would have abolished all the assemblies. Perhaps this represented a transatlantic version of what James would have liked to do at home. It would certainly have been good for military organisation, and for the enforcement of the trade laws. Had any attempt been made to implement it, the wars of independence might have happened a century earlier, but the Revolution of 1689 consigned it to the dustbin. The ministers of William III recognised that, even in the new situation, London was not strong enough to impose effective imperial government in North America, and that the popular assemblies were the heart of the self-governing system. After 1690, in the context of endemic war with France, and aware of the extensive French colonial presence, from Canada in the north to Louisiana in the south (where Fort Prudhomme was founded on the Mississippi in 1682), attempts were made to pull the English colonies into a tighter association. In May 1690 representatives from New York, Massachusetts, Plymouth, Connecticut and Maryland met in New York. A small combined military operation was planned and carried out, but it was a complete failure.[68] This insignificant experiment was not repeated, but optimistic commentators have occasionally referred to it as the first American Congress. A few years later, in 1697 and 1700, William Penn came up with a number of well-thought-out proposals for representative meetings of all the colonies under the presidency of a royal commissioner. Such meetings would have coordinated defence, resolved disputes between colonies, and established a common coinage. Sensible as this plan was, it came to nothing, partly because of deeply entrenched separatism, and partly because the perceived need was not sufficiently pressing. Instead William III actually reduced royal control by restoring the charter of Massachusetts in 1691, incorporating into it Plymouth, Maine, and what was later to be New Brunswick.[69] Only in the remote Leeward Islands did the pressure of war produce a short-lived experiment in federalism.

The importance of the American colonies in 1690 was not military, or even political, but economic. The population had risen dramatically since 1650, and had reached about 400,000 – more than that of Wales.[70] This was achieved partly by immigration, but largely by natural increase. The climate was healthy, the land fertile, and the space almost unlimited. In Newfoundland the scattered fishing settlements, which no one particularly wanted to encourage, acquired a new importance after 1660 as a base for contraband trade with New England. In New England itself the most important town was Boston, and nearly all the settlements were within 30 miles of the coast, except in the valley of the Connecticut, where the penetration was about 80 miles. To the north were the French settlements in the St Lawrence valley and Nova Scotia, while to the south-west were the New Netherlands. Maryland and Virginia were still shallow settlements around the main estuaries and inlets, and communication with the English colonies to the north was entirely by sea. Carolina was established to the south of Virginia, on land which Spain theoretically claimed, but over which it had never established any control. The proprietors of this new venture included not only important noblemen such as the Earl of Clarendon and the Duke of Albemarle, but also the current Governor of Virginia and at least one Barbados planter.[71] The intention was not to compete with Virginia or Barbados by producing tobacco or sugar, lucrative as these were, but to grow citrus fruits, olives and other commodities previously imported from the Mediterranean. In other words, it was a deliberate piece of economic planning, but the result was disappointing. Two distinct settlements were created, which later became north and south Carolina, but the population, which came mainly from other colonies, particularly in the West Indies, grew only slowly until the arrival of significant numbers of Huguenots in the late 1680s. Most of the food which was grown was exported to the West Indies rather than to England, and the main secondary industries were smuggling and piracy.[72]

The acquisition of the New Netherlands during the second Dutch war was, however, a different matter entirely. The tidy fact that it linked Virginia and Maryland with New England into a continuous territory was more important to the map-makers than to the settlers, because overland communication remained slow and difficult. Nevertheless the economic significance of the gain was very great. New York was already second only to Boston among North American towns, and it controlled the trade route which came down the Mohawk and the Hudson from the Great Lakes.[73] Transfer of control from the Dutch to the English was the last thing that the French authorities in Canada wanted, and the *Intendant* tried to insist that his government should amend the Treaty of Breda in that respect. His intention was clearly either to seize or to purchase it himself in due course, but Louis did not support him.[74] The former Dutch lands were subsequently divided into two colonies, which became New York and New Jersey, and proprietary systems of control were established for them. In the process both acquired representative assemblies, which had not been features of the Dutch system. One of the proprietors was William Penn, the son of that admiral who had commanded Cromwell's abortive 'Western Design', and who partly for that reason was keen to invest some of his considerable wealth in America. Not satisfied with his stake in New Jersey, some fifteen years later he persuaded the king to give him a new proprietary grant of lands inland from New York and Maryland, and he established the town of Philadelphia on the Delaware river.[75] Of all the English colonies in America, Pennsylvania, as it later became, was the most instant success. The land was so fertile and the management which Penn established so wise that the settlement grew by leaps and bounds, attracting both from England and the other colonies. Later, it was to have a significant German presence, but that was not until the following century.

By contrast, the Hudson's Bay Company had to fight its way into the far north, against determined French opposition. By 1682 it had established a number of fortified trading posts around the south and south-eastern shores of the bay, but in that year a French expedition from Quebec attacked and captured a number of them. These were subsequently returned, but the climate of hostility remained, and there was a further clash in 1686, until the issue was subsumed in the general Anglo-French wars at the end of the century.[76] Newfoundland also contained a mixture of both English and French settlements, but the English were more numerous, thanks to the contraband trade already noticed, and included one village of some significance, at St Johns. In 1680 Charles II decided to pre-empt any further problems by establishing a regular colony, and a governor was appointed. This also was to be a bone of contention in the later wars.[77] The Hudson's Bay forts changed hands several times between 1695 and 1697, and in the latter year Newfoundland was overrun. The peace of Ryswick restored Newfoundland, but many of the forts remained in French hands for the time being.

None of the lands upon which these colonies were planted were actually empty at the time, and starting with the major Indian revolt in Virginia in 1622, the process of settlement involved constant tensions and occasional bloody hostilities. In North Carolina a few hundred Indians were even enslaved, but this was contrary to the wishes of the proprietors, and was not imitated elsewhere.[78] From Maryland southward the colonists learned many valuable skills from the indigenous population, particularly in the cultivation of unfamiliar crops, but relations were seldom amicable. This was partly because of the settlers' insatiable appetite for land, but also because of their ambivalent attitude towards relatively primitive peoples, which led to constant fraud and deceit in their dealings with them. Such deceptions frequently provoked a violent response, which the settlers then used to justify further seizures. Only in Pennsylvania did this pattern not develop, because although the need for land was just as great, Penn succeeded in insisting upon honest dealing at all times. There were tensions, as elsewhere, but not the same cycle of violence. Further north, and particularly in Canada and the Hudson Bay territories, the problem was rather different. Here land was less of an issue, and the Indians were principally trading partners. They provided some food, but mainly the furs and pelts for which there was a high demand in Europe. They were paid, partly in manufactured goods such as pots and pans, but more often in guns and alcohol. The guns were ostensibly for hunting, but both commodities caused endless problems.[79] Attempts by the colonial authorities to control this traffic were futile, and in the later Anglo-French wars tribes such as the Algonquins and the Iroquois were deliberately armed by both sides as auxiliary allies.[80]

In New England the colonies attempted to regularise relations with their tribal neighbours by insisting that there should be no private dealing for land. All transactions should be public, and should relate to the settlement of organised communities. In principle this was admirable, because it cut out piratical operations which were the most frequent cause of violence, and enabled the authorities to insist upon an acceptable level of fair dealing. Until about 1675 this policy was also accompanied by an evangelical missionary campaign, aimed at both education and conversion. It enjoyed some success, because the 'praying Indians' enjoyed a special protected status, but it could not check the expansion of the colonies, and however honest and even philanthropic the intentions, they did not disguise the imperative need for land.[81] The missionary effort collapsed in 1675 when a chief known as 'King Philip' decided that only full-scale war could turn back the encroaching white man. A confused and savage struggle followed which lasted about three years, and at the end of it the defeated Indians were more open to exploitation than before, because it was felt that their own actions had invalidated the moral scruples which had hitherto informed official dealings with them. While the New England struggle was at its height, in 1676 another and rather different conflict had broken out in Virginia. This originated in small thefts and other petty crimes by Indians, for which disproportionate revenge was exacted, including the treacherous murder of six Indian chiefs at a conference. When the Governor, Lord Berkeley refused to act, some of the settlers themselves took the law into their own hands to assist the Indians in obtaining redress. The Governor then declared them to be rebels, and used the colonial militia to suppress them. There were a number of casualties among both the dissidents and their Indian allies, and 40 executions.[82] The punishments were unnecessarily severe, but there were to be no further troubles of a similar nature, and indeed no further Indian wars, except in the context of struggles between the Europeans themselves.

By 1690 the American experience was already beginning to feed back some influences into England, beyond the trade which enriched all the parties who dealt in it. The most important was probably the practice of religious freedom. Although some colonies, particularly in New England, were as narrowly intolerant as the worst European regimes, in most this was far from being the case. In America the automatic link which joined secular and ecclesiastical authority, in England or Sweden just as much as in France or Spain, did not exist, or was so tenuous as to be meaningless. Congregations in isolated settlements worked out their own ways and means, and frequently found among them families from completely different backgrounds, force of circumstances driving them into a cooperation which they would have rejected if they had remained in Europe. The frontier fostered many undesirable qualities for civilised living, but it bred some rugged survivors who were worthy of imitation. Intellectually, the colonies had as yet little to offer. Harvard College produced some worthy theologians and preachers, but none who had much influence in England. The most influential 'feedback' from New England came at first from the soldiers and seamen who embraced the Commonwealth cause, and from sharp businessmen like Sir George Downing. Cambridge, Massachusetts, had the first printing press in the New World by 1675, but its products were subject to a strict censorship which would not have been tolerated in London, and the first American newspaper failed for the same reason in 1690.[83] Nevertheless, things were moving. Philadelphia had a printing house by 1687, and New York by 1693. The *Boston Newsletter* was successfully launched in 1704. The smaller southern colonies could at this stage make little contribution. William and Mary College had aspirations, but in its early days was little more than a secondary school.

However, the most important effect of the development of the New World was the experience of success. Just as the exploits of the *conquistadores* had fired the enterprise of Spain in the sixteenth century, and had created an aura of confidence, even invincibility, the flourishing state of its American colonies generated confidence in England. By 1690 this confidence was percolating through every aspect of English life. The enormous success of the commercial revolution, the great wealth and financial sophistication of London, the size and power of her navy, and not least her ability to resolve a major constitutional crisis without civil war or the forfeiting of any of these advantages, was convincing Englishmen that God looked on them with particular favour. It was this period also which saw the origins of what has recently been called the 'gentry culture'.[84] The Tudors had turned England from a 'feudal' monarchy, in which the Crown had to deal primarily with noblemen and their affinities, into a gentry commonwealth, where the power of the community lay mainly in the county commissions and the House of Commons. The seventeenth century saw this process extended, via the heavy interpenetration which already existed between the landowning aristocracy and the City of London. Capitalist farming finally replaced the older customs of land use, again following Tudor precedents, and steered major aristocratic investment, first into trade (and privateering), then into industry. Consequently, as the Empire came into existence, it was run, not by a new or culturally distinct class of entrepreneurs, but by the same substantial gentlemen who had formed the backbone of the political nation for over a hundred years. The consequences of this for the later imperial regime are incalcuable.

In 1690 it must also be remembered that it was England which was the power, and Wales was a part of England for all the purposes with which we are here concerned. Ireland was a troubled dependency of England, and although in theory a separate kingdom was in fact a large colony. Positively it provided a modest but healthy trade; negatively it was a backdoor for enemies and a haven for pirates. Scotland, however, was a different matter. If James's imaginative scheme of union had been accepted in 1605, it would have participated in a modest way in all the developments we have been examining. As it was, its importance was mainly confined to the civil war, and after being reluctantly incorporated into the English republic, it regained its autonomy in 1660.

Attempts to revive the Scottish navy foundered for lack of resources, and the Navigation Acts excluded Scottish merchants from many lucrative trades. By 1690 Scotland's small-scale economy was in recession, and the merchants of Edinburgh and Glasgow tried to break out and create their own commercial revolution. There were already many Scots settled in the English colonies of North America, but Scotland had no colonies, and no major trading companies of its own. However, autonomy could create opportunities as well as problems, and a number of London merchants (some of whom were Scots) floated a scheme to circumvent the monopolies of the African and East India companies by registering new companies in Scotland. The Scots parliament passed enabling acts in 1693 and 1695, and a new company was registered. The capital was fixed by the London promoters at £600,000, half to be raised in London and half in Scotland. Unfortunately there had been irregularities in the 1695 Act, and the existing London companies reacted strongly. As a result of the political storm, the London investors in the Scottish company backed out. The registration, however, was not invalidated, and the Edinburgh merchants decided to continue on their own. By an enormous effort £400,000 was pledged in Scotland, and some £190,000 actually subscribed. About 1,300 people contributed, from every walk of life, in what many saw as a patriotic enterprise. However, without London expertise the inexperienced directors floundered. They failed to obtain the king's consent to obtain ships in Hamburg and Amsterdam, and he disavowed them; they infringed the monopoly of the Bank of Scotland; and worst of all, they decided to sink their capital in a colony on the Darien peninsula, about 150 miles south of Panama. This was territory claimed by Spain, at that time England's ally, and William III, whose approval had not been sought, denounced the colony as an illegal enterprise. Three attempts were made to establish a settlement in 1698 and 1699, but a combination of Spanish hostility, storms, and the vile climate defeated them all. With the exception of a single trading voyage, which returned a profit of about £4,000, every penny of the investment had been lost by 1700.[85] It was a totally avoidable disaster, and although the first reaction was to blame the English for not supporting them, the more astute of the Scottish investors realised that it had been caused by incompetence and inexperience.

The important lesson which both sides learned was that the constitutional relationship between England and Scotland would have to be addressed if the Scots were going to be put in a position to emulate their southern neighbours. Injured pride and recriminations would have to be set aside, and the salutary experience of the Darien scheme was to be a significant motivator in promoting the Act of Union in 1707. Given the later contribution the Scots were to make to the British Empire, the Darien fiasco had its positive side, and the South Sea Bubble was soon to demonstrate that even London was not immune to investment folly.

Notes

1. For a wide-ranging discussion of the economic problems of these years, see E.E. Rich and C.H. Wilson, eds, *The Cambridge Economic History of Europe*, V (Cambridge, 1977).

2. 12 Charles II, c.18. M. Jensen, ed., *English Historical Documents: American Colonial Documents to 1776*, IX (London, 1955), 354–6.

3. 15 Charles II, c.7. Ibid., 356–8.

4. Sir George Downing, *A Discourse* [16 December 1664] (London, 1664). S.C.A. Pincus, *Protestantism and Patriotism: Ideologies and the Making of English Foreign Policy, 1650–1668* (Cambridge, 1996), passim.

5. R. Davis, *The Rise of the English Shipping Industry in the Seventeenth and Eighteenth Centuries* (London, 1962), 15.

6. G.S. Pryde, ed., *The Treaty of Union of Scotland and England, 1707* (Edinburgh, 1950). W. Ferguson, 'The making of the Treaty of Union, 1707', *Scottish Historical Review*, 43, 1964, 96–110. T.C. Smout, 'The Anglo-Scottish Union of 1707: I; The economic background', *Economic History Review*, 2nd series, 16, 1964, 455–67.

7. About 1,500 Dutch prizes were taken during the first war, more than in the second and third wars combined. Frank Fox, *Great Ships: The Battlefleet of King Charles II* (London, 1980).

8. G. Holmes, *The Making of a Great Power, 1660–1722* (London, 1993), 441.

9. W.G. Hoskins, 'Harvest fluctuations and English economic history, 1620–1759', *Agricultural History Review*, 16, 1968, 15–31. D.C. Coleman, *The Economy of England, 1450–1750* (London, 1977), 112.

10. C.G.A. Clay, *Economic Expansion and Social Change: England 1500–1700. II: Industry, Trade and Government* (Cambridge, 1984), Table 16.

11. Dr Edward Chamberlayne, *Angliae Notitia, or the Present State of England* (London, 1694), 68.

12. R. Davis, 'English foreign trade, 1660–1700', *Economic History Review*, new series, 7, 1954, 150–66.

13. W.E. Minchinton, ed., *The Growth of English Overseas Trade in the Seventeenth and Eighteenth Centuries* (London, 1969), 66–7. Davis, 'English foreign trade, 1660–1700'.

14. Clay, *Economic Expansion*, 150. R. Davis, *Aleppo and Devonshire Square* (London, 1967), 42.

15. Holmes, *The Making of a Great Power*, 442.

16. M.W. Flinn, *History of the British Coal Industry* (London, 1984), II, 26–7.

17. K.N. Chaudhuri, *The Trading World of Asia and the English East India Company* (Cambridge, 1978).

18. Davis, 'English foreign trade, 1660–1700'; Clay, *Economic Expansion*; Minchinton, *Growth of English Overseas Trade*.

19. R.S. Dunn, *Sugar and Slaves: The Rise of the Planter Class in the English West Indies, 1624–1713* (London, 1973), 203.

20. Clay, *Economic Expansion*, 160.

21. P.D. Curtin, *The Atlantic Slave Trade: A Census* (Madison WI, 1969), 54–5.

22. Davis, 'English foreign trade, 1660–1700'.

23. E.E. Rich, *The Hudson's Bay Company. I: 1670–1763* (London, 1968).

24. J. Thirsk, *Economic Policy and Projects* (Oxford, 1978).

25. G.N. Clark, *The Later Stuarts, 1660–1714* (Oxford, 1949), 42–3.

26. Holmes, *Making of a Great Power*, 198–9.

27. G.D. Ramsay, *English Overseas Trade during the Centuries of Emergence* (London, 1957).

28. D.G. Barnes, *History of the English Corn Laws from 1660–1846* (London, 1930). E. Kerridge, *Textile Manufactures in Early Modern England* (Manchester, 1985), 241–2.

29. Davis, *The Rise of the English Shipping Industry*; Ver Steeg, *The Formative Years*.

30. Oliver Goldsmith, *The Deserted Village*.

31. B. Coward, *The Stuart Age* (London, 1994), 481.

32. E. Kerridge, *Trade and Banking in Early Modern England* (Manchester, 1988), 76.

33. A. Heal, *The London Goldsmiths, 1200–1800* (Cambridge, 1935), 51 et seq.

34. A.V. Judges, 'The origins of English banking', *History*, 16, 1931, 138–45. J.M. Holden, *The History of Negotiable Instruments in English Law* (London, 1955).

35. Kerridge, *Trade and Banking*, 78–9. T.S. Ashton and R.S. Sayers, *Papers in English Monetary History* (Oxford, 1953).

36. Kerridge, *Trade and Banking*, 77.

37. J.A.S.L. Leighton Boyce, *Smiths the Bankers, 1658–1958* (London, 1958). W.T.C. King, *History of the London Discount Market* (London, 1936). J.K. Horsefield, 'Beginnings of paper money in England', *Journal of European Economic History*, 6, 1977, 117–32.

38. Horsefield, 'The "Stop of the Exchequer" revisited', *Economic History Review*, 2nd series, 35, 1982, 511–28.

39. Holmes, *The Making of a Great Power*, 270–2.

40. J.H. Clapham, *The Bank of England*, 2 vols (Cambridge, 1944). B.L. Anderson and P.L. Cottrell, *Money and Banking in England: The Development of the Banking System, 1694–1914* (London, 1974).

41. J. de Vries, *The Economy of Europe in an Age of Crisis, 1600–1750* (Cambridge, 1976).

42. W. Foster, *East India House: Its History and Associations* (London, 1924). *The English Factories in India: A Calendar of Documents*, ed. W. Foster, C. Fawcett and P. Cadell, vols 1–17, 1618–84 (London, 1906–55).

43. *English Factories in India*, ed. Foster, Fawcett and Cadell.

44. B.M. Malabari, *Bombay in the Making, 1661–1726* (London, 1910). S.A. Khan, *Anglo-Portuguese Negotiations Relating to Bombay, 1660–1677* (Bombay, 1922).

45. 'Relation of the retaking of . . . St Helena . . . 1673', in E. Arber, *An English Garner* (London, 1877–96), II, 431.

46. R. and O. Strachey, *Keigwin's Rebellion (1683–4)* (Oxford, 1916).

47. P. Anderson, *The English in Western India* (London, 1854).

48. Cited in Clark, *Later Stuarts*, 338.

49. J.H. Rose, A.P. Newton *et al.*, *Cambridge History of the British Empire* (Cambridge, 1926–59); IV: *British India, 1497–1858*.

50. Clark, *Later Stuarts*, 339–40.

51. R. Davis, 'English foreign trade, 1700–1774', *Economic History Review*, 2nd series, 15, 1962, 285–99.

52. E. Donnan, ed., *Documents Illustrative of the History of the Slave Trade to America*, 3 vols (Washington, 1930–32). K.G. Davies, *The Royal Africa Company* (London, 1957).

53. G.F. Zook, 'The Company of Royal Adventurers trading into Africa [1662–72]', *Journal of Negro History*, 4, 1919, 134–231.

54. Davies, *Royal Africa Company*.

55. Holmes, *The Making of a Great Power*, 296.

56. A.P. Newton, *European Nations in the West Indies, 1493–1688* (London, 1933).

57. C.H. Haring, *The Buccaneers in the West Indies in the Seventeenth Century* (London, 1910). V. Barbour, 'Privateers and pirates in the West Indies', *American Historical Review*, 16, 1911, 529–66.

58. *Les particularitez de la defaite des Anglois . . . dans l'Isle de S. Cristophe, en l'Amerique, par les Francois* (Paris, 1666).

59. E.A. Cruikshank, *The Life of Sir Henry Morgan; with an Account of the English Settlement of the Island of Jamaica, 1655–1688* (London, 1935). Haring, *The Buccaneers*.

60. R. Davis, *The Rise of the Atlantic Economies* (London, 1973), 126–7.

61. A.M. Whitson, *The Constitutional Development of Jamaica, 1660–1729* (Manchester, 1929).

62. Clark, *Later Stuarts*, 321.

63. C.M. Andrews, *The Colonial Period of American History*, 4 vols (New Haven, 1934–38).

64. Ibid.

65. L.W. Labaree, *Royal Government in America* (New Haven, 1930). Clark, *Later Stuarts*, 323–4.

66. R.L. Morton, *Colonial Virginia* (Williamsburg, 1960).

67. Andrews, *Colonial Period*.

68. Clark, *Later Stuarts*, 324.

69. Ibid.

70. Davis, *Rise of the Atlantic Economies*, 127.

71. W.F. Craven, *The Southern Colonies in the Seventeenth Century* (Louisiana, 1949).

72. Ibid.

73. J.A. Williamson, *A Short History of British Expansion. I: The Old Colonial Empire*, 2nd edn (London, 1945).

74. C. Lucas, *The Historical Geography of the British Dominions: Canada and Newfoundland* (London, 1921).

75. Andrews, *Colonial Period*. C.O. Peare, *William Penn* (Philadelphia and New York, 1957).

76. E.E. Rich, *The Hudson's Bay Company. I: 1670–1763* (London, 1958).

77. Lucas, *Canada and Newfoundland*.

78. Clark, *Later Stuarts*, 332–3. M.E. Sirmans, *Colonial South Carolina, a Political History, 1663–1763* (Chapel Hill, 1966).

79. Rich, *The Hudson's Bay Company*.

80. Clark, *Later Stuarts*, 333–4.

81. Andrews, *Colonial Period*.

82. Morton, *Colonial Virginia*.

83. H.F. Kearney, *Scholars and Gentlemen* (London, 1970), 67–70. John Winthrop, 'Reasons . . . justifying . . . the plantation in New England', in J.P. Greene, ed., *Settlements to Society, 1584–1763* (New York, 1966), 62–3.

84. See particularly P.J. Cain and A.G. Hopkins, *British Imperialism: Innovation and Expansion 1688–1914* (London, 1993).

85. Clark, *Later Stuarts*, 334.

It is often pointed out that England at the end of the seventeenth century was still a predominantly agrarian society. Apart from the great city of London, its towns were still of modest size. London, in 1690 held about 500,000 people, out of a total in England and Wales of some 5.5 million. Norwich had about 30,000, Bristol about the same. Perhaps as many as 1.5 million lived in towns of 3,000 or more, but a large proportion of them remained directly dependent upon the rural economy.[1] Probably as much as 80 per cent of the population lived directly or indirectly off the land. The population of Scotland at the same time was a fraction over one million, of whom approximately 100,000 lived in the burghs.[2] The enormous social and economic changes which are normally called the Industrial Revolution were not to begin for another generation. Most people were as dependent as their ancestors had always been upon the vagaries of the weather, and as vulnerable to the random depredations of disease. For all these reasons, some have placed that magic watershed 'the end of the middle ages' in 1714.

While such an economic perception is factually accurate, it nevertheless creates a most misleading impression. The commercial revolution had given England the financial muscle not only to wage war on a scale never hitherto contemplated, but also to finance the ingenious experiments in farming and manufacture which were to transform the country over the next 150 years. At the same time, for reasons which were quite unconnected with prosperity, and still remain mysterious, the plague cycle which had been running since the fourteenth century petered out. The Great Plague of London in 1665 was the last major outbreak, and by the end of the century the scourge had almost disappeared. For equally mysterious reasons, this did not produce a demographic surge; indeed the population level in the late seventeenth century was relatively static.[3] The demographic changes had come earlier. From a low of less than 2.5 million in 1450, the population of England and Wales had climbed steadily to about 3 million by 1550, leaped to over 4 million by 1600, and peaked at 5.6 million in 1657, before falling back slightly over the following decades.[4] Whatever may be said of the sixteenth century, the economic changes of the seventeenth century were not demographically driven.

The changes which transformed England from an ancient but relatively modest kingdom in 1490 to a major imperial power 200 years later were complex and interrelated. They were also at least as much political and cultural as they were economic. In the first place the country was uncharacteristically deflated at the beginning of the Tudor period. In the tenth century the King of England had held a loose but acknowledged overlordship over the rest of the British Isles. From the eleventh to the fifteenth century he had been the ruler of a fluctuating dynastic empire, which at its widest extent had embraced almost half of France. By 1490 all that remained was a firm control over Wales, a less firm control over a small part of Ireland, and Calais. Claims to the Crown of France and to suzerainty over Scotland represented no more than the detritus of obsolete ambitions. Moreover for half a century before 1490 the country had been plagued with factional strife and short periods of chronic misgovernment. By the time Henry VII died in 1509, England had recovered its unity, and a measure of self-confidence. Although English military power was little regarded, even in Scotland, the Tudors could do business on equal terms with the Valois, the Habsburgs and the Trastamara, the ruling House of Spain, and even inter-marry with them. Moreover English wool and woollen cloth made her a major element in the north European trading pattern, and London a significant city. Secondary commerce was fluctuating, as it had done for generations. Spanish and Mediterranean trade was doing well, Hanseatic trade declining. Bristol merchants were eyeing the New World, but the Cabots' one famous voyage was of no immediate consequence.

The first major change was brought about by nothing more substantial than Henry VIII's enormous egotism. Greatly admiring the achievements of his predecessor Henry V, and determined to play in the major league, he created for himself a powerful standing navy. This achievement was a little like the royal supremacy over the church; it was created to enable him to get his own way over a particular matter, and ended up by making a major, and permanent, change to his kingdom. Henry was not interested in trade, except as a means to obtain money for the gratification of his other ambitions. His imperial vision was confined to seizing vulnerable bits of France and recovering an ancient (and partly imaginary) ascendancy over Scotland.[5] He was interested in guns and warships, partly to gratify these ambitions, and partly as symbols of power and honour. Whether he had any statesmanlike view of the consequences of his own actions is debatable. By allying with parliament to subdue the church, he transformed the role of that institution in government; by allying with the gentry to protect himself against dissident nobles, he altered the political function of the aristocracy; and by dissolving the monasteries to fund his military ambitions, he altered the distribution of wealth across the whole country. At the same time, by creating a powerful navy to grab a bit of France, he gave his successors the means to transform the international standing of his kingdom. Only two things suggest that Henry may have been able to see a little further than the end of his own nose. One is his refusal to renegotiate his relations with the papacy once the immediate causes of the breach had disappeared, to which may be added the manner in which he protected the supremacy during his son's minority. The other is the creation of the Council for Marine Causes. Fleets might come and go, as they had done for centuries, but a properly organised and funded infrastructure was the best guarantee of continuity. Henry's fleet was powerful, and its weaponry up-to-date, but no more so than the fleets of France, Flanders, or the Hanseatic League. Where England had the edge was in her capacity to mobilise, service and maintain her fighting ships efficiently and at a manageable cost. Whether either of these visions should be attributed to the king himself, rather than his advisers, is interesting, but not really relevant. The important thing is that they happened.

The test came when Henry died, and his oversized ego disappeared from the scene. The governors of his son's minority would have had every excuse to abandon the exposed positions which he had taken up, and demobilise the fleet as their grandfathers would have done. However, they did no such thing, and that is why the short reign of Edward VI should be seen as a 'turning point'. Somerset clung on to Boulogne (Henry's only conquest in France) and insisted, most unwisely, on continuing his attempts to bully Scotland. He also pressed ahead with a religious policy which might have been calculated to cause maximum annoyance, not only to the Pope but also to the Holy Roman Emperor. In consequence, military expenditure continued to be high, and debt levels increased. Somerset also continued Henry's rash practice of debasing the coinage, and the exchange rate in Antwerp began to falter. When the Protector was removed in October 1549, and his successor the Earl of Warwick quickly brought the wars to an end, again a generally low-key policy of retrenchment might have been expected. Instead the Protestant policy continued, and tension with the Emperor remained high. At the same time, the sterling exchange rate collapsed, and there was a slump in the all-important cloth trade. Whether this crisis caused some fresh thinking to take place, or merely coincided with it, is difficult to understand. However, as Thomas Gresham struggled with the exchange rate in Antwerp, some very fruitful seeds were being sown in London. Sebastian Cabot, the Emperor's Pilot Major, had been brought back to England after an interval of more than 30 years, and was working along with an interested City group, John Dee, William Cecil and Warwick himself, to initiate a search for a northern route to China.[6] Similar ideas had been mooted in the past, and individual merchants had tried to break out of the established European patterns, but nothing had come of their efforts. Now, however, for the first time, there was sufficient interest (and money) available in London, and sufficient involvement by the government, to turn the ideas into reality. The Willoughby/Chancellor voyage of 1553/54 represented a new departure in a way which the Cabot voyages of 1496/97 and the William Hawkins venture of 1535 had not.

The Antwerp trade revived, and quantitively remained dominant for many years to come, but it lacked its former security and the new spirit of adventure was not to be denied. In spite (or perhaps because) of the fact that Philip as King of England from 1554 to 1558 tried to stifle the interest of London merchants in southward and westward ventures, their appetite was whetted. The Muscovy Company was a safe option in the circumstances, but it was not a false dawn. Although it was shaken by the political tensions which accompanied Edward's death and Mary's accession, the Council for Marine Causes continued to function smoothly, and carried the navy safely through the lapse of royal interest which followed that crisis. Not only did Mary's French war bring a fresh level of expenditure and commitment, it also brought a reform of the institution itself from which it benefited. By the time of Elizabeth's accession in 1558 no one thought of the navy as an optional extra, or even a temporary wartime device (like an army), but rather as a part of the normal machinery of the state, like parliament or the Court of Kings Bench. At the same time, the return of William Cecil and of Warwick's son Lord Robert Dudley to positions of power guaranteed that the initiatives of 1553 would be picked up again. The first decade of Elizabeth's reign saw a dramatic upsurge of interest and investment, by both merchants and councillors, in long-distance trading ventures and voyages of exploration. Between 1560 and 1580 the whole maritime culture changed. Levels of skill and navigational education improved; men like Drake and Hawkins became heroes; and although the queen's attitude was not consistent, her willingness to invest both ships and money did more than anything else to create the 'enterprise partnership' which was characteristic of these years. In this respect, as in other ways, Elizabeth picked up and developed initiatives which had shown themselves first in her brother's reign, and the whole period from 1550 to 1580 should be seen as one of radical reorientation. The eccentric and prophetic voice of John Dee was an authentic expression of this extraordinary period.

The time of war which followed, although in a sense it saw the consummation of the 'enterprise partnership', a number of new companies formed, and important developments in Levantine trade, was much less innovative. England's relative success against Spain was as much a consequence of Philip's overstretched resources and creaky bureaucracy as it was of English effectiveness. Elizabeth's ships were good, and her guns and gunners better, but her resources were limited and partnership had its price as well as its advantages. Colonies were attempted, but did not succeed, and the naval administration which had served the country so well for over half a century began to fall apart. On the other hand, the sea began to grip the imaginations of Englishmen in a way which it had never done before, and Richard Hakluyt's *Principall navigations, voiages and discoveries* was a clarion call which no earlier generation would have issued, or heeded.[7] What followed in the early seventeenth century, both good and bad, arose naturally from the achievements and failings of Elizabeth's reign. Between 1604 and 1630 the navy lost the script. It did not disintegrate, much less disappear, but it lost the capacity to do its job effectively, and fell seriously behind both the French and the Dutch. A generation had grown up which seemed to believe that seafaring should pay for itself, and an impoverished crown was unable to maintain it as a state-of-the-art public enterprise. On the other hand, commercial ventures multiplied, particularly in the Levant and the Far East, and the first viable colonies were established, the latter success representing the second major 'turning point'. By contrast with the earlier period, the Crown and the Privy Council played almost no part in this; indeed it was those who were opposed to the Crown, or trying to escape from it, who were most creative.

The fact that the Crown and the political nation were beginning to pull in different directions for the first time since the fifteenth century was of ominous significance. When Charles I took the navy in hand after 1633, he was not looking back to the reign of Elizabeth, but abroad, particularly to France. 'Partnership enterprise' had disappeared, partly because of the storm of recrimination which had followed the fiascos of the 1620s, and partly because the king was no longer trusted to act in the best interests of his country as most of his subjects understood it. It was no accident that when Charles was at loggerheads with the Scots in 1639, he was also trying to annul the charter of Massachusetts. The 'Ship Money fleet' has to be seen in this context. The ships were well found, but funded by a special levy which was soon to provoke high-profile defiance. They were a useful asset to a king who was trying to restore his prestige at sea, and might have given a good account of themselves if put to the test, but they were very much the king's own property and as such were objects of potential political controversy. When Charles's relationship with his parliament finally broke down in 1642, most of his navy deserted him, and many of the New England colonists came back to fight against him. In the violent confrontation of the civil war the partnership government which the Tudors had created finally disappeared, and the loser was the king.

This essentially political and religious struggle put commercial and colonial developments on hold, but did nothing to turn them back, or change their direction. The execution of Charles I in 1649 sent shock waves through

Europe, but it also had the very positive effect of forcing the English to invent a new type of executive power. This was based, not on any form of Divine mandate, nor on widespread popular consent, but upon a coalition of interest groups, particularly the army and the City of London. The influence of the latter was critical, because for the first time it was acknowledged that it was the wealth generated by trade which underpinned the state. The Rump parliament was in an excellent position to squeeze taxation out of a reluctant country, but it was the liquidity provided by the merchants and bankers of London which got the bills paid on time. In 1649 the navy was a somewhat ramshackle affair, consisting mainly of a miscellaneous collection of small and medium-sized ships, some state-owned, some privately 'taken up', which was designed for small-scale in-shore fighting, and chasing privateers.[8] The great warships of 1638 were largely laid up. But the Admiralty administration had been adapted to the new political circumstances, and when the republic faced up to the need to defend itself as a viable state, it was able to respond. Over the next ten years, while trade stagnated and colonial affairs continued to mark time, the navy was transformed; and this must count as the third 'turning point'.

Charles I's royal fleet had harked back to that of Henry VIII, but the navy of the republic quickly became one of the major spending departments of the state, and a premier instrument of policy. Elizabeth had seen her navy primarily as defensive, and had left the aggression to private enterprise. Now the navy became the servant of an aggressive policy, particularly designed to seize control of international trade. It was not at first conspicuously successful, but it did manage to dent the Dutch supremacy, and even to make an impression on the North Africans. By 1660 it was a massive, state-of-the-art fighting force, committed to the acquisition of a global political and commercial status; it was also by all previous standards vastly expensive. In spite of political and financial fluctuations, that situation appertained down to the end of the century, and well beyond, and it was largely as a result of that policy that the final turning point, the commercial revolution, was reached. This was not achieved by happy accident, nor by the random efforts of individual and group enterprise, but by the consistent effort of the state, coordinated and directed through the City of London. The fact that England was ruled by a king again after 1660 affected the style in which this was done, and often determined the details of particular policies, but did not fundamentally change the stance first taken up by the republic. It is sometimes said that Oliver Cromwell's principal legacy was a hatred of standing armies and Independency, and it is true that constitutionally and socially the republic left little behind. However, to take such a negative view is extremely misleading. Cromwell and his servants shifted the whole orientation of English public policy, and the fact that Charles II stole his clothes should not be allowed to conceal that fact. The huge expansion of trade, the consequent growth of the merchant marine, the rapid development of the colonies, and the transformation of the East India Company, all took place between 1650 and 1690 as a direct result of these policies.

In medieval Europe, the bases of power were land and *manred*, the capacity to command military service. Ship service, upon which medieval fleets were based, was a specific adaptation of the latter. Early modern states, such as France, Russia, and even Spain, continued to operate on this basis, which became easier as the power of the monarchs increased. Such a style of warfare was based, not on trade, but on land revenue, and it was this fact which caused the 'cash flow' problems which were such a feature of sixteenth- and seventeenth-century government. It also made (and broke) such great banking houses as the Frescobaldi and the Fuggers. Philip II was still largely reliant on ship service when he was assembling the Armada, which is why his efforts were so clumsy and expensive. In this context, Henry VIII was not an innovator. In creating his navy he was emulating the French and the Scots, and he continued to raise most of his ships by requisitioning, which was an adaptation of the traditional ship service. Where he did innovate was in the creation of his Council for Marine Causes. The developments of Edward VI's reign, although crucial to this story, were again not innovative. Warwick and Cecil were only doing what the kings of Spain and Portugal and the republic of Venice had been doing for a hundred years. However, Elizabeth's 'partnership enterprise' was rather different, and began the crucial process of encouraging a land-based aristocracy to interest itself, and invest its money, in commercial and maritime ventures. As applied to warfare, it was a brilliant device to overcome the perpetual problems of a small country with inadequate resources. Partnership was far more effective than state power (which she did not have) in enabling Elizabeth to mobilise the resources of her subjects.

Consequently the English had moved away from the medieval system by the beginning of the seventeenth century, but this meant that when partnership began to break down (for a variety of political and religious reasons), there was nothing much left for the king to draw on. Clumsy and insensitive attempts to overcome this problem led directly to civil war. The civil war finally and symbolically destroyed feudal tenure in England, but it also unveiled the fact that commercial wealth had made the city of London a political force capable of separate and focused mobilisation. The English did not invent a power system based on money rather than *manred*; the Dutch had been forced into that innovation by their own wars of independence over half a century before. London, however, was keenly envious of the commercial success of Amsterdam, and eager to mobilise the power of the English state to remedy that situation. The demise of the monarchy, with its huge baggage of traditional systems and attitudes, created the opportunity. When Charles II returned in 1660, he was quite intelligent enough to understand the significance of what had happened, and in accepting it endeavoured to mould it to his own requirements. He enjoyed a fair measure of success, and certainly made the new priorities compatible with monarchical government, until his brother undermined that achievement for reasons quite unconnected with this story. After 1690 the Crown was taken down another peg, and the Whig ascendancy provides a suitable plateau upon which to bring this evolutionary story to an end. Although neither 1689 nor 1707 were significant dates in the history of any particular colony, they did mark rites of passage which transformed the English colonies of the seventeenth century into the British Empire of the eighteenth.

Notes

1. E.A. Wrigley and R.S. Schofield, *The Population History of England, 1541–1871: A Reconstruction* (Cambridge, 1981), 531–4, 566. G. Holmes, *Making of a Great Power, 1660–1722* (London, 1993), 404–7.

2. R.H. Campbell and J.B.A. Dow, eds, *Source Book of Scottish Economic and Social History* (New York, 1968), 1, 2, 8ff. M. Flinn *et al.*, *Scottish Population History from the Seventeenth Century to the 1930s* (Cambridge, 1977), 191.

3. Holmes, *Making of a Great Power*, 403.

4. E.F. Jacob, *The Fifteenth Century* (Oxford, 1961), 369; Wrigley and Schofield, *Population History*, 528. All statistics before the mid-sixteenth century are rough approximations.

5. For Henry's vision of a matrimonial alliance between Prince Edward and Queen Mary, see J.J. Scarisbrick, *Henry VIII* (London, 1968), 436–44.

6. Sir William Foster, *England's Quest of Eastern Trade* (London, 1933), 3–13.

7. K.R. Andrews, 'New light on Hakluyt', *Mariners Mirror*, 37, 1951, 299–308. G.B. Parks, *Richard Hakluyt and the English voyages* (New York, 1928).

8. N.A.M. Rodger, *The Safeguard of the Sea* (London, 1997), 411–26.

SELECT BIBLIOGRAPHY

Abbey, W.B.T., *Tangier under British Rule, 1661–1684* (Jersey, 1940)

Acts of the Privy Council, ed. J.R. Dasent *et al.* (London, 1890–1907)

Adams, S., 'New light on the "Reformation" of John Hawkins: the Ellesmere naval survey of January 1584', *English Historical Review*, 105, 1991, 97–111

Adams, S., 'The outbreak of the Elizabethan naval war against the Spanish Empire, and the embargo of May 1585', in S. Adams and M-J. Rodriguez Salgado, eds, *England, Spain and the Gran Armada, 1585–1604* (London, 1991)

Adams, S., 'The Dudley clientele, 1553–1563', in G.W. Bernard, ed., *The Tudor Nobility* (London, 1993)

Alsop, J.D., 'A regime at sea: the navy and the 1553 succession crisis', *Albion*, 24, 1992, 577–90

Anderson, P., *The English in Western India* (London, 1854)

Anderson, R.C., 'Henry VIII's Great Galley', *Mariners Mirror*, 6, 1920, 274–81

Anderson, R.C., *Oared Fighting Ships* (London, 1962)

Andrews, C.M., *British Committees, Commissions and Councils of Trade and Plantation, 1622–1675* (Baltimore, 1908)

Andrews, C.M., *The Colonial Period in American History*, 4 vols (New Haven, 1934–38)

Andrews, K.R., 'New light on Hakluyt', *Mariners Mirror*, 37, 1951, 299–308

Andrews, K.R., *Elizabethan Privateering, 1585–1604* (London, 1964)

Andrews, K.R., *The Spanish Caribbean: Trade and Plunder 1530–1630* (London, 1978)

Andrews, K.R., *Trade, Plunder and Settlement: Maritime Enterprise and the Genesis of the British Empire, 1480–1630* (London, 1984)

Andrews, K.R., *Ships, Money and Politics: Seafaring and Naval Enterprise in the Reign of Charles I* (London, 1991)

Andrews, K.R., Canny, N.P. and Hair, P.E.H., eds, *The Westward Enterprise* (Liverpool, 1978)

Ashton, T.S. and Sayers, R.S., *Papers in English Monetary History* (Oxford, 1953)

Aylmer, G.E., 'Slavery under Charles II: the Mediterranean and Tangier', *English Historical Review*, 114, 1999, 378–88

Barbour, V., 'Privateers and pirates in the West Indies', *American Historical Review*, 16, 1911, 529–66

Battick, J.F., 'Cromwell's diplomatic blunder: the relationship between the Western Design of 1654–5 and the French alliance of 1657', *Albion*, 5, 1973, 279–98

Baumber, M.L., 'Parliamentary naval politics, 1641–49', *Mariners Mirror*, 75, 1989, 255–68

Bayley, C.A., ed., *The Raj: India and the British, 1600–1947* (London, 1990)

Bigges, Walter, *A summarie and true discourse of Sir Francis Drakes West Indian voyage* (London, 1586)

Bisson, D.R., *The Merchant Adventurers of England: The Company and the Crown, 1474–1564* (London, 1993)

Black, J.B., *The Reign of Elizabeth* (Oxford, 1936)

Bogucka, M., 'Amsterdam and the Baltic in the first half of the seventeenth century', *Economic History Review*, 2nd series, 26, 1973, 433–47

Bosher, R.S., *The Making of the Restoration Settlement: The Influence of the Laudians* (London, 1951)

Bovill, E.W., 'The Madre de Dios', *Mariners Mirror*, 54, 1968, 129–52

Boxer, C.R., *The Dutch Seaborne Empire, 1600–1800* (London, 1965)

Boxer, C.R., 'The taking of the Madre de Dios, 1592', *Mariners Mirror*, 67, 1981, 82–4

Braddick, M.J., 'An English military revolution', *Historical Journal*, 36, 1993, 965–75

Brenner, Robert, *Merchants and Revolution, 1550–1653* (Cambridge, 1993)

Bridenbaugh, C., *Vexed and Troubled Englishmen* (Cambridge MA, 1974)

Burwash, D., *English Merchant Shipping, 1460–1540* (Toronto, 1947)

Bush, M.L., *The Government Policy of Protector Somerset* (Manchester, 1975)

Cain, P.J. and Hopkins, A.G., eds, *British Imperialism: Innovation and Expansion 1688–1914* (London, 1993)

Calendar of State Papers, Spanish, ed. Royall Tyler *et al.* (London, 1862–1954)

Canny, N.P., *The Elizabethan Conquest of Ireland: A Pattern Established, 1565–1576* (London, 1976)

Capp, Bernard, *Cromwell's Navy* (Oxford, 1989)

Carlton, Charles, *Charles I: The Personal Monarch* (London, 1995)

Carus Wilson, E.M., 'The origin and early development of the Merchant Adventurers', *Economic History Review*, 2nd series, 4, 1932, 147–76

Carus Wilson, E.M. and Coleman, O., *England's Export Trade, 1275–1547* (London, 1963)

Challis, C.E., *The Tudor Coinage* (Manchester, 1978)

Chandaman, C.D., *English Public Revenue, 1660–1688* (Oxford, 1975)

Chaudhuri, K.N., *The English East India Company* (Cambridge, 1965)

Chaudhuri, K.N., *The Trading World of Asia and the English East India Company* (Cambridge, 1978)

Chrimes, S.B., *Henry VII* (London, 1972)

Clapham, J.H., *The Bank of England* (Cambridge, 1944)

Clark, G.N., 'The Navigation Act of 1651', *History*, 7, 1922, 282–6

Clark, G.N., *The Later Stuarts, 1660–1714* (Oxford, 1949)

Clark, P., ed., *The Early Modern Town: A Reader* (London, 1976)

Clay, C.G.A., *Economic Expansion and Social Change: England 1500–1700* (Cambridge, 1984)

Clayton, N., 'Naval administration, 1603–1628' (University of Leeds Ph.D., 1935)

Coleman, D.C., *The Economy of England, 1450–1750* (London, 1977)

Colvin, H.M., *The History of the King's Works*, 4 vols (Oxford, 1963–73)

Connell Smith, G., *The Forerunners of Drake* (London, 1954)

Corbett, J.S., *Successors of Drake* (London, 1900)

Corbett, J.S., *England in the Mediterranean, 1603–1713* (Navy Records Society, London, 1904)

Corbett, J.S., ed., *Fighting Instructions, 1530–1816* (Navy Records Society, London, 1905)

Coward, Barry, *Oliver Cromwell* (London, 1991)

Coward, Barry, *The Stuart Age* (London, 1994)

Craven, W.F., *The Dissolution of the Virginia Company: The Failure of a Colonial Experiment* (New York, 1932)

Craven, W.F., *The Southern Colonies in the Seventeenth Century* (New York, 1949)

Cruikshank, C.G., *Elizabeth's Army*, 2nd edn (Oxford, 1966)

Cruickshank, E.A., *The Life of Sir Henry Morgan; With an Account of the English Settlement of the Island of Jamaica, 1655–1688* (London, 1935)

Cunich, P., *The Dissolution of the Monasteries and the growth of royal patronage in England 1536–1547* (Cambridge Ph.D, 1989)

Curtin, P.D., *The Atlantic Slave Trade: A Census* (Madison, Wisconsin, 1969)

Davies, C.S.L., 'The administration of the navy under Henry VIII: the origins of the Navy Board', *English Historical Review*, 80, 1965, 268–8

Davies, C.S.L., 'England and the French War, 1557–9', in J. Loach and R. Tittler, eds, *The Mid Tudor Polity* (London, 1980)

Davies, G., *The Restoration of Charles II* (Oxford, 1955)

Davies, J.D., 'Pepys and the Admiralty Commission of 1679–84', *Historical Research*, 62, 1989, 34–53

Davies, J.D., *Gentlemen and Tarpaulins* (London, 1991)

Davies, J.D., 'The navy, parliament and political crisis in the reign of Charles II', *Historical Journal*, 36, 1993, 271–88

Davies, K.G., *The Royal Africa Company* (London, 1957)

Davies, K.G., *The North Atlantic World in the Seventeenth Century* (London, 1974)

Davis, R., 'English foreign trade, 1660–1700', *Economic History Review*, new series, 7, 1954, 150–66

Davis, R., 'England and the Mediterranean, 1570–1670', in F.J. Fisher, ed., *Essays in the Economic and Social History of Tudor and Stuart England* (London, 1961)

Davis, R., *The Rise of the English Shipping Industry in the Seventeenth and Eighteenth Centuries* (London, 1962)

Davis, R., *Aleppo and Devonshire Square* (London, 1967)

Davis, R., *English Overseas Trade, 1500–1700* (London, 1973)

Davis, R., *The Rise of the Atlantic Economies* (London, 1973)

de Beer, E.S., 'The secret treaty of Dover', *English Historical Review*, 39, 1924, 86–9

Dee, John, *General and rare memorials* (London, 1577)

Dietz, B., 'The Huguenot and English corsairs during the third civil war in France, 1568–1570', *Proceedings of the Huguenot Society*, 19, 1952–58, 278–94

Dietz, B., 'Overseas trade and metropolitan growth', in A.L. Beier and R. Finlay, eds, *London 1500–1700* (London, 1986)

Dietz, F.C., *English Government Finance, 1485–1558* (Urbana IL, 1921)

Dietz, F.C., *English Public Finance, 1558–1640* (New York, 1932)

Donald, Peter, *An Uncounselled King: Charles I and the Scottish Troubles, 1637–41* (Cambridge, 1990)

Donnan, E., ed., *Documents Illustrative of the History of the Slave Trade to America*, 3 vols (Washington, 1930–32)

Doran, Susan, *Monarchy and Matrimony* (Stroud, 1996)

Dunn, R.S., *Sugar and Slaves: The Rise of the Planter Class in the English West Indies, 1624–1713* (London, 1974)

Dyer, F.E., 'Reprisals in the sixteenth century', *Mariners Mirror*, 21, 1935, 187–97

Dyer, F.E., 'The Ship Money fleet', *Mariners Mirror*, 23, 1937, 187–97

Ellis, S.G., *Tudor Ireland* (London, 1985)

Evelyn, John, *Navigation and Commerce: Their Original and Progress* (London, 1674)

Falls, Cyril, *Elizabeth's Irish Wars* (London, 1950)

Ferguson, W., 'The making of the Treaty of Union, 1707', *Scottish Historical Review*, 43, 1964, 96–110

Firth, C.H., 'The capture of St Iago by Capt. Myngs, 1662', *English Historical Review*, 14, 1899, 536–40

Firth, C.H. and Rait, R.S., *Acts and Ordinances of the Interregnum* (London, 1911)

Fisher, F.J., 'Influenza and inflation in Tudor England', *Economic History Review*, 2nd series, 18, 1965, 120–30

Fisher, F.J., 'London as an engine of economic growth', in P. Clark, ed., *The Early Modern Town: A Reader* (London, 1976)

Flinn, M.W., *A History of the British Coal Industry* (London, 1984)

Foster, Sir William, *England's Quest of Eastern Trade* (London, 1933)

Foster, W., Fawcett, C. and Cadell, P., eds, *The English Factories in India: A Calendar of Documents*, vols 1–17, 1618–84 (London, 1906–55)

Fox, Frank, *Great Ships: The Battlefleet of King Charles II* (London, 1980)

Foxe, John, *Actes and Monuments of these latter and perillous days* (London, 1563)

French, P.J., *John Dee: The World of an Elizabethan Magus* (London, 1973)

Friel, Ian, 'The documentary evidence for maritime technology in later medieval England and Wales' (University of Keele Ph.D., 1990)

Friel, Ian, *The Good Ship: Ships, Shipbuilding and Technology in England, 1200–1520* (London, 1995)

Friis, A., *Alderman Cockayne's Project: The Commercial Policy of England in its Main Aspects* (London, 1927)

Fudge, J.D., *Cargoes, Embargoes and Emissaries: The Commercial and Political Interaction of England and the German Hanse, 1450–1510* (Toronto, 1995)

Fulton, T.W., *The Sovereignty of the Sea* (London, 1911)

Gammon, S.R., *Statesman and Schemer: William, First Lord Paget, Tudor Minister* (Newton Abbott, 1973)

Gee, H., 'The Derwentdale plot, 1663', *Transactions of the Royal Historical Society*, 3rd series, 11, 1971, 125–42

Glasgow, T., 'The navy in Philip and Mary's war', *Mariners Mirror*, 53, 1967, 321–42

Glasgow, T., 'The navy in Elizabeth's first undeclared war, 1559–60', *Mariners Mirror*, 54, 1968, 23–37

Glasgow, T., 'The navy in the Le Havre campaign of 1562–4', *Mariners Mirror*, 54, 1968, 281–96

Glasgow, T., 'A list of ships in the Royal Navy from 1539 to 1588', *Mariners Mirror*, 56, 1970, 299–307

Gould, J.D., *The Great Debasement* (London, 1970)

Gould, J.D., 'Cloth exports 1600–1640', *Economic History Review*, 2nd series, 24, 1971, 249–52

Gray, Todd, 'Turks, Moors and Cornish fishermen: piracy in the early seventeenth century', *Journal of the Royal Institution of Cornwall*, new series, 10, 1987–90, 457–75

Gray, Todd, 'Turkish piracy and early Stuart Devon', *Transactions of the Devonshire Association*, 121, 1989, 159–71

Greene, J.P., *Settlements to Society, 1584–1763* (New York, 1966)

Grose, C.L., 'The Anglo-Portuguese marriage of 1662', *Hispanic American History Review*, 10, 1930, 313–52

Grose, C.L., 'England and Dunkirk', *American Historical Review*, 39, 1933, 1–27

Grose, C.L., 'The Dunkirk money', *Journal of Modern History*, 5, 1933, 1–18

Hakluyt, Richard, *The principall navigations, voiages and discoveries of the English nation* (London, 1589)

Hagthorpe, John, *England's Exchequer, or a discourse of the sea and navigation* (London, 1625)

Hammond, W.N., 'The administration of the English navy, 1649–1660' (University of Columbia Ph.D., 1973)

Hammond, P.W., ed., *Richard III: Loyalty, Lordship and Law* (London, 1986)

Haring, C.H., *The Buccaneers in the West Indies in the Seventeenth Century* (London, 1910)

Harlow, V.T., ed., *The Voyages of Captain William Jackson, 1642–46* (Camden Miscellany, 13, London, 1924)

Hebb, D.D., *Piracy and the English Government, 1616–1642* (Aldershot, 1994)

Holden, J.M., *The History of Negotiable Instruments in English Law* (London, 1955)

Holmes, Geoffrey, *The Making of a Great Power, 1660–1722* (London, 1993)

Horrox, Rosemary, *Richard III: A Study in Service* (London, 1989)

Horsefield, J.K., 'The beginnings of paper money in England', *Journal of European Economic History*, 6, 1977, 117–32

Horsefield, J.K., 'The Stop of the Exchequer revisited', *Economic History Review*, 2nd series, 35, 1982, 511–28

Hoskins, W.G., 'Harvest fluctuations and English economic history, 1620–1759', *Agricultural History Review*, 16, 1968, 15–31

Houlbrooke, R.A., 'Henry VIII's wills: a comment', *Historical Journal*, 37, 1994, 891–900

Hutton, R., *The Royalist War Effort, 1642–46* (London, 1982)

Hutton, R., 'The making of the secret treaty of Dover', *Historical Journal*, 29, 1986, 297–318

Imray, J., 'The Merchant Adventurers and their records', *Journal of the Society of Archivists*, 2, 1964, 457–67

Inwood, Stephen, *A History of London* (London, 1998)

Ives, E.W., 'Henry VIII's will: a forensic conundrum', *Historical Journal*, 35, 1992, 779–804

Ives, E.W., 'Henry VIII's will: the Protectorate provisions, 1546–7', *Historical Journal*, 37, 1994, 901–13

Jamieson, Alan, 'The Tangier galleys and the wars against the Mediterranean corsairs', *The American Neptune*, 23, 1963, 95–112

Jensen, M., ed., *English Historical Documents: American Colonial Documents to 1776* (London, 1955)

Jordan, W.K., *The Chronicles and Political Papers of Edward VI* (London, 1966)

Jordan, W.K., *Edward VI: The Young King* (London, 1968)

Jordan, W.K., *Edward VI: The Threshold of Power* (London, 1970)

Judges, A.V., 'The origins of English Banking', *History*, 16, 1931, 138–45

Junge, H-C., *Flottenpolitik und revolution: Die Enstehung der englischen Seemacht wharend der Herrschaft Cromwells* (Stuttgart, 1980)

Kamen, Henry, *Philip of Spain* (London, 1997)

Kelsey, H., *Sir Francis Drake: The Queen's Pirate* (New Haven, 1998)

Kelsey, S., *Inventing a Republic: The Political Culture of the English Commonwealth, 1649–1653* (London, 1997)

Kennedy, D.E., 'The English naval revolt of 1648', *English Historical Review*, 77, 1962, 247–56

Kerridge, E., *Textile Manufacture in Early Modern England* (Manchester, 1985)

Kerridge, E., *Trade and Banking in Early Modern England* (Manchester, 1988)

Khan, S.A., *Anglo-Portuguese Negotiations Relating to Bombay, 1660–1677* (Bombay, 1922)

King, W.T.C., *A History of the London Discount Market* (London, 1936)

Kingsbury, S.M., *The Records of the Virginia Company of London*, 4 vols (London, 1906–35)

Kingsford, C.L., 'The taking of the Madre de Dios, 1592', *Naval Miscellany*, 2, 1912, 85–121

Kirsch, P., *The Galleon* (London, 1990)

Kupperman, Karen, 'Apathy and death in early Jamestown, 1607–1618', *Journal of American History*, 66, 1979, 24–40

Labaree, L.W., *Royal Government in America* (New Haven, 1930)

Land, Aubrey, C., *Colonial Maryland: A History* (New York, 1981)

Larkin, J.F. and Hughes, P.L., *Tudor Royal Proclamations*, 3 vols (New Haven, 1964–69)

Lawson, Philip, *The East India Company: A History* (London, 1993)

Letters and Papers, Foreign and Domestic . . . of the Reign of Henry VIII, ed. James Gairdner *et al.* (London, 1862–1910)

Letters and Papers relating to the War with France, 1512–14, ed. Alfred Spont (Navy Records Society, London, 1897)

Lewis, M., *Armada Guns* (London, 1961)

Lewis, M., *The Hawkins Dynasty* (London, 1969)

Libell of Englyshe Polycye, The, ed. Sir George Warner (Oxford, 1926)

Lloyd, C., *English Corsairs on the Barbary Coast* (London, 1981)

Lloyd, Howell, 'Corruption and Sir John Trevor', *Transactions of the Honorable Society of Cymmrodorion*, 1974–75, 77–102

Loades, David, 'The king's ships and the keeping of the seas, 1413–1480', *Medieval History*, 1, 1991, 93–104

Loades, David, *The Reign of Mary Tudor* (London, 1991)

Loades, David, *The Tudor Navy* (Aldershot, 1992)

Loades, David, *John Dudley, Duke of Northumberland* (Oxford, 1996)

Loades, David, ed., *John Foxe and the English Reformation* (Aldershot, 1997)

Lockyer, Roger, *Buckingham* (London, 1981)

Lowe, Ben, *Imagining Peace: A History of Early English Pacifist Ideas* (Philadelphia, 1997)

Lucas, C., *The Historical Geography of the British Dominions: Canada and Newfoundland* (London, 1921)

Lyell, L. and Watney, F., eds, *Acts of Court of the Mercers Company, 1453–1526* (London, 1936)

MacCaffrey, W., *The Shaping of the Elizabethan Regime* (London, 1969)

MacCaffrey, W., *Elizabeth I* (London, 1993)

MacCulloch, D., *Thomas Cranmer* (London, 1996)

McCusker, J.J. and Merard, R.R., *The Economy of British America, 1607–1789* (Chapel Hill, 1985)

MacDougall, N., *James IV* (Edinburgh, 1989)

MacDougall, N., '"The greattest scheip that ever saillit in Ingland or France": James IV's Great Michael', in *Scotland and War, AD 79–1918* (Edinburgh, 1991)

McGowan, A.P., *The Jacobean Commissions of Enquiry, 1608 and 1618* (Navy Records Society, London, 1971)

McGurk, John, *The English Conquest of Ireland: The 1590s Crisis* (London, 1997)

Malabarie, B.M., *Bombay in the Making, 1661–1726* (London, 1910)

Maltby, W.S., *The Black Legend in England* (Durham NC, 1971)

Markham, C.R., *The Hawkins Voyages* (Hakluyt Society, London, 1879)

Miller, J., *James II: A Study in Kingship* (Brighton, 1978)

Minchinton, W.E., ed., *The Growth of English Overseas Trade in the Seventeenth and Eighteenth Centuries* (London, 1969)

Morgan, E.S., 'The labour problem at Jamestown, 1607–1618', *American Historical Review*, 76, 1971, 595–611

Morton, R.L., *Colonial Virginia* (Williamsburg, 1960)

Muñoz, Andres, *Viaje de Felipe II a Inglaterra* (Zaragoza, 1554)

Newton, A.P., *European Nations in the West Indies, 1493–1688* (London, 1933)

Nichols, Philip, *Sir Francis Drake Revived* (London, 1626)

Ogg, David, *England in the Reign of Charles II*, 2nd edn (Oxford, 1955)

Oppenheim M., *Naval Accounts and Inventories of the Reign of Henry VII, 1485–88, 1495–97* (Navy Records Society, London, 1896)

Oppenheim, M., *The History of the Administration of the Royal Navy, 1509–1660* (London, 1896)

Oppenheim, M., ed., *The Naval Tracts of Sir William Monson*, 5 vols (Navy Records Society, London, 1902–14)

Outhwaite, R.B., *Inflation in Tudor and Early Stuart England* (London, 1969)

Padfield, P., *Guns at Sea* (London, 1973)

Padfield, P., *Maritime Supremacy and the Opening of the Western Mind* (London, 1999)

Palmer, M.A.J., 'The "military revolution" afloat: the era of the Anglo-Dutch Wars', *War in History*, 4, 1997, 123–49

Parker, G., *The Dutch Revolt* (London, 1977)

Parker, G. and Martin, C., *The Spanish Armada* (London, 1988)

Parks, G.B., *Richard Hakluyt and the English Voyages* (New York, 1978)

Pearl, Valerie, *London and the Outbreak of the Puritan Revolution* (Oxford, 1961)

Peck, Linda, 'Problems in Jacobean administration: was Henry Howard, Earl of Northampton, a reformer?', *Historical Journal*, 19, 1976, 831–58

Pepys, Samuel, *Diary . . . 1660–1669*, ed. N.B. Wheatley (London, 1893–99)

Pepys, Samuel, *Memoirs relating to the State of the Royal Navy of England, 1679–1688*, ed. J.R. Tanner (London, 1906)

Pepys, Samuel, *Private Correspondence and Miscellaneous Papers . . . 1679–1703*, ed. J.R. Tanner, 2 vols (London, 1926)

Perrin, W.G., ed., *The Autobiography of Phineas Pett* (Navy Records Society, London, 1918)

Pettegree, A., *Foreign Protestant Congregations in Sixteenth-Century London* (Oxford, 1986)

Petty, R., 'The rebellion of Sir George Booth, August 1659', *Journal of the Chester and North Wales Archaeological and Historical Society*, new series, 33, 1939, 119–37

Pincus, S.C.A., 'Popery, trade and universal monarchy: the ideological context of the outbreak of the second Anglo-Dutch war', *English Historical Review*, 107, 1992, 1–29

Pincus, S.C.A., *Protestantism and Patriotism: Ideologies and the Making of English Foreign Policy, 1650–1668* (Cambridge, 1996)

Plumb, J.H., *The Growth of Political Stability in England, 1675–1725* (Cambridge, 1967)

Porter, H.C., *The Inconstant Savage: England and the North American Indian, 1500–1660* (Cambridge, 1979)

Powell, J.R., *Robert Blake* (London, 1972)

Powell, J.R. and Timings, E.K., eds, *Documents Relating to the Civil War, 1642–48* (Navy Records Society, London, 1963)

Powley, E.B., *The English Navy in the Revolution of 1688* (Cambridge, 1928)

Pryde, G.S., ed., *The Treaty of Union of England and Scotland, 1707* (Edinburgh, 1950)

Purchas, Samuel, *Hakluytus Posthumous or Purchas his Pilgrimes*, 4 vols (London, 1625; Hakluyt Society Glasgow, 1905–07)

Quinn, D.B., 'Edward IV and exploration', *Mariners Mirror*, 21, 1935, 275–84

Quinn, D.B., *The Voyages and Colonising Enterprises of Sir Humphrey Gilbert* (Hakluyt Society, London, 1940)

Quinn, D.B., *The Roanoake Voyages, 1584–90* (Hakluyt Society, London, 1955)

Quinn, D.B., 'The argument for the English discovery of America between 1480 and 1494', *Geographical Journal*, 127, 1961, 227–85

Quinn, D.B., 'The Munster plantation: problems and opportunities', *Cork Historical and Archaeological Society Journal*, 71, 1966, 19–40

Quinn, D.B. and Ryan, A.N., *England's Sea Empire* (Liverpool, 1983)

Quintrell, B., 'Charles I and his navy in the 1630s', *The Seventeenth Century*, 3, 1988, 159–79

Rabb, T.K., *Enterprise and Empire, 1575–1630* (New Haven, 1967)

Rabb, T.K., *Jacobean Gentleman: Sir Edwin Sandys, 1561–1629* (London, 1998)

Ramsay, G.D., *English Overseas Trade during the Centuries of Emergence* (London, 1957)

Ramsey, P.H., 'Overseas trade in the reign of Henry VII', *Economic History Review*, 2nd series, 6, 1953, 173–82

Ramsey, P.H., *The Price Revolution in Sixteenth-Century England* (London, 1971)

Ramsey, R.W., *Richard Cromwell: Protector of England* (London, 1935)

Read, Conyers, 'Queen Elizabeth's seizure of Alba's pay ships', *Journal of Modern History*, 5, 1933, 443–64

Redworth, G., *In Defence of the Church Catholic: A Life of Stephen Gardiner* (Oxford, 1990)

Rich, E.E., *The Hudsons Bay Company. I: 1670–1763* (London, 1968)

Richardson, W.C., *Stephen Vaughan: Financial Agent of Henry VIII* (Baton Rouge, 1953)

Richmond, C.F., 'Royal administration and the keeping of the seas, 1422–1485' (University of Oxford D.Phil., 1962)

Richmond, C.F., 'English naval power in the fifteenth century', *History*, 52, 1967, 1–15

Richmond, Sir Henry, *The Navy as an Instrument of Policy, 1558–1727*, ed. E.A. Hughes (Cambridge, 1953)

Robertson, F.W., 'The rise of the Scottish navy, 1460–1513' (University of Edinburgh Ph.D., 1934)

Rodger, N.A.M., 'The development of broadside gunnery, 1450–1650', *Mariners Mirror*, 82, 1996, 301–24

Rodger, N.A.M., *The Safeguard of the Sea* (London, 1997)

Rodriguez Salgado, M-J., *The Changing Face of Empire: Charles V, Philip II and Habsburg Authority, 1551–1559* (Cambridge, 1988)

Roots, Ivan, *The Great Rebellion, 1642–1660* (London, 1966)

Rose, S.E., *The Navy of the Lancastrian Kings* (Navy Records Society, London, 1982)

Ross, C., *Richard III* (London, 1981)

Russell, C., *Parliament and English Politics, 1621–29* (Oxford, 1979)

Rymer, T., *Foedera, conventiones, literae . . . et acta publica* (London, 1704–35)

Salisbury, W., 'A draught of a Jacobean three-decker: the Prince Royal?', *Mariners Mirror*, 47, 1961, 170–7

Scammell, G.V., *The World Encompassed: The First European Maritime Empires, c.800–1650* (London, 1981)

Scammell, G.V., 'The English in the Atlantic Islands, 1450–1650', *Mariners Mirror*, 72, 1986, 295–317

Scammell, G.V., *The First Imperial Age* (London, 1989)

Scarisbrick, J.J., *Henry VIII* (London, 1968)

Schantz, G., *Englische Handelspolitik gegen Ende des Mittelalters*, 2 vols (Leipsig, 1881)

Schofield, R.S., 'The geographical distribution of wealth in England, 1334–1649', *Economic History Review*, 2nd series, 18, 1965, 483–510

Scott, W.R., *Joint Stock Companies: The Constitution and Finance of English, Scottish, and Irish Joint Stock Companies to 1720*, 3 vols (London, 1910–12)

Seaward, P., *The Cavalier Parliament and the Reconstruction of the Old Regime, 1661–67* (Cambridge, 1989)

Senior, C.M., *A Nation of Pirates: English Piracy in its Heyday* (London, 1976)

Simpson, P., ed., *Danziger Inventar: Inventare Hansischer Archive des 16. Jahrhunderts* (Aalen, 1913)

Sirmans, M.E., *Colonial South Carolina: A Political History, 1663–1763* (Chapel Hill, 1966)

Smith, A.G.R., *The Emergence of a Nation State, 1529–1660* (London, 1984)

Smout, T.C., 'The Anglo-Scottish Union of 1707: the economic background', *Economic History Review*, 2nd series, 16, 1964, 455–67

Speck, W.A., *Reluctant Revolutionaries: Englishmen and the Revolution of 1688* (London, 1988)

Spence, R.T., *The Privateering Earl: George Clifford, Earl of Cumberland* (Stroud, 1995)

Spurr, J., *The Restoration Church of England, 1646–1689* (New Haven, 1991)

Statutes of the Realm, ed. A. Luders *et al.* (London, 1810–28)

Stearns, S.J., 'The Caroline military system, 1625–27' (University of California, Berkeley, Ph.D., 1967)

Strachey, R. and O., *Keigwin's Rebellion, 1683–4* (Oxford, 1916)

Supple, Barry, *Commercial Crisis and Change in England, 1600–1642* (London, 1959)

Sutherland, N.M., *The Massacre of St Bartholomew and the European Conflict, 1559–1572* (Oxford, 1973)

Taylor, E.G.R., *Tudor Geography, 1485–1583* (London, 1930)

Taylor, E.G.R., *Later Tudor and Early Stuart Geography* (London, 1934)

Thirsk, J., *Economic Policy and Projects* (Oxford, 1978)

Thirsk, J. and Cooper, J.P., eds, *Seventeenth-Century Economic Documents* (Oxford, 1972)

Thompson, I.A.A., 'The invincible Armada', in *Royal Armada* (London, 1988)

Twiss, Sir Travers, *The Black Book of the Admiralty* (London, 1871–76)

Tyacke, N., *Anti-Calvinists: The Rise of the English Arminians, 1590–1640* (Oxford, 1987)

Usherwood, S. and E., *The Counter-Armada, 1596* (London, 1983)

Van der Wee, H., *The Growth of the Antwerp Market and the European Economy* (London, 1963)

Vries, J. de, *The Economy of Europe in an Age of Crisis, 1600–1750* (Cambridge, 1976)

Waters, D.W., *The Art of Navigation in England in Elizabethan and Early Stuart Times* (London, 1958)

Webb, S.S., *The Governors General: The English Army and the Definition of Empire, 1569–1681* (Chapel Hill, 1979)

Wernham, R.B., *The Making of Elizabethan Foreign Policy, 1558–1603* (London, 1980)

Wernham, R.B., *The Expedition of Sir John Norris and Sir Francis Drake to Spain and Portugal, 1589* (Navy Records Society, London, 1988)

Western, J.R., *Monarchy and Revolution: the English State in the 1680s* (London, 1972)

Wheeler, J.S., 'Navy finance, 1649–1660' *Historical Journal*, 39, 1996, 457–66

Whitson, A.M., *The Constitutional Development of Jamaica, 1660–1729* (Manchester, 1929)

Williams, Penry, *The Later Tudors, 1547–1603* (Oxford, 1995)

Williamson, J.A., *The Cabot Voyages and Bristol Discovery under Henry VII* (London, 1962)

Wilson, C.H., *England's Apprenticeship 1603–1763* (London, 1965)

Wilson, Derek, *Sweet Robin: A Biography of Robert Dudley, Earl of Leicester* (London, 1981)

Woolrych, A., 'The Good Old Cause and the fall of the Protectorate', *Historical Journal*, 13, 1957, 133–61

Woolrych, A., 'Last quests for a settlement, 1657–1660', in G.E. Aylmer, ed., *The Interregnum: The Quest for a Settlement, 1646–1660* (London, 1972)

Wrigley, E.A. and Schofield, R.S., *The Population History of England, 1541–1871: A Reconstruction* (Cambridge, 1981)

Young, A.R., *His Majesty's Royal Ship* (New York, 1990)

Zook, J.F., 'The Company of Royal Adventurers trading into Africa [1662–72]', *Journal of Negro History*, 4, 1919, 134–231

INDEX

Mary, Queen of Scotland 42, 61, 73, 82,
    83, 86, 91, 93, 94, 97, 98, 109, 110,
    130
Maryland 142, 144–6, 174, 186, 231, 233
Massachusetts 145, 216, 231, 232, 248
  Bay 143, 144
  Company 143, 144
  colony 144–6, 232, 233
    charter 145, 231
Masulipatam 226
Maximilian, Holy Roman Emperor 28
Mechlin 40
Medina Sidonia, Duke of 131
Mediterranean, sea 8, 92, 99, 141, 169,
    173, 210
Medway, river 147, 202, 205, 206
Mendoza, Bernadino de, Spanish
    Ambassador 113
Mercantilist theory 140, 176, 218, 222
Mercator, Gerhard 112
Mercers Company 30, 49
Merchant Adventurers 16–18, 26, 28–30,
    36–8, 43, 45, 47–9, 53, 54, 57,
    59–61, 63–7, 76, 91, 92, 98, 101,
    106, 107, 116, 117, 140, 147, 218,
    219
  Antwerp house 53
  charter 17
  court 30
Merchant marine 41, 146, 168, 215, 217,
    250
  naval auxilliaries 86, 122, 130, 167
Mercia 4
Middleburg 140
Milburne, John, of London 13
Military revolution 201, 213, 214
Moghul Empire 226, 227
Mokha 226
Moluccas 120
Monaghan 138
Monastic lands 45, 71, 245
Monck, George, Duke of Albermarle 182,
    183, 234
Monson, Sir William 105, 118, 134, 135,
    149, 170
Montague, Edward, Earl of Sandwich 180,
    181, 183, 198
Montague, William, Earl of Salisbury 6
Montgomeryshire 137
Moorish Emirates, North Africa 199
Mordaunt, Charles, Earl of Pembroke 195
More, Sir Thomas 37
Morgan, Sir Henry 200, 201, 213, 230,
    242

Morley, Lord 3
Moscow 68, 69
Moulton, Robert 170
Mounts Bay, Cornwall 97
Mowhawk river 234
Munster, Ireland 138, 160
Munster, Germany, Bishop 203
Murad III, Sultan 117
Muscovy Company 58, 59, 92, 102, 148,
    220, 247
  trade 67, 68, 87, 92, 101, 140
Mynges, Christopher 179, 200, 212

Namur 225
Naples 179
Naseby, battle (1645) 158
Navigation Acts 177, 220, 231, 232
  1486, 1489 28
  1650 171, 175, 176, 216
  1651 171, 175, 176, 185, 186, 216
  1660 216, 217, 232, 238
Navigational science 20, 215
'Navy Board circle' 87–9, 114, 125, 127,
    128, 137
Navy, English 61, 62, 71, 72, 74, 76, 78,
    83, 85, 86, 98, 101, 105, 122, 148,
    154–7, 159, 163–7, 169–71, 176,
    178–81, 185, 186, 188, 193, 198,
    199, 204, 207, 210, 247
  dockyards 43
  finance and debt 126, 156, 158, 159,
    166, 167, 169, 183, 184
  firepower 150
  fraud and corruption 127, 149, 150, 166
  mutiny (1659) 182
  patronage 149, 155
  'petty navy royal' 111, 112, 131
  policy 71, 126, 127, 158, 176, 183,
    191–3, 201, 209, 210–13, 245, 249
  politicisation 170
  ratings 168
  recruitment 128, 153, 169
  stores 175, 216, 222
  strategy 167, 179, 210
    'blue water' 131, 136, 178
    summer and winter guards 167
  victualling 83, 125, 126, 150, 155, 156,
    169, 183
    Surveyor General, office 62, 73, 126
  wages 150, 152, 169, 182
  warfleet 130, 152, 158, 189, 197, 201,
    207, 210, 211
  workforce 43, 83, 190
Navy, Scottish 40, 47, 137, 160, 238